Intellectual Property and Open Source

Intellectual Property and Open Source

Van Lindberg

O'REILLY®
Beijing · Cambridge · Farnham · Köln · Sebastopol · Taipei · Tokyo

Intellectual Property and Open Source
by Van Lindberg

Printed in the United States of America.

Published by O'Reilly Media, Inc., 1005 Gravenstein Highway North, Sebastopol, CA 95472.

O'Reilly books may be purchased for educational, business, or sales promotional use. Online editions are also available for most titles (*http://safari.oreilly.com*). For more information, contact our corporate/institutional sales department: (800) 998-9938 or *corporate@oreilly.com*.

Editor: Andy Oram
Production Editor: Sumita Mukherji
Copyeditor: Amy Thomson
Proofreader: Nancy Reinhardt
Indexer: Ellen Troutman Zaig
Cover Designer: Karen Montgomery
Interior Designer: David Futato
Illustrator: Robert Romano

Printing History:
July 2008: First Edition.

ISBN: 978-0-596-51796-0

[M]

1215097554

CONTENTS

PREFACE

I have a workbench in my garage where I keep some of my woodworking tools. While I am not a great carpenter—actually, I'm a pretty terrible carpenter—I still enjoy building things and working with the wood.

Although I have had my workbench set up for several years, I am always a little bit tentative when I first use a new power tool. I have learned to respect the fact that tools can be useful, but they can also be difficult or dangerous if not used correctly. To adopt a phrase used with some other tools, it can be too easy to shoot yourself in the foot.

This book is about a tool that we use called intellectual property—IP for short. We use IP to allocate value and create incentives in society. Just like many other powerful tools, IP can be very useful, but it can also be difficult to work with. You can (easily!) shoot yourself in the foot with intellectual property if you don't understand how and why this tool works.

Unfortunately, there are few topics quite as misunderstood as intellectual property. Take a detour through the comments section of almost any recent Slashdot discussion. Many contributors begin their comments with, "IANAL, but..." ("I am not a lawyer, but...") and then attempt to describe a legal principle, often incorrectly.

Part of my job each day is to work as a translator—translating from "lawyer" to "engineer" and back. For lawyers, I describe the interactions between computers, networks, and code. For engineers, I describe how to work with the legal system. My goal for this book is to raise the level of understanding and discussion about intellectual property and software. If we understand the function and rationales behind IP law, we can work with IP more easily, discuss it more fluently, and work together to improve it where necessary.

What This Book Is...and Is Not

This book is meant to be a developer's documentation for the legal system. As with any other tool, the workings and results of the legal system can seem inscrutable until the assumptions and processes underlying the code are laid bare. This book will unravel the United States' intellectual property system by showing how it is composed of a number of interlocking, interoperating parts—patents, copyrights, trademarks, trade secrets, and some contracts, all of which act according to their own internal logic and demands. As much as possible, the minutiae of case names, Latin terms, and general legalese will be laid aside as implementation details; instead, the focus will be on the concepts and rules driving the overall system.

This book is designed to help anyone who interacts with other people through creative expression, particularly code. For example, those in commercial contexts will find it useful to learn how their day-to-day jobs brush up against IP law. Entrepreneurs will be particularly interested in who "owns" the code and the concepts behind their companies. Open source developers will find it a useful handbook to one of the more esoteric but important parts of their software project.

This book is *not* meant to be legal advice about what you should do in any specific situation. One difficulty with writing about intellectual property (or any legal topic) is that it is essentially impossible to be absolutely comprehensive. Legal disputes are generally fact-intensive, and superficially similar cases can lead to very different outcomes. Moving up to a higher level of abstraction allows individually distinguishable cases to coalesce into recognizable and useful principles. Generally following these principles should help to guide your understanding and keep you out of trouble. If specific legal issues do arise, however, it is best to consult a lawyer about your own situation.

How to Read This Book

This book can be approached as a story or as a reference manual, depending on how you want to use it. I would suggest reading it as a story first; later sections will build upon earlier explanations. After you have read this book in its entirety, individual chapters will be much more useful as you look for guidance on particular IP issues.

This Book As a Story

Different parts of the IP laws developed as responses to particular societal and economic problems; understanding those problems will help you understand the methods that IP law uses to accomplish its ends. IP laws have also been developed in response to (or in order to enable) certain business models. Understanding the business models will also help explain the use and expansion of IP law in society.

Thus, I will start by showing how economics, politics, psychology, and other disciplines all made their mark on IP law. I will show how each branch of IP law was designed to deal with different issues in slightly different ways.

After looking at each type of IP in isolation, I will then examine how they work together in real life. To do this I will bring in the concepts of contracts and licensing, and we will take a detour into open source/free software licensing as an embodiment of IP principles.

I will then present a series of situations showing the interaction of IP law with an idea as the idea moves from conception to realization and is communicated to others. These situations will be presented roughly in the chronological order in which they would occur in the development of the idea.

This Book As a Reference

This book is also designed to work as a desk reference for those generally interested in intellectual property issues. The individual chapters on patents, copyrights, trademarks, and trade secrets should be useful to those who come into close contact with those constructs for the first time or after an extended absence. While I don't pretend to tell you all you would need to know as a lawyer, I hope that those sections will also be of use when you need to work with lawyers to develop or manage IP issues.

The sections on open source (*http://opensource.org*) licensing are also intended to be of use to those becoming familiar with open source licenses or needing to pick a license. I will also spend some time dealing with the particular difficulties that can arise when using the GNU GPL.

Each chapter in the latter half of this book is written to work as a standalone response to a particular typical situation, even though those chapters will assume the base level of knowledge about IP law given in the first half of the book. Chapters in the latter half of the book will also have, as appropriate, sample forms, procedures, or language that can be used to address the legal situation presented. Once again, however, you cannot assume that any particular form, procedure, or language will be applicable and effective for your particular situation. If you have any questions at all, it is best to consult a licensed lawyer in your local jurisdiction.

A Note About Terminology

There are many developers who bristle at the very use of the term "intellectual property." The Free Software Foundation (FSF) places it among "Phrases that are Worth Avoiding" (*http://www.gnu.org/philosophy/words-to-avoid.html#IntellectualProperty*) and Richard M. Stallman writes frequently against its use on the grounds that it covers many concepts (copyrights, patents, trademarks, and so on) that have very distinct legal policies and histories (see *http://www.gnu.org/philosophy/not-ipr.html*).

Whether or not developers agree with the current legal system, however, those who build software are on the front lines of creating and using intellectual property. We are already in the workshop, using the legal tools provided by our society. We need to understand how they work, if only to avoid having our rights cut off.

As discussed further in Chapter 8, I am aware of the important philosophical differences implied in the use of the term "free software" as opposed to "open source." Where applicable, I will use the correct term to describe how they are both socially and legally different. Nevertheless, because open source software is a strict superset of free software, I will generally use the more inclusive term when discussing legal elements common to both.

The Rest of This Book

This book is divided into two parts. The first part, comprising Chapter 1–Chapter 8, is an introduction to intellectual property law. The second part, comprising Chapter 9–Chapter 14, is more of an intellectual property handbook for developers, particularly those working in the open source space. It is also applicable to those working commercially, but more often than not your experience with intellectual property will be constrained by your employer's IP policies. The quick outline is as follows:

An Introduction to IP Law

- Chapter 1 introduces the four basic types of intellectual property—patents, copyrights, trademarks, and trade secrets, as well as the philosophical and economic foundations of intellectual property in general.
- Chapter 2 and Chapter 3 dive into the law by examining the world of patents. The nuts and bolts of patent documents are explained in Chapter 2, and the process of writing and *prosecuting* (obtaining) a patent is examined in Chapter 3. This chapter also examines patent-specific issues such as *priority, prior art, obviousness,* and the difficulties inherent in software patents.
- Chapter 4 transitions to the subject of copyrights. After laying out the history, protections, and limitations of copyright, this chapter will show how those protections both restrict and enable code sharing and licensing. Particular attention will be given to the definition and problem of *fair use* and the separation of functional and creative works.
- Chapter 5 looks at trademarks and their role in society. The essential requirements for a trademark are discussed, as well as the process for obtaining, registering, and defending a mark. This chapter also discusses the permissible uses of a mark and the evolving area of trademark dilution.
- Chapter 6 analyzes trade secrets as a mechanism for protecting knowledge and describes the ways in which trade secrets are relevant to today's enterprises. This chapter also takes some time to talk about what can and cannot be considered a trade secret in a software company, particularly in an open source software company.
- Chapter 7 brings together the different types of IP and shows how they can all interact within a single software project or product. I also examine the role of contracts and licenses in IP—what the IP law taketh away, a license giveth (at least sometimes). Contracts are discussed as the mechanism by which private agreements are given the force of law.
- Chapter 8 turns to open source and places it in context. This chapter reexamines some of the social and economic issues associated with intellectual property, and then looks at how the mechanism of open source licensing provides a different way of addressing those concerns.

An Intellectual Property Handbook for Developers

- Chapter 9 starts with your idea. Who owns it? The answer to that question might be you or it might be your employer. This chapter discusses IP assignment agreements, covenants to not compete, and some of the other papers that you signed but didn't read when you started working at your job. You will also learn about *works for hire* and how to determine who owns what.
- Chapter 10 assumes that you will be releasing code under a source available, open source, or free software license. How do you apply a license to your code? The different kinds of licenses will be compared, and the specter of license compatibility will be raised. This chapter will also discusses dual (or multiple) licensing and the business models associated with different types of licenses.
- Chapter 11 discusses what happens when you get your first patch. Who owns the patch? Do you have the right to use it? This chapter examines your right to accept and use patches and proposes several different alternatives depending on the level of formality in your project structure.
- Chapter 12 is a dive into the specifics of working with GPL'd code. Building on the licensing discussions in Chapter 10, this chapter will talk about the special issues raised by the GPL. This chapter provides answers to some of the most common questions about the GPL, particularly with regard to linking.
- Chapter 13 is an applied guide to reverse engineering. This chapter takes a look at some case studies in reverse engineering, and then provides a procedure for pursuing reverse engineering projects (mostly) safely. Along the way we will discuss the process of test-driven development as an effective method for managing reverse engineering.
- Chapter 14 concludes with the process of formalizing your project by establishing a non-profit foundation to guide it. As you will see through the book, the "growing up" of a project is in part about the process of adopting legal formalities. As your project starts to acquire contributors and users, you and your users will want to establish the formalities that will keep your project viable for the long term. This chapter discusses the when, why, and how of incorporating a non-profit entity to hold and manage the intellectual property for your project.

Appendixes

A few appendixes are included with this book:

- Appendix A contains a sample proprietary information agreement, the use of which is covered in Chapter 9.
- Appendix B–Appendix D contain lists of licenses certified by the Open Source Initiative (OSI), Free Software Foundation, and the Fedora Project.

- Appendix E–Appendix M contain recommended licenses and declarations:
  - — Public domain declaration
  - — Simplified BSD License
  - — Apache License, version 2.0
  - — Mozilla Public License, version 1.1
  - — GNU Lesser General Public License, version 2.1
  - — GNU Lesser General Public License, version 3
  - — GNU General Public License, version 2
  - — GNU General Public License, version 3
  - — Open Software License

Safari® Books Online

When you see a Safari® Books Online icon on the cover of your favorite technology book, that means the book is available online through the O'Reilly Network Safari Bookshelf.

Safari offers a solution that's better than e-books. It's a virtual library that lets you easily search thousands of top tech books, cut and paste code samples, download chapters, and find quick answers when you need the most accurate, current information. Try it for free at *http://safari.oreilly.com*.

Acknowledgments and Disclaimers

I want to acknowledge the substantial help I have received on this book. First and foremost, I need to thank my wife Susie and my children for giving me many months of Saturdays and evenings to write. I also want to thank the many others who were also supportive of this project.

This book is considerably better because of the help of many good people at O'Reilly. My editor, Andy Oram, provided extensive feedback and assistance throughout the process; Isabel Kunkle was a model of patience as I worked (too slowly) to get my drafts into production; Amy Thomson provided valuable help copyediting and clarifying the text; and Mike Hendrickson was willing to take a chance on a slightly different kind of book.

I also want to thank the people who helped out as technical reviewers on the text. Matt Asay, James Grimmelmann, Leslie Hawthorn, Glyph Lefkowitz, Lawrence Lessig, Stephana Patton, Richard Salgado, Julie Steele, and Luis Villa all gave valuable feedback on earlier drafts. Nevertheless, all errors in this text are mine alone.

Finally, a disclaimer: I work for a law firm and I represent clients. The views presented here are mine alone and should not be imputed to my firm, any clients of the firm, friends, enemies, or anyone else. This book is not legal advice, is not complete, and in most cases omits technicalities and simplifies complex situations. No person should act, or fail to act, on any legal matter based on the contents of this book. In short, it is a work of fiction, any resemblance to characters living or dead is purely coincidental, etc.

I hope you enjoy it.

CHAPTER ONE

The Economic and Legal Foundations of Intellectual Property

When programmers get together to talk, the conversation is likely at some point to turn from .NET frameworks or memory usage patterns to copyrights, patents, or trade secrets. People in the computer field realize that a cluster of legal concerns known as *intellectual property* (IP) plays a big role in its development. Consider just a few of the headline-making legal issues in technology over the past decade, most of which will be remembered by readers of this book:

- One of the most explosively popular applications in modern times, Napster, was shut down by a copyright infringement lawsuit in 2000. The founders of Napster thought they were safe from copyright infringement charges because the service itself never copied music files. But because its *users* shared copyrighted music without authorization from the copyright holders, the Supreme Court took down Napster a theory of "contributory copyright infringement."
- Around the same time, a promising new file-sharing service called Aimster was temporarily shut down on a different IP basis: America Online claimed infringement on its AIM trademark.
- The shutdown of Napster (and Aimster) fostered a sudden interest by the public in new or previously obscure peer-to-peer file-sharing protocols. The changing technical and legal landscape has forced the music recording industry to shift its enforcement efforts to individuals, leading occasionally to lawsuits against six-year-olds and grandmothers, and

sparking debates over whether colleges should collaborate in making students obey music industry restrictions on network use.

- The SCO Group, a tiny computer company formerly prominent in the field of Unix, sued the most famous computer company in the world, IBM, in 2005. SCO put forward a cluster of complaints (soon taken up in lawsuits and countersuits involving other companies) covering just about every area of IP: abuse of its UNIX trademark, copyright infringement, and theft of trade secrets. (The trademark is officially on the uppercase name UNIX, but most of the computer field uses the casual spelling "Unix".)

  Although legal and technical experts scoffed at the claims, many industry analysts worried that the suit would stunt the growth of the open source operating system Linux, which was becoming increasingly important to IT departments in large corporations.

  As the SCO cases proceeded, they turned up a range of bizarre claims and debates, including questions of who owns Unix, the enforceability of open source licenses, and what constitutes "copying" of programming source code.

  Most of the claims in SCO's case were rejected in August 2007, and SCO filed for bankruptcy the following month, but the case is still winding its way through the courts.

- A series of court rulings in the 1980s and 1990s established that software and business methods could be patented in the United States. The rulings decided that software could be considered a "process" or "machine" (both of which are patentable) instead of an "idea" or "algorithm" (which are not patentable). This resulted in a 3,000% increase in software and business patent filings between 1995 and 2001 alone.

  Software patents have been the subject of high-profile lawsuits such as *NPT, Inc. v. RIM* (which nearly shut down the widely used email service on Blackberry handhelds) and *Eolas v. Microsoft* (which claimed ownership of a key concept in web browser navigation). In 1999, Unisys decided it held a patent that entitled it to payment from any web site that used a picture in GIF format; GIF was and remains one of the most popular formats for online pictures.

There are so many opinions about IP that just starting the discussion opens the proverbial can of worms. There are IP maximalists who argue that intellectual property is at the foundation of our society, a fundamental building block of our economy. Others tie the right to control our creative expression to our rights and identities as creators. For them, intellectual property is intrinsic to who we are.

There are IP minimalists who argue that intellectual property doesn't exist; that the very concept is a contradiction in terms because "knowledge cannot be owned." Others argue against intellectual property because it restricts our range of creative expression. Still others oppose IP on more pragmatic grounds, pointing out that the term "intellectual property" puts many separate laws and concepts into a single indefinite box.

Intellectual property law is, in many ways, a study in contradictions. I think that it is easiest to understand, however, by thinking about intellectual property law as *code*.

Law and Code

Imagine you are a software developer embarking on a new project with a large existing codebase and an active group of developers. On first impression, the code is messy and contradictory. It is plagued by corner cases and inexplicable design decisions. Your first thought might be to discard all of it and start over fresh. Indeed, some of the long-time contributors agree.

With time, however, you begin to understand some of the design decisions that went into the code. Many of the pure abstractions failed, and the previous contributors patched the code in order to achieve workable results in particular circumstances. In most cases, the original design was roughly followed, but parts of the code were extended or trimmed to accommodate for bugs or adjust to new circumstances. There are some new users of the code, as well—other groups have started using the code to do things that the original developers had never foreseen. Those new users have to be accommodated. The code may be messy, but at least it is understood, and it works where it needs to.

This scenario, which any programmer would dread, is like the current state of intellectual property law. The law is a code, just like computer code. It is even described that way; the books that hold the laws are described as the United States *Code* (USC). There are definitions, reserved words, and code sections. There are the rough equivalents of subroutines, symbol tables, and linkers. Lawyers and judges act as interpreters. (Lawsuits concerning single passages of the code often take years, making other interpreted languages look like a lap of the Indianapolis 500 in comparison.)

It gets worse: *every* line of the legal code was written by committee, and *almost* every line of it has been patched by a later piece of legislation or modified by a court. Indeed, IP law is rooted in a more than 200-year-old codebase. Is it any wonder that it is a mess?

Nevertheless, there is usually logic behind the apparent messiness (or even madness) in the law. Just as with the long-time developers above, the original design of the intellectual property code has been stretched in some places and squeezed in others to make it fit new circumstances and changed priorities. Also, like the developers above, new laws have come to depend on the specific structures defined as intellectual property. We even have courts to carry out a form of test-driven development for new laws. Like the code described above, it may be messy, but at least it is understood, and it usually works where it needs to.

IP is a broad, nuanced, and difficult subject. This book is not about the debates and extremes in intellectual property. It is not meant to argue for or against any particular laws. Rather, this book is an attempt to describe and provide tools for working with the IP system as it currently exists.

The Types of Intellectual Property

There are four main branches of intellectual property, each designed to protect a different type of intellectual product. Later chapters will focus on individual types of intellectual property. For now it is enough to introduce the four primary systems that constitute IP.

Patents

Patents are time-limited statutory monopolies designed to protect inventions and technological developments. In return for full disclosure of your idea, you are granted the ability to prevent anyone else from making, using, selling, offering for sale, or importing the invention. Patents last for a maximum of about 20 years, after which the invention becomes part of the public domain.

During its life, the patent protects *all* implementations of a particular idea. You have the right to prevent other people from practicing (either making or using) your invention, even if they independently invent or re-implement the advancement described in your patent (in other words, even if they didn't copy your idea).

Because patents offer such strong protection, they are designed to be hard to get. A patent must disclose an invention that is "useful," "novel," and "non-obvious." Unfortunately, this doesn't mean that all granted patents are useful, novel, and non-obvious! Further, the patent must completely describe the best way to implement the invention using highly technical language. Well-drafted patents usually cost from $10,000 to $50,000 to obtain and generally require the assistance of a registered patent lawyer.

Copyrights

Copyrights are limitations on the *expression* of an idea. They are designed to protect paintings, sculptures, writings, boat hulls, dramatic works, architectural drawings, and anything else that shows individual creative expression. According to the copyright statute, copyright protection *automatically* attaches to anything you create as soon as it is "fixed in a tangible medium of expression"—basically, as soon as it is written down or recorded somewhere. Copyrights can last from 90 to about 150 years, depending on the circumstances.

Generally, copyright protection is not as strong as patent protection. Copyright protection does not prohibit other expressions of the same idea. As an extreme case, identical works created completely independently do not infringe the others' copyright. Further, copyright law has some built-in exceptions that allow other people to use copyrighted materials without the consent of the copyright owner.

Copyright law is applicable to software as a *non-dramatic literary work*. Although copyright law does not cover purely functional expressions, most code has enough originality to receive at least weak copyright protection.

Trademarks

Trademarks protect the *association* of a provider of goods or services with a picture, word, slogan, or tune, known generically as a *mark*. Trademarks were originally developed as an extension to the concepts of unfair competition and consumer protection; trademarks were used to protect consumers by preventing the counterfeiting of goods and to protect the reputations of individual artisans. In the past century, the role of trademarks has expanded to include the concepts of branding and customer loyalty.

You can gain a trademark for free simply by using it, although registration of the trademark with the United States Patent and Trademark Office (the USPTO or PTO) gives additional rights. Registration with the PTO generally requires the assistance of a lawyer and can cost from $2,000–$8,000 (or more) including all fees.

Trademarks are unusual in several respects. First, certain trademarks can last forever, as long as they are actually used. For example, it is highly unlikely that anyone will ever be able to open a steakhouse named McDonald's. That name is too attached to the well-known fast food chain, and it is quite conceivable that it will be used and associated with that chain for at least the next thousand years.

Second, trademark protections must not overlap. Two companies cannot use the same mark in the same market for the same goods. This is to ensure that there is always a clear association between a particular mark and the associated trademark holder.

Third, trademarks must be defended. Copyrights and patents don't have to be asserted to still have value. Trademarks, though, will die if they are not defended when they are infringed.

Trade Secrets

Trade secrets are the oldest form of intellectual property. A trade secret is just information that derives value from being kept a secret. For example, Apple keeps information about its future product plans a secret—this helps increase the excitement around each product release and Apple show. Trade secrets last as long as their *secret* status is actively protected.

The Intellectual Property System

Even from these brief descriptions, it should be obvious that the term "intellectual property" encompasses a number of divergent and even contradictory bodies of law. Returning to the law and code analogy above, intellectual property isn't really analogous to just one program. Rather, it is more like four (or more) programs all possibly acting concurrently on the same source materials. The various IP "programs" all work differently and lead to different conclusions. It is more accurate, in fact, to speak of "copyright law" or "patent law" rather than a single overarching "IP law." It is only slightly tongue in cheek to say that there is an intellectual property "office suite" running on the "operating system" of U.S. law.

With so many different moving parts in the system, simply naming and describing the different types of intellectual property doesn't do enough to explain *why* the intellectual property system works the way it does. To understand the reasons behind the messiness of intellectual property, it is necessary to stand back and look at the system as a whole, as well as the problems intellectual property was designed to fix.

Intellectual Property and Market Failure

Intellectual property starts with economics. Intellectual property law is, at its most basic, an attempt to remedy a failure in the market for knowledge. We want more knowledge in society, but the nature of knowledge tends to discourage (or technically, underencourage) efforts to create and share new ideas.

Normally, economists analyze society in terms of preferences, markets, and incentives. We all have preferences—things that we want and things that we don't want. A market is the place where we exchange goods and services with others, making decisions about how to best satisfy our preferences. There are costs (incentives) associated with getting what we want; the "price" of something is the result of balancing how much we want some good (our demand) with how much other people are willing to provide that good (the supply).

The interesting thing about markets is that they involve tradeoffs. Because we have limited resources, we have to make choices between different goods. If something costs very little, we tend to substitute the low-cost goods for high-cost goods.

Normally, the balancing of costs and preferences results in an optimal aggregate distribution of goods. Every once in a while, however, we encounter a *market failure*, a situation where balancing costs and preferences results in overproduction or underproduction of a certain good.

In this particular case, the good that we want is knowledge. As we will see, creating new knowledge is costly, and normal markets tend to discourage the creation of new knowledge. Intellectual property is the tool that we use to remedy this market failure. That is, intellectual property is the tool we use to change incentives to increase the amount of knowledge in society.

More specifically, intellectual property law is designed to fix the problems that arise because: 1) knowledge costs more to create than it costs to copy (or consume); and 2) secret knowledge is more valuable to individuals, but shared knowledge is more valuable to society.

The Cost of Creating Knowledge

Thinking is work. It is sometimes hard to compare thinking to other kinds of work—at the end of the day, there are no holes dug, or products made, or rooms cleaned, but anyone who has worked over a particularly hard problem all day knows that it takes time and effort to create solutions to problems. Although we embody our solutions in code or in writing, the real effort is the cost of creation. The code we write is simply an artifact that allows us to share the products of our thinking.

Once a person has paid the cost of creation, however, the economic cost of a second person using that knowledge moves down to essentially zero. The SSL libraries used to encrypt HTTP traffic are a good example. The cost of creating SSL was (and is) enormous; it includes the cost of developing the theories and algorithms governing SSL, as well as the cost of translating those algorithms into fast, efficient, and correct code.

For those who want to understand the technical details of SSL, there is still effort involved in learning and understanding the code. Nevertheless, the cost of acquiring that knowledge via OpenSSL and its documentation is vastly smaller than the cost of originally creating that information. Even Isaac Newton, generally regarded as a genius for his creative effort, acknowledged that his work built upon the work of others. When Newton stated in a letter to Robert Hooke in 1676, "If I have seen a little further it is by standing on the shoulders of Giants," he was acknowledging the mental work expended by others to raise his base level of understanding. The difference in cost between acquiring knowledge from another person and originally creating that knowledge is substantial.

For those who just want to use the fruits of other people's knowledge, the cost is essentially zero. For example, millions of people use SSL many times each day, and never think about the hundreds of thousands of hours of effort expended to make SSL work.

This is the first basic dilemma of information: high-quality information tends to have a very high cost to create, a much lower cost to acquire, and almost no cost to use. Therefore, our incentive is to use other people's knowledge frequently and to create new knowledge rarely.

The Value of Secrets

Secrets are valuable, but they have value only for those holding them. For example, the PIN associated with my debit card has value to me only as long as it remains a secret. Both public-key and symmetric encryption rely on secrets for their value. On a grander level, wars have been fought and lives have been lost over secrets; we have multiple government agencies dedicated to keeping our secrets and uncovering the secrets of other people.

Although some secrets are of little value to society, other secrets could have great value if they were revealed. For instance, one of greatest ceramic makers in Renaissance Florence (the Delia Robbia family) found a secret way of making particularly bright and resilient colors. Many others could have used this knowledge to create beautiful ceramics as well. When the founders of the studio died, however, the secret was lost for centuries (porcelain-making, itself, was a secret known only to the Chinese for a long time). The Delia Robbia family profited because it kept its chemical formulae secret, but society also suffered because other competent ceramics makers could not use the technique.

Shared knowledge is especially valuable because knowledge is generally susceptible to *network effects*: the more people who possess a particular piece of knowledge, the more valuable that knowledge becomes because it gets pooled with other knowledge to lead to new applications. For example, the success of the scientific method is based upon sharing hypotheses and experimental results. Industrial advances are generally the result of incremental progress by multiple groups working on the same problem. Economic markets are driven by and depend on the sharing of information.

This is the second basic dilemma of information: information has higher individual value when it is kept secret, but higher societal value when it is shared. Those who create new knowledge often have an incentive to keep their work a secret so that they can keep the benefits of that knowledge to themselves; if society wants to reap the greater benefits of sharing, it must counter that incentive with others.

The Nature of Information

We want more knowledge (or more generally, more information) in society. As discussed above, however, normal market mechanisms do not provide incentives for individuals to create and share new knowledge. Economists classify information as a *public good* that is susceptible to the *free rider problem*. Before getting into the law, therefore, we will take a brief detour into economic theory.

It's All Good(s), or Information in Economic Theory

Economic theory divides goods according to two axes: *rivalrousness* and *excludability*. Different rules apply for different categories of goods.

Rivalrous goods

A rivalrous good is something that only one person can have at a time. For example, food, cars, and physical goods generally are examples of rivalrous goods. If I eat a banana, nobody else can eat it. Another rivalrous good familiar to anybody with teenagers is the mirror in the bathroom; if one person is getting ready for the day, nobody else can use it. (OK, technically this is not rivalrous, since more than one person can look in the mirror at one time, but the common use makes this rivalrous—see the further explanation under the upcoming "Excludable goods" section.)

Information, on the other hand, is a non-rivalrous good. If I have a piece of information that I share with you, then we both have the benefit of that information. Thomas Jefferson, most famously the third president of the United States, but also the first patent examiner in the United States, described it as follows in *The Writings of Thomas Jefferson* (Derby & Jackson, 1859):

> [The] peculiar character [of an idea] is that no one possesses the less, because every other possesses the whole of it. He who receives an idea from me, receives instruction himself without lessening mine; as he who lights his taper at mine, receives light without darkening me.

A non-rivalrous good, therefore, is something that people can share at the same time without any single person having to even temporarily give up part of it. In the words of Thomas Jefferson, each person "possesses the whole of it."

You can further break down the definition of rivalrous goods. Some things are rivalrous in ownership only, and others are rivalrous in use. As noted above, a banana (in its convenient prepackaged form) is rivalrous in its *use*—only one person may eat the banana. The banana is also rivalrous in its *ownership*. Many people may "own" a banana in the legal sense (they may have some legal control over or claim on the banana), but there still must be a known, countable number of banana owners.

Excludable goods

An excludable good is something that another person can be prevented from obtaining. I can stop you from obtaining my banana by eating it myself. No matter what you do, it is impossible for you to get the banana after I have consumed it (at least, it is impossible for you to get it in the same convenient prepackaged form). Putting a lock on the bathroom door makes the bathroom mirror an excludable good. Even though the bathroom mirror is not used up like the banana, the lock keeps anyone else from using the mirror at the same time.

As might be expected, however, information is not like a banana. Quoting again from *The Writings of Thomas Jefferson*:

> If nature has made any one thing less susceptible than all others of exclusive property, it is the action of the thinking power called an idea, which an individual may exclusively possess as long as he keeps it to himself; but the moment it is divulged, it forces itself into the possession of every one, and the receiver cannot dispossess himself of it.

A non-excludable good, therefore, is a good that I cannot prevent you from consuming. Shared knowledge possesses this quality of non-excludability; there is no general method of teaching something to someone with the intended result that he or she does not learn it.

The four types of goods

Goods can therefore be categorized into four different types based upon whether they are rivalrous and exclusive. The four types of goods are *private goods, common-pool goods, club goods,* and *public goods.*

	Excludable	Non-excludable
Rivalrous	*Private goods* (cars, houses, computers, MP3 players, bananas)	*Common-pool goods* (fishing stocks, the rainforest, the air)
Non-rivalrous	*Club goods* (cable television, golf courses, group discounts, Wi-Fi access)	*Public goods* (the environment, national defense, lighthouses, information)

Private goods. Private goods are both rivalrous and excludable. Most things that you would think of as "property" fall into the category of private goods. It doesn't matter if it is portable, like an MP3 player, or fixed, like your house. If only one person (or a finite, countable number of people) can possess the good at one time, and the owner of the good has the power to keep others away, then it is a private good.

One way to think about private goods is to analogize them to locks or mutexes in a multithreaded program. A number of different threads may want to use a protected resource, but control of the lock around the resource is rivalrous; only one thread can hold it at a time. You can pass around control of the lock to different threads so that each holds the lock in turn, but no two threads can hold the lock at precisely the same moment. In fact, the point of using locks in a multithreaded program is to make certain resources excludable; locks are put around critical sections precisely to keep other threads out.

Club goods. Club goods are non-rivalrous and excludable. They get their name from the context in which they frequently show up—clubs that provide some sort of benefit for their members.

For example, I have at times been a member of a CD club, one where you can get 7 or 10 CDs for the price of one. The CD promotion *could* theoretically be applied to an infinite number of people, since there is nothing in the nature of the CD promotion that requires that only one person or group possess it at a time (although the record-keeping and billing systems of the CD club would have a hard time dealing with an infinite number of subscribers).

To better illustrate the unlimited nature of club goods, consider the "locals" discount given by Disneyland to the residents of Southern California. Any person that presents proof of local residence can receive a specially discounted annual pass to the park. When considered over time, the movement of people into and out of Southern California makes the total number of people eligible for this discount both uncountable and infinite.

The park discount example also illustrates another quality of club goods—they are excludable. To receive the discount, you must provide proof that you live in Southern California. No proof, no discount, even though the total number of people that may eventually provide proof is infinite.

When considering information, club goods are interesting because they show how excludability can solve the problem of non-rivalrousness in some circumstances. By putting a gate around Disneyland, the Disney corporation is able to ensure that it is compensated for all visits to the park.

Common-pool goods. Common-pool goods are rivalrous and non-excludable. The name "common-pool" is used because the classic examples usually revolve around commonly held resources. For example, schools of fish migrate all over the ocean, so it is very difficult to prevent people from catching them in different places. However, the use of the fish is rivalrous —a fish can only be caught and eaten once.

The most famous example of a common-pool good is a town *commons* used for grazing animals. In the agrarian societies of the 17th and 18th centuries, town dwellers usually retained land for small personal farms. The individual farmers, however, did not generally own enough land to provide grazing area for all their animals.

The solution adopted by some towns was to provide a large town commons, or grazing area, available to all residents. Each day the individual farmers would bring their animals to the commons for a period of time to graze. Each night they would bring the animals home to sleep in their personal barns.

The result of this arrangement has become known as the *tragedy of the commons*. Individual landowners used the common area to support more animals than they would otherwise keep. Grazing area maintained on the personal farm was relatively expensive—it was space that couldn't be used to grow more crops or house more animals. In contrast, the grazing area was relatively free—there was no additional cost associated with using the commons. Faced with an expensive choice (use personal land) and a cheap choice (use the commons), people used the commons as much as possible. As a result, the commons was degraded from overuse.

That is the essence of the tragedy of the commons. Because no individual person or group "owns" the common-pool goods, people perceive that anything taken from the common pool is free, or at least lower in cost. This creates an incentive to overuse the common-pool goods at the expense of other goods. As common-pool goods are rivalrous, some potential users of the good are crowded out and receive much less than their share.

Public goods. Public goods are non-rivalrous and non-excludable. These are goods that we want more of in society, like a clean environment or defense from national enemies, but they are goods that by their nature cannot be owned, controlled, or provided by any single person. Private goods can be managed naturally because each owner has an incentive to preserve the resource or consume it in a useful way. Public goods have no such controlling entity; they are diffuse.

Although public goods are diffuse, they can still be costly. Taking a clean environment as an example, it may be easy to remove 90% of the pollutants from a particular area. It is harder to remove 99% of the pollutants. It may be extremely difficult to remove 99.99% of the pollutants, and may be essentially impossible to remove 99.9999%. Dealing with these problems is like dealing with computer problems that have exponential complexity. The simple cases may be doable, even trivial, but the harder cases become very hard very quickly. The only difference is that computer problems use up time and space, and public goods problems use up time and money.

Like common-pool goods, public goods are not excludable, so they suffer from a form of the tragedy of the commons. Public goods are free to use, so people feel the incentive to use as much of them as possible. Additionally, since public goods are not rivalrous, they don't suffer from crowding out, but they can be *degradable*. The overuse of degradable goods tends to destroy some of their value.

It gets worse—public goods are also susceptible to a particular type of market failure called the *collective action* or *free rider problem*. The free rider problem exists because public goods are not only non-excludable, but are also costly to produce.

The free rider problem gets its name from the most common example used to illustrate this problem. Imagine that each day there are many city buses available to take people where they need to go. There is a catch, however: the first person to get on the bus pays $10,000, covering the fares for everybody else. The second, third, and all others getting on the bus get to ride for free.

In this situation, there is a high cost for being the first person to get on the bus, but a low cost for everybody else. The incentive is for everybody to hang back; nobody wants to be the person who pays the fare. Once somebody has paid the fare, however, everybody crowds on. After all, the ride is free—it has been paid for by someone else.

One way of looking at this situation is that the free rider problem is the incentive not to pay the cost for public goods (nobody wants to be the first person on the bus). Once somebody has paid the cost for the public good, however, the situation changes into a variant of the tragedy of the commons (everybody tries to ride the "free" bus, resulting in a crowded and smelly ride).

Information As a Public Good

Information is a public good that is susceptible to both the free rider problem and the tragedy of the commons. Specifically, these problems are seen in the cost of creating knowledge and the value of secrets.

The cost of creating knowledge is high, but the cost of consuming it is low. This is the free rider problem. There is a cost associated with creating new and useful knowledge that people don't want to pay, especially if there is a way to gain the knowledge from someone else. Therefore, there is a societal incentive to not create as much knowledge as we would ideally like to have.

Secrets are more valuable to you personally, but shared knowledge is more valuable to society. This is the tragedy of the commons. As long as you are the only one who knows a secret, it is as if you are the only person who has a key to the gate around part of the town commons. The resource is valuable to you because you have the key, but it is worthless to everybody else. The only way for others to get any value from that part of the pasture is to get the key from you.

Changing the Nature of Information

We can now hone in on the subjects of real concern to this book: frameworks governing the production and use of information.

Algorithms for creating knowledge

Faced with the public-good problems of information, there are a number of alternative ways in which we can, as a society, increase the production of knowledge. The first and most obvious answer is to handle information like we handle other public goods; that is, by working collectively to create knowledge by directly paying people to create new knowledge. Just as we use collective action (government) to provide environmental protection and national defense, we can also use the government to fund scientists, engineers, and inventors.

We do this already. Government grants are a major source of funding for scientists, and we have government agencies like the National Institute of Science and Technology that directly employ scientists. Tax-supported public universities are another means by which we publicly fund the creation of knowledge.

The bad news is that direct funding of knowledge creation doesn't always work. The reason is that government-directed funding is the real-life equivalent of a procedural algorithm in code. Procedural decisionmaking, like other procedural algorithms, works best when there is a relatively constrained problem space and the procedure for moving forward is widely known. Thus, government funding works best for broad scientific knowledge and general engineering problems. The search strategy (the scientific method) is known; all that remains is the application of the strategy to specific problem domains.

Other types of information are not so straightforward; they suffer from a massive problem space with many local maxima. For example, what is the formula for creating a great novel, a winning slogan, or a piece of sculpture? While many great works of art and culture have been created using public funding, it is not possible in general to direct the creation of the next great American novel. Our best efforts aren't much better than random chance. There is a similar problem with groundbreaking inventions. By definition, they are new—they are not piecewise refinements of existing solutions. They frequently arise out of new and unusual ways of addressing problems.

Markets, on the other hand, are like parallel or evolutionary algorithms. They are designed to find solutions in massive problem spaces by attempting many different solutions and testing each of them for success or failure in the market. Therefore, they could provide an alternative method of funding the creation of knowledge—if not for the free rider problem and the tragedy of the commons.

Making public goods private

If you recall, I used bathroom mirrors and shared resources in programs as examples of private goods. As I hinted above, this is not exactly true. More than one person can look in the bathroom mirror at one time, and more than one thread can use the shared resource at one time. In both cases, though, the result of multiple simultaneous use is a mess—somebody or something blows up.

The solution, for both the bathroom door and the shared resource, is a lock to make these sharable goods private. This illustrates an important point: legal or technological controls (that is, code) can change the nature of goods.

This is also a solution for information. Legal controls are added to the information to convert it from a public to a private good. By making some aspects of the information private, normal market mechanisms can be used to make investment choices and to allocate resources; the parallel algorithms of the market can be used to find and fund the creation of more knowledge for society.

If we could share our secret knowledge and still prevent it from being used or understood by others, there would likely be no secrets; no particular advantage would be gained by keeping the knowledge away from other people. The function of intellectual property law is just that —it allows us to share our secrets while still controlling how they are used.

The bargain

The price that inventors and authors pay for receiving exclusive control over their knowledge is that control is only granted for a limited period. Article I, Section 8 of the United States Constitution makes this bargain explicit: "To promote the progress of science and useful arts, by securing for limited times to authors and inventors the exclusive right to their respective writings and discoveries."

SCIENCE AND USEFUL ARTS

It is not generally known that most people understand the phrase "Science and Useful Arts" backward. "Science" was the natural sciences, including writing and philosophy; this phrase spurred the creation of the copyright act. The "useful arts" referred to crafts, the product of *art*isans; this phrase spurred the creation of the patent act. Thus promoting "the progress of science" led to the protection of art, and promoting the "useful arts" led to the protection of science.

The result of this bargain is that knowledge is temporarily mixed with law to create a hybrid good called "intellectual property." After the limited times decreed by the Constitution and by Congress, the knowledge reverts to its natural state as a public good; the freed knowledge is then said to be in the "public domain." The intended consequence of this process is an ever-increasing store of knowledge that is freely accessible to the public.

The purpose of intellectual property in economic terms

Modern intellectual property law has two objectives, first, to allow individuals to be compensated for the costs and risks inherent in knowledge creation, and second, to balance and align the interests of individuals and society by providing individual incentives to develop and share knowledge and societal protection for certain types of secrets.

Intellectual property law accomplishes these objectives by creating IP out of information; it takes intangible products of the mind and imbues their creators with special legal rights over their creations. These legal rights make certain aspects of the underlying information excludable, allowing private markets to allocate the appropriate resources to knowledge creation.

The rights granted under IP law are sometimes called *negative rights*, which are actually the rights to prevent other people from taking a particular action. In other words, the most consistent effect of the IP laws is to make some piece of knowledge excludable.

OTHER THEORIES OF INTELLECTUAL PROPERTY

The economic and philosophical arguments provided here are commonly known as the utilitarian justification for intellectual property. The underlying rationale is the economic concept of *utility*—that is, generalized happiness or usefulness. Under this theory, placing temporary restrictions on the use of information over time leads to the production and dissemination of knowledge.

This is the most common American justification for intellectual property and it is the justification that most closely fits with the patent and copyright portions of our intellectual property system. It is not, however, the only justification for intellectual property and it does not neatly match up to some other parts of our legal system.

Another justification for intellectual property comes from John Locke's natural rights perspective. Under a Lockean theory of intellectual property, a person owns what he creates by his own effort. "Whatsoever, then, he removes out of the state that Nature hath provided and left it in, he hath mixed his labor with it...and thereby makes it his property" (John Locke, *Two Treatises on Government, Third Edition*, 1698). If the working of the land and raw materials is "labor" that justifies ownership of the result, then working toward the creation of a new idea should justify ownership of that idea.

The trade secret laws in force across the United States tend to adhere most closely to a Lockean model of intellectual property. Trade secrets are recognized, at least in part, because of the labor spent in creating and maintaining them.

By way of contrast, the utilitarian model embraced by the copyright law explicitly disregards the amount of effort required to create a new original work; what matters is the creativity involved in arranging or generating the work. In one famous case (*Feist Publications, Inc. v. Rural Telephone Service Co.*), the United States Supreme Court held that a telephone book was not protected by copyright despite the substantial work expended to create it. Putting the names in alphabetical order was insufficiently creative to warrant protection.

A third justification for intellectual property is the *personhood* perspective. Under this theory, all works are bound up in the identities of their creators. Because the creator is solely responsible for the work—the work is, after all, just an extension of the creator's identity—no one would be harmed if the work were completely withheld from society. As a corollary, the creator has the right to withhold his works to any degree. The creator's right of absolute control continues for as long as the works exist.

This perspective is especially common in Europe, where it is expressed as the *droit moral* or the *droit d'auteur* (the moral right or the author's right). Interestingly, the *droit moral* only applies in the case of cultural works—things that can be protected by copyright. Patentable, technological innovations do not enjoy a similar *droit d'inventeur*.

The personhood perspective is less common in the United States, but it shows up as the *termination* right—the ability of authors to terminate a copyright license unilaterally 35 years after the creation of a work, and in certain specialized protections for sculptures and visual arts. It also frequently appears in arguments for longer terms of copyright protection.

About "Property"

There are two basic misconceptions to address before continuing. First, thinking of "property" as an inherent part of an object rather than artifact of the legal system, and second, thinking of property as a singular right rather than a collection of various rights.

Property as a legal concept

A "good" is an item. It has an independent existence regardless of the law. Land, trees, books, bananas, clean air, and information all are goods. They may not all be tangible, but they exist in some sense outside of any system of laws. They would still exist on Mars, where there are no governments or laws (yet).

"Property," on the other hand, is a legal concept only. Property is the name that we give to something that we have legal control over. The land on Mars is not anybody's property. It won't be anybody's property until there is a system of laws that allows some entity to claim it, control it, and use force to evict people from it.

Among the IP minimalists mentioned at the start of this chapter, some go so far as to denounce the very use of the term "intellectual property." The Free Software Foundation (FSF) places it among "Phrases that are Worth Avoiding" (*http://www.gnu.org/philosophy/words-to-avoid.html#IntellectualProperty*). Others scoff at the idea that using an idea, song, or algorithm could ever be "stealing."

There are some IP maximalists, on the other hand, who find it ridiculous that an idea could ever be "free." They would argue that using someone else's idea is *always* stealing, that you just can't always enforce your rights.

Both of these extremes represent opposite sides of the same fundamental misunderstanding. Intellectual property is a hybrid good made up of equal parts information and law. The IP minimalists look at the hybrid and see only the underlying information; the IP maximalists look at the hybrid and see only the legal controls. In this hybrid sense, at least, the term "intellectual property" is appropriate: it acknowledges both the informational and legal aspects of the combined good.

As a corollary, it is interesting to note similar confusion around the term "stealing." Stealing is the violation of a legal property right, so unauthorized use of intellectual property *is* stealing. However, once that property right expires, it is impossible to steal the remaining information. No matter how attached the creator may be to a particular piece of knowledge, everyone in the world "possesses the whole of it."

Property as a bundle of rights

The second major misconception about property rights is that they are singular. The truth is that any kind of property is a collection of separate and independent rights. Each one of those rights may be individually sold, licensed, given away, or destroyed.

One common analogy is to compare property rights to a bundle of sticks. Each stick represents a different legal claim that you have on the underlying good. For example, land has a number of rights associated with it: there are separate rights associated with being on the land, drilling or mining on the land, building on the land, living on the land, and walking or driving across a particular portion of the land. In some cases there may be other rights, such as the right to build a tall building on the land (separate from short building rights), the right to use the water on the land, and the right to fish or hunt on the land. Each one of these rights (and almost any other rights you might be able to come up with that concern the use of the land) is an individual property right. Many times people own the whole bundle of rights, but just as many times they don't. For example, most people in Texas don't own the mineral rights to the land underneath their houses. That is, they don't own the right to anything more than 500 feet down from the bottom of their houses.

You get a different bundle of rights when you own IP, but you still get multiple rights. For example, the United States code specifies that a copyright owner gets exclusive rights to:

- Reproduce the copyrighted work in copies or phonorecords.
- Prepare derivative works based upon the copyrighted work.
- Distribute copies or phonorecords of the copyrighted work to the public by sale or other transfer of ownership, or by rental, lease, or lending.
- Perform the copyrighted work publicly.

- Display the copyrighted work publicly.
- In the case of sound recordings, perform the copyrighted work publicly by means of a digital audio transmission.

In addition, each one of these rights can be broken down further into even smaller "bundles." Take the right "to reproduce the copyrighted work in copies or phonorecords." That right can be broken down temporally (you may reproduce the work for one year), geographically (you may reproduce the work in your own state), by format (you may reproduce the work on compact disc only), or by almost any other restriction you might care to dream up.

There is no obligation to be consistent about how you slice and dice your bundles of rights. You may sell the same right to different people, you may license different rights for different amounts, or you may keep all of the rights to yourself.

Property rights and enforcement

Despite the negative associations some people have with the idea of intellectual output being termed "property," the status of intellectual property as property has an important function in our legal system. Specifically, property rights can be enforced with an *injunction*. That means that the courts will enforce the property owner's rights to exclude others from using the intellectual property; they will order any infringing users to stop. This is in contrast to equity rights, which will be enforced by the courts only by requiring an infringing user to pay damages (usually money).

Evaluating the System

So, does intellectual property work? Yes...and no. In one sense, our intellectual property system has been phenomenally successful in encouraging people to create intellectual property. For the past 50 years—and especially the past 30—there has been a tide of stronger intellectual property protections across industries. This growth in IP has encouraged people to invest heavily in the development of new intellectual property, and has moved IP to the core of many business strategies. For most businesses in the United States, in fact, the intellectual property part of the business is the most valuable aspect of the business.

Nevertheless, people's attitudes about intellectual property are changing. We are starting to see a swing away from stronger intellectual property protections, and toward more openness and collaboration. As things change, it is important to understand not only the current intellectual property laws, but also the structure and purpose of the underlying system. Part of this swing toward openness is reflected in the growing acceptance and importance of open source software.

Whether or not people agree about the desirability of intellectual property, it still has to be acknowledged as an independent discipline and a major force in the computing industry. For example, there are intellectual property divisions in law schools, intellectual property departments in corporations, and intellectual property lawyers in the telephone book.

Furthermore, different concepts under the intellectual property umbrella work together and it takes a lawyer to help you understand how they are coordinated and apply to your specific situation. For instance, should a particular inventor rely on a trade secret or a patent for protection? Is copyright enough to protect a cartoon character, or should it be registered as a trademark as well? These concepts become entwined through use.

The next chapters take a deeper dive into the specifics of each branch of intellectual property. Except where necessary, I will not return again to the broader foundations of intellectual property law. As you read, however, it would be valuable to consider the philosophical foundations as they relate to each branch of the law. In some cases, the original intent has been frustrated by later developments in the law. In other cases, the utilitarian bargain is more or less working as expected.

Either way, intellectual property is in a state of flux. The development of IP law and the ability to enforce IP rights usually lags behind the technologies that both enhance and threaten those who define their lives and their businesses in terms of intellectual property. Keeping an eye on the fundamentals is one way to predict the ways in which IP law and technology in general will move in the future.

CHAPTER TWO

The Patent Document

Imagine you are a programmer learning a new computer language. When you are given a program in the new language, the syntax is usually obscure even if the overall constructs are familiar. Repeated exposure and study may alert you to reserved words and give you an idea of their meaning, but fully understanding the program requires you to know the *syntax* and *semantics* of the language as well as the problem domain addressed by the code.

Patents are the type of intellectual property that most closely resemble code in this context. A well-written patent document is highly structured, with required sections, definitions, reserved words, and "program flow" constructs.

As a result, patent documents tend to be very boring, somewhat ungrammatical, and only semi-intelligible to an ordinary competent English speaker. Even when you understand the problem domain addressed by a particular patent (i.e., the area of technology described within the patent) you do not fully understand the patent until you also have a handle on the specificities of the patent language.

In fact, patents are specifically like pattern-matching code such as regular expressions. Instead of matching text, however, patents match technology. As anyone who has used regular expressions can tell you, though, very complex regular expressions don't always match what you think they should when you first run them. Patents are similar; in truth, nobody (not even patent lawyers) knows *exactly* what a patent will match until the patent is tested by running it through a court.

Patent law differs from other forms of intellectual property in its substantial focus on the patent document itself. The limits and bounds of the patent grant are almost entirely defined by the words and phrases used in the patent instrument.

This chapter is one of two in this book that look at patents, one of the most controversial topics at the crossroads of computers and intellectual property. Because patent law is so intimately concerned with the language and structure of the patent document, it is valuable to begin by looking at the patent document itself. Only after we understand the patent document can we begin to look at getting and using the patent.

The Construction of a Patent

Pattern-matching code usually has a compact form used to represent the range of possible inputs matched by a particular expression. Examples include regular expressions, tag tables, document type definitions (DTDs), and schema. State machines or automata can also be used to represent patterns.

As noted earlier, patents are very similar to code, pattern-matching code in particular. It should not be surprising, then, that a patent document has a detailed file format, not unlike the file formats used by your computer.

For example, the standard file format for Linux is called the *Executable and Linking Format*, or ELF for short. Every ELF file begins with a structure called the *ELF header*. This structure contains information that describes the contents of the file. It includes the file's magic-number signature, with flags indicating whether the contents are 32-bit or 64-bit, little-endian or big-endian, etc.

After the ELF header comes the *program header table*, which points to the various parts of your program. This is followed by one or more code segments and (usually) a section header table used for linking your program.

The format of a patent is surprisingly similar to the format of an ELF file. The first page of the patent is called the *face* of the patent and acts like a header for the patent file. It contains information about the patent. For example, it includes the patent number, the list of inventors, the patent's magic dates, a list of cited references, and an abstract describing the contents of the file.

After the face of the patent come the *figures* and *short descriptions*, designed to illustrate the various parts of your invention. This is followed by the *detailed description*, a series of paragraphs describing the implementation and functioning of your invention as illustrated by the figures. The final part of the patent consists of the *claims*, a series of sentences describing the bounds of legal protection granted by the patent.

The similarities are illustrated in Figure 2-1.

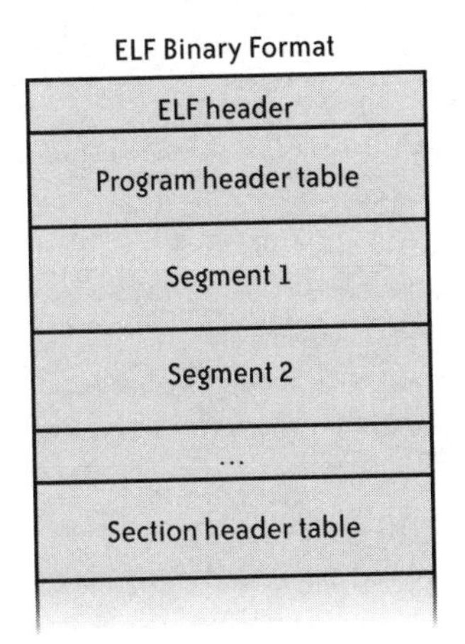

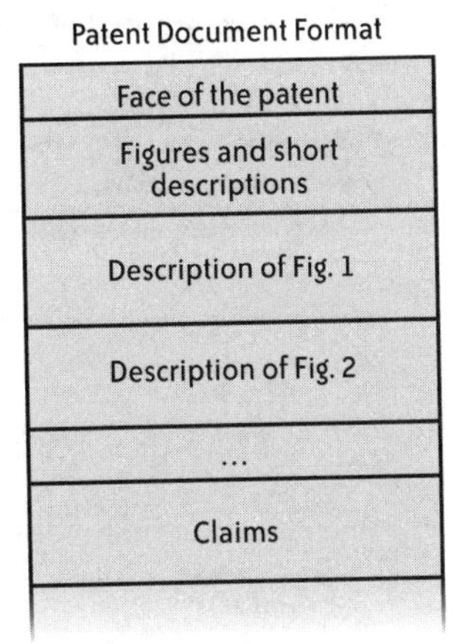

FIGURE 2-1. ELF versus patent file format

Figure 2-2 shows the front page of a typical patent. In fact, this is Amazon.com's famous *1-click* patent. I will use this patent to illustrate certain general features of patents by calling out individual portions of the document. In particular, we will pull apart the first and last pages (the face of the patent and the claims), which hold most of the legally relevant information.

We will also talk about the structure, content, and significance of the middle of the patent, called the *specification* or *disclosure*. The point of the disclosure, as its name suggests, is to teach people how to recreate the invention (even though some inventors do better than others with that requirement). But just as the code segments in an ELF file will vary between programs, so will the specifications in various patents vary from each other. So, instead of talking about the specific contents of the detailed description, we will talk in general about how the descriptions are structured and how they relate to the rest of the patent document.

The Face of the Patent

The face of the patent contains metainformation about the patent—required dates, numbers, outside references, etc. We will examine certain portions of the face in detail.

The Patent Number

The largest feature on the face of the patent (aside from the designation of the document as a United States Patent) is the assigned patent number. Patent numbers are assigned in order as patent applications are approved. Therefore, the assigned patent numbers not only provide unique identifiers for each invention, but also serve as a running tally of all patents approved

US005960411A

United States Patent [19]

Hartman et al.

[11] **Patent Number: 5,960,411**

[45] **Date of Patent: Sep. 28, 1999**

[54] **METHOD AND SYSTEM FOR PLACING A PURCHASE ORDER VIA A COMMUNICATIONS NETWORK**

[75] Inventors: **Peri Hartman; Jeffrey P. Bezos; Shel Kaphan; Joel Spiegel**, all of Seattle, Wash.

[73] Assignee: **Amazon.com, Inc.**, Seattle, Wash.

[21] Appl. No.: **08/928,951**

[22] Filed: **Sep. 12, 1997**

[51] **Int. Cl.**[6] **G06F 17/60**
[52] **U.S. Cl.** **705/26**; 705/27; 345/962
[58] **Field of Search** 705/26, 27; 380/24, 380/25; 235/2, 375, 378, 381; 395/188.01; 345/962

[56] **References Cited**

U.S. PATENT DOCUMENTS

4,937,863	6/1990	Robert et al.	380/4
5,204,897	4/1993	Wyman	380/4
5,260,999	11/1993	Wyman	384/4
5,627,940	5/1997	Rohra et al.	395/12
5,640,501	6/1997	Turpin	395/768
5,640,577	6/1997	Scharmer	395/768
5,664,111	9/1997	Nahan et al.	705/27
5,715,314	2/1998	Payne et al.	380/24
5,715,399	2/1998	Bezos	705/27
5,727,163	3/1998	Bezos	705/27
5,745,681	4/1998	Levine et al.	395/200.3
5,758,126	5/1998	Daniels et al.	395/500

FOREIGN PATENT DOCUMENTS

0855659 A1	1/1998	European Pat. Off.	G06F 17/30
0855687 A2	1/1998	European Pat. Off.	G07F 19/00
0845747A2	6/1998	European Pat. Off.	G06F 17/60
0883076A2	12/1998	European Pat. Off.	G06F 17/60
WO 95/30961	11/1995	WIPO	G06F 17/60
WO 96/38799	12/1996	WIPO	G06F 17/60
WO 98/21679	5/1998	WIPO	G06F 17/60

OTHER PUBLICATIONS

Jones, Chris. "Java Shopping Cart and Java Wallet; Oracles plans to join e-commerce initiative." Mar. 31, 1997, InfoWorld Media Group.

"Pacific Coast Software Software creates virtual shopping cart." Sep. 6, 1996. M2 Communications Ltd 1996.

"Software Creates Virtual Shopping Cart." Sep. 5, 1996. Business Wire, Inc.

Terdoslavich, William. "Java Electronic Commerce Framework." Computer Reseller News, Sep. 23, 1996, CMP Media, Inc., 1996, pp. 126, http://www.elibrary.com/id/101/101/getdoc . . . rydocid=902269@library_d&dtype=0-0&dinst=. [Accessed Nov. 19, 1998].

"Internet Access: Disc Distributing Announces Interactive World Wide." Cambridge Work-Group Computing Report, Cambridge Publishing, Inc., 1995, http://www.elibrary.com/id/101/101/getdoc . . . docid=1007497@library_a&dtype=0-0&dinst=0. [Accessed Nov. 19, 1998].

(List continued on next page.)

Primary Examiner—James P. Trammell
Assistant Examiner—Demetra R. Smith
Attorney, Agent, or Firm—Perkins Coie LLP

[57] **ABSTRACT**

A method and system for placing an order to purchase an item via the Internet. The order is placed by a purchaser at a client system and received by a server system. The server system receives purchaser information including identification of the purchaser, payment information, and shipment information from the client system. The server system then assigns a client identifier to the client system and associates the assigned client identifier with the received purchaser information. The server system sends to the client system the assigned client identifier and an HTML document identifying the item and including an order button. The client system receives and stores the assigned client identifier and receives and displays the HTML document. In response to the selection of the order button, the client system sends to the server system a request to purchase the identified item. The server system receives the request and combines the purchaser information associated with the client identifier of the client system to generate an order to purchase the item in accordance with the billing and shipment information whereby the purchaser effects the ordering of the product by selection of the order button.

26 Claims, 11 Drawing Sheets

FIGURE 2-2. Page 1 of the 1-click patent

by the United States Patent and Trademark Office (USPTO or PTO) since the organization of the office on July 4, 1836. (Patents were approved prior to this date by the secretary of state; there were about 10,000 patents between the first patent act in 1790 and 1836.)

There is not any necessary correspondence between a patent's number and its application date, its issue date, or any other date associated with the patent. Because numbers are issued in order of approval, however, you can get a rough idea of the age of a patent by looking at its number. At the time of writing, the most recently issued patent is number 7,278,169, for "Controlling the downloading and recording of digital data." The oldest enforceable patent is number 4,739,880 for a "Laundry Hamper." Patents with numbers lower than that have fallen into the public domain. By the time you read this, however, the Laundry Hamper will be old news, and many other patents will also have entered the public domain.

Some patents have letter codes at the start of the number, for example, D552,191 for a "Dragon" design or RE39,316 for a "Sliding visor." These codes refer to specific categories of patents as opposed to standard utility patents. Table 2-1 shows the various specialized patent types.

TABLE 2-1. Specialized patent categories and their numbers

Example patent numbers	Specialized category
RE39,325, RE36,424, RE 41,027	Reexamined patents
PP17,133, PP15,888, PP18,011	Plant patents
D552,191, D485,981, D506,743	Design patents
H2,204, H1,986, H2,034	Statutory Invention Registrations
T1,012, T2,875, T1,843	Defensive publications

These specialized types of patents are not as common as utility patents, but they do show up occasionally. The most common type of specialized patent is the design patent, which can be used to protect computer housings (like the iMac), GUI elements, and font designs. Note that a Statutory Invention Registration (SIR) is not a patent. Rather, it is a document that affirmatively places some advance in the public domain. It has drawings and a description like a patent, but it is not required to be new, useful, and non-obvious. SIRs have defensive value, but they do not make the invention excludable.

One thing to note about the patent number is that it provides useful shorthand for referring to the patent. The last three digits of the patent number (411 for the Amazon patent, for example) are like a hash value, and are commonly used as a contraction for the patent number. Thus, the 1-click patent is sometimes referred to as the *'411 patent*.

Mathematicians and statisticians note: this works because the subject matter of the patent is largely uncorrelated to the patent number as a whole and is completely independent relative to the last three digits of the patent number. The birthday paradox applies for groups of patents larger than 37, but patents are not usually dealt with in very large groups. When two patents in the same legal proceeding have the same last three digits, other means, like the short inventors' names, are used to distinguish between them.

Inventors and Inventorship

A patent is said to define one or more inventions made by one or more inventors. The inventors are listed in two places on the patent. Right underneath the "United States Patent" designation at the top is the short list of the inventors. The full listing of inventors is given right under the title (see Figure 2-3 and Figure 2-4).

United States Patent [19] [11] **Patent Number: 5,960,411**
Hartman et al. [45] **Date of Patent: Sep. 28, 1999**

FIGURE 2-3. Patent header showing short list of inventors

[75] Inventors: **Peri Hartman; Jeffrey P. Bezos; Shel Kaphan; Joel Spiegel,** all of Seattle, Wash.

FIGURE 2-4. Full list of inventors

The listing of inventors

As shown in Figure 2-4, all inventors on the patent are shown in the full listing right underneath the title of the patent. If a patent contains multiple inventions (as most do—we will get to that later), it must list all inventors for each invention. Each inventor has separate rights to the patent; to "own" a patent, a company must get an agreement from every inventor.

The short list of inventors is not particularly important except that it determines the "inventor" of the patented invention in the public's mind. Among those in the know, there is a subtle jockeying to become the first named inventor on the patent application. If you can be the first named inventor, your name will be the name that shows up in the short list at the top of the patent.

For example, Jeff Bezos, CEO of Amazon.com, was a co-inventor of the 1-click method. Many legal filings, though, refer to this as the "Hartman" patent, because Peri Hartman is the first named inventor.

Inventorship: becoming an inventor

The process of becoming an inventor is called *inventorship*. Although inventorship is a relatively simple concept, it can be difficult to get right in some situations. Getting it right is important because failing to list all inventors or mistakenly listing a non-inventor can make a patent invalid (and thus unenforceable).

According to the definition, an inventor is a person who *conceives* and, either personally or through directing someone else, *actually* or *constructively* reduces an invention to practice. Unpacking that definition a bit, there are two separate acts that go into becoming an inventor:

conception, or coming up with the specifics of the idea, and reducing the idea to practice—legalese for making it work.

Conception of the Invention

Conceiving an invention is more than just "thinking it up." For example, most of us have "thought up" teleportation. What we haven't thought up are the specifics of a working idea. Even if we assume that someone already came up with a machine that would be theoretically capable of teleportation, but they just didn't realize that the machine could be used for teleportation, that person would still not have conceived teleportation in the legal sense. To be an inventor, you must come up with and recognize that you have a working idea.

The conception of an invention is complete if an inventor *can* provide a description that would enable a person having ordinary skill in the art to actually make the invention without extensive research or experimentation. This is sometimes called an *enabling disclosure*.

Reduction to practice

Reducing an invention to practice involves the process of filling in the technical details necessary to make the invention work. Sometimes the process of stating an idea makes the reduction to practice obvious; many times it does not.

A good example showing the distinction between conception and reduction to practice is the story of Thomas Edison and the lightbulb. Very early on, Edison had a working idea—that passing electricity through a resistant material could cause it to glow, providing light. Turning that conception into a workable lightbulb, however, was difficult. Edison tried over 6,000 different materials before trying the carbonized cotton thread filament that resulted in patent number 223,898.

A reduction to practice can be either *actual* (you actually build the invention) or *constructive*. I stated earlier that the conception is complete when the inventor *can* make an enabling disclosure. Constructive reduction to practice is complete when the inventor *actually makes* that disclosure.

Practical considerations in inventorship

In many circumstances, there is no question about inventorship. Either one person or a small number of people conceives, designs, and builds the invention. When there is more than one person, all of them are listed as co-inventors. Nevertheless, there are two recurring issues that complicate real-world inventorship discussions: political and business pressures, and determining contributions.

The first issue is political. Sometimes it is good office politics to include your boss in the list of inventors. Other times, especially when bonuses are given for successful patent applications, there is an incentive to include or not to include other people that may have had a part in the invention. This issue also raises its head when someone outside the company, like an independent contractor, is responsible for part of an invention. Business policies may indicate that outsiders do not qualify as inventors.

If you are tempted to cave in to this sort of political pressure regarding inventorship, *don't*. At best you will cost yourself a couple thousand dollars to fix the problem later. In other situations, you will cost yourself hundreds of thousands (or even millions) of dollars when someone else fixes the problem for you. At worst, you will lose the patent.

For example, I am familiar with one situation where a person was kept off the inventor list for a patent because of political considerations like these. Many years later, the patent was the subject of a lawsuit for hundreds of millions of dollars worth of damages. When the existence of the unlisted inventor came up during the lawsuit, the defendant company contacted the unlisted inventor and obtained a separate license to the patent. Instead of winning hundreds of millions of dollars, the accusing company had to drop the lawsuit and swallow its (multimillion-dollar) costs.

The second issue in inventorship is practical. Sometimes it is hard to distinguish between somebody who just worked on an invention under the direction of the inventor and somebody who actually contributed to the invention itself. A person who merely builds the invention based on the inventor's detailed conception is not an inventor. The implementer may have to be counted as an inventor, though, if the conception was changed during construction or if there was an original contribution beyond the guidance from the original inventor that allowed the conception to be successfully reduced to practice.

Legally, inventorship is considered on a claim-by-claim basis (the claims are short, discrete statements about the invention at the end of the patent—we will discuss them more later). Anyone who comes up with an idea or implementation detail that is important enough to be included in the claims should be listed as an inventor.

Ownership of a Patent

As discussed further in Chapter 7 and Chapter 9, one distinction common to the various types of intellectual property is that the *creator* of a protected work is not always the same person as the *owner* of the protected work. In patent law, that means that inventorship is separated from ownership. The default rule in the United States is that the inventor owns the patent unless there are contracts that change this arrangement. But just like a piece of tangible property, the patent can be sold, licensed, or destroyed.

Selling a patent

When people talk about selling a patent, what they are really talking about is *assigning* the rights granted by the government to another person (or entity). This assignment allows a non-inventor to exercise all the rights originally held by the inventor, including the all-important right of excludability. In most corporate circumstances, employees are required to assign all of the intellectual property they create, including patents, to their employer. In other circumstances, the inventor can assign the patent to someone else in exchange for a payment. Figure 2-5 shows the *assignee* (the entity receiving the assignment) of the '411 patent as Amazon.com.

[73] Assignee: **Amazon.com, Inc.**, Seattle, Wash.

FIGURE 2-5. Assignment of the '411 patent

Patents can be assigned many times throughout their lives. While there are databases that keep track of the current assignee of each current patent, the face of the patent and the text provided to the USPTO patent search engine reflect only the assignment in force when the patent was issued. Therefore, you cannot be sure of who owns any particular patent simply by looking at its face. The easiest way to check a patent's ownership is to look at the USPTO's Public PAIR web site at *http://portal.uspto.gov/external/portal/pair* or the public assignment database at *http://assignments.uspto.gov/assignments/q?db=pat.*

Licensing a patent

In legalese, a patent license is a limited grant to exercise one or more of the limited rights granted to the patent holder. In English, a patent license means that you are not forbidden from building, selling, using, or importing the invention covered by the patent. This is phrased in the negative because patents only grant negative rights. Patents make knowledge excludable; a patent license stops the legal exclusivity from applying to someone. There are two primary distinctions between a patent license and a patent assignment or sale. First, a licensee usually only gets a subset of the rights granted to the patent holder. Second, the patent does not actually change hands; the assignee still owns the patent for legal purposes.

Although most patents are assigned at least once in their lives, licenses are by far the most common type of intellectual property transaction. This is because the patent instrument itself is a private good; only one entity (or a countable, finite number of entities) can own the patent at one time (Chapter 1 has an extensive discussion of the economic principles underlying these labels). The rights associated with the patent, however, are a club good; they can be licensed to many people simultaneously.

Destroying a patent

A patent is destroyed if the patent holder dedicates it to the public domain. Although this is not very common, it does happen occasionally. The most well-known example in recent times is probably RSA patent 4,405,829, "Cryptographic Communications System And Method," covering public-key cryptography. The '829 patent was due to expire September 20, 2000, but the RSA Corporation dedicated it to the public domain on September 6, 2000—two weeks early. As a result of RSA Corporation's dedication, all of the rights associated with the patent were destroyed two weeks earlier than they would have been otherwise, and the RSA Corporation received a wave of good publicity.

Patents can also be destroyed as a result of legal action. If a court (or in certain circumstances, the PTO) is convinced that certain claims of a patent are *anticipated*, that is, if someone else created them first, then those claims can be declared unenforceable. Even more serious is *inequitable conduct*. Inequitable conduct is a broad term for deceiving, misleading, or concealing information from the PTO. If a court finds that a patent holder engaged in inequitable conduct, the entire patent can be declared unenforceable.

Inventions as a public good

While most modern inventors work for companies that require them to assign all of their inventions to their employers, the separation of inventorship and ownership still serves to emphasize the utilitarian bargain inherent in patent law. U.S. patents are granted only to *people*, never to corporations or other artificial entities. Even if the patent is assigned many times throughout its life, the face of the patent always reflects the names of the people who invented it.

The reason that patents are granted only to people goes back to the economic rationale underlying the U.S. Patent Act. Patents are designed to reward the creation of new knowledge, an essentially *human* act. Assignees are usually corporations—economic actors with no inventive capacity. The patent law thus recognizes and rewards human inventiveness by giving inventors that disclose their inventions the first right to control their creations, regardless of company affiliation.

In practice, however, companies usually require all employees to sign assignment agreements that hand over full control of all patent rights to the company. See Chapter 9 for a much more extensive discussion of employee assignment agreements.

This can get a little difficult if there are multiple inventors—particularly in situations where some of the inventors on a patent are not employees of the company. In that case, each inventor has full ownership of the patent rights associated with the patent, and each inventor can use or assign rights to the patent as she sees fit.

Patents and Dates

One of the most important features of patent law is a time limit on the rights granted by a patent. This limitation comes directly from the constitutional authorization for the Patent Act; the act is authorized only to provide exclusive rights for limited times. Therefore, the dates associated with a particular patent are of supreme importance, as those dates define the temporal boundaries of the patent protection.

For those seeking patent protection, the patent dates serve another function. Usually, many people are working in the same area of study and sometimes a couple of people "invent" the same thing at around the same time. Patent dates are used to determine who gets priority when two inventors' applications overlap in time.

With that in mind, there are three magic dates associated with a U.S. patent, all of which appear on the face of the patent document. In reverse chronological order, they are the *issue date*, the *application date*, and the *priority date*.

The issue date

The issue date is the date that the patent was officially granted by the USPTO. It is listed in the header for the patent as the "Date of Patent" (Figure 2-6).

United States Patent [19]	[11] **Patent Number:**	**5,960,411**
Hartman et al.	[45] **Date of Patent:**	**Sep. 28, 1999**

FIGURE 2-6. '411 patent header showing the issue date

A patent becomes official only after it has been issued. Even granted applications (applications that have been reviewed by the PTO and judged worthy of a patent) do not acquire any legal force until they have been published by the government. Thus the issue date (or patent date, as it is sometimes called) does not relate to date of invention; rather, it only marks the start of the patent holder's exclusive rights over that invention.

A person can still try to license an idea before the patent is granted, or warn potential competitors not to start developing products that could be considered infringing when the patent is granted later. After filing, therefore, the inventors can publicize their invention as *patent pending*.

A note for those who have participated in the patenting process and are awaiting the official publication of the patent: check the PTO web site Tuesday afternoon. New patents are always published Tuesday morning.

The application date

The application date marks the day when a sufficiently complete *application* for a *utility patent* entered the PTO's examination system. Under most circumstances, it also serves as the priority date (as discussed next). It is recorded on the face of the patent, as shown in Figure 2-7.

[22] Filed: **Sep. 12, 1997**

FIGURE 2-7. Application date

The United States application date is not set by provisional applications (preliminary applications that "keep your place in line") or applications filed before a different government body (such as the European or Japanese patent offices). The application date frequently serves as the *earliest filing date*.

The priority date

The priority date in the U.S. patent system is usually date of the earliest patent filing, unless you need to and can prove that you officially created your invention earlier. Usually this priority date is the same as the application date. If a patent *claims priority* to some document that was filed earlier than the utility patent application, however, and there is support in the earlier document for what is claimed in the application, then the date of the earlier document is used as the priority date.

FIRST TO FILE VERSUS FIRST TO INVENT

The United States patent system is unusual because it is presently a *first to invent* system, not a *first to file* system. A first to invent system grants patent rights to the person who can prove the *earliest reduction to practice*. A first to file system grants patent rights to the *first person who files a patent application* describing the invention. Most patent systems outside the United States use a first to file model.

First to file systems are much easier to manage because there is no ambiguity about which of several competing patent applications should be granted priority. On the other hand, first to file systems are criticized because the eventual patent rights are granted based upon a "race to the patent office" rather than on the true date of invention. This is seen by some as unfair to small inventors, who cannot file applications as quickly as well-funded corporations. In reality, a lot of large corporations take months to prepare and file their applications, so smaller, more nimble inventors can have an edge.

With the growing number of patent applications, however, the additional cost and complexity of the first to invent system is drawing fire. There is currently pending legislation to move the United States to a first to file system. Many industry watchers believe that the U.S. will move to a first to file system in the next several years.

The priority date matters because this is the magic date that divides *prior art* from new ideas. Prior art is the patent law term for everything known to the public before you conceived your idea. Your priority date is, in effect, your "place in line" on the inventor's timeline.

As described earlier, although the priority date is frequently the same as the application date, this is not always the case. For example, look at U.S. Pat. No. 6,996,836, shown in Figure 2-8.

(22) Filed: **Nov. 19, 2002**

(65) **Prior Publication Data**

US 2003/0126618 A1 Jul. 3, 2003

Related U.S. Application Data

(63) Continuation of application No. 09/137,448, filed on Aug. 11, 1998, now Pat. No. 6,484,317, which is a continuation of application No. 08/638,280, filed on Apr. 26, 1996, now Pat. No. 5,841,468.

FIGURE 2-8. '836 patent priority information

The specific application leading to the '836 patent was filed on November 19, 2002. The application filed in 2002, however, had a "parent" application filed in 1998, and the 1998 parent had a parent of its own filed in 1996. That means that the priority date, or legal date of invention for this 2006-issued patent, officially occurred all the way back in 1996.

Remember, the priority date is the dividing line between prior art (which can be used to challenge a patent) and ideas that are not prior art (which rarely help challenge a patent, and might infringe the patent). For example, competitors trying to work around or challenge this particular patent are generally restricted to prior art published before the 1996 priority date.

More broadly, if someone files for a patent on a technology that later becomes mainstream, there will be many applications that use the technology by the time the patent issues. That is one reason why many people complain when patents are issued; by the time the patent issues, the technology is old and obvious to ordinary practitioners. To properly judge new advances, however, patents must be judged by the circumstances existing at the time the invention was created.

The patent term

The application date and issue date (and in some cases the earliest filing date/priority date or international application filing date) work together to determine the length of a patent's lifetime, called the patent's *term*. The end of a patent's enforceable period is called the *expiration date*.

The rules for calculating expiration dates changed in 1995 when the United States passed laws to implement the Agreement on Trade Related Aspects of Intellectual Property Rights (TRIPS agreement). Before TRIPS, a patent expired 17 years after the issue date. After the TRIPS agreement, the formula was changed so that patents expire 20 years after their earliest non-provisional priority dates.

Rather than making a retroactive change, the United States chose to adopt a phased strategy for implementing the new patent terms. Accordingly, we are currently in a period of transition between the different methods of calculating a patent's expiration date. As a result, calculation of the expiration date can be somewhat complicated.

To figure out the term of a patent, the two most important pieces of information are the issue date and the *earliest filing date*. The issue date was discussed earlier. The earliest filing date is the earliest one of:

- The date of the first utility patent application from which the current application claims priority
- The date of a Patent Cooperation Treaty (PCT) international filing

Just to make things confusing, the earliest filing date is *not* the date of a provisional application, nor is it the date of a patent application filed in a foreign country (those two filings provide a priority date, but not a filing date).

Sometimes, there can be more than one application in the same patent *family*. Patents in the same family use the same (or part of the same) specification to describe a number of logically distinct or overlapping inventions. The first patent application in the family is the *parent* application. The application date of the parent is the earliest filing date.

As mentioned, all recent patents (filed as of June 8, 1995) generally have an expiration date 20 years after the earliest filing date. This 20-year term is mostly consistent between nations; eventually, all patents, including patents in foreign countries, will all share the 20-year-term calculation. U.S. patents filed before June 8, 1995 have a term that is the longer of 17 years from the issue date of the application, or 20 years from the earliest filing date of the application.

Exceptions to the rule

Even within these rules, individual patent terms are subject to exceptions. The two most important of these are *terminal disclaimers*, where an applicant is forced to give up part of the patent term, and *patent term adjustments*, extra time added to the term because of PTO delay or a few other permitted reasons. Terminal disclaimers and patent term adjustments are normally listed on the face of the patent, but individual checking is necessary if you have to calculate the exact term for a particular patent.

Other Information on the Face of the Patent

The rest of the information on the face of the patent can be generally divided into two parts: an outline of the history of the patent and a synopsis of the patent document itself.

The historical outline

During the PTO's examination of a patent application, the examiner keeps a record of all the arguments, references, and statements made during the examination process. This information becomes public after a patent is issued and is known as the *file history* or the *file wrapper*. The entire course of examination is laid bare in the file history. The examiner puts forth prior art and can make rejections based on the prior art, after which the applicant points out the distinguishing features included in the claims that are not taught by the prior art references.

This patent history can be seen in miniature on the face of the patent. Not only are the application number and examiners' names listed, but also every piece of prior art that was considered by the examiner during the course of the examination. This prior art is referred to as being *listed on the face of the patent*. Figure 2-9 shows some of the prior art references for Amazon's '411 patent.

[56] **References Cited**

U.S. PATENT DOCUMENTS

4,937,863	6/1990	Robert et al.	380/4
5,204,897	4/1993	Wyman	380/4
5,260,999	11/1993	Wyman	384/4
5,627,940	5/1997	Rohra et al.	395/12
5,640,501	6/1997	Turpin	395/768
5,640,577	6/1997	Scharmer	395/768
5,664,111	9/1997	Nahan et al.	705/27
5,715,314	2/1998	Payne et al.	380/24
5,715,399	2/1998	Bezos	705/27
5,727,163	3/1998	Bezos	705/27
5,745,681	4/1998	Levine et al.	395/200.3
5,758,126	5/1998	Daniels et al.	395/500

FOREIGN PATENT DOCUMENTS

0855659 A1	1/1998	European Pat. Off.	G06F 17/30
0855687 A2	1/1998	European Pat. Off.	G07F 19/00
0845747A2	6/1998	European Pat. Off.	G06F 17/60
0883076A2	12/1998	European Pat. Off.	G06F 17/60
WO 95/30961	11/1995	WIPO	G06F 17/60
WO 96/38799	12/1996	WIPO	G06F 17/60
WO 98/21679	5/1998	WIPO	G06F 17/60

OTHER PUBLICATIONS

Jones, Chris. "Java Shopping Cart and Java Wallet; Oracles plans to join e–commerce initiative." Mar. 31, 1997, Info-World Media Group.

FIGURE 2-9. Prior art references cited in Amazon's 1-click patent

Having prior art listed on the face of the patent is a little like receiving a vaccination against a disease. When you receive a vaccination, you are injected with a small amount of a potentially dangerous virus. In overcoming the virus, your body develops defenses against that specific bug; it becomes very unlikely that the exact same virus will ever hurt you again.

In similar fashion, it is very unlikely that any prior art listed on the face of the patent can be used against you again. The prior art listed on the face of the patent has been reviewed by the examiner, and there is a strong presumption that the examiner was doing his job. Therefore, just like exposure to a virus immunizes you against that bug, exposure to a particular piece of prior art helps immunize you against that art.

The Synopsis of the Patent

The information on the face of the patent is also designed to give a quick summary of the contents of the patent. There are three different parts of this synopsis: the *title*, the *abstract*, and the *representative figure*.

The title

The title of the invention must be shorter than 500 characters in length and must be as short and specific to the invention as possible. Certain words are not allowed in the title. Specifically, the patent's title may not begin with the articles "a," "an," or "the," or include the phrases "new," "improved," "improvement of," or "improvement in." See Figure 2-10 for an exemplary patent title.

[54] **METHOD AND SYSTEM FOR PLACING A PURCHASE ORDER VIA A COMMUNICATIONS NETWORK**

FIGURE 2-10. Official title of Amazon's '411 patent

The abstract

The abstract of the patent is a single paragraph of 150 words or less that provides a short description of the invention described in the patent. See Figure 2-11 for an example of a patent abstract.

The official purpose of the abstract is to "enable the United States Patent and Trademark Office and the public generally to determine quickly from a cursory inspection the nature and gist of the technical disclosure." As you will notice from the abstract in Figure 2-11, however, patent abstracts are not generally amenable to cursory inspection. Rather than short statements of invention, patent abstracts have been described as a "word salad." (The '411 patent abstract is actually better than most—it can get much worse than this.)

One reason patent abstracts are unclear is that statements in the abstract have been used against patent holders in past court cases. As a result, abstracts try to describe the specific details of an invention in a very general fashion. Unsurprisingly, the outcome of this forced marriage of generality and specificity will put the average person to sleep faster than typical over-the-counter medications.

[57] **ABSTRACT**

A method and system for placing an order to purchase an item via the Internet. The order is placed by a purchaser at a client system and received by a server system. The server system receives purchaser information including identification of the purchaser, payment information, and shipment information from the client system. The server system then assigns a client identifier to the client system and associates the assigned client identifier with the received purchaser information. The server system sends to the client system the assigned client identifier and an HTML document identifying the item and including an order button. The client system receives and stores the assigned client identifier and receives and displays the HTML document. In response to the selection of the order button, the client system sends to the server system a request to purchase the identified item. The server system receives the request and combines the purchaser information associated with the client identifier of the client system to generate an order to purchase the item in accordance with the billing and shipment information whereby the purchaser effects the ordering of the product by selection of the order button.

FIGURE 2-11. Abstract of the '411 patent

The representative figure

Of all three elements in the patent synopsis, the representative figure is probably the most useful. In the U.S., the representative figure is chosen by the patent examiner, not the applicant, and is intended to best represent the patent as a whole. The figure usually provides a top-level view of the process, method, or product described by the patent; it puts the patent in context. In the '411 patent, for example, the examiner felt that the flowchart in Figure 2-12 best illustrated the gist of Amazon's 1-click system.

Applicants are required to provide a figure where necessary for the understanding of the invention. If the drawing is necessary to understand the invention (and for mechanical or computer-related inventions, it almost always is) the examiner can request one, and the patent will not be issued until the applicant provides a drawing. Even if a figure is *not* necessary to understand the invention, but the invention *can* be depicted in a figure, the examiner has the right to require that a figure be provided.

The Body of the Patent

The body of the patent is commonly called the *specification*. It makes up the bulk of the patent document, and is the part of the document most people refer to when they talk about the patent. On first glance, this seems reasonable; after all, the specification contains all of the

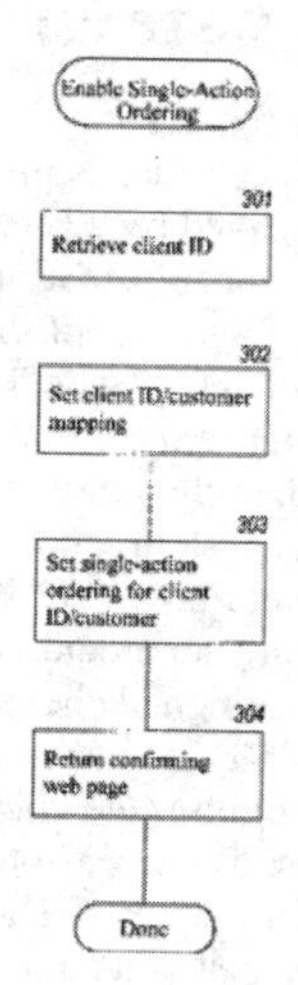

FIGURE 2-12. The representative figure for Amazon's '411 patent

pictures, equations, method descriptions, and assorted details necessary to make the invention work.

It doesn't matter; much of what is written in the specification has *relatively little effect* on what is covered by the patent. Most experienced patent lawyers will skip right to the claims when interpreting a patent. This is changing, however; there are some recent cases that held patents invalid based on screwy comments or poor drafting in the specifications. Further, any ambiguous claim terms are interpreted by referring to the specification and patent history. Nevertheless, the fact remains that the specification is one of the least legally significant parts of the patent.

So why include a specification at all? One answer goes back to the utilitarian bargain inherent in the patent law. The specification preserves and communicates to society the knowledge held by the inventor. The technical know-how contained within the specification gives the patent long-run value by enabling others to make and use the invention after the patent expires. The short-run value (the boundaries of the right to exclude) are largely defined by the dates on the face of the patent and the claims at the back.

With that said, the specification, while not great reading by any means, is the most interesting part of the patent. It generally includes the drawing sheets, the background and summary of the invention, descriptions of the drawings, and a detailed description of various aspects of the invention.

The Drawing Sheets

The drawing sheets are placed right below the face of the patent. As described earlier in the section titled "The representative figure," a patent usually has at least one figure. Most patents have many figures, varying in type according to what they are intended to show.

For example, mechanical devices frequently contain engineering-style drawings showing the parts of the invention. The first figure may be an exploded view, followed by front, side, and top views of the various necessary components. Systems frequently use entity diagrams to show the different parts of the system and the relationships between the parts. Processes are illustrated using flowcharts or decision trees.

Each figure usually contains many reference numbers. *Every* individual part of the drawing is referenced by its own number so that the written description can be cross-referenced with the drawings. Later drawings reuse the same numbers if later parts of the specification describe the same part. Figure 2-13, Figure 2-14, and Figure 2-15 show typical drawing sheets.

The Written Description

As mentioned earlier, the description usually contains the information that gives the patent educational value and helps the patent comply with the legal requirement to fully disclose the invention.

The technical field

The body of many patent specifications begins with a declaration of the field of invention. For example, in Amazon's '411 patent, the invention "relates to a computer method and system for placing an order and, more particularly, to a method and system for ordering items over the Internet." This declaration is not essential, and some patents omit it. It is primarily there as a guide for the Patent Office; when they originally receive the application, it is assigned to an examiner according to the subject matter of the patent. By declaring the technical field, applicants can help ensure that the application will be assigned to an examiner with an appropriate background.

The background and summary of the invention

The background section is a brief discussion of the state of the art in the technological area, including any earlier attempts to solve the problem addressed by the invention. Along the way, the background also serves to introduce common terms that, although not essential to the invention itself, are helpful for understanding the technical problems addressed by the patent. Prior relevant patents (or other references) known to the inventor can also be cited. When provided, the summary provides context for the invention, gives an overview of the specific solutions provided, and presents some specific advantages.

U.S. Patent   Jan. 4, 1994   Sheet 3 of 6   5,276,703

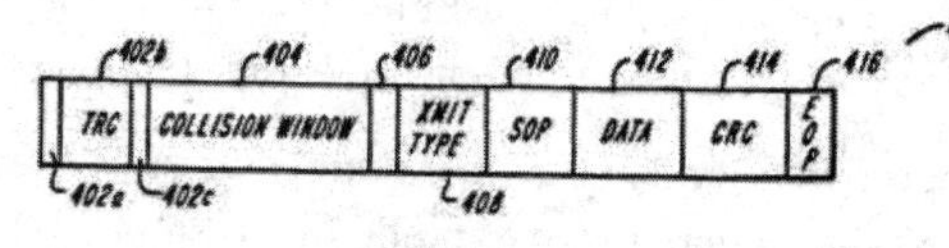

FIG. 4

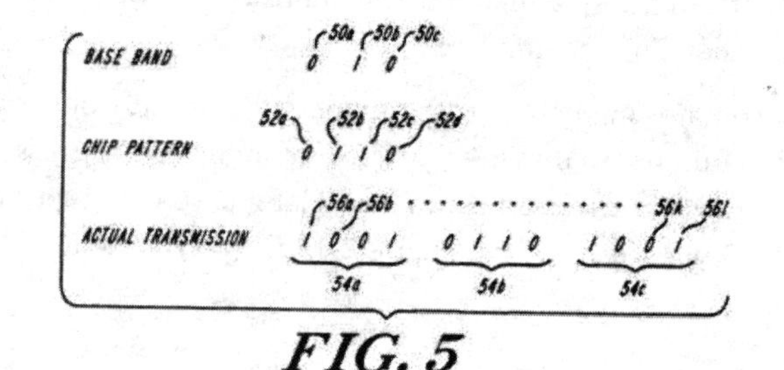

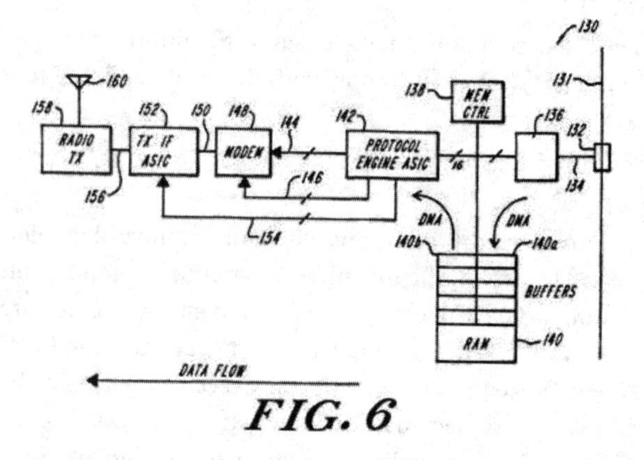

FIGURE 2-13. Drawing sheet for U.S. Pat. No. 5,276,703, "Wireless Local Area Network Communications System"

The background and summary sections were once the easiest places to see and appreciate the invention described in the patent. Unfortunately, the background and summary sections, like the abstract before them, have become less useful in the face of recent court decisions. Specifically, anything in the background is deemed to be *admitted prior art*—that is, prior art that can be used against the inventor without having to provide any other reference. Some patents have been invalidated or otherwise restricted because they mixed together the summary of the invention with the background; their own inventive descriptions were held against them as admitted prior art and they lost the protection over part or all of their inventions.

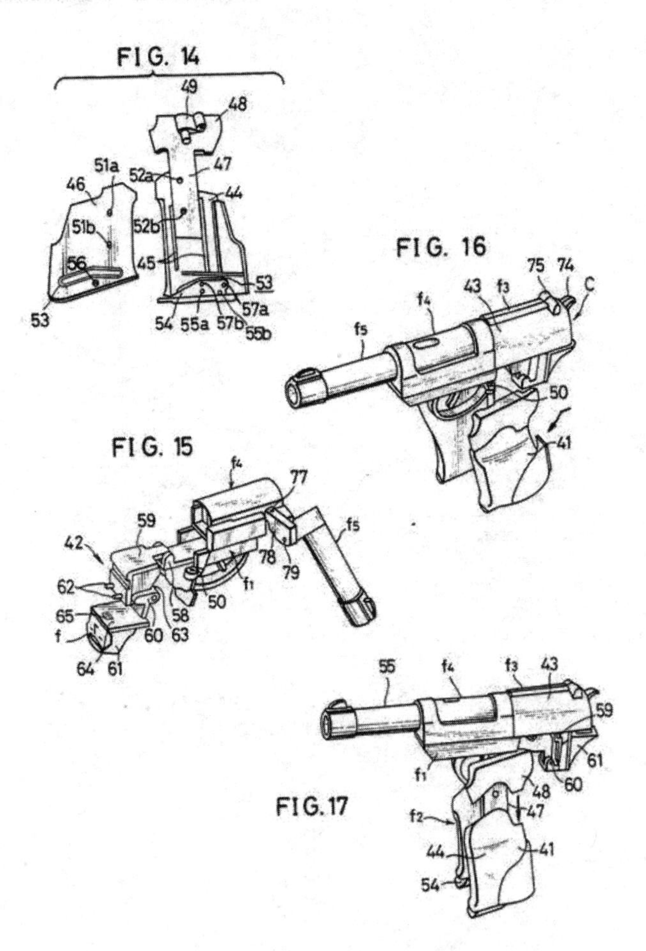

FIGURE 2-14. Drawing sheet for U.S. Pat. No. 4,571,201, "Toy Gun Convertible Into Robotic-Humanoid Form"

Similarly, the description of the uses and advantages of the invention has been cut back because of various court decisions. Recall that a patent covers all implementations of an idea; various implementations are called *embodiments*. However, an embodiment *is not* the invention—it is an implementation of the inventive idea in the real world. Patent inventors have rights to embodiments that they didn't list in the application, as long as the patent claims (to be discussed shortly) are considered to cover those embodiments.

Historically, summaries would usually state that the invention had certain uses or certain advantages, rather than saying that particular embodiments had certain uses or certain

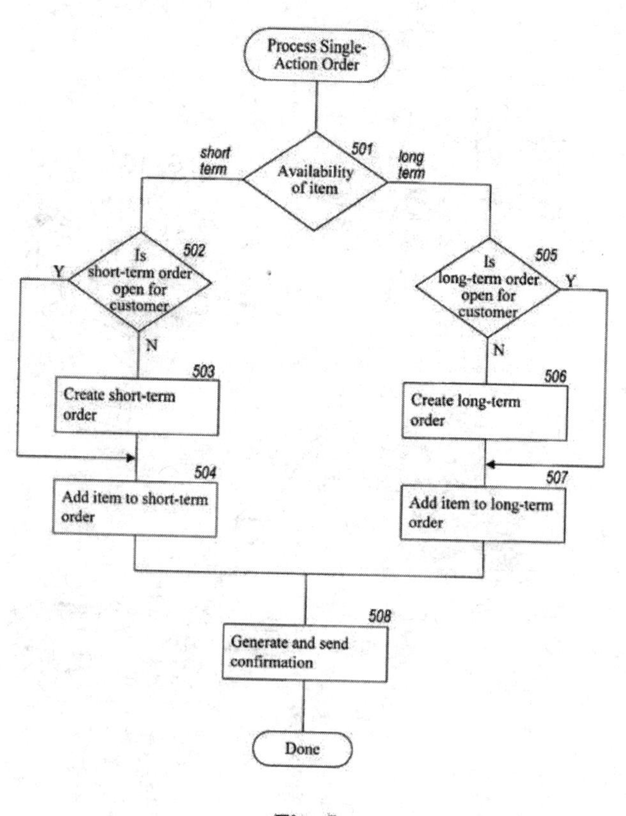

FIGURE 2-15. Drawing sheet for U.S. Pat. No. 5,960,411, Amazon.com's 1-click patent

advantages. This sometimes led to competitive products being declared outside the scope of the patent because they failed to provide one of the uses or advantages.

As a result, many new patent applications have either cut down on backgrounds and summaries or have eliminated them completely. Even when these sections are included in new patent applications, they are very carefully neutral and vague—more word salad.

The description of the figures

The remainder of the written description is usually provided by the short and long descriptions of the figures. The short descriptions are required, but are otherwise not extraordinary—they are generally composed of one sentence (if that).

The detailed description is different. The detailed description must describe the invention with enough specificity that someone who is of ordinary skill in the same art can reconstruct the invention from the knowledge provided by the description and the drawings alone. To return to an earlier phrase, the detailed description and drawings must together provide an enabling disclosure of the invention.

One item of relevance to computer-related patents is that no code listings have to be provided to the patent office as part of the disclosure. Rather, only the program flow (as shown in flowcharts), program architecture (as shown in diagrams), and algorithmic functioning must be provided. According to a case called *Fonar Corp. v. General Electric*, the code implementing an invention is *merely* an implementation detail and can be provided by anyone with ordinary skill in programming.

The detailed description refers to the drawings. As I stated earlier, each part depicted in the figures is associated with an individual reference number. The detailed description follows these numbers; as the drawings are broken out into separate components, so too are the parts of the detailed description.

There is no particular order imposed by law for the figures or detailed description, but well-written patents are generally tree-structured. For example, assume a patent has nine figures, as shown in Figure 2-16.

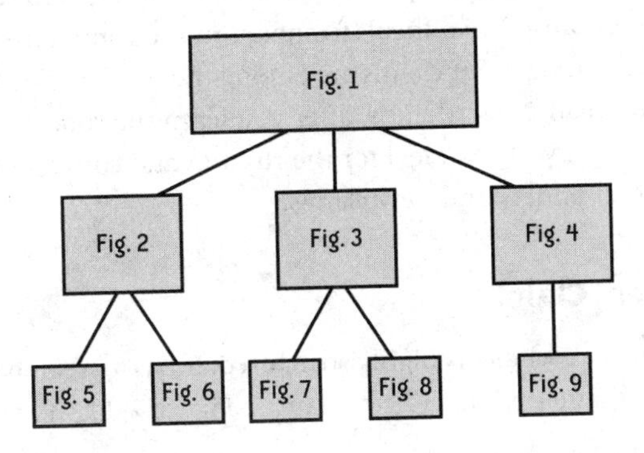

FIGURE 2-16. Detailed description as a tree structure

In this example, assume Fig. 1 is used to provide a high-level view of the invention and detail its interaction with outside systems. Figs. 2, 3, and 4 show component-level views of various parts illustrated in Fig. 1. Figs. 5 and 6 show subcomponents previously identified in Fig. 2. Figs. 7 and 8 show subcomponents previously identified in Fig. 3, etc. Each one of these subcomponents can have sub-subcomponents, until sufficient detail is provided regarding the invention as a whole.

REFERENCING A PATENT

Each patent is set up as a simple row-column grid to assist readers in referencing specific portions of the patent. The text is arranged into two columns on each page and each column in the patent has its own number. Similarly, the rows of text in the patent are numbered, with a reference numeral showing up every five lines. In citing a patent, you can refer others to a specific spot by describing the location of the reference in the grid, as in, "See Patent 4,583,212, col. 3, lines 44–54."

The Claims

The claims are the legal heart of the patent. Just as the patent dates define the temporal boundaries of patent protection, the language of the claims defines the intellectual boundaries of the patent. As described by 35 U.S.C. § 112:

> The specification shall conclude with one or more claims particularly pointing out and distinctly claiming the subject matter which the applicant regards as his invention.

Translated, this means that the claims *are* the invention. Each separate claim is a separate invention and represents a separate grant of rights from the government.

Patent claims appear at the end of the patent as a series of numbered sentences. Each patent claim is one sentence. Because it is difficult to shoehorn the complete subject matter of the patent into a single sentence, patent claims are among the most awkward and ungrammatical sentences you will ever read. Nevertheless, after you learn the ropes and work your way through a few patents, you will get a feel for the rhythm and conventions of claim language and will be better able to understand new claims.

Structure of a Patent Claim

A claim, like the patent as a whole, is highly structured. It has a preamble, transitional phrase, one or more limitations, and optional effects clauses. Figure 2-17 shows claim 1 for Amazon's '411 patent.

INDENTATION

Another similarity between patents and code is that indentation is used to make the logical structure of the claims more apparent. There are no official formatting standards for claims, but the formatting of the '411 patent claim is typical. Each noun phrase starts on its own line, and subparts are indented to show their relationship to their parent elements.

1. A method of placing an order for an item comprising:
under control of a client system,
    displaying information identifying the item; and
    in response to only a single action being performed,
        sending a request to order the item along with an identifier of a purchaser of the item to a server system;
under control of a single-action ordering component of
    the server system,
    receiving the request;
    retrieving additional information previously stored for
        the purchaser identified by the identifier in the received request; and
generating an order to purchase the requested item for the
    purchaser identified by the identifier in the received request using the retrieved additional information; and
fulfilling the generated order to complete purchase of the
    item
whereby the item is ordered without using a shopping cart
    ordering model.

FIGURE 2-17. Claim 1 of Amazon's 1-click patent

The preamble

The preamble has only one requirement: it must specify the type of invention being described by the claim. For example, the preamble may recite a system, an apparatus, a method, a composition of matter, or any other type of patentable advance.

In addition to defining the type of invention described by the claim, the preamble may also state a goal or introduce terminology. For example, Amazon's 1-click patent states, "A method for placing an order for an item" (see Figure 2-18). Other patents may specify a "A wireless networking system for connecting mobile computers to the Internet."

1. A method of placing an order for an item comprising:

FIGURE 2-18. Claim 1 preamble for Amazon's 1-click patent

The transitional phrase

The transitional phrase is a word or short phrase defining the relationship of the invention as a whole to the noun clauses immediately following. The most important transitional phrase in patent law is the word "comprising." The word "comprising" is favored by patentees because it is an *open-ended* transition. Other transitional phrases, such as "consisting of," "composed of," and "consisting essentially of," are *closed* transitions.

The best way to understand the effect of open versus closed transitions is to consider an imaginary claim covering a peanut butter sandwich. A sandwich "comprising" peanut butter could also have jelly; in other words, more items can be added to the basic technology covered by an open transition without removing the technology from the scope of the patent claim.

By way of contrast, a sandwich "composed of" peanut butter could include peanut butter only. A sandwich "composed essentially of" peanut butter could have incidental other ingredients, but the one and only *main* ingredient would still have to be peanut butter.

In other words, "comprising" can be translated as "having at least the following," whereas "composed of" can be translated as "having only the following."

The limitations

Just as the claims are the heart of the patent, the limitations are the heart of the claim. Each limitation is a statement describing a single step, component, or part of the invention. Figure 2-19 shows the first limitation of claim 1 of Amazon's '411 patent.

under control of a client system,
displaying information identifying the item; and

FIGURE 2-19. First limitation of claim 1 of Amazon's 1-click patent

Of course, an inventor wants to place as few limitations on her invention as possible. But if she skimps on limitations, she risks having the examiner find prior art and rejecting her claim. A patent must be novel, and therefore must differentiate itself through limitations. As described more fully in Chapter 3, patent applications usually go through one round (and occasionally more) of a tug-of-war between the applicant and examiner, with the examiner rejecting claims on the basis of prior art and the applicant adding limitations to differentiate the claims from the prior art.

Each limitation can be further subdivided into individual terms—individual words or short phrases that must be interpreted together. For example, fully analyzing the limitation in Figure 2-19 would require analysis of "control," "client system," "displaying information," "identifying," and "item." Anytime substantial analysis is required, lawyers will typically create a *claim chart*, a grid showing claim terms on one side and commentary or quotes from other sources on the other side. For patents with long or complicated claims, a single claim chart can reach into hundreds of pages.

An optional effects clause

A claim may also include one or more effects clauses. Effects clauses are added either to more precisely define a particular preceding claim term or to assert that a certain result is caused by the system. A typical effects clause uses the word "wherein," but "whereby" is also a common choice. Figure 2-20 shows the effects clause from claim 1 of Amazon's '411 patent. Amazon's use of the effects clause to add a limitation to the system as a whole is typical.

> whereby the item is ordered without using a shopping cart
> ordering model.

FIGURE 2-20. Effects clause in claim 1 of Amazon's 1-click patent

Independent and Dependent Claims

Within a patent, there are two basic types of claims: independent and dependent. Independent claims have enough limitations to meet two statutory requirements: first, they completely describe the working invention, and second, they are unique. Amazon's claim 1 is an independent claim.

Dependent claims, on the other hand, have a modified preamble compared with independent claims. Instead of reciting a "system," for example, they would recite "the system of claim 1" (or claim 10, or just some other claim). Dependent claims work by latching onto an independent claim and further limiting it by adding further language and claim terms. Dependent claims can also refer in cascading fashion to other dependent claims.

If a claim is rejected or invalidated later in court, all the claims that depend on it may be invalidated as well. Those trying to attack a patent get the most bang for their buck by invalidating an independent claim (it depends on the situation, though; invalidating a dependent claim automatically invalidates the linked independent claim).

Other Resources

There are a number of resources available on the Internet for looking up patent documents. The best overall search interface is provided free by the USPTO at *http://www.uspto.gov/patft/index.html*. There are a number of searches, such as the quick search and the patent number search, but the real jewel is the advanced patent searching capability. The PTO has divided up and indexed all U.S. patents granted since 1976. A nestable Boolean search is available, including operators for each field of the patent and range operators for the dates. Results are provided as HTML rather than in the standard patent document format, but the database is always up-to-date.

Google also has an excellent patent search interface available at *http://www.google.com/patents*. Google's search doesn't have the same per-field granularity provided by the PTO and its information can sometimes be spotty due to the necessity of using OCR to recognize many old patents. Nevertheless, Google's full-text searching can't be beat and it offers easy PDF downloads of each patent.

Finally, patents in PDF format can be downloaded either through Google's patent search, *http://www.pat2pdf.org* or Free Patents Online (at *http://freepatentsonline.com*). For the latter two services, however, you will need to know the number of the patent you are looking for first; neither of these services really provides a way to search or browse the patents.

CHAPTER THREE

The Patent System

One of the first assignments frequently given to new programming students is the Fibonacci function: given a number *n*, return the *nth* number in the Fibonacci sequence. A typical response to this assignment might be coded as follows:

```
def fib(n):
    if n == 0: return 0
    elif n == 1: return 1
    else: fib(n-1) + fib(n-2)
```

Unfortunately, this code has a trick: trying to compute *fib(n)* any numbers larger than 40 or so results in incredibly long running times. In algorithmic terms, this code has complexity $O(2^n)$. In other words, the running time increases exponentially as the number requested goes up. Before *n* gets very large, the running time is too long to be feasible.

The reason why the fib function is so expensive is because it redoes the work each time. If you ask for *fib(5)*, the function also works out *fib(4)* and *fib(3)*. The calculation of *fib(4)* in turn works out *fib(3)* and *fib(2)*. The calculation of *fib(3)* works out *fib(2)* and *fib(1)*, etc. There is a lot of duplicated effort, and that duplicated effort takes work and time.

One technique for speeding up this function is *memoization*. Memoization works by caching the results of each call in a lookup table. The first time a function is called with certain arguments, the memoized function computes the result and associates the function arguments with the result value. When the function is called later with the same arguments, the memoized function returns the cached value rather than spending time and processing power computing the results again.

For example, a memoized Fibonacci function might look like the following:

```
memo = {0:0, 1:1}

def memo_fib(n):
    if n in memo: return memo[n]
    else:
        result = memo_fib(n-1) + memo_fib(n-2)
        memo[n] = result
        return result
```

Unlike the original *fib* function, this function can be called with very large numbers and will return almost instantly.

It is important to note that a memoized function is *always* slower than a normal function the first time it is run. The functions associated with memoization—the value lookup, cache miss, and association of the result with the argument list—all take time and processing power. Nevertheless, memoization is a critical optimization tool. If the cost of creating the result is much greater than the cost of the caching machinery, returning a cached result is much cheaper than re-creating the result for each function call.

The Patent System As a Knowledge Cache

The patent system as a whole can be compared to applying memoization to the process of invention. Creating a new invention is like calling an expensive function. Just as it is inefficient to recompute the Fibonacci numbers for each function invocation, it is inefficient to force everyone facing a technical problem to independently invent the solution to that problem. The patent system acts like a problem cache, storing the solutions to specific problems for later recall. The next time someone has the same problem, the saved solution (as captured in the patent document) can be used.

Just as with memoization, there is a cost associated with the patent process, specifically, the approximately 20-year term of exclusive rights associated with the patent. Nevertheless, the essence of the utilitarian bargain is that granting temporary exclusive rights to inventions is ultimately less expensive than forcing people to independently recreate the same invention.

Thus, patents are an expression of the utilitarian model for intellectual property described in Chapter 1. They can be viewed as a contract between society (represented by the government) and an inventor. In return for the development of new technology and its eventual dedication to the public domain, the government agrees to grant a roughly 20-year exclusive right to make, use, sell, or import the invention. After the patent expires, the patent is dedicated to the public domain for anybody to make, use, or sell.

Further, the patent system can also be viewed as an optimization of our collective inventive capacity. The invention process is expensive. Even though many inventions seem obvious in retrospect, it is very difficult to come up with the original breakthrough idea. The patent system catalogs these inventions—solutions to problems—as patents, making them available for others to use.

Returning to the comparison we made in Chapter 2 between regular expressions and patents, it is interesting to note that regular expression evaluation is one of the most frequently memoized operations in languages that support regular expressions. Just as described above, the regular expression is evaluated and the result cached; subsequent use of the regular expression reuses the cached version.

In this chapter, we will take a walk through the land of patents by focusing first on the requirements for getting a patent, then the process of getting a patent, and finally the business end of using patents and negotiating with patent holders.

Requirements for Getting a Patent

Patentable subject matter is set out by four sections of the U.S. Code: sections 101 (subject matter and utility), 102 (novelty), 103 (obviousness), and 112 (enablement). Each of these sections has thousands of pages of interpretation in books and court cases; we will whittle these four horsemen of the patent act into a general framework that we will use to explain the structure and mechanics of the patent law.

Section 101: Subject Matter and Utility

Because this section is so short and so important, it is reproduced here in its entirety:

> §101. Inventions patentable
>
> Whoever invents or discovers any new and useful process, machine, manufacture, or composition of matter, or any new and useful improvement thereof, may obtain a patent therefore [sic], subject to the conditions and requirements of this title.

The first important point to note is that the law is written such that it assumes that a patent should be granted *unless* certain conditions apply. Although the conditions for getting a patent are frequently stated in the negative ("You can't get a patent unless..."), the default position in the law is that anything "new and useful" is patentable.

Statutory subject matter

Section 101 defines what is considered *statutory subject matter*: processes, machines, items of manufacture, and compositions of matter. Processes are defined as any "process, act or method" and are directed to technical and industrial processes (who says legislators don't understand recursion?). Machines don't have to be wholly tangible and can include systems and devices. "Items of manufacture" describes items that are made somehow via human effort. "Compositions of matter" are chemical compounds and mixtures.

These statutory categories can interlock. For example, the inventor of a new kind of peanut butter sandwich could receive three different patents: a process patent on the method of making the sandwich, a machine patent (or device patent, as they are frequently called) on the sandwich-making contraption, and an article of manufacture patent on the sandwich itself.

With such a broad definition of what is patentable (the judicial interpretation of these phrases is "anything under the sun made by man"), it is instructive to consider what cannot be patented. Patents cannot be granted on preexisting discoveries, scientific theories or mathematical algorithms, aesthetic creations (like stories, musical compositions, and performances), purely mental acts, and basic information.

There are common threads between the various things that cannot be patented:

- You cannot patent things that you did not invent. Discoveries, natural laws, and algorithms all fall into this category. Even if you are the first person to formulate a particular theory, or find a particular chemical element that exists in nature, your discovery existed before you found it. Thus, you did not invent your discovery and you are not entitled to a patent.
- You cannot patent things that in themselves have no real-world effects or real-world embodiments. Theories, algorithms, information, and purely mental acts fall into this category. Even if a manner of thinking is completely new, it must be tied to a particular set of real-world actions (a process) or a particular real-world result (an article of manufacture) before it becomes a patentable advance.
- You cannot patent basic things that did not require inventive work. Basic information and discoveries fall into this category. It may require work to discover a new naturally existing element, just like it requires work to compile a phone book. Nevertheless, patent law (and copyright law, incidentally) is not designed to simply reward work; the result must be something inventive. While it may be economically useful to bring together facts that were previously stored separately, facts are not the public good that IP law was designed to support. Unless your creation entails new knowledge, you are not entitled to a patent.
- Finally, you cannot patent things that are purely aesthetic—things that derive their value from the particular expression of an abstract idea. Patents cover all expressions of abstract idea, not just particular forms of that idea. By analogy, consider the distinction between genres and books in literature. A patent can be compared to a very narrow genre: everything contained within that genre is excludable. (Copyright, on the other hand, makes the opposite distinction: the genre, or underlying idea of a creation, is not protectable, only the particular expression of that idea as contained in a book.)

The current controversy in patent law over software patents is tied to this idea of what is and is not patentable. Software straddles the line between algorithms and processes. On one hand, software inventions have some physicality—they run on physical computers, employ real electrical signals to do work, and can have real-world effects. On the other hand, the computer is simply scaffolding that speeds up the evaluation of a wholly intangible algorithm.

To address these concerns, the patent office requires that applications describe how their inventions produce either a "physical transformation" or a "useful, concrete, and tangible result." According to the PTO, a physical transformation occurs when the claimed invention transforms a physical object to a different structural state or thing. However, data is intangible, so manipulation of data in a data structure is not enough to make the invention patentable. Instead, the structure and effect of the invention as a whole is examined. If the claimed invention is tangible when considered as a whole, or if the end result of running a process is physical or tangible, then the claim as a whole is considered to be statutory subject matter.

In practice, the "useful, concrete, and tangible" guideline is mostly toothless. Software can be implemented in hardware, and vice versa; the patent claims are simply written to apply to a "computing device" that can be implemented either way. Another tactic is to specify an output on some device; a particular display on a monitor or combination of electrical signals in a circuit is enough to bring a computer-implemented invention into the real world.

An alternative tactic for bringing a computer-implemented invention under the statute is the *Beauregard style* claim. Beauregard claims are named after the court case in which they were declared to be acceptable, *In re Beauregard* (53 F.3d 1583, Fed. Cir. 1995). In that case, Beauregard's invention was a method for filling in the area defined by a polygon displayed on a raster display system. One particular claim accepted by the court recited "a computer usable medium" on which was stored "computer readable program code means," (i.e., code), which executed the fill algorithm. Because the invention considered as a whole was functional (i.e., not just a description of the invention) and included a physical part (the "computer usable medium"), the claim as a whole was held to be patentable under section 101.

THE GIF PATENT

U.S. Patent 4,558,302, commonly known as the "GIF patent," is a patent describing the application of Lempel-Ziv-Welch (LZW) compression to a string of symbols; this technique was eventually adopted as part of the 1987 GIF graphics standard. In August 1999, the owners of the '302 patent, Unisys, announced that anyone using GIFs on an "Intranet Web site or an Internet Billboard Web site" would have to license the GIF patent for a one-time fee of $5,000-$7,500.

One result of the public outcry over Unisys' patent licensing announcement was the creation of web sites purporting to demonstrate why software patents should not be allowed. These sites included a short tutorial on mentally performing the LZW method on a 1-pixel GIF. After completing the tutorial, the site visitor was informed that his or her brain infringed the GIF patent. To continue thinking, the visitor should be prepared to pay the proper license fee.

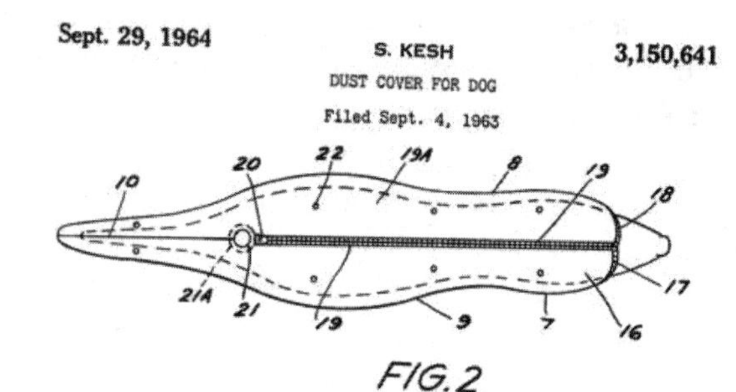

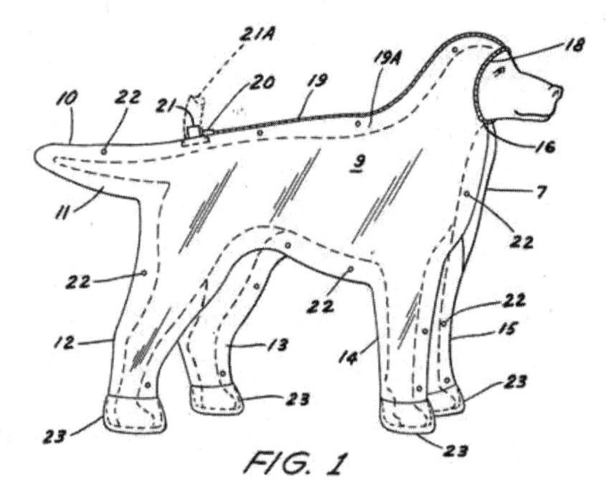

INVENTOR
SEROUN KESH
BY Edward M. Apple
ATTORNEY

FIGURE 3-1. Patent No. 3,150,641, "Dust Cover for Dog"—another useful invention

Utility

The second function of Section 101 is to define the requirement of *utility*; the invention must be useful. The primary thing to remember when evaluating utility is that it does not mean "useful" as most people would define it (serviceable for an end or purpose, valuable or productive). Instead, "useful" is roughly synonymous with "has an intended use," and bears little relation to the common definition of the term (see Figure 3-1).

In modern patent practice, the only time the utility requirement is invoked is when the claimed invention is something like a perpetual motion machine, where the operation of the machine is against the accepted laws of physics. In that case, the invention is rejected for lack of utility because it will not work. Applicants are free to overcome this objection by submitting a working model; no one has yet done so.

Section 102: Novelty

Officially, Section 101 imposes the requirement that patentable inventions must be new, or "novel" in the patent jargon. Nevertheless, it is Section 102 that defines what "new" means in terms of the patent law: it means that a particular invention is not disclosed within the prior art.

Prior art

Prior art can be defined generally as everything that was public knowledge before you conceived of your invention. There is no limit on the timeframe. For example, one Supreme Court case (*Jungersen v. Ostby & Barton Co.*, 335 U.S. 560, 1949) cited the works of a 16th-century metalworker as prior art in a case involving a method of making jewelry.

Eligible prior art is defined in Section 102. Section 102 says that a person "shall be entitled to a patent" unless one of seven conditions apply. Each condition is laid out in its own paragraph.

The first and second paragraphs are similar. They deal with situations where somebody else created the same invention first:

> (a) the invention was known or used by others in this country, or patented or described in a printed publication in this or a foreign country, before the invention thereof by the applicant for patent, or
>
> (b) the invention was patented or described in a printed publication in this or a foreign country or in public use or on sale in this country, more than one year prior to the date of the application for patent in the United States

Prior art that matches one of these descriptions is called 102(a) prior art or 102(b) prior art, respectively. In these situations, somebody else got there first. These paragraphs allow for the possibility that the invention was just "known," but usually it is the existence of a written record (either the printed publication or the patent application) or a physical artifact (the item on sale or in public use) that serves as proof of prior invention.

The difference between these two paragraphs has all to do with the one-year time period cited in paragraph (b). In the United States, there is a one-year grace period between the time of invention and the time when you have to file your patent application. If somebody comes up with the same invention, or if you have yourself published the details of your invention, within a year of the time you file your patent application, it is considered 102(a) prior art. You can overcome that prior art by showing evidence of your own invention's existence before the other person's publication date.

For example, imagine that you invented a new mashed potato-throwing machine on January 1. On June 1, your competitor in the flying foodstuffs business started selling a new mashed potato-throwing machine, which happens to be essentially identical to yours. On December 31, you finally filed for a patent.

In this situation, your competitor's machine is 102(a) prior art. When your competitor's machine is cited against you, you can maintain the novelty of your invention by providing proof that your own invention existed six months before he started selling his machine.

Now lets modify the situation. Imagine your competitor also described his forthcoming mashed potato-throwing machine in his business newsletter in November of the previous year, two months before you invented your machine. You never read your competitor's newsletter, so you didn't know about his description.

In this modified situation, your competitor's machine is 102(a) prior art, but his description is 102(b) prior art because it was published more than a year before you filed your patent application. In U.S. patent law, there is a one-year *absolute bar* to patenting; one year before the filing date is known as the *critical date*. There is no way to overcome this 102(b) prior art; your invention is not novel and your patent should not be granted (if it is granted by accident, it will be invalid).

Let's modify the situation one more time. Let's assume that *you* invented and published the newsletter description of the potato-throwing machine in November, but didn't file for a patent until December, 13 months later. The newsletter description is still 102(b) prior art that you can't overcome. It doesn't matter that *you* published the newsletter description rather than someone else; if it was published more than a year before the filing date, the absolute bar will prevent you from getting a patent.

Be aware that other countries generally do not have the same one-year grace period as the United States. If you describe your invention to anybody before you file for a patent, you will usually be giving up your foreign patent rights.

Similar situations are presented in paragraphs (d) and (e) of Section 102.

> (d) the invention was first patented or caused to be patented, or was the subject of an inventor's certificate, by the applicant or his legal representatives or assigns in a foreign country prior to the date of the application for patent in this country on an application for patent or inventor's certificate filed more than twelve months before the filing of the application in the United States.

This paragraph describes a situation where you first filed for a patent in a foreign country, and then let more than 12 months pass before filing an application in the United States. The one-year absolute bar prevents you from getting a patent in the United States.

> (e) the invention was described in...an application for patent...before the invention by the applicant[...].

To simplify this paragraph, it describes the situation where there are inventions overlapping in time from two different inventors. The two inventors do not know each other and do not know of the overlapping patent applications. This paragraph specifies that the inventor with the earliest date of invention (as determined between the two applicants) is the winner; the winner's patent application can frequently be applied as prior art against the loser's application.

Paragraph (f) provides a catchall provision, barring a patent if the inventor "did not himself invent the subject matter sought to be patented."

Paragraphs (c) and (g) address situations in which inventions are kept from the public. Paragraph (c) forbids the granting of a patent if the inventor "has abandoned the invention." Paragraph (g) forbids the granting of a patent if somebody else created the invention first and the invention was "not abandoned, suppressed, or concealed."

Paragraphs (c) and (g) hearken back to the utilitarian bargain of patent law: temporary excludability is granted by the government in return for full disclosure of the new invention. These two paragraphs prevent people from "double dipping" their IP protections by keeping something secret at first and patenting it later.

In theory, any public knowledge is fair game for prior art; if another person thought of your invention first, their conception should serve as prior art. In practice, prior art must be proven, so it consists of anything described in a written publication, demonstrated, or sold to the public before the conception of your invention. Of all of these, only written descriptions are really useful as prior art before the Patent Office. In the Patent Office itself, prior art searches by patent examiners are usually limited further to just patents, published patent applications, and available literature.

This is important for two reasons. First, not all relevant literature is *available*. Software development, unlike many other areas of technology, is unique in its oral tradition. Basic software development knowledge was (and still is) most often passed through teams; the underlying software principles are only rarely written down. The Jargon File, for example, is hacker oral history that has only relatively recently been put down in writing. Although this is changing due to the Internet, particularly the World Wide Web, the "easy" innovations in software development were usually not written down in an accessible fashion.

When software was judged to be fully patentable in the U.S. in the 1990s, the effect of maintaining software knowledge as an oral history was that many of the easy and obvious aspects of software development were not readily available as prior art to the PTO. Thus, there are many patents that have been granted on techniques that are not novel in the software field; the prior art was essentially invisible to the PTO.

The second reason this is important is a side effect that I call the "problem of the missing four-legged dog." Certain things are so obvious that they aren't written down—like the fact that a dog has four legs. Thus, it can be very difficult to find prior art on techniques that are, in fact, well known.

Element-by-element comparison

One of the tricky parts of patent law is determining whether a particular publication or patent can serve as prior art. Assume that you are examining a patent, and you find a publication that was printed more than a year before the filing date of the patent (i.e., the publication is 102(b) prior art). How can you tell whether the publication *anticipates* the patent?

The procedure for evaluating prior art is claim-by-claim, element-by-element comparison. First, each claim is considered alone. Then each clause in the claim is considered as an independent *limitation*, or necessary feature. Within each limitation, each individual element (word or short phrase) is compared to the publication.

The tool that lawyers use most frequently to do comparisons is the *claim chart*. A claim chart is a two-column table with individual claim elements on the left and equivalent words or phrases from the prior art document (or documents) on the right. A claim is anticipated if, and only if, every element of every limitation is "disclosed" by the applied prior art. Table 3-1 shows an excerpt from a claim chart.

TABLE 3-1. Sample claim chart

Claim element	Prior art element
[1.2a] a plurality of mobile transceivers	[1.2a]: "*a plurality of mobile transceivers.*" Mitzlaff teaches mobile transceivers: "At the microwave frequencies considered here, signal blockage due to *moving people and equipment* is the main source of intermittent behavior in a typical office environment." (Mitzlaff, Pg. 21, "Radio Channel Characteristics: Intermittence"). In Fig. 2.1, Mitzlaff shows the mobile transceivers (the "User Modules" or "UM") attached to individual pieces of equipment, including PCs ("Personal Computers"), which are mobile. Mitzlaff describes the User Modules (UMs) as follows...

This element-by-element comparison is designed to make the comparison between a patent and another piece of technology rigorous. As described in Chapter 2, the patent document is a type of pattern recognizer. The elements in a claim work like the base "atoms" in a regular expression: they provide an irreducible core of technological elements that, when brought together carefully, match a piece of outside technology.

Section 103: Obviousness

One result of the element-by-element claim match strategy is that it can sometimes be difficult to find a single piece of prior art that discloses the same invention as that claimed in a patent. What is more likely is a partial match, either that the prior art substitutes something similar but not identical to the claim, or that multiple pieces of prior art, when assembled together, match all elements in the claim. In these situations, Section 103 may render the combination *obvious*.

Section 103 states:

> 35 U.S.C. 103 Conditions for patentability; non-obvious subject matter.
>
> (a) A patent may not be obtained though the invention is not identically disclosed or described as set forth in section 102 of this title, if the differences between the subject matter sought to be patented and the prior art are such that the subject matter as a whole would have been obvious at the time the invention was made to a person having ordinary skill in the art to which said subject matter pertains.

The test imposed by this section is whether a person of ordinary skill, knowing the prior art, would have found the patented invention obvious at the time the invention was made, without using any hindsight.

In practice, Section 103 does not bring anything new into the field of prior art. Instead, it allows multiple pieces of prior art to be considered together at the same time. The only restriction is that the person tying the various pieces of art together must be able to present a persuasive argument as to why a *P*erson *H*aving *O*rdinary *S*kill *I*n *T*he *A*rt (a PHOSITA) would possibly consider thinking of the two or more references together.

There are a number of standard arguments for considering multiple pieces of art together under Section 103. If two pieces of art are analogous or solve the same problem, they can be considered together. If one piece of art solves a problem put forward by the other piece of art, then those two pieces of art would be more likely considered together. If someone suggests that two pieces of art can be used together, then they likely can be considered together under Section 103.

Section 112: Enablement

Section 112 relates back to the utilitarian bargain presented in Chapter 1. This is the section that requires that patent applicants pay for their patent protection by disclosing new inventions to the public. Quoted in part:

> 35 U.S.C. 112 Specification.
>
> The specification shall contain a written description of the invention, and of the manner and process of making and using it, in such full, clear, concise, and exact terms as to enable any person skilled in the art to which it pertains, or with which it is most nearly connected, to make and use the same, and shall set forth the best mode contemplated by the inventor of carrying out his invention.
>
> The specification shall conclude with one or more claims particularly pointing out and distinctly claiming the subject matter which the applicant regards as his invention.

As discussed earlier, a patent requires an *enabling disclosure*; this is the statutory demand that raises that requirement.

Getting a Patent

So, you have come up with a new invention: you have invented a mousetrap that can read email (Zawinski's Law states that every program attempts to expand until it can read mail—programs that cannot so expand are replaced by ones that can). The process of protecting your email-reading mousetrap will usually vary depending on whether you are in a typical corporate environment or in a startup/solo inventor environment.

A Typical Corporate Patent Process

Corporate patent processes vary from company to company. Some procedures may be essentially ad hoc, while others may be completely formalized. Generally, the more established the company, the more formal the patent process. In most cases, corporate patent processes go through four stages: disclosure, evaluation, application, and prosecution.

Disclosure

The first stage in the corporate patent process is disclosure—letting your company know that you have come up with a new and possibly patentable idea. Informally, disclosure may be as easy as sticking your head into your boss's office to tell him about your idea. In most cases, though, your disclosure will require a written record, known as an *invention disclosure form.*

The disclosure form serves a couple of purposes. First, it serves as a record of the invention. Second, it allows your company to evaluate the invention for patentability, and third, it serves as an initial disclosure for the patent attorney.

Most disclosure forms have two parts, bookkeeping data and a description of the invention. The bookkeeping data is generally basic, consisting of a title, conception date, and list of inventors. Your company may also ask about the relationship of your invention to current development, both at your company and at competitors' companies. They will also probably ask about whether you have told anybody else about your invention.

The description of the invention forms the bulk of the disclosure. Typical forms ask for background on the invention and a detailed description of how the invention works. You may be asked to provide code, examples, engineering specifications, design diagrams, and flowcharts, basically anything necessary to describe the invention to another engineer.

Evaluation

Once you have submitted your disclosure, most companies use an evaluation process to determine whether they will file for a patent on your invention. Because filing for a patent is a lengthy (two to five years) and expensive ($10,000–$50,000) process, most companies want a chance to estimate the value of your idea before they commit time and money to patenting it.

Evaluation of patent disclosures may be decentralized, in which case each manager performs his own evaluations, or it may be centralized, in which all evaluations are performed by a central committee. Evaluators will normally look at two things: novelty and importance.

As discussed earlier, patents are required to be novel to survive the patent process. Companies don't usually perform extensive prior art searches to determine if there are applicable patents in a subject area. Nevertheless, expert review by other engineers is usually a good yardstick to determine whether a patent has novelty problems. If other engineers can think of products or patents that do the same thing as what is described in your disclosure, it is more likely that spending the money to create a patent application would not be worth it.

Expert review also performs another function: if the invention is described well enough that other experts can review and judge the disclosure, then the disclosure is probably *enabling*; that is, it probably has sufficient detail to allow other similarly situated engineers to *practice* (build or use) the invention.

The second thing that is evaluated is the prospective importance of the invention. Not all inventions are equal—some are tremendously important, and others are trivial. Although there is value to be gained by holding any granted patent, most companies want to be more strategic with their patenting dollars.

Application

If an invention is judged worthy of patenting, it moves into the application process. This is the first step in which lawyers typically come into the process. A patent attorney reads your disclosure and usually performs a supplementary interview to resolve any questions he may have about exactly how the invention works.

The patent attorney then takes your disclosure and his interview notes and produces the patent application, typically a 12- to 40-page document suitable for filing in the Patent Office. The application contains drawings, claims, and a detailed description of your invention—in short, everything that is needed to evaluate the application and create the final patent document. After this application is prepared, it is typically sent back to you, as the inventor, for your approval and signature.

Upon receiving the draft application, the typical response is to wonder at the 30-page mass of legalese created out of a relatively svelte 3-page invention disclosure. Nevertheless, that 30-page mass of legalese, if drafted correctly, is probably a better *legal* description of your invention than the clear and simple 3-page disclosure.

The reason for this paradox has to do with the competing aims of a good patent: abstraction and detail. Both of these aims ultimately have the same mission—to increase the *scope* of your patent. In other words, they are both meant to increase the area of technological development described by your patent document.

Detail

Officially, a patent is written so that it is intelligible to a PHOSITA. The patent doesn't have to mention any details that would be immediately obvious to an intelligent, trained, but otherwise ignorant developer or engineer. Most developers and engineers take a broad view of what is obvious in their field, making patents sometimes look ridiculously overspecified for simple inventions.

When lawyers write a patent document, however, they use a different set of heuristics. First, a patent must *fully* describe how to make or use the invention. That means that many types of details that would be disregarded in a technical report should be included in the patent. If an omitted detail later turns out to be important, a court could decide that the patent was not enabling and declare the patent invalid. Therefore, if there is a question as to whether a particular detail could conceivably be considered important by a 68-year-old non-technical judge in 2020, that detail should be included.

Second, patents can sometimes bring additional implementations under the claim scope by including a few details. For example, imagine a hypothetical patent application, filed in 1990, describing document transfer via a symbolic address. If the patent only talked about memory addresses, then it could be restricted to intracomputer applications. If the patent mentioned network addresses, then it could conceivably implicate the entire World Wide Web. The hypothetical inclusion of that single detail could dramatically increase the scope and value of the patent.

Abstraction

Abstraction, loosely defined, is the process of grouping some details together into categories and ignoring the rest. Developers and engineers are familiar with abstraction; it is fundamental to both hardware and software. Transistors are grouped together into gates, ignoring the details of P-N junctions and doping; gates are grouped together into functional units; functional units are exposed as system calls, ignoring the specifics of the hardware; system calls are grouped into APIs, ignoring the underlying bit-twiddling to make things work.

It is important to note that abstraction allows encapsulation; with perfect abstraction, different underlying implementations can be used interchangeably. For example, the WINE project allows applications using the Win32 API abstraction to run unmodified on Linux.

Invention abstraction works the same way. By defining functional units in the invention in a very abstract way, the patent scope can be expanded. For example, a computer-implemented invention may include an awkward-sounding "computing device including interpretable instructions and an evaluator for evaluating the instructions and returning a result." This "computing device" describes a PC, but it also describes a bare processor, a hypervisor, an operating system, and a programming language virtual machine. Just as WINE allows more than one operating system to support a given application, this "computing device" allows more than one type of device to serve as the platform for a given invention.

Prosecution

Once you have signed off on the application, it moves into the final stage, prosecution (the official term for pursuing a patent application is *prosecuting* the patent). This stage is handled almost exclusively by your patent lawyer.

To start the prosecution process, your application is filed with the PTO along with the prescribed fees. Your application is given a number. Congratulations! You can now officially claim that your product or process is *patent pending*.

Then you wait. And wait.

Two to four years later, your patent comes into the hands of a PTO examiner. The examiner is chosen based on the area of technology to which your invention belongs. There are design examiners, plant examiners, biotech examiners, engine examiners, and software examiners. Some examiners may specialize even further; for example, one examiner may only handle valves.

The examiner studies your application and usually responds with a series of complaints in an official form called an *Office Action*. The examiner has three basic areas of concern: the subject matter, the prior art, and the form.

First, it is the examiner's responsibility to make sure that your invention is directed to *statutory subject matter*. In other words, the examiner will reject your patent if your claims purport to cover an algorithm, law of nature, or expressive work.

Second, the examiner is responsible for making sure that your invention is novel and not obvious. The examiner will search the prior art to find anything that *anticipates* your claims or renders them *obvious*. If he finds anything that is arguably similar to your claims, he will reject your application.

Third, the examiner is responsible to make sure that your application complies with all the formalities required by the patent law and the PTO rules. Given the thousands of pages of rules available, there is almost always something to complain about.

As a practical matter, the first Office Action will almost always be a rejection. Part of the job of a patent attorney is to expand your patent's scope to cover everything that isn't already known. The process of generalizing the claims to cover foreseeable variations, however, will usually result in the initial application for a patent being too broad compared to the disclosure in the specification or the prior art.

To deal with the examiner's complaints, patent attorney files a written *response* to the Office Action. There are two basic tools in the attorney's toolbox, arguments and amendments.

When presenting an argument, the patent attorney responds that the rejections are not supported by the prior art presented by the examiner. For example, imagine a hypothetical patent claim for a chair, including "a seat and four legs." The examiner may respond with a patent for a table, pointing out the flat top (equivalent to the seat) and four legs. An attorney may present various arguments in response. For example, he may argue that the table is not analogous to the chair. The attorney could also assert that sitting on the table would destroy the primary purpose of the table—serving food.

Alternatively, the attorney can amend the claims. An amendment changes the text of the claims by adding a *limitation*—a necessary feature of the invention. For example, the patent attorney might be able to change the description of the chair to include "a seat from 12 to 24 inches in height and four legs." In this case, the description of the chair would no longer match the description of the table, and the prior art is *overcome*.

Referring again to the discussion of claim charts in Chapter 2, this "give and take" is the reason why each individual element and limitation in a claim must be addressed. Every single word and phrase in the claim can be essential to the uniqueness of the claim.

If and when the examiner agrees that the form and the substance of the application are acceptable, he sends a *Notice of Allowance* indicating that the application is ready to be issued as a patent. Once you pay the issue fee, the patent is printed and released.

Filing As an Inventor

Given the substantial costs associated with getting a patent attorney, the obvious question is whether you can file your own patent and avoid the cost. Inventors are allowed to file patents on their own inventions, and many do, leading to the success of books like *Patent It Yourself* by Nolo Press (2008). The rationale is that nobody understands the invention better than the inventor, and that each person should have the right to represent him or herself before the government.

Nevertheless, the best advice is that you shouldn't do it (for experts only: you shouldn't do it *yet*). It takes a lot of practice to become proficient with both the syntax and the idioms of patent law. To better illustrate, consider the situation of a programmer writing a first application a new language or framework.

Problem 1: Syntax

When writing in a new language, often the first challenge is simply getting your program to compile. Seemingly small syntax errors can prevent your code from becoming an executable binary. Further, even when your program compiles, that doesn't mean it is correct; many binaries segfault as soon as you try to run them. Little bugs in the source code can prevent the binary executable from fulfilling its function.

Patents are similar. As discussed earlier, patents have a highly specified form, similar to the syntax of a programming language. Inventors filing for themselves are not given any slack regarding the PTO's rules and procedures. Like getting a program through the compiler, getting an application through the patent office requires that all the syntactical rules be obeyed.

Further, even if you have successfully gotten your application through the PTO, you can still encounter the legal equivalent of having your patent segfault. Deviating from Patent Office procedures—even in very small ways that don't prevent your patent from being granted—can result in your patent being declared *invalid* or *unenforceable* after the grant. Unlike code, which can be fixed and recompiled, patent claims that have been declared invalid are gone forever.

Problem 2: Idioms

The second reason for not filing your own patent is more subtle—it concerns knowing common idioms. In the software world, this is usually associated with code that works for a narrow range of situations, but which is too convoluted, too inflexible, or just too *ugly* to work in the general case. One common cause of ugly code is, ironically, prior programming experience in another language. For example, you may have known people who could "write C (or Java, or Perl) in any language."

The root cause of this ugliness is a lack of familiarity with the idioms of the new language. Each language has its own ways of expressing solutions to problems; part of becoming an expert is learning which expressions are the most powerful and efficient in your language of choice.

You happen to know one language, English, which is substantially related to the legalese used in patent documents. Nevertheless, there are important idioms in patent law that, if not used correctly, can affect the strength and utility of your patent. For example:

- Patent claims should in some cases avoid the word "or." Using "or" can sometimes render your claim *indefinite*, and thus unenforceable. Instead, alternatives are described as "one of x, y, and z." Phrases like "such as" and "for example" are also legally ambiguous.
- Patent claims that include the word "means" have a different interpretation than claims that use any other word. For example, "a web browser including a module for rendering HTML" would be interpreted differently than "a web browser including a means for rendering HTML."
- Paradoxically, patents should be careful using the word "invention" to describe an invention. The word "embodiment" is used instead. This is because the patent covers all implementations of a particular technological idea. For example, if your patent states that "the invention includes a database," then the courts say that anything that doesn't include a database is by definition not your invention, even if it is otherwise identical.

Even if you do decide to file the patent yourself, it is usually a good investment to have a patent attorney carefully review it before you file.

Patent Proliferation

Patents are the most expensive and powerful weapons in an IP arsenal. For some companies, particularly pharmaceutical companies, patents are the lifeblood of invention and the key to

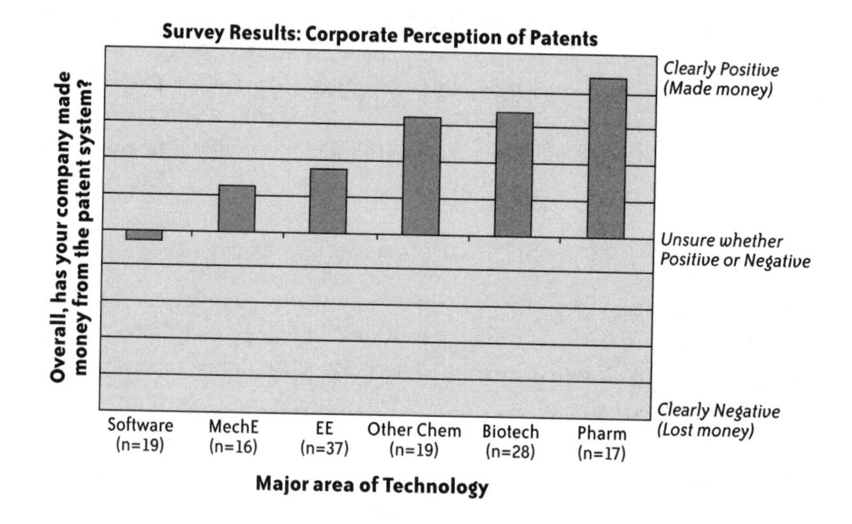

FIGURE 3-2. Corporate perception of patents across industry groups (used by permission of Dennis Crouch)

profitability. For other companies, particularly software companies, patents are the rough equivalent of madly proliferating nuclear weapon arsenals.

For example, an unscientific survey was performed on the popular patent blog "Patently-O" in late 2007. Readers were asked whether the patent system, taken as a whole, had been positive (made money) or negative (lost money) for their companies. Figure 3-2 shows the results from 131 corporate employees, all of who were highly involved in their companies' patents and patenting processes.

These results merge responses from small corporations with those from large corporations. It also excludes individuals at law firms, government entities, and educational institutions. Individuals responded to the question, "Overall, has your company made money from the patent system?" There were three potential responses: "Clearly positive (made money)," "Unsure whether positive or negative," and "Clearly negative (lost money)." For the graph shown in Figure 3-2, these responses were converted to a simple numerical scale: 1, 0, and −1, respectively. The y-axis ranges from −1 to 1.

The most interesting aspect of this graph is that software companies consider participating in the patent system to be a money-losing proposition—but they still do it. Even companies that are highly successful in getting software patents can have an uneasy relationship with the patent system. During Patent Office hearings*concerning software patents and industry, Adobe's principal scientist, Douglas Brotz, stated:

* (Patent and Trademark Office, Department of Commerce, Docket #931222-3322: Use of the Patent System to Protect Software Related Inventions, 1994)

> Good morning, Mr. Secretary and members of the Panel. My name is Douglas Brotz. I'm Principal Scientist at Adobe Systems, Incorporated, and I am representing the views of Adobe Systems as well as my own....
>
> Let me make my position on the patentability of software clear. I believe that software per se should not be allowed patent protection....
>
> The problems inherent in certain aspects of the patent process for software-related inventions are well-known, the difficulties of finding and citing prior art, the problems of obviousness, the difficulties of adequate specifications for software are a few of those problems. However, I argue that software should not be patented, not because it is difficult to do so, but because it is wrong to do so.

Nevertheless, at the time this statement was made, Adobe had 35 granted or pending applications for patents. It now has over 500 granted or published applications for patents.

The "nuclear arsenal" quality of patents is even clearer when India's nuclear weapons policy is compared to Red Hat's patent policy statement. Table 3-2 compares statements from the Embassy of India's article "Evolution of India's Nuclear Policy" (*http://www.indianembassy.org/pic/nuclearpolicy.htm*) with statements from Red Hat's "Statement of Position and Our Promise on Software Patents" (*http://www.redhat.com/legal/patent_policy.html*).

TABLE 3-2. Nuclear policy versus patent policy

Common message	Red Hat's patent policy	India's nuclear policy
We think the world would be better off if these [weapons, patents] were abolished . . .	"Red Hat has consistently taken the position that software patents generally impede innovation in software development and that software patents are inconsistent with open source/free software.... We will continue to work to promote this position and are pleased to join our colleagues in the open source/free software community, as well as those proprietary vendors which have publicly stated their opposition to software patents, in that effort."	"A nuclear weapon-free-world would, therefore, enhance not only India's security but also the security of all nations. This is the principle plank of our nuclear policy."
But we live in the real world, where a relatively small number of other players are building up a large number of these [weapons, patents]....	"At the same time, we are forced to live in the world as it is, and that world currently permits software patents. A relatively small number of very large companies have amassed large numbers of software patents."	"At the global level, there is no evidence yet on the part of the nuclear weapon states to take decisive and irreversible steps in moving towards a nuclear-weapon-free-world. Instead, the NPT [Nuclear Non-Proliferation Treaty] has been extended indefinitely and unconditionally, perpetuating the existence of nuclear

Common message	Red Hat's patent policy	India's nuclear policy
		weapons in the hands of the five countries who are also permanent members of the UN Security Council."
Thus, we must build up and maintain our own stores of [weapons, patents]....	"One defense against such misuse is to develop a corresponding portfolio of software patents for defensive purposes.... [P]rudence dictates this position."	"In the absence of universal and non-discriminatory disarmament, we cannot accept a regime that creates an arbitrary division between nuclear haves and have-nots."
That we promise shall not be used except in defense.	"[T]o the extent any party exercises a Patent Right with respect to Open Source/Free Software which reads on any claim of any patent held by Red Hat, Red Hat agrees to refrain from enforcing the infringed patent against such party for such exercise ("Our Promise").... Our Promise does not extend to any party who institutes patent litigation against Red Hat with respect to a patent applicable to software."	"[T]hese are weapons of self-defence.... The Government on this occasion reiterates its readiness to discuss a "no-first-use" agreement with that country, as also with other countries bilaterally, or in a collective forum."

The Patent As a Property Right

The tremendous power of the patent comes from two foundations. The first is the scope of coverage, as discussed earlier; a patent covers all implementations of the invention. It is the inventive concept that is protected, not any particular set of code, gears, plant seeds, genes, chemicals, or processes.

The second foundation is the recognition of the patent grant as a property grant. As described in Chapter 1, *property* is a legal term for a bundle of rights granted over a good. In the case of patents, the rights included in the bundle are particularly powerful, powerful enough to make or break entire companies. There are two rights in particular that are worth discussing: the right to exclude and the right to injunctive relief.

The right to exclude

We have already discussed how patents place a legal lock around otherwise public knowledge by giving patent holders the right to exclude. However, the right to exclude is a *negative* right. There is no complementary right to practice (use) the invention described in the patent.

To understand the difficulty that this purely negative right presents, recall the example in Chapter 1 of the lock around a shared resource in a program. The reason for the lock is to allow a single process to use or access the shared resource. No other processes are allowed to hold the lock at the same time.

In the patent world, things are different. Imagine a "patent lock" in a program that worked the same as a regular exclusive lock, except that *multiple processes could acquire the lock at the same time*. The result of multiple processes acquiring the patent lock would be deadlock: none of the processes could proceed, because they would each be holding a resource needed by the others. It would just happen that the processes would be holding onto the same resources.

For a slightly more patent-centric example, imagine two people, Abel and Bert, each vying for control of the lucrative peanut butter sandwich industry. Abel recognizes the competitive threat posed by Bert and patents his peanut butter sandwich. Abel uses open-ended "comprising" language in his claim: "I claim a peanut butter sandwich, the sandwich comprising two slices of bread and a smear of peanut butter."

Bert, on the other hand, also recognizes a competitive threat in Abel and applies for a patent. Bert patents an improvement to the basic peanut butter sandwich (a sandwich with peanut butter and jelly): "I claim a peanut butter sandwich, the sandwich comprising two slices of bread, a smear of peanut butter, and a smear of jelly."

While they wait for their patents to issue, both Abel and Bert have success in the marketplace. In the process, Abel copies Bert's wildly successful method of placing jelly on a sandwich. When the patents issue two years later, Abel and Bert sue each other.

The right to injunctive relief

At this point, it is important to note a second property right granted with a patent: the right to *injunctive relief*. A person who is entitled to injunctive relief has the power to ask a court to *enjoin* another person's conduct, that is, to force the second person to stop doing whatever it is that trespasses on the first person's property right. In the case of patents, that means that a court can order you to stop making, selling, importing, or offering for sale anything that infringes on another person's patent.

Mutually assured destruction

Returning to Abel and Bert, each patent holder sues the other. Who wins?

The answer is both...and neither.

From Abel's perspective, remember that open-ended language allows more things to be added to a patent claim. Thus, Bert's peanut butter and jelly sandwich infringes Abel's peanut butter sandwich patent. Abel can receive an injunction against Bert, shutting down his sandwich business.

From Bert's perspective, competitive pressures have forced Abel to adopt the superior peanut butter *and* jelly technology. Thus, Abel's peanut butter and jelly sandwiches infringe Bert's peanut butter and jelly sandwich patent. Bert can receive an injunction against Abel, shutting down his sandwich business.

Patent cross-licensing

The story of Abel and Bert illustrates the fundamental power and difficulty of patents. For any sufficiently large company, you can use your patent power to drive competitors out of business, but your competitors also usually hold enough patents to drive you out of business.

The result of this situation has been a unique form of negotiation called *patent cross-licensing*. In most cases, large companies do not bother to examine individual patents. Instead, the two companies meet together, each bringing their own "stack" of patents. All patents in both stacks are licensed to both parties, and a balancing payment is given to the party with the bigger stack.

CHAPTER FOUR

Copyright

The movie *Antitrust* came out at the height of the dot-com boom. *Antitrust* was Hollywood's take on the geek chic of the late 1990s: the story of a few heroic open source hackers taking on an evil, grasping corporation situated in the Pacific Northwest.

Predictably, it was awful.

Buried among all the things that this movie got wrong, though, was one thing it got right: early in the movie, the protagonist is seen wearing a t-shirt that labels him a "code poet." In one phrase, they captured why software is subject to copyright law—because it is a form of personal expression, not just a means of accomplishing some function.

Understanding the subtle distinctions inherent in that statement is essential to understanding the storms of controversy that inevitably arise around copyright issues.

Copyright in Context

Copyright is probably the most difficult of the four major branches of intellectual property law. Although patent documents (and some aspects of patent practice) are more complex and intricate than the copyright equivalents, the underlying mechanics of the patent system are relatively simple.

Patents can be seen as a straightforward exchange: describe your invention to society and in return receive exclusive control over the use of the invention. After a while, the period of exclusive control ends and everybody receives the benefit of your inventive effort.

Copyright is superficially similar but fundamentally different. Like patent law, copyright is part of the grand bargain discussed in Chapter 1. In return for the creation of knowledge, we also grant to authors a time-limited property right over the fruits of their intellectual efforts.

However, copyright has a far more human dimension than the mechanical results of inventive effort; it is much more about who we *are* than about what we *do*. As a result, copyright is much more subtle than patent law. In particular, there are two fundamental differences between patents and copyrights:

- Patent law covers *function*; copyright law covers *expression*.
- You have to work to get your invention *into* the protected space of patents. You have to work to get your expression *out of* the protected space of copyright.

The social and legal difficulties of copyright law can mostly be traced to one or both of these fundamental principles.

Expression

The first fundamental principle is that copyright protects personal expression in all its varieties. This is both the great strength and compelling weakness of copyright.

To understand why, think again about the economic difficulty of knowledge creation. In Chapter 1, we discussed how knowledge has network effects; the more people who possess a piece of information, the more valuable the information becomes. Nevertheless, people sometimes don't want to share their knowledge because they lose the personal advantages that come from keeping the information a secret. The result is a market failure, because the incentives that promote secrecy tend to reduce knowledge-sharing below the optimal level.

Copyrighted content is in an analogous position. Instead of secrecy, though, the problem is *control*. The copyright model creates strong incentives to expand the creator's control in many directions, despite the significant societal benefits that come from sharing copyrightable expression.

Expression and personality

Copyrightable expression, by design, is closely tied to the personality of its creator. As a result, people often feel much more strongly connected to their copyrighted works than other forms of intellectual property. Copyright law respects the intimate tie between creator and creation, in part by giving the authors of copyrighted works a very long term of protection—currently the life of the author plus 70 years for most works. During this term, the author is granted control over almost all use of the work as well as rights in *derivative works* (works adapted from the originally copyrighted item).

This tight control is generally accepted in our society, perhaps because of the personal link between expression and authorship. If you have ever felt ripped off when someone took your idea, your words, or your work and called it their own, you have felt the strong personal pull of copyright.

Expression and society

On the other hand, shared creative expression plays an important role in our society. Human beings are social animals, and we connect with each other through our personal expressions. Considered as a whole, *culture* is just the product of many personal expressions mixed together.

This is true both on a micro and on a macro level. On the micro level, consider the well-known movie *Monty Python and the Holy Grail*. This movie is not the result of a single personal expression; rather, it is a collective expression, the result of many people working together. Most obvious is the writing and acting of the Monty Python comedy troupe. There were also, however, creative and expressive inputs from animators, camera operators, costumers, lighting and sound designers, musicians, møøse trainers, and many others. The name "Monty Python and the Holy Grail" is just a shorthand for the collective expressive efforts that went into the movie.

The various movie awards ceremonies are good examples of recognizing the individual creative expressions that went into the whole. In those ceremonies, the collective expression is only recognized once, with the "Best Movie" award. Every other award is given for individual creative expressions incorporated into the whole—the best actors, costumers, editors, directors, and others.

On a macro level, our culture as a whole is tied inseparably to the many bits of expression, both individual and collective, that it contains. Just like *Monty Python and the Holy Grail*, our "culture" is a shorthand for the expressive efforts of many people. It is not just Picasso, Jane Austen, J.K. Rowling, George Lucas, and Tim Burton. It is not limited to the writers of blogs, the composers of music, the choreographers of plays, and everyone else whose work involves creating copyrighted content. Our culture is also created by you and all the people around you as you talk, write, work, and live each day. It consists *entirely* of shared copyrightable expression.

Expression and communication

Further, copyrighted expression has become a cultural and symbolic shorthand for communication. For example, saying that someone "is a Homer Simpson" invokes copyrighted expression to communicate a personal point. In a more extreme example, there are people who primarily communicate by quoting other people's expressions; think of those who respond to almost every question with quotes from *Monty Python* or *Napoleon Dynamite*.

As Danah Boyd points out in the article "When Media Becomes Culture: Rethinking Copyright Issues," (*http://zephoria.org/thoughts/archives/2005/09/29/when_media_beco.html*), we appropriate more than just words for communication. People use photos and animated "smilies" to show their moods. We associate different ringtones with different people. We display our attitudes, affiliations, and personality by putting logos, pictures, and quotes on our t-shirts. Hip-hop in particular has a long history of *sampling*—using little bits of other songs remixed into a new composition. We have become like Mrs. Who (from Madeline L'Engle's *A Wrinkle In Time*) or Bumblebee (from the 2007 *Transformers* movie), using other people's expressions to express ourselves. (It is amusing that this paragraph is itself an example of the point it seeks to communicate.)

Boyd's point is that, to a certain extent, the "content" industries are victims of their own success. They have successfully managed to get their work incorporated into popular culture. They have done this in part by building upon the cultural heritage of prior shared expression, and in turn, their works have become part of our shared culture, available for a new generation of authors and artists to use.

The problem of control

The problem is that the strong personal protections of copyright are in conflict with the shared nature of culture. The economic benefits of copyright discussed in Chapter 1 are built on controlling expression, while the social and cultural benefits of copyright are based upon sharing expression.

This problem of control puts copyright into a difficult economic position, comparable to the original market failure that prompted the development of copyright. Of course this is an issue with patents too, but the much shorter term of patent protection mitigates the problem. In the copyright world, the combination of strong controls, long terms, and widespread incentives to share sets up a persistent unstable dynamic.

The state of copyright

The powerful individual inclination toward control of copyrightable material has resulted in political pressure for the strengthening of copyright protection. In fact, the story of copyright from the 1700s until about 1990 has been almost entirely a story of lengthening terms (from 14 years to life plus 70 years), increasing scope (from only particular types of works to almost all works), and stronger protections (from restrictions on publishing rights only to restriction of almost all uses).

Only recently have people started feeling a contrary pull toward less restriction on copyrighted material. The primary reason for this shift is the Internet, and more broadly, the rise of digital media. This new technology has empowered a larger percentage of the population to create new works and express themselves artistically, but as new people have entered into the creative space, they have found the well of our common culture increasingly dry.

The "content" industries, having ridden a century-long wave of popular support of strong copyright, have established legal and business models that depend on the existing copyright regime. Meanwhile, popular sentiment is shifting away from support of strong copyright, and people are "voting with their feet" by sharing music and movies, remixing and mashing up content from other providers, and generally disregarding many of the established boundaries of copyright.

The Power of Defaults

The second primary driver of copyright is that expressions are copyrighted *by default*. This is a relatively new development, and it has changed the fundamental balance of copyright in our economy and in our society.

Defaults have enormous power. Just ask Microsoft; its enormous market share in operating systems and web browsers is almost entirely due to the power of defaults. When you buy a computer, it is possible to get any operating system you want. You can go to apple.com and get a Macintosh, or find someplace that is willing to sell you a computer with Linux (or even other operating systems) preinstalled.

But if you take no unusual steps and just buy the first acceptable computer that you see, you will end up buying Microsoft Windows. It is the default choice, and because it works well enough, and is available, it has become most people's preferred choice.

Similarly, when Internet Explorer came out in the mid-1990s, most people agreed that it wasn't as good a browser as Netscape Navigator. Besides, those who were interested in the Internet had already downloaded Netscape; there was usually no reason to change.

As people upgraded their computers and their operating systems, however, they were faced with a choice: go to extra trouble to download Netscape onto the new computer, or just use the pre-installed Internet Explorer. The key market share driver for Internet Explorer, at least initially, wasn't the quality of the browser; it was the browser's simple presence on the desktop. It may not have been the best, but it was there, it was good enough, and it worked. In three years' time, Internet Explorer went from an also-ran to overwhelmingly dominant, largely by the power of being the default.

Defaults are also a key part of the history of copyright. There are two aspects of copyright where the default has changed over time: in the application of copyright protection to a work, and in the nature of works eligible for protection.

Defaults in the Application of Copyright

It used to be that expressions were not copyrighted by default. As with patents, the creator had to explicitly register the work with the United States Copyright Office. Failure to register the work didn't only mean that it was not copyrighted when it was published, it meant that it could not ever be copyrighted, even later.

Further, copyrighting the work took effort. Not much effort, but it was not economically profitable to spend the few dollars required to copyright each work unless your business model depended upon your legal control of the expression. Therefore, the great majority of the stories, songs, jokes, sayings, and paintings that imbued American culture were in the public domain and freely shared.

This changed with the Copyright Act of 1976. The 1976 act removed the requirement that new works be registered to receive copyright protection. Instead, the act created a system of protection for all "original works of authorship," published or unpublished, from the moment they were "fixed in a tangible medium of expression."

Copyright as the default state

This change in defaults was profound; it shifted the landscape around copyright. Before the act, people needed to expend time and effort to have copyright applied to their works. This minimal barrier of registration resulted in a significant drop-off in the application of copyright —only a percentage of all works were copyrighted. Immediately after the implementation of the 1976 act, people needed to expend time and effort to keep copyright from applying to their works. The result was that essentially all new works were copyrighted. Copyright became the natural state of new creative expression.

The change in expectations was so pervasive that a few people started to argue about the existence of the public domain. Under the new law, the public domain was defined in the negative as the *absence* of copyright protection. According to one scholar, you couldn't place works into the public domain; you could only decline to enforce your copyright. Similarly, works with expired copyrights weren't in a place called the "public domain" because there was no such place. Instead, they were works with no-longer-enforceable copyrights.

Defaults and complexity

I mentioned in Chapter 2 that the patent document is the most complex document in the field of intellectual property. The complexity of the patent document is a direct result of the defaults that are applied to technological works.

The scope of a patent's protection is spelled out in the patent claims. Anything outside those claims is free for someone else to use; the patent language defines an island of protection in the sea of prior art. The patent document is complex because it must deal with the linguistic and legal complexity inherent in defining the boundaries of protection. When people argue about patents, they argue about whether the accused technology lies *inside* the scope of the patent language.

Copyright is exactly the opposite. Everything is copyrighted by default, so people don't argue whether the copyright statute is applicable to the problem; it is always applicable. Therefore the documents that deal with copyright grants are simple and straightforward.

Instead, people in copyright lawsuits argue about the *exceptions* in copyright law. The exceptions are complex because they define the boundaries where copyright becomes inapplicable—oases of unencumbered use in the land of copyright control. When people argue about copyrights, they argue about whether the accused work lies *outside* the scope of the copyright grant.

Defaults in the Applicability of Copyright

The second change to the defaults in copyright has been the types of works that are eligible for copyright protection. This is a different issue from the defaults in the application of copyright law, but the changes are similar in their reach.

By way of analogy, think of defaults in the area of network security. Assume that you have a default that "a security policy must be applied to all incoming traffic." That is like the default application of copyright discussed earlier; every new work is measured against the copyright standard, just as every incoming packet is inspected as it comes into a secure network.

On the other hand, simply saying that, "a security policy must be applied" does not tell you anything about which traffic will ultimately be allowed through the firewall. That depends on a completely different set of factors that must be analyzed independently.

When deciding which sort of traffic should be allowed through your firewall, there are two basic choices. You can have a *default allow policy*, which grants access unless there is a rule in place *denying* the connection, or you can have a *default deny policy*, which forbids access unless there is a rule *allowing* the connection. Default deny policies are considered safer, but they are more work to configure and maintain; any time some new application has to access the network, the firewall rules must be changed to allow the new connection.

Defaults in the scope of works eligible for copyright

The history of copyright in the United States can also be seen as a movement from a default deny to default allow policy for copyright. Under previous copyright acts, only specifically enumerated types of works were eligible for copyright protection. For example, the Copyright Act of 1790 (the first copyright act instituted in the United States) only allowed protection for books, maps, and charts. If you created something else, it was ineligible for copyright protection.

This was the default deny policy of copyright at work. Unless there was a specific provision in the law allowing copyright protection for your category of work, you had no protection at all.

The result of this policy was tremendous pressure on Congress to amend the Copyright Act to allow new types of protections and new types of works. For example, the Copyright Act was amended in 1802 to allow "historical and other prints." Then it was amended to provide protection for paintings and musical compositions. It was amended again to provide protection for dramatic works, photographs, and sculptures. Each time a new medium came to the forefront of the copyright scene, the law had to be amended to allow protection.

The tipping point came in the early 1900s. You may be familiar with player pianos that read *piano rolls*—sheets of paper with perforations representing different notes. Although piano rolls allowed the reproduction of pieces of music, a 1908 court case called *White-Smith v. Apollo* decided that they were not in the allowed category of sheet music, and were thus not protectable. The court stated:

> These perforated rolls are parts of a machine which, when duly applied and properly operated in connection with the mechanism to which they are adapted, produce musical tones in harmonious combination. But we cannot think that they are copies within the meaning of the copyright act.

Sheet music publishers were outraged. Partially as a result of this decision, Congress passed a revision to the Copyright Act the next year. The Copyright Act of 1909 gave the copyright owner of a musical work the exclusive right "to make any arrangement or record in which the thought of an author may be recorded and from which it may be read or reproduced." Recording studios are still vigorously applying the controls this act granted them when they prosecute people for exchanging MP3 files.

In addition, the 1909 act took the first step toward a default allow policy for copyright. Rather than just setting up a new protected statutory category for piano rolls, Congress decided to try to handle this situation in a more flexible and permanent manner. Specifically, the 1909 Copyright Act was much more expansive in its language when it described what would be considered a "Copyrightable Work" (some individual classifications are omitted here; emphasis in original):

> The works for which copyright may be secured under this Act shall include all the writings of an author.
>
> [The] application for registration shall specify to which of the following classes the work in which copyright is claimed belongs: Books, ... Periodicals, ... Works of art, ... Photographs, ...
>
> *Provided nevertheless,* That the above specifications shall not be held to limit the subject-matter of copyright as defined in section four of this Act, not shall any error in classification invalidate or impair the copyright protection secured under this Act.

Under this new, more flexible language, all works were swept into one basic category—the "copyrighted work." All copyrighted works received the same basic protection. There were a few classes of works, such as dramatic works, that received additional protection. However, the creation of an omnibus class of copyrighted works significantly simplified the administration of copyright under the 1909 act. When new forms of art were developed, such as films, they could be included under "all the writings of an author" and would be covered by copyright.

The Copyright Act of 1976 was the culmination of this evolution. Just as the 1976 act changed the defaults for the *application* of copyright to new works, it also completed the transition from a default deny to a default allow policy for the *types* of works eligible for copyright protection. The 1976 act declared that copyright protection could apply (and would apply) to all "original works of authorship." This intentionally broad and inclusive language was designed to include any work that showed *originality*—the result of decisionmaking by a creative mind.

Copying and the History of Copyright

Many people don't realize that for most of the history of copyright, it was legal for people to make as many personal copies of books works as they wanted, as long as it was strictly for personal use. The restriction on personal copying is of relatively recent vintage, only dating back to 1915 or so.

The reason is that "copy" has multiple meanings: it is both a noun and a verb. As a verb, copy has the common meaning, "to reproduce or imitate." As a noun, copy is "a collection of written material or a complete work." The word is still used in the noun sense in the publishing industry: a "copy editor" is somebody who edits written material (the "copy"), not somebody who manages the reproduction of content.

In its original sense, copyright was a *publishing* right. Only somebody who had rights over the work as a whole (the "copy" as a noun) was able to publish and distribute the work. Individual use was not even addressed; if a person wanted to copy (the verb) an entire book, he or she was free to do so. Individual reproduction was not an economic threat to content publishing because it didn't scale.

Section two of the Copyright Act of 1831 makes this clear: those granted a copyright had "the sole right and liberty of printing, reprinting, publishing, and vending" the work (in other words, all publishing-related rights). Obviously, reproduction (copy as a verb) was required for publication of the work (copy as a noun), but they were two different things. This small distinction is important to understanding the state of copyright today.

Copying (the verb) and copyright

When paintings and statues were added to the list of works that could be copyrighted, there was some concern as to how the copyright on something like a statue might be infringed. Statues couldn't be mechanically reproduced and "published" like books.

The problem was that a second artist could get around the exclusive rights granted under the law by creating a new work that was for all intents and purposes a copy—a republication—of the existing copyrighted work. To prevent this sort of gaming of the system, Congress inserted the word "copy" (verb sense) into the Copyright Act of 1870 as a specific protection against the violation of the rights of artistic reproduction. Figure 4-1 is from the Restated Copyright Act of 1874.

A contemporary reading of this passage would suggest that all copying would be prohibited. However, there were different penalties imposed for the infringement of books and the infringement of other artistic works. Significantly, copying was not listed as a trigger for the infringement of books. Therefore, the turn-of-the-century understanding of copyright law was

SEC. 4952. *Any Citizen of the United States or resident therein who shall be the author, inventor, designer, or proprietor of any book, map, chart, dramatic or musical composition, engraving, cut, print, or photograph or negative thereof, or of a painting, drawing, chromo, statue, statuary, or of models or designs intended to be perfected as works of the fine arts, and the executors, administrators, or assigns of any such person shall, upon complying with the provisions of this chapter, have the sole liberty of printing, reprinting, publishing, completing, copying, executing, finishing, and vending, the same; and in the case of a dramatic composition of publicly performing or representing it, or causing it to be performed or represented by others. And authors may reserve the right to dramatize or to translate their own works.*

FIGURE 4-1. Copyright eligibility in 1870

that artistic works could not be copied, but there was no limitation on the private copying of books—only on publication.

More specifically, only copies of books that were sold *in competition to the publisher* were considered to infringe the copyright. Figure 4-2 shows an excerpt from an influential copyright treatise at the time:*

SECTION II.—PROHIBITED ACTS, AND REMEDIES.

It is an infringement, subject to the remedies stated below, to do any of the following acts in respect of a copyright work.

In the case of :—

I. *Books* :[5] without the consent of the proprietor in writing signed in the presence of two witnesses.
   1. To print or publish.
   2. To dramatize or translate.
   3. To import.
   4. Knowingly to sell or expose for sale copies unlawfully made or imported.

FIGURE 4-2. 1902 excerpt on copyright infringement of books

In contrast, the rights reserved to authors and creators of artistic works were much broader. Figure 4-3 shows the difference.

* Evan James MacGillivray, *A Treatise Upon the Law of Copyright: In the United Kingdom and the United States*, J. Murray, 1902, at 287–288.

II. *Maps,*[1] *charts, dramatic or musical compositions, prints, art engravings, photographs, chromos, paintings, drawings, statues, statuary models and designs for the fine arts:* without the consent of the proprietor in writing signed in the presence of two witnesses.

1. To engrave, etch, work, or copy.
2. To print or publish.
3. To dramatize or translate.
4. To import.
5. Knowingly to sell or expose for sale copies unlawfully made or exported.

FIGURE 4-3. 1902 copyright infringement of artistic works

The significant difference between these two passages is that all *copying* of artistic works was explicitly forbidden, but there was an implicit acceptance of private, personal-use copies of books and other literary materials.

This ignores state common law copyright, which applied to works immediately upon fixation (and sometimes even before). Nevertheless, publication terminated all common law rights, and after publication, the work became either public domain or federally copyrighted and governed by the law quoted above.

The Copyright Act of 1909

This changed with the Copyright Act of 1909. The 1909 act was the first step toward the "protectable by default" standard described earlier, and as such, it was much more expansive in its language when it described what would be considered a "copyrightable work." Again from the act:

> The works for which copyright may be secured under this Act shall include all the writings of an author.
>
> [The] application for registration shall specify to which of the following classes the work in which copyright is claimed belongs: Books, ... Periodicals, ... Works of art, ... Photographs, ...

Notice that books, periodicals, works of art, and other sorts of works were all included under the same "copyrighted work" umbrella. Further, *all* copyrighted works received the same basic protection; they were subject to the copyright holder's exclusive right "to print, reprint, publish, *copy*, and vend the copyrighted work" (Copyright Act of 1909, Section 1a, emphasis added).

In one stroke, the creation of a single base standard for copyrighted works reserved to copyright holders the right to restrict *all* copies of literary works, even those made exclusively for personal, unpublished use.

Stepping aside from the history for a moment, I noted before that this situation is not too different from designing a security policy or writing a regular expression. Having personally made the mistake of being overinclusive in those other contexts, it is my personal opinion that the 1909 prohibition on private copying of literary works was a mistake. Not necessarily a mistake in the sense that "they should not have done that," but rather a mistake in the sense that it was an *unintended* extension of the law.

It is possible that the expansion of the prohibition on personal-use copying was an intended consequence of the 1909 act, but there is no discussion in the Congressional Record about that change. Instead, the discussions were focused on the simplification of the statute and the mechanical reproduction of music, specifically, on reversing the *White-Smith* decision about piano rolls.

Regardless of whether it was a mistake, however, the language of the statute made copying in all contexts subject to the restrictions of copyright. In the 1917 publication of *A Treatise on the Law of Copyright and Literary Property* (American Law Book Co.), William Benjamin Hale noted that, "Strictly, even a single copy made for private use is an infringement." By the mid-1920s, restrictions on personal copying were regularly upheld by the courts.

Copying and software

The restriction on personal-use copying of books is essential to the copyright protection of software today. Software is copyrighted as a literary work, in the same category as books. There is no restriction, even today, on *reading* or *using* a copyrighted work.

In the computer world, the analogue to reading is executing a program. As a result, there is no restriction whatsoever in copyright law on executing a program written and copyrighted by someone else. However, to read or execute something on a computer, you must copy it. Copying, in fact, is one of the most fundamental operations of a computer.

For example, imagine you are using your web browser to read something on the Internet. The text you are reading had copyright applied to it when it hit the disk, or maybe even the RAM, on the author's computer. Then a copy of that information was brought into memory and sent over the network to the web server. The web server put a copy in RAM and then another copy on disk. When you asked for a copy of the HTML file, the web server copied the information into RAM again, sent another copy over the network (creating intermediate copies in caching servers) until it got to your computer. Your computer made a copy in RAM, maybe cached a copy on the disk, and then sent another copy to the video memory, where it finally shows up for you to read.

The copyright statute tries to deal with this issue by allowing "the owner of a copy of a computer program to make or authorize the making of another copy or adaptation of that computer program provided...that such a new copy or adaptation is created as an essential step in the utilization of the computer program in conjunction with a machine and that it is used in no other manner." Nevertheless, some companies (and courts) have used the existence of these various copying mechanisms to apply copyright protections to the running of software.

For example, Vivendi Universal and Blizzard software have sued a company called MDY to prevent the distribution of a program that automates certain aspects of Blizzard's *World of Warcraft* game. Blizzard argues that its license agreement prohibits the use of unapproved software connected to the game. Under this interpretation, any use of MDY's program violates the license, because making a copy of the game residing in RAM is an infringement on Blizzard's copyrights. This case is still in the courts and will probably be decided sometime in 2008.

The Terms of Copyright

So with the context of history, it is time to start looking at the terms in the law to see how they are applied today. The basic rules for copyright are set forth in Title 17 of the U. S. Code, which is largely still based on the Copyright Act of 1976.

The Copyright Act gives protection to "original works of authorship fixed in any tangible medium of expression, now known or later developed, from which they can be perceived, reproduced, or otherwise communicated, either directly or with the aid of a machine or device."

Works of authorship include:

- Literary works
- Musical works, including any accompanying words
- Dramatic works, including any accompanying music
- Pantomimes and choreographic works
- Pictorial, graphic, and sculptural works
- Motion pictures and other audiovisual works
- Sound recordings
- Architectural works

These categories are flexible. As noted above, software is considered a literary work. Unless you are *sure* that some type of expression is outside the bounds of copyright, then you should assume that copyright applies.

Defining "Expression"

The first core principle of copyright is that it applies only to an *expression*. So, what is an expression?

- In math, an expression is a combination of symbols (numbers, operators, and variables) that can be evaluated.
- In a computer context, an expression can also refer to some representation of a value or something that can be evaluated to return a value.
- In language, an expression is a communication in speech or writing.

The common thread between these (and other) definitions is that they all make reference to something *concrete*, usually a specific sequence of words or symbols. Different symbols are used to illustrate a particular thought or convey a particular idea.

Broadening this definition, an expression is *any artifact used to convey an idea*. The artifact may be ink on a paper, code in a file, paint on a canvas, or words on a page; the important aspect is that concrete physical representation communicates an idea from one person to another.

By way of contrast, a patent covers the *idea* behind an invention. The idea may be embodied in many different machines, processes, or products, each of which is a concrete expression of the patented concept. This is what makes patents so powerful—many different things can be covered by the description in a single patent.

On the other hand, 1+3, 3+1, and 2+2 are all different expressions that happen to evaluate equally. If these could be copyrighted (they can't), all three of these expressions would have independent copyright status.

Ideas and Expressions

The distinction between concepts (say, "a series of numbers that sum to four") and a particular expression ("2+2") is called the *idea/expression dichotomy*. This principle is at the core of copyright law precisely because copyright covers personal expression and patents cover technical knowledge.

Judging technical expression

When we are judging technical knowledge, there are very basic criteria for deciding whether something has any worth. Does it work? Does it work better than existing solutions in some way? Is it feasible? Anyone with some knowledge of the field can try to answer these questions in a reasonable and objective way.

It is also possible to define technical concepts precisely enough that a suitably skilled person can look at a particular machine and understand whether it expresses a particular idea. That is the patent law in a nutshell; the patent document defines an idea with specificity (in theory), and patent suits reflect an objective mapping between the patent and a particular system (again, in theory). That is why the different types of machines described in a single patent are called *embodiments*—they each individually concretely express or "embody" some aspect of the inventive concept.

Judging personal expression

On the other hand, it is much more difficult to judge personal expressions. What is great art? What is a good book? What is a funny joke? As the saying goes, you can put these questions to three people and get four opinions. Complicating the situation further are the many examples of personal expression that were not considered noteworthy when they were made, but were later recognized as great art. There is no *objective* way to classify personal expressions into those that are good and bad, so there is no way to design a law that would allow for copyright protection only of good expression.

Further, there is no platonic ideal expression of a particular concept. Many people can have the same idea and express it in different ways. For example, which banana in Figure 4-4 is the true banana? Which is the best expression of the idea "banana?"

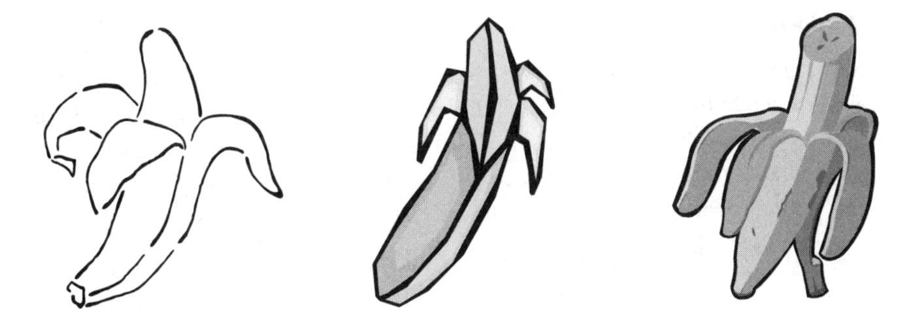

FIGURE 4-4. Going bananas

Ideas, expressions, and Turing machines

Although software has a functional, technical component, the idea/expression dichotomy also applies to code. Even when an idea is almost purely functional, there are different ways in which the code can be expressed.

To understand the idea/expression dichotomy in a software context, think of the Turing machine. A Turing machine is a simple machine with just two parts: a "tape" that can store symbols, and a "head" that moves back and forth across the tape, reading and writing symbols. Alan Turing, one of the pioneers of computer science, proved that this simple mechanical device is *computationally equivalent* to the computers we use each day. That means that although the Turing machine wouldn't necessarily be very fast, it is *possible* to make it run all the same programs as the newest Intel microchip.

Many people have created Turing machines, both in software and with real heads and tapes, but the fundamental breakthrough was more than the physical machine—it was the *idea* of the Turing machine. This *Universal Turing Machine*, as the hypothetical machine is sometimes called, has an infinite tape and can take an infinite amount of time to run that tape. It exists only as a platonic ideal.

One way in which this Universal Turing Machine has affected computer science is the idea of *Turing completeness*. A language or device is Turing complete if it can express the same range of computations as a Universal Turing Machine.

If the Turing machine were patented, all computer languages (as well as a number of file formats and logic games) would be covered under the patent, as they are all Turing complete —an alternative expression of the fundamental idea of computing as expressed by the Universal Turing Machine.

Under the copyright law, however, the Universal Turing Machine as a concept would not be protectable. Instead, only your particular implementation of a Turing machine could be protected by the law. Another person could create his own implementation of the idea, as long as he didn't just take yours.

The merger doctrine

One result of the idea/expression dichotomy is that there is no copyright protection in basic facts. This is known as the *merger doctrine*. Under the merger doctrine, courts will not protect a copyrighted work from infringement if the idea underlying the work can be expressed only in one or a limited number of ways. In such an instance, the idea and expression are said to merge; you cannot separate the idea from the way in which it is expressed.

The rationale for this rule is straightforward. It would be very difficult, for example, to have a discussion about general relativity without mentioning the equation $e=mc^2$. It doesn't matter that $e=mc^2$ took a long time to develop, and it doesn't matter that creative *problem solving* was required to discover it. Copyright is designed to protect original creative expression, and mere recitation of facts is not creative. Following the same principle, collections of facts are not generally copyrightable. A written list of national capitals is no more creative than a list of numbers.

Similarly, it is not possible to copyright expressions consisting of just a few words or a short phrase. For example, there is really only one way to say "Good morning," even if you made an original, creative decision to speak those particular words. The courts have decided that it would be against public policy (not to mention foolish and unenforceable) to grant copyright control over simple phrases to just a few people.

Scenes à faire

A similar doctrine applies when examining common elements across a genre. A good example is the use of elves in fantasy literature. J.R.R. Tolkien set the archetype with the publication of *The Hobbit* and *The Lord of the Rings*, and elves have been a standard non-human character type ever since. Tolkien's elves were tall, thin, and long-lived; these characteristics were carried forward in other books and in role-playing and computer games.

The French phrase *scenes à faire* ("the scenes to be made") is used to describe these recurring story elements in copyright law. These story elements are considered part of the *idea* of a fantasy story and as such are not copyrightable. Individual descriptions of particular characters are protectable, but the existence of elves and their general characteristics are not.

This has become a particularly important topic with the rise of the World Wide Web. "FanFic" (fan fiction) stories take an existing world and characters, (like the world of Harry Potter) and use the characters and circumstances of that world to create new stories. In the case of fan fiction, the boundary between copyrightable expression and scenes à faire is unclear, at least in part because it is unclear whether a "Harry Potter story" is a genre. Most courts have held that a character is independently copyrightable if the character is *distinctly delineated.* Generic or undeveloped characters are not protected. "Distinctly delineated," though, is a term that still has to be more clearly defined.

Mostly functional expression

The merger doctrine also applies in cases where there is a very thin line between functional expression and creative expression. The copyright statute explicitly excludes from protection "any idea, procedure, process, system, method of operation, concept, principle, or discovery." When there are both creative and functional aspects to a work, copyright "is limited to those aspects of the work—termed 'expression'—that display the stamp of the author's originality."

This is the awkward middle ground inhabited by software. Anyone who has worked extensively with code knows that there are both expressive and functional aspects to any codebase, but it is frequently difficult to separate the two.

The law in this case is unsettled, at least in part because the expressiveness in code is hard for many judges to appreciate. For example, in *Sega v. Accolade* (1992), the court said:

> Computer programs pose unique problems for the application of the "idea/expression distinction" that determines the extent of copyright protection. To the extent that there are many possible ways of accomplishing a given task or fulfilling a particular market demand, the programmer's choice of program structure and design may be highly creative and idiosyncratic. However, computer programs are, in essence, utilitarian articles - articles that accomplish tasks. As such, they contain many logical, structural, and visual display elements that are dictated by external factors such as compatibility requirements and industry demands...
>
> In some circumstances, even the exact set of commands used by the programmer is deemed functional rather than creative for the purposes of copyright. When specific instructions, even though previously copyrighted, are the only and essential means of accomplishing a given task, their later use by another will not amount to infringement.

In fact, some people argue that many pieces of code are not expressive at all, or if they are expressive, they are expressive in the sense that they capture a piece of functionality in a particularly elegant way. However, technical elegance is different from personal expression, and doesn't trigger the application of copyright.

COPYRIGHT IN HEADER FILES

One particularly difficult issue concerns copyright protection of header files. An individual name or symbol in a header file is cannot be copyrighted, but the particular selection of symbols may be. The selection of symbols to be exported is inherent to API design, which could be a copyrightable creative decision. If you have ever heard programmers talking about "beautiful" or "ugly" APIs, you have wandered into the tricky middle ground of barely copyrightable expression.

In my opinion, the most likely scenario is a case-by-case determination. A bunch of constants would probably not support copyright. The entirety of an exported API is more likely copyrightable, but the header files would probably only support a "thin" copyright, where even trivial changes would be enough to avoid infringement. No one really knows, though, because the law of copyright is changing day by day.

For header files in particular, the rationale for copyright protection is substantially weakened when there is a second compatible implementation of a library. In that case, the headers, as creative as they might be, would probably merge into the functional interface supported by many concrete implementations.

For example, take the C++ standard template library (STL). There are a number of different implementations of the STL, all copyrighted by different authors. The STL headers themselves, however, have become just *functional* descriptions of the underlying copyrighted implementations. All STL implementations must use identical function definitions in the header files, or they would not be source-compatible with each other.

The issue of header files also arises in the context of GPL-licensed software. Chapter 12 discusses this issue in more detail.

Fixation

An idea must have a concrete expression to be protectable. The copyright statute is fairly literal in this regard, saying that copyright protects "original works of authorship fixed in a tangible medium of expression." *Fixation* is the legal term used to refer to the necessity that an expression must be grounded in a physical object.

A work is fixed in a tangible medium of expression when it is written down, recorded, or otherwise made permanent enough that it can be perceived and reproduced by other people. It doesn't matter where or in what medium the expression is fixed; as long as it is recorded *somewhere*, copyright protection applies.

For those wondering about the copyright notices at the end of ball games, game performances can be copyrighted because they are recorded at the studio at the same time they are transmitted over the air. If the performance was broadcast live and never recorded, no copyright protection would apply. Modulating the radio waves is not enough; the artifacts protected by copyright must be tangible and not transitory.

One open question has to do with the applicability of copyright law to copies in RAM. Some people argue that the contents of RAM are not permanent enough to allow for copyright protection to apply, but the current trend is toward allowing RAM copies to count as fixations for copyright purposes.

Because the fixation requirement applies to both the initial establishment of copyright and the later determination of when infringing "copies" are made, RAM copies have become increasingly important. As noted earlier, almost every operation in a computer results in a copy being made; these temporary RAM files may be both copyright protected and infringing.

Originality

Because copyright is designed to provide incentives for the creation of new works, the law requires that the work be new. In patent law, this requirement is called novelty; in copyright law, it is called *originality*.

Therefore, originality/novelty is one principle common to both copyrights and patents, but its application in copyright serves only to underline the fundamental difference between these two branches of law.

In particular, patent law requires that an invention be *absolutely* novel. In theory, each new patent should describe a system or method that has never existed before in any form on Earth. Even though the patent system isn't ironclad, and everybody admits that many non-novel patents make it through the patent office, the PTO at least expends effort to try to find any systems, methods, or machines that are essentially equivalent to your patent claims. It does not matter if the prior system was properly appreciated or understood by its creator; if an equivalent prior system existed, your invention cannot be patented.

On the other hand, copyright originality is all about the specific decisions that you made when you were fixing the work, i.e. moving the concept from an idea to an expression. The end result may be *exactly the same* as another work made by someone else, but if the work is the result of an original, creative decision process, then you have sufficient originality to claim copyright protection on the work.

Original copies

Although it does happen sometimes, it is usually difficult to come up with the exact same expression as another person. For that reason, duplicates or near-duplicates of someone else's work are presumed to result from copying. However, if you can prove that you did not have access to the other work or that you went through a different decision process in creating your work, then your identical (or nearly identical) work will be considered original. This is essentially the strategy used in reverse engineering (discussed in Chapter 13).

Minimal originality

Although copyright requires that an original decision be made when expressing the work, it is hard to underestimate the amount of actual originality required before copyright kicks in. For example, I have a map of the world that was stitched together from different satellite passes. Deciding which satellite photos to use was the original decision that permitted the mapmaker to copyright the map.

Another example is the famous musical piece "4'33". The composer, John Cage, made the single original decision *not* to play any music for the duration of the piece. This was enough to establish copyright in the piece.

An unusual epilogue to the story of *4'33"* came in July 2002. The descendants of John Cage sued composer Mike Batt for copyright infringement when he released the track "A Minute's Silence" and credited "Batt/Cage." Batt defended his originality, saying, "I certainly wasn't quoting his silence. I claim my silence is original silence...it's digital. [Cage's silence] is only analog." The case was settled a few months later; both parties refused to comment on whether Batt's silence was original or not.

Compilations

Compilation copyrights are a special type of copyrighted work. They are created when a person collects or assembles "preexisting materials or...data...in such a way that the resulting work as a whole constitutes an original work of authorship."

This is a tricky area because in some cases there is very little distinction between a collection of facts (not copyrightable) and a compilation (copyrightable). Compilations of facts, such as a phone book or a map, must contain evidence of some creative spark to qualify for copyright protection. For example, phone books are not considered original enough to merit copyright protection, even though they cost a lot of time and money to make. This is because they only contain collections of facts (not original in themselves) and their alphabetical organization is mechanical, not original. Originality requires creativity; alphabetization is not creative.

In practice, almost any work that is created by an author will meet the originality requirement. Unless the information is organized purely mechanically, such as by alphabetization, the selection of the individual facts is frequently enough to support a copyright claim.

Even when the arrangement of information is purely mechanical, there are things that can instill copyright. For example, map and phone book publishers insert a small amount of made-up information into the listings—non-existent addresses with fictitious names. This small amount of original creativity is enough to support a copyright on the whole work, even though the individual facts in the book are not by themselves protectable.

The compilation copyright is separate from any copyright protections that may apply to the individual works in the compilation. For example, a collection of the best of Shakespeare's plays might be subject to copyright even though the individual plays would be old enough to have no protection; the selection and organization of the plays could constitute enough creativity to support a compilation copyright claim if the choosing was not purely mechanical.

This is the same principle that allows Linux distributors such as Red Hat to claim copyright protection on their installation disks. Even if Red Hat did not provide any of the packages on the disk directly, Red Hat would still have a copyright on the compilation of programs chosen for the installation disk.

Copyright protection of forms and databases

One current issue in copyright law is the protection of individual forms. The rule right now is that blank forms are not copyrightable. There may be individual bits of the form that could be protected, like a logo, but the basic form fields themselves are not eligible for copyright.

The "blank forms" rule is important to software developers because of the clear analogue between blank forms and all sorts of schema. For example, a database schema is very similar to an electronic representation of a paper form. An XML schema is used similarly to describe the structure of other data. The ability to copyright bare schemas is an open issue that needs to be resolved.

The blank forms doctrine comes from an old Supreme Court case called *Baker v. Selden*. As sometimes happens in these cases, the important aspect of that case was not the final determination of who won or lost, but a passing statement made by the court in the discussion of the case: "blank account-books are not the subject of copyright." This statement was expanded over time into the current rule, "blank forms such as time cards, graph paper, account books, diaries, blank checks, scorecards, address books, report forms, order forms and the like, which are designed for recording information and do not in themselves convey information," are not protectable by copyright.

However, the real-world application of this rule is much more complicated. Some forms have been denied copyright protection because of the blank forms rule. However, a number of court cases have found *some* protectable elements in forms, particularly in collections of forms. Instead of automatically denying copyright to blank forms, the court will determine whether the form is sufficiently original to qualify for a compilation copyright. If the court finds that the arrangement of headings and selection of sentences meets the originality requirement, the form will be copyrightable (and copyrighted).

Further muddling the issue, the Copyright Office also regularly grants copyright registrations for forms. As explained by the office (*http://www.copyright.gov/*), "there is no way to secure copyright protection for the idea or principle behind a blank form...[but] an original literary work...is subject to copyright registration even though it is published in conjunction with a blank form...not protected by copyright." However, the copyright registration does not say, "the logo on this form is copyrighted." Instead, it says that copyright applies to the form without specifically designating subparts that are protectable. As a result, the copyright status of any particular form is very unclear.

With regard to *populated* databases, copyright protection has been granted to collections that display original creative expression. For example, a database containing information about the best restaurants in a city can be protected by copyright because the particular selection of restaurants is guided by the subjective and original criterion of being the "best." Therefore, the populated database can receive copyright protection even if all of the facts contained within the database (addresses, phone numbers, etc.) are individually unprotectable.

The Copyright Term

As with patents, the patchwork of laws affecting copyright has made it somewhat complicated to figure out the copyright status of some works. For this issue, there are three different laws to consider: the Copyright Act of 1909, the Copyright Act of 1976 (which went into force on January 1, 1978), and the Sonny Bono Copyright Term Extension Act of 1998. The duration of a copyright depends on when the copyrighted work was first created, when it was first published, and where the work was created. For our purposes, we will assume that all works were created in the United States.

Starting from the oldest works, anything that was registered or published before 1923 is in the public domain. These works can be used by anyone for any purpose; their use cannot be controlled, despite the fact that some publishers put copyright symbols on reproductions of public domain works.

If a work was published between 1923 and 1963, a two-term system was applied, with a renewal required 28 years after the initial registration to maintain the copyright. If the copyright owner did *not* apply for copyright renewal, the copyright expired and these works are now in the public domain. If the copyright owner did renew the copyright registration, these works had their terms automatically extended to 95 years. These works will enter into the public domain no sooner that 2018 (95 years from 1923).

If a work was published between 1964 and 1977, there is no renewal requirement. These works will automatically have a 95-year term and will enter the public domain no sooner than 2059.

The Copyright Act of 1976 established new, much longer copyright terms for all new works. For all works fixed on or after January 1, 1978, the copyright term extends for the author's life plus an additional 70 years after the author's death. If it is a *joint work* (a work made by more than one author), the term extends to 70 years after the last surviving author's death. For *works for hire* (works created in the course of employment) or anonymous/pseudonymous works, the copyright extends for 95 years from publication or 120 years from creation, whichever is shorter.

If a work was created before 1978, but not published, it was automatically given copyright protection under the Copyright Act of 1976. The copyright term for these works is computed based on the same life-plus-70-year or 95/120-year terms applied to works created after 1978.

The law further specifies that for unpublished works created before 1978, the copyright extended at least until December 31, 2002. For works that were formerly unpublished but were later published before January 1, 2003, the term of copyright will not expire before December 31, 2047.

Owning a Copyright

By default, authors own their copyrights. This may seem natural now, but it was actually a substantial change made in the 1976 law; under all previous iterations of the Copyright Act the copyright was owned by the publisher (remember, this was a *publishing* right). In most situations under the current law, you own the rights to your personal creative expression.

One important distinction is that owning a reproduction of someone's expression (the result of the verb "copy") doesn't give any rights to the underlying creative expression (the noun "copy"). For example, if you own a CD of the Muppets' Greatest Hits, your ownership is limited to the particular piece of plastic that you bought in the store. It so happens that the piece of plastic you own can be read in a certain way to reproduce the Muppets' music, but your rights over the music are limited to reading the disc.

Unpublished Works

When the 1976 Copyright Act flipped the default from "works are not copyrighted unless they have been registered" to "works are copyrighted unless an exception applies," it created a broad new category of copyrighted works: unpublished copyrighted works. Under previous Copyright acts, there was no concept of copyright for an unpublished work, because copyright applied only to published works.

Unpublished copyrighted works are by far the most common category. If you doodle in school, you create an unpublished copyrighted work. If you take notes in a meeting, you create an unpublished copyrighted work. If you sing "Happy Birthday" for the video camera at a party, you create an unpublished copyrighted work. Just as the Turing machine proceeds through its computations leaving symbols on its tape, so too, do we move through life leaving behind us a trail of miniscule copyrighted artifacts.

Joint Authorship

Although we have talked about personal expression so far, more than one person can be considered the author of a work. When several people work together to create a single work, the result may be a *joint work*. According to the Copyright Act, a joint work is "a work prepared by two or more authors with the intention that their contributions be merged into inseparable or interdependent parts of a unitary whole." This is clearly applicable to many computer programs and other copyrightable works created by programmers.

The important aspect of a joint work is that *all authors intend* their contributions to be considered together. It doesn't matter if one person contributed more to the work, or that the many authors contributed to different parts of the work. For example, musical groups usually create joint works when they work together on an album. It doesn't matter that there may be more drum work in one song and more vocals in another. It also doesn't matter if they are even in the studio at the same time. As long as all parties worked with the intention of creating the disc together, they are joint authors of the final work.

In a software context, the result of pair programming would usually be considered a joint work. This is in contrast to code written by one programmer and later patched by another. In that case, the original author did not have the intention to create a joint work, even though the second author did. The result of this second situation is called a *derivative work*, and will be discussed later in this chapter.

Joint authorship matters because joint authors get equal rights to the final work; each author can use or license the work without permission from any other author. This is in contrast to derivative works, where the original author has superior rights over the work and can control the distribution of the later work.

Works for Hire

One of the most commercially important classifications under copyright law is the category of *works for hire*. The majority of works in the commercial market contain at least some element that was created as a work for hire.

A work for hire is created when someone, either a person or a business, directs another person to create an original work in the course of employment or under the direction of the first person. For example, when you write code for your work, you are creating a work for hire. In this situation, the author of the work is *not* the person who created the work, but instead the person who directed the creation of the work.

Think again about *Monty Python and the Holy Grail*. This movie is the result of many people working together, but it is not a joint work. Instead, it is owned by the producers of the film —the people who paid all the other workers to come together for the writing, filming, and editing that went into the final result. (As an aside, that is why the awards for "Best Picture" go to the producers of a film; they are the legal "authors" of the picture.)

The Copyright Act recognizes a work for hire in two specific situations:

- The work is created by an employee acting within the scope of his or her employment.
- The work is specially ordered or commissioned for use:

  — as a contribution to a collective work

  — as a part of a motion picture or other audiovisual work

  — as a translation

— as a supplement to another work

— as a compilation

— as an instructional text

— as a test or as answer material for a test, or

— as an atlas

The first situation applies to ordinary employment; if you are an employee, anything you create in the ordinary course of your job is a work for hire. The only wrinkle is whether somebody is actually an "employee." In general, if your boss determines your schedule, directs how you do your work, provides the equipment for your use, and pays taxes for employing you, you are an employee. Anything you create belongs to your employer.

If some or all of these don't apply to you, however, you may be in the second situation. In that case, the law tries to protect authors by making it significantly more difficult to have something considered a work for hire. In that case, works for hire must be specially ordered or commissioned and they must come within one of the categories listed above. Even then, a work will be a work for hire only if a *written agreement* says that the work will be a work for hire.

Implied licenses and ownership of works for hire

Figuring out whether something is a work for hire is important because it determines who can use and control the work after it is done. When you hire a wedding photographer, for example, the default is that the photographer is the author of the work and retains the copyright *even though you paid him (or her) to take the pictures.* As a result, the photographer retains the film negatives (or the digital files, these days) and each copy of the pictures must be individually purchased.

This is an especially important issue for software companies. If a company hires non-employee independent contractors to create an essential piece of infrastructure, then, by default, those independent developers are the owners of the software. There is an *implied license* for the company to use a copy of the software, but the developers have the legal right to do what they like with any other copies, including selling them to a competitor. Further, the purchasing company may not have any rights to build on (or even fix bugs in) the software.

Further, the law doesn't explicitly say that software can be created as a work for hire. Even if the software is specially ordered or commissioned, it doesn't easily fit within any of the allowed categories. While it is unlikely that a court would decide that software couldn't be considered a work for hire, especially if there was a written agreement signed by the independent developers, this issue has not been decided for certain.

Accordingly, most employee contracts and development agreements take a belt-and-suspenders approach: employees are required to sign agreements specifying that all their works are works for hire, and promising to transfer their copyrights to the employer if a court ever decides that their work product doesn't count as a work for hire.

Copyright Formalities

Before the Copyright Act of 1976, publishers had to comply with certain requirements to have copyright protection applied to a work. They had to register new works, send copies of the work to the Library of Congress, and include the copyright symbol (©) and year of publication on each copy of the work. While it is still a good idea to include the copyright symbol and year on each copy, it is no longer necessary. It is necessary to formally register your copyrights only if you are going to sue someone for infringement.

The Rights Granted by Copyright

Copyright, like other forms of intellectual property, reserves to its owners certain exclusive rights. In the case of copyright, Section 106 of the Copyright Act grants the owners of copyrights the exclusive right to do (or allow someone else to do) the following:

- *Reproduce* the copyrighted work
- *Prepare derivative works* based upon the work
- *Distribute* copies of the work to the public
- *Perform* the copyrighted work publicly
- *Display* the copyrighted work publicly

Reproducing a Work

The first and (now) most fundamental reserved right is the right to reproduce a copyrighted work. Some people believe that any private copying within a home is acceptable under copyright law. Under the strict terms of the statute, there is no provision for copying of any kind, private or not. This is why, for example, the RIAA (the Recording Industry Association of America) argues that putting MP3s on your iPod is a copyright violation. In their view, any copying must be explicitly authorized.

This argument does not hold up in many circumstances because of *fair use* (which we will discuss further below), but there is support for their position that any copying infringes their copyrights.

PHONORECORD

You may occasionally see the terms "Phonorecord" and "sound recording" applied to copyrighted works. A "Phonorecord" is the physical object that embodies a work of authorship, like a CD, DVD, or hard drive. According to the Copyright Act, a "sound recording" is any work that results "from the fixation of a series of musical, spoken, or other sounds, but not including the sounds accompanying a motion picture or other audiovisual work." Phonorecords usually (but do not necessarily) contain sound recordings.

Preparing Derivative Works

One of the more important reserved rights under copyright law is making derivative works. According to the Copyright Act, a derivative work is:

> ...a work based upon one or more preexisting works, such as a translation, musical arrangement, dramatization, fictionalization, motion picture version, sound recording, art reproduction, abridgment, condensation, or any other form in which a work may be recast, transformed, or adapted.

The rule about derivative works applies when there is *partial* copying, transformation, or adaptation of a copyrighted source. For example, software development usually involves the creation of a long chain of derivative works; everything after the initial check-in of the code creates a new derivative work. Most parts of the codebase don't change, but each new patch creates a new derivative work.

This copying doesn't have to be literal. For example, the legal difficulties of FanFic arise because they necessarily involve copying some of the names, characters, and situations from the original copyrighted works, even if the stories themselves are otherwise completely original.

Further muddying the waters are *de minimis* changes—changes that are so minimal that the changed work should be considered identical to the original work. De minimis changes can actually be quite extensive if they don't involve any originality. For example, if a person republished a copy of a Harry Potter novel with all instances of "Harry Potter" replaced by "Parry Hotter," the textual changes would be substantial, but the total effect would be a de minimis change.

The right to prepare derivative works should be understood as an anti-gaming provision of the copyright law. Before the law included this provision, a number of people tried to profit off other people's works by selling derivative works that had just enough changes to evade the earlier, more literal copyright provisions. One good example of this was the creation of piano rolls from copyrighted musical works. Tired of this sort of gaming of the system, Congress included rights over derivative works in the 1976 Act.

Derivative works are difficult because they represent an amalgam of different and supposedly exclusive rights. A derivative work results from a transformation or adaptation of an original work, and that transformation is itself an original copyrightable (and copyrighted) contribution. Therefore, both the original author and the transformer have independent copyright interests in the work. The original author has an overriding right to veto the distribution of the derivative work, but any subsequent distributor must receive permission from both the original author and the transformative author.

The copyright complexity of open source software systems is in large part due to the rules surrounding derivative works. A large project like the Linux kernel has hundreds or thousands of authors. It is essentially impossible to figure out which patches were purely functional (and thus not copyrighted), which patches were de minimus (not affecting copyright status), and which patches were new and original (resulting in a derivative work). As a result, *nobody* really owns the Linux kernel; the best description of its status is that it is owned jointly by its developers.

One consequence of this fact is that it would be very difficult to move the kernel to a new license, even if Linus Torvalds or the bulk of developers decided they wanted to. This is not a problem with FSF software because it used a more disciplined approach to gathering copyrights. The centralization of copyrights is discussed further in Chapter 11 and Chapter 14.

Originality and derivative works

For a mixed work to qualify as a derivative work, the new portion must have enough originality to qualify as a copyrightable work itself; adding de minimis or purely functional expressions to a copyrighted work does not create a derivative work. Similarly, copying de minimis or purely functional expressions from an otherwise copyrighted work does not create a derivative work.

For example, copying most of a "Hello World" program into your own "Goodbye Cruel World" program would not make your "Goodbye" code a derivative work of the "Hello" code, even though there was substantial literal copying between the two programs. Especially in small codebases, there are only a few ways to express certain concepts, and the expressions may be constrained by the functional requirements of the program. Larger programs, of course, offer a wider variety of expression and so direct copying of code is more likely to create a derivative work.

Non-literal copying is governed by the *abstraction-filtration-comparison* test. This test works by *abstracting* the structure of a program from the specific syntax used to express the program. Elements that cannot be copyrighted, such as purely functional or public domain algorithms, are *filtered* out, and the remaining original expressive elements are *compared* to the supposedly infringing work.

In theory, the abstraction-filtration-comparison test elegantly isolates copyrightable expression from the rest of the code. In practice, it usually provides highly idiosyncratic and unrepeatable results.

Distributing a Work

One of the exclusive rights granted under the 1976 act is the right to distribute (or control distribution of) a work. This was a broadening of the publishing rights associated with copyright. The 1909 act granted the exclusive rights "to print, reprint, publish, copy, and vend the copyrighted work." The 1976 act went further by reserving to copyright holders the right to "distribute" the work in any fashion.

This subtle broadening of language has had a direct impact on the new world of peer-to-peer software. In an April 2008 decision, one court held that having a shared files folder on a computer and thereby making files *available* for distribution is sufficient to infringe the exclusive rights of distribution granted under copyright law. Thus, not only the transfer of a copy, but also the intent to transfer or displayed invitation to transfer a copy can violate the exclusive right of distribution. The law is still unsettled, though. It remains to be seen whether other courts will decide similarly.

The first sale doctrine

One limitation on the exclusive right of distribution is that it only applies the first time a particular copy is sold. For example, think of a book. The copyright holder, probably the author, is able to dictate who gets to publish the book and how much the book costs to buy. Once a reader has bought a copy of the book, however, the copyright holder's exclusive control over *that copy* is exhausted. The reader is then able to keep the book, give it away, resell the book, or bury it in his backyard. The first sale doctrine allows the development of used bookstores, libraries, and the sale of kitschy memorabilia on eBay.

Nevertheless, the first sale doctrine does not apply if there is anything less than a complete sale. Software companies usually do not sell copies of their software; they only license them (allow their use). These license terms can be (and usually are) more restrictive than the default rules of copyright in this regard. As a result, there isn't a significant resale market in software like there is in books. For example, if you give a friend an install disk for Microsoft Windows, he may not be legally allowed to install it, even if you delete your copy and let him reregister with the same license number. Again, however, the law may be changing. A June 2008 decision stated that some shrinkwrapped software "licenses" are actually sales, subject to the first sale doctrine.

Performance or Display of a Work

The public performance and display rights allow a copyright holder to control when a work is performed publicly. A public performance occurs when the work is displayed or performed in a place open to the public or when the work is transmitted to multiple locations. For example, it would be a violation of this right to rent a movie and display it in a city park or stream the movie over the Internet without permission.

These rights generally apply to software because software is a literary work. For example, public performance of a video game without permission would probably violate this right, although the parameters of public performance of software have not been well established.

Fair Use

The primary limitation on copyright owners' control of the use of copyrighted material is a principle called *fair use*. In general, fair use allows the copying, distribution, and use of copyrighted material, without permission, for *transformative* or important purposes. Courts created the doctrine of fair use in an effort to balance the rights of copyright holders with the rights of society at large. Courts recognized there was value in allowing some copying of copyrighted material, particularly for important functions such as teaching, scholarship, and political speech. Some of the principles around fair use were finally codified as part of the Copyright Act of 1976, which gave four principles for determining whether something was a fair use:

- The purpose and character of the use, including whether such use is of commercial nature or is for non-profit educational purposes
- The nature of the copyrighted work
- The amount and substantiality of the portion used in relation to the copyrighted work as a whole; and
- The effect of the use upon the potential market for or value of the copyrighted work

Despite this seeming exactitude, it is difficult to say exactly what counts as a fair use. Both courts and Congress wanted the definition of fair use to be flexible enough to deal with new situations. The Copyright Act actually allows consideration of factors other than these, but these are the only four that are usually considered.

Most fair use is either commentary or parody. If you are commenting on a copyrighted work, for example, writing a book review, you can (in most cases) copy parts of the work so that those reading your review have the necessary context to understand it. Educational use—scholarship—is just a special case of commentary. Greater leeway is allowed in the use of copyrighted material when there is an educational or non-profit purpose.

Even in the case of a book review, however, there is no bright line test that indicates how much of a work you can copy. In one famous case, an excerpt of 200 words (out of 30,000) was not considered fair use because it revealed the essence of the entire book.

Courts have generally allowed much more substantial copying of copyrighted material in the case of parody. Parody is closely tied to the principle of free speech. We have traditions and laws that are designed to place a high value on the existence of many different kinds of expression. Courts have recognized that sometimes the most important discourse is the most cutting. As a result, they have sometimes allowed large amounts of copyrighted material to be incorporated into a parody...but not always.

The most important factor in fair use analysis is the fourth, the effect of the use upon the market (or potential market) for the original work. This factor is more important than all the others, and copyright holders can almost always make an argument that any particular use of copyrighted material can negatively affect the market, or again, a potential market, for the copyrighted work.

In one case, for example, a sculptor made a sculpture based upon a photograph from another artist. Even though the original photographer could not sculpt and therefore could not have created the sculpture, the court ruled that this was not a fair use because it negatively affected the market for authorized sculptures related to the photograph.

A Rule of Thumb

To make things simpler, the easiest way to reason about copyright is assume that *any* use of a copyrightable work is legally reserved to the copyright owner. That is the power of defaults at work. The control granted by copyright isn't quite that broad, but identifying specific uses as being outside of copyright can be difficult and tricky, and the law can change under you if your application pushes the boundaries of what is acceptable.

For example, you may be familiar with the Grokster case, *MGM Studios, Inc. v. Grokster, Ltd.* When the Grokster peer-to-peer network was created, the established rule in copyright law was that a technology sometimes used for copyright infringement would not be prohibited if it had *substantial non-infringing uses* as well (the "Sony" rule, named after *Sony Corp. v. Universal City Studios*). The owners of the Grokster network felt that they were safe, because the underlying peer-to-peer technology was used for legitimate content, swarm distribution of material, and dissident political expression—all substantial non-infringing uses.

In the Supreme Court's decision in this case, the court created the new doctrine that *inducing* copyright infringement was prohibited under the same terms as copyright infringement itself. Because Grokster encouraged and derived revenue from the massive amounts of copyright infringement happening during use of its system, Grokster itself was liable and had to shut down.

...and a bit about legal interpretation

It is unfortunate that under the current copyright law, the most accurate predictions about prospective cases usually come from borrowing from the branch of academia known as *legal realism*. Legal realism is a cynical interpretive strategy that sees all law in terms of political power structures; the reasoning behind individual decisions is nothing more than window dressing for underlying political biases and power struggles.

Under a legal realist analysis, any use of copyrighted material that was objectionable or questionable would be struck down as infringing. Non-objectionable use of copyrighted material would be allowed only if the political and economic interests in support of the use were more powerful than the political and economic interests against the use. Unfortunately, this is, in my opinion, the best guide to the outcome of any future copyright case.

CHAPTER FIVE

Trademarks

In June of 2001, Slashdot led with the headline, "More Trouble With AOL And GAIM" (*http://yro.slashdot.org/article.pl?sid=01/06/25/2115200*). Mark Spencer, the author of GAIM (later renamed "Gaim") explained it in his own words:

> Well, AOL is at it again. In 1998, I wrote a program called GAIM which provided Linux users with a way to participate in AOL's Instant Messenger (tm) service. GAIM is one of the best examples of Open Source software in action....
>
> In July of 1999, I received a letter from AOL's Legal Representation requesting that we remove their AOL trademark and logo from our web site and product name, which we promptly did. Now, in 2001, the same firm has sent us notice requiring that we change the name of the product...because they believe GAIM's name to be confusingly similar to the AIM trademark....

The legal challenges from AOL continued for almost six years. A settlement was finally reached, but one of the conditions was that the project be renamed. Gaim was renamed *Pidgin* in April, 2007. The code continued, but the name had to go. And the reason was trademark law.

Trademarks Defined

The traditional definition of a *trademark* is a word, name, or symbol used to identify particular products or services offered by a particular manufacturer or coming from a particular source. Trademarks have their roots in manufacturing—in the *trades* (hence the name). As soon as people began to specialize in the manufacture of certain goods, they wanted a method of distinguishing their wares from others offering similar goods. Thus, they began to "mark" their products with some sort of identifying symbol or name.

Over time, the concept of the trademark was expanded to include other types of commercial enterprises—services, trade associations, certifications, and so forth. These alternate marks are all considered under the category of trademark law, but they have their own individual names. *Trademarks* (as opposed to the general category of trademark law) have been maintained for use in connection with goods. *Service marks* are used in connection with services. *Collective marks* are used by associations, cooperatives, or other groups to indicate membership. *Certification marks* are used to indicate the approval or endorsement of a third-party product or service. Because these all cover different types of products, services, and situations, lawyers discussing trademark law talk generally about "marks" when they are referring to any of the different types. Table 5-1 gives common examples of each kind of mark.

TABLE 5-1. Types of marks

Type of Mark	Examples
Trademark	Linux, Exxon, Coca-Cola, Chevrolet, KitchenAid, Special K
Service marks	Flickr, Netflix, FedEx, Sharper Image, TruGreen Chemlawn
Collective marks	Girl Scouts, Better Business Bureau, SEIU, PGA, American Heart Association
Certification marks	Good Housekeeping Seal of Approval, TRUSTe, Hacker Safe, Open Source

The problem with this definition of trademarks is that it conveys a lot of information without conveying a lot of understanding. So perhaps a better way to appreciate trademarks is to think about the shortcut icons on the desktop of your computer. Figure 5-1 shows a typical shortcut icon.

This icon shares many of the attributes of a typical trademark. The icon pictured in Figure 5-1 actually contains two trademarks, the Fox-and-Earth logo associated with Firefox (trademark registration no. 3408321), and the name "Firefox" itself (trademark registration no. 2974321). The association between shortcut icons and trademarks, however, goes much farther than that.

Trademarks As Pointers

The shortcut in Figure 5-1 is not the Firefox web browser itself. Rather, this icon is associated with a shortcut, or link. It points to the real executable file, which is located somewhere else on the disk. Without the linked application, the shortcut has no purpose. In fact, in Windows, a shortcut without a properly linked application reverts to a generic icon. It is the linked application that gives the shortcut both its appearance and its meaning.

Like the shortcut icon, a trademark is a symbol that is linked in the mind of consumers with a real company or with real products and services. Without the association of the symbol with

FIGURE 5-1. The shortcut icon for Firefox

a real product, service, or company, the symbols that we currently recognize as trademarks would be nothing but small, unrelated bits of art. The purpose of the trademark is to be a pointer to the larger, "real" entity that the trademark represents. It is the larger entity that defines the trademark and gives it form and meaning.

Trademarks As Distinguishing Identifiers

Shortcut icons provide an easy-to-distinguish symbol to help the user recognize linked applications. The picture associated with a shortcut—its icon—is designed to be easily recognizable and instantly associated with the appropriate application. Part of the value of the shortcut comes from the fact that it is instantly distinguishable from the other icons on the desktop. If all the icons looked the same, they would be much less useful; somebody wanting to start the web browser would have to inspect all the available shortcuts and choose the correct one. This would take much more time and be much less efficient.

Trademarks serve a similar function in the commercial world. These marks, or *brands* more generally, distinguish and authenticate the product of a particular manufacturer and set those products apart from similar products offered by others. For example, think of the advertisement, "Powder Milk Biscuits—the ones in the blue box." In this case, the blue box is serving a trademark function by setting apart one particular manufacturer's biscuit mix from all others.

Trademarks As Objects of Focus

A related computer concept applicable to the world of trademarks is the idea of *focus*. When you are using a computer, one application is in the foreground; it is said to have the focus. All other applications are in the background. The computer uses this idea of focus in several different ways. It sends your keystrokes only to the focused application, the menus are only active on the focused application, and in general, you can only interact with the focused application.

The same idea also applies to computer shortcuts. When you are choosing from a number of different possible actions or programs that are each represented by an icon on the desktop, pressing the Enter key will invoke the action or program associated with the currently focused icon. The idea of focus allows users to better concentrate their attention on the particular task at hand.

In similar fashion, trademarks allow us to better concentrate our attention on particular products or services in the marketplace. By better allowing us to differentiate between various products or manufacturers, trademarks allow us to focus our attention on one product at a time, excluding others from our concentration.

Trademarks Build Associations with Their Targets

On a computer desktop, shortcuts usually are used for more than just accessing programs. File types are also associated with certain programs, and the shortcut icons for those file types reflect both the file type and the associated application.

For example, MP3 files (usually with the file extension *.mp3*) usually have an associated music player program. This music player program could be iTunes, Windows Media Player, VLC, or some other program entirely. If you change the music player program associated with *.mp3* files on your computer, though, the icon for the *.mp3* files change, even though there hasn't been any change in the underlying information contained within the files. What *has* changed is the association. The changed icon is representative of the underlying shift in the system.

This change in the shortcut icon is similar to what happens in the world of trademarks. When the shortcut icon for the *.mp3* file changes, we understand that there has been a change in the associated application. This is an important logical leap; we instantly have a different set of expectations about the same *.mp3* file *just because it has changed its visual representation.*

In the trademark realm, we also develop a set of expectations (and associations) that we associate with different brand-related visual (or auditory) representations. Just like the shortcut icons on a computer desktop, the trademarks associated with a particular company come to have more than just the ordinary meaning; they develop *secondary meaning* to those who view the mark. When dealing with well-known marks, this secondary meaning can be quite strong. For example, almost everybody would associate a "McBurger" or "McKids" with the McDonald's chain of fast food restaurants.

The Economic Function of Trademarks

Trademarks are not rooted in a utilitarian public goods bargain like patents and copyrights. One reason is that trademarks are just too old; some forms of trademark-like marking go back almost 4,000 years. (The foundations of the utilitarian bargain underlying patent and copyright law only go back four or five hundred years at the most.) However, the difference between trademarks and patents and copyrights is much more fundamental than just age.

TRADEMARKS AND THE UNITED STATES CONSTITUTION

The trademark laws are actually quite specific regarding the source of the authority used to pass federal trademark-related laws. The first national trademark law, passed in 1870, cited the patent and copyright clause of the United States Constitution as the basic authority for trademark law. This law was overturned by the Supreme Court as beyond the power of Congress; the patent and copyright clause contained no explicit or implicit provision enabling Congress to establish trademark protection. Undeterred, Congress tried again in 1881, this time basing the statute in the Commerce clause of the Constitution. The Commerce clause rationale stuck, and is the explicit basis for Federal Trademark law today.

Specifically, patents and copyrights were developed to combat a public goods problem. There are disincentives to developing or sharing patentable or copyrightable knowledge because the knowledge is non-excludable. Those same economic fundamentals, however, aren't driving trademark law. Putting aside any question of trademarks as an art form, there just is no public goods justification for encouraging the development of new words for the English lexicon (like Exxon or Flickr), tiny repetitive melodies (like the Windows startup sound) or small, stylized drawings (like the Firefox icon).

Nevertheless, trademark-like markings developed spontaneously in many civilizations across the world. The independent development of trademarks in so many places suggests that there are underlying causes that tend to encourage their creation. Two theories are used to explain the development and function of trademarks in economic terms.

Trademarks As Advertising

One analysis of trademarks treats them as essentially indistinguishable from advertising. In this view, trademarks have two functions, both of which are generally negative for customers.

First, trademarks are a way of getting customers to provide free advertising for goodsmakers. One example of this type of trademark usage is the stickers, license plate holders, and faux-metal attachments that car dealerships attach to every car they sell. The car dealerships are able to gain additional exposure and implied goodwill from all of their customers by attaching these miniature trademark/advertisements to their customers' cars. The cost imposed for each customer is small, but the potential gains for the dealership are large. And just to tilt the scales, some dealerships make it very difficult to remove their additions without marring the paint on your car.

The second advertising-based justification for trademarks is that they are created to distinguish commodity products and "fool" consumers into paying monopoly-level prices for commodity-level products. An example of this sort of trademark usage is the branding of common food products, like ketchup or water. For example, Dasani brand bottled water is almost nothing more than tap water from local municipal water supplies, literally the exact same product that comes out of the faucet. However, the bottled water is almost 100 times more expensive. Sometimes people are willing to buy the more expensive water to display wealth or show status. Other times people buy the bottled water because they are misled into believing that the higher-priced products are of correspondingly higher quality.

Trademarks As Information Shortcuts

The trademark-as-advertising view was very common through the early 1900s, and still has a number of adherents. The more common modern view, however, has a more pro-consumer focus on transaction costs. In this view, trademarks reduce information-gathering costs by consumers. When it is difficult or time-consuming for consumers to perform their own searches and reach their own conclusions, trademarks serve as information shortcuts, just as the icons on computer desktops serve as application shortcuts.

The trademarks-as-information theory has gained ground because it has greater predictive power. The advertising theory gives a reason why trademarks might be developed, but market forces would tend to limit the spread of purely advertising-driven trademarks because of their consumer-negative effects. The information theory, on the other hand, provides an explanation for the continuation of trademarks because, under the trademarks-as-information framework, both producers and consumers receive some benefit.

Producer benefits of trademarks

There are two primary producer-side benefits of trademarks under the information theory. First, producers benefit because they are able to more easily associate their products with their advertising.

This point is related to, but not exactly the same as, the producer advantage described under the trademarks-as-advertising theory. Under the advertising theory, the trademarks *are* the advertisements. Under the information theory, producers have outside advertisements for their products that feed into the overall brand association for the products. The correspondence between the branded advertising and the branded products allows consumers to more quickly and accurately associate the advertising claims with the correct products.

For a more concrete example, think again about the advertisement for Powder Milk Biscuits ("the ones in the blue box"). It is very easy for consumers to associate the trademark blue box with the blue box on the shelf at the store. On the other hand, think of the alternate advertisement, "the ones with lot numbers 2092937, 2095829, 2059239, or 2039395." Without the identifying blue box trademark, it would be too difficult and time-consuming to find out which products were made by which manufacturer.

A second benefit to producers is that they are better able to capture the market benefits of improvements to the product. For example, one reason why the Firefox web browser has been able to capture market share is because it offered an important benefit over Internet Explorer: security. Users of the Firefox browser needed to worry less about security issues and exploits when they were browsing the Internet.

Increased security is important to users, but security improvements are very difficult for most computer users to judge. Firefox is open source, but only a small number of people are qualified to read through the code and vet it for security issues. The source code of Internet Explorer is not available for the same sort of external review. Further, most computer users are not aware of security alert services like CERT, and they wouldn't have the time or the background to understand the security alerts even if they knew where to find them.

Nevertheless, Firefox was able to gain and maintain a reputation for increased security. Those who did have the background to properly understand some of the security issues were able to make their findings known, and Firefox's market share increased. This is really a special case of the advertising benefit described above. The benefit of being "the safer web browser" became associated with the Firefox marks.

More broadly, the trademark "Firefox" started to acquire secondary meaning with customers. The word "Firefox" didn't just refer to the literal web browser software provided by the Mozilla organization; it also began to reflect a reputation for increased safety and security for web browser users. Thus, the Firefox marks gave consumers an easy way to distinguish between different web browsers on the basis of their security reputations.

Customer benefits of trademarks

Under the information theory of trademarks, customers benefit from trademarks because the marks reduce information and search costs and allow for reputational consistency over time.

The first benefit to consumers is increased search and information efficiency. For example, in the Powder Milk Biscuits example, it would be very difficult for consumers to look through many similar boxes to find the preferred biscuit mix, just as it would be very difficult to search through many identical icons to find the preferred application. We work more quickly and efficiently when we are able to distinguish alternatives easily. Trademarks provide consumers with a set of distinguishing characteristics, making product identification more efficient.

The second benefit is related to the first. Because trademarks are consistent over time and between customers, the marks allow customers to maintain reputational information for products and companies in the market. Specifically, trademarks allow many consumers to coordinate product and company information. For example, last year Apple announced that it was going to introduce a new consumer product, which it would call the iPhone. This announcement resulted in considerable press attention and general interest, even though the phone hadn't been released yet and wouldn't be released for nearly nine months. On opening day, hundreds of people lined up outside Apples' stores to buy the new product.

It is true that people had seen some pictures of the iPhone and watched Steve Jobs demonstrate it on stage at MacWorld. However, none of these users lining up to buy the phone had ever actually used or seen the phone in person. Nevertheless, they were still willing to spend a considerable amount of time and money to get the phone, essentially sight unseen. One reason for this was Apple's trademark—its brand.

Apple has a reputation for high-quality, well-designed consumer electronics. Many people have had positive experiences with other Apple products. The existence of the Apple brand identifier allowed prospective iPhone purchasers to pool and coordinate their Apple-specific information, allowing many people to make the decision to buy the phone without requiring any previous personal interaction with the product.

The information-sharing aspect of trademarks also helps when companies or products have a bad reputation, as well. For example, one difficulty faced by Microsoft in the current marketplace is the reputation that the newest release of its operating system, Microsoft Windows Vista, has poor quality. For example, Vista was listed by *PC World* as the biggest tech disappointment of 2007 and by *InfoWorld* as the number two all-time tech flop. Although many people have had positive experiences with Windows Vista, the operating system's reputation has directly contributed to reduced sales.

The discussion provided in this chapter is, itself, a testament to the power of this reputational tracking; even in this metadiscussion of trademarks and product reputation, it is essentially impossible to disentangle the trademarks from the products they represent. Upon reading the trademarked names "iPhone" and "Vista" in this discussion, you have likely automatically thought of the particular physical phone and the particular software product that those trademarked names represent. The "pointers" in your mind between those trademarked words and the corresponding products are so strong that it is very hard to make any other association.

Modern Trademark Law in the United States

Keeping in mind the analogy of trademarks to computer shortcut icons, the contours of trademark law are easier to understand. Trademark law is designed to allow users to exclusively identify the commercial source or origin of their products or services. Trademark rights arise through actual use of the mark in a commercial context; that is, trademark rights first start to accrue when consumers first have the opportunity to make the necessary mental associations. Those who hold trademarks are allowed, and in fact required, to protect the mental association between the mark and the associated service, product, or company. Failure to protect the

FIGURE 5-2. Well-known business logos

customer associations connected with the mark removes the distinctiveness of the mark as an identifier, resulting in the termination of the trademark rights.

Talking About Trademarks

So far, our discussion of trademarks has focused on word marks (like the word "Firefox") and visual symbols (like the Fox-and-Earth icon used for Firefox). Figure 5-2 shows a number of these well-known business marks.

While these types of marks are by far the most common, any distinctive symbol, word, shape, sound, scent, color, or texture may be used as a mark if it performs the necessary source-identifying function. For example, Owens Corning has a trademark on the color pink as applied to home insulation; NBC has a trademark on the three note musical phrase often heard on that network; and the grocery retailer Food4Less has a trademark on pyramid-shaped roof ornaments.

Establishing Trademark Status

Although trademark law doesn't arise out of the same theoretical foundation as patents and copyrights, it is similar to them in that it grants a bundle of exclusive rights—specifically, *property* rights—in products of the mind.

A trademark is born

Like copyrights, trademark property rights arise naturally, with no need for formalities. When you create an expressive work, the copyright immediately applies; when you start to use a distinctive mark, trademark rights automatically apply.

Specifically, in the United States, trademark rights are established when a commercial user begins to use a particular distinctive symbol *in commerce*. Those who wish to inform others of their intent to claim a particular symbol as a trademark can begin by placing a trademark ™ sign next to the claimed mark. Using the ™ symbol does not by itself create the trademark and it does not convey any additional rights. The ™ symbol is helpful, however, to put others on notice that the mark is considered to be intellectual property.

Hearkening back to the comparison of trademarks with shortcut icons, the appropriate comparison is the "create new shortcut" menu item in the right-click menu. Trademarks, like shortcuts, don't exist in isolation—they have to point to something. Starting to use a trademark is like establishing the link between the shortcut and the associated application for the first time.

The limits of trademark protection

Trademark protection, unlike some other forms of intellectual property protection, can last forever—as long as the mark remains in active use. Offsetting the very long life of trademark protection, however, are the geographic and market limits on the use of the mark.

Trademark law was established in a time when communication between different parts of the country was very slow and national-scale commerce was very rare. In these circumstances, many different artisans could unknowingly start using the same mark at the same time. To accommodate this situation, three rules were created to limit the reach of trademark protection.

First, trademark rights were (and are) established according to geographic boundaries. For example, one person can use a mark in California without interfering with the use of the same mark in Texas. Where there is a question, the boundaries are determined by market reach. Therefore, many different people can exclusively use marks like "Cooper's Barrels" and

"Fletcher's Arrows" at the same time. (Etymologists note: the original meanings of "cooper" and "fletcher" are now sufficiently obscure that these aren't just descriptive anymore.)

Of course, markets are not static, and so competing users of a mark can wind up in the same geographic region. Therefore, the second rule is that the earliest user of a mark (called the *senior* user) will always be able to maintain the use of the mark at the expense of a later-established user (called the *junior* user). This "earliest use wins" rule always takes precedence in the senior user's geographic area.

One famous application of this "earliest use wins" rule is in the case of *Nissan Computer v. Nissan Motor Company*. Nissan Computer was established by Uzi Nissan, an immigrant who used his last name as a business name for a variety of enterprises, including a computer company established in 1991. Mr. Nissan registered the domain name Nissan.com in 1994 for use in association with his computer business.

Initially, there was no conflict between Mr. Nissan's business and Nissan Motor Company because Nissan Motors was at that time known in the United States as Datsun. As Nissan Motors started to use the same mark, however, the computer company and the car company were inevitably drawn into conflict.

Despite Nissan Motors' best efforts, Nissan Computers was ruled to be the senior user of the "Nissan" trademark on the Internet. Nissan Computers' earlier use of the Nissan.com domain name allowed it to maintain its web site at that address. To this day, Nissan Motor Company is at NissanUSA.com, not at the more desirable Nissan.com.

The third rule is that trademark usage is generally segregated by market. For example, there is Delta Airlines and Delta Faucets; Eagle Brand Sweetened Condensed Milk and Eagle Brand Medicated Oil; the Monster job board and Monster cables. These uses of the same brand name are not considered to be overlapping because they are used in different industries and serve different markets.

There are exceptions to the segregation-by-market rule. Certain brands are so well known and so famous that consumers could reasonably, but mistakenly, infer a connection between the well-known brand and the unrelated product. For example, imagine a person selling snorkeling suits at McSwim.com. The McDonald's mark is so well known that some customers could get false impression that the swimming gear was associated with or endorsed by the McDonald's fast food chain, despite the dissimilar nature of the goods.

Registration: Making the trademark formal

As with copyrights, formalization and registration of a mark confers a number of additional rights. All marks that have successfully gone through the federal registration process are allowed to display the ® registration symbol alongside the mark (such a mark is not necessary, but is recommended for use). The registration symbol (or the phrase "Registered in the U.S. Patent and Trademark Office") should be placed somewhere near the mark or placed conspicuously referencing the mark.

State registration of trademarks is also available, and can confer some additional rights within the state. The requirements and benefits of state registration of marks vary from state to state. In contrast, federal registration of trademarks gives rights across the United States.

For example, the first and most important of the rights provided by federal registration is a nationally recognized right to exclusive use of the mark in relation to the products or services for which it is registered. All registered marks are published by the United States Patent and Trademark Office (PTO), and are available for search and inspection. Therefore, everyone is considered to be "on notice" relative to marks that have been published. This means that while two people could use identical unpublished marks in mutual ignorance of each other, people are presumed to be aware of any marks that have been published by the PTO.

Comparing trademarks with shortcut icons, federal registration would be like changing the association for all *.mp3* files computer-wide. Rather than having a single shortcut to a music player program, all *.mp3* files on the system would by default be associated with the chosen and registered music player application.

The second important right associated with registration is the presumption of validity and ownership that registrations legally carry. In the absence of trademark registration, the company trying to enforce its mark must first prove that its mark is valid and properly owned before trying to prove infringement. Registration eliminates this need.

The third important right associated with registration is the ability to make your mark *incontestable*. Once a trademark has been federally registered and used for five years, the owner of the mark can petition for the mark to be made incontestable. The power of an incontestable mark is that certain aspects of the mark, such as the mark's validity, ownership, or registration, cannot be argued any more in front of a court. The mark can still be challenged for other reasons, but incontestability raises the bar and makes the most common trademark attacks useless.

To draw a suitable analogy to the shortcut icons in a computer system, having a mark become incontestable is like putting all the music file type associations into read-only mode after assigning a certain player to be the default player across the system. While it might be possible to play *.mp3* files with another music player application, it becomes significantly harder to do.

Distinctiveness: The Essential Quality of a Trademark

As discussed earlier, one of the essential aspects of a trademark is distinctiveness. The information-providing benefits of trademarks are dependent upon trademarks being good source identifiers. If a mark is associated with a single product, service, or company, then consumers can use that mark to reduce information-gathering and search costs. If the mark is not distinctive, customers cannot use it in that fashion.

Before getting into the distinctiveness of a mark, note that some categories of marks are defined as inherently not registrable. A mark is not eligible to be registered if it is:

- Immoral, deceptive, or scandalous
- A flag, coat of arms, or other insignia of the United States, (or of a state or other political body)
- The name, portrait, or signature identifying a particular living individual, except with consent
- The name, signature, or portrait of a deceased President of the United States during the life of the President's spouse, except with the spouse's written consent

These categories of marks are excluded because they have significant negative societal costs compared with the benefits of their registration. Because the registration of these marks would be a net societal negative, they are simply not allowed.

Looking at the marks that are left, only sufficiently distinctive marks can be registered. Because the distinguishing function of trademarks is so critical to their function, marks are judged based upon their ability to distinguish the goods and services of one provider from the goods and services of another. In day-to-day terms, this means that trademarks are graded based upon their visual (or aural) distinctiveness. A mark cannot be registered if it resembles one that is already registered and is likely to cause confusion, mistake, or deception.

This principle also makes sense when applied to the computer shortcut icon analogy. If the icons for the various shortcuts are not distinctive, the user has to spend time searching among the icons for the correct one.

Finally, marks that would be overgeneralized—or worse, misleading—are not allowed. For example, "California Cheese" is not very distinctive when referring to cheese from California; it would not be allowed. "California Cheese" would be deceptive if applied to cheese made in New York; this deception would thwart the information-gathering function of trademarks and is thus not allowed.

The only exception to this "merely descriptive" rule occurs when a particular descriptive term, geographic designation or surname has been associated with certain goods for so long that the otherwise simply descriptive mark has acquired secondary meaning.

A good example of this exception is McDonald's hamburgers. The surname McDonald as applied to any particular sort of good would generally be considered descriptive; but McDonald's restaurants have been around for such a long time that the meaning associated with McDonald's is not "McDonald's the surname," but rather is "McDonald's the restaurant."

Even discounting these exceptions, there are still a wide variety of possible marks. These possible marks vary in strength depending upon their inherent distinctiveness.

Traditionally, trademarks can be classified into four different categories: generic, descriptive, suggestive, and arbitrary or fanciful.

Generic marks

Generic marks are simply the name of the category of product. For example, if the Mozilla organization had attempted to trademark "Web Browser" as the name of its web browser, it would be rejected as generic.

There are two reasons behind this. The first is that the name of a category of goods, like "Web Browser," is inherently not distinctive. Because all products in that category are also web browsers, such a mark would not reduce the search and information-gathering costs for potential consumers.

The second reason is that allowing a single company or organization the exclusive right to use the category name would unfairly restrict competition in that segment of the market. Competitors could not accurately describe their products without infringing on the "Web Browser" mark.

Because generic marks are inherently non-distinctive and anticompetitive, they are never protectable as trademarks. One interesting exception to this policy are the words "Olympic" or "Olympics." The United States Olympic Committee has been granted super-trademark authority covering many uses of that word, even in contexts not related to sports.

Descriptive marks

Descriptive marks don't try to name the category of their associated goods, but instead describe the nature of or features of the goods. Descriptive marks are generally not protectable.

Some open source projects have adopted this sort of descriptive name. For example, there is the "Simple Blog" blog application. While "Simple Blog" isn't a generic category encompassing all blogs, the name isn't sufficiently distinctive to allow consumers to distinguish the "Simple Blog" blog application from any other blog that happens to be simple to use.

As in the McDonald's case, it is possible to eventually gain trademark protection for a merely descriptive name—if the descriptive name has been used long enough or advertised widely enough to gain *acquired distinctiveness*. For example, the term "Windows" has been used widely enough to make this otherwise descriptive name a reliable indicator of the source of operating system products.

Nevertheless, it is difficult to achieve acquired distinctiveness, so adopting descriptive marks is generally discouraged.

Suggestive marks

A suggestive mark requires the user to make some sort of logical leap to associate a particular good or service with the mark. For example, imagine that the Mozilla organization had named its browser "Wolf Spider" and used a stylized picture of a wolf spider as the icon.

A "Wolf Spider" browser does not immediately describe the functionality of the browser. However, it is easy to see the association: spiders generally crawl along webs. The "Wolf Spider" browser would crawl the World Wide Web.

The dividing line between "descriptive" and "suggestive" marks depends upon the imagination and thought that is required to make the connection between the good and the mark. If the mark describes the good itself, then it would be considered descriptive. If the mark describes or suggests some abstract aspect related to the good or its use, then the mark would be considered suggestive. The "Wolf Spider" browser would be suggestive because the web browser is not literally a spider. However, the connection with spiders suggests the overall function of the browser—to surf the web. Thus, this suggestive mark would require enough of a logical leap to make it inherently distinctive and would be protectable.

Arbitrary and fanciful marks

Arbitrary marks are known words that have no apparent connection with the associated product. For example, apples have nothing to do with computers, making the "Apple Computer" mark arbitrary and protectable. Doves have nothing to do with soap, so the association established by the mark "Dove Bar" is arbitrary and protectable.

Fanciful marks, on the other hand, are marks that are entirely made up—they are brought into the English lexicon just to serve as trademark identifiers. For example, "Google," "Exxon," and "Firefox" had no meaning before they were coined by their various creators. Arbitrary and fanciful marks have no association outside of their designated products, so they are always highly protectable.

Defending a Trademark

One last peculiarity of trademark law is that trademarks must be vigorously defended or they will be lost. To better understand the reason why, think again of the file associations and shortcut icons associated with our music player application.

During the late 1990s, one area of substantial commercial concern was the increasing use of compressed audio files like *.mp3*s. A number of people saw *.mp3* files as a business opportunity, and several companies developed proprietary music player applications designed to steer users toward favored music stores and online properties.

In the midst of this business skirmish, one of the common tricks used by new (and old) companies was to steal the file associations associated with your files. That is, if you installed a new application that had a music player component, the application installer changed the file type association of all your *.mp3* files to point them to the newly installed music player. Savvy users learned that they had to be careful about the order in which they installed software; preferred software had to be installed last so that its file associations wouldn't be overwritten.

To deal with this situation, the makers of several audio players introduced a new feature—a checkbox usually labeled "Defend these file associations." When this feature was enabled, the software would store a record of the user's preferred file associations, and restore those associations whenever another newly installed program tried to change them. The introduction of this file association defender feature meant that programs were able to largely maintain the status quo (and the user's preferred settings). Programs that didn't adopt this feature generally lost their file associations over time and fell out of favor.

Trademark law is similar in many ways to these competing programs. Different companies are all competing for market share, and more specifically, for part of your attention as a consumer. Some of the best tools these companies have are their trademarks. These marks are strongly associated with their companies and they are all competing with each other for your attention.

In this very competitive market, each trademark holder has to spend the time defending the distinctiveness of his own mark. As with the music player file associations, the removal of the distinctive relationship between a trademark and its associated product weakens the product and makes the mark less distinctive and less representative of a single source. In trademark law this is called *dilution.* Anti-dilution provisions in trademark law are designed to prevent the weakening of brand focus around each trademark.

Further, trademark law has traditionally been concerned with distinguishing counterfeit goods on the market. For a maker of lower-quality goods, it is cheaper to impersonate a high-quality producer than to attempt to raise the quality of one's own goods. Therefore, it makes more sense to try to pass off lower-quality goods as higher-quality goods that have manufactured by someone else. In trademark law this is called *passing off,* and it has a corrosive effect upon the reputation associated with the other producer's products and marks.

The trademark law recognizes that the positive economic functions of trademarks can only generally be maintained when each trademark holder vigorously defends the mental focus associated with each mark, so it makes the vigorous defense of trademarks a legal requirement. Trademark holders are required to police each and every infringement of their trademarks (that they are aware of).

To return finally to Gaim and America Online, it becomes obvious why trademark law was at the center of the AOL/Gaim controversy. It was more than just a simple situation of some developers disagreeing over a particular development project; rather, the requirements of the trademark statute required AOL to police its trademark as vigorously as possible.

It is certain that AOL pursued the Gaim developers extremely aggressively, and going after each individual developer was probably a tactical decision that allowed AOL to apply its significant resources more effectively against the smaller and financially weaker Gaim developers. Nevertheless, and contrary to some of the suggestions by free software developers at the time, it was not in AOL's ability to just ignore Gaim. Once maintaining the AIM trademark became a high-level priority, America Online had no other choice.

CHAPTER SIX

Trade Secrets

Trade secrets are the oldest form of intellectual property. According to some experts, trade secret law dates back at least to the Roman Empire, where the Roman courts recognized lawsuits for an *actio servi corrupti*, literally, an action for corrupting a slave. The *actio servi corrupti* was used to protect slaveholding tradesmen or landholders from the harm caused by rivals "corrupting" a slave, usually through bribery or intimidation, and causing that slave to turn over confidential information. Anyone found guilty of corrupting a slave was liable to the slave owner for twice the amount of damages.*

Partially because of its ancient heritage, trade secret law doesn't include modern 17th-, 18th-, and 19th-century notions such as utility and the public domain. Therefore, trade secrets don't work under the same framework as other types of intellectual property. Instead, trade secrets are just *valuable information* that you *keep secret*. We as a society have decided that, in some cases, we will honor and protect your right to keep your business to yourself. As a result, basic trade secret law is relatively uncomplicated.

Basic trade secret law is important because almost all of the information created or handled by employees is initially a trade secret. This includes source code, product plans, marketing documents, customer lists, procedure manuals, and internal telephone directories—if it is

* For more information, see A. Arthur Schiller, Trade Secrets and the Roman Law: The Actio Servi Corrupti, 30 Colum. L. Rev. 837 (1930). Recent scholarship has cast doubt on this interpretation of the *actio servi corrupti*—see Alan Watson, Trade Secrets and Roman Law: The Myth Exploded, 11 Tul. Eur. & Civ. L.F. 19 (1996), but I prefer the more colorful, earlier account. See also Merges et al., *Intellectual Property In the New Technological Age*, 3d. ed., Aspen, 2003.

written down or only known by employees, then it is probably considered a trade secret by the company. (That also means that its use is probably restricted—see the discussion in Chapter 9 about proprietary information agreements.) It doesn't matter that those secrets may also be protected by copyrights or patents; trade secret law is the first line of defense.

Trade Secrets Defined

There is no single definition for "trade secrets" within the U.S. because each state has its own trade secret law. However, trade secrets are typically understood to include any information (formulas, processes, designs, compilations, programs, instructions—in short, anything) that is *secret, valuable,* and *derives part of its value from being secret.* Trade secrets are fragile; they must be protected and will terminate if they are made available to the public.

Despite this fragility, trade secrets include some of the most valuable intellectual property in the world. For example, the formula for Coca-Cola is famously a trade secret. So are the eleven secret herbs and spices in KFC's original recipe for fried chicken. Particularly of interest to software developers is the fact that most source code produced in the computer industry is also considered a trade secret. My favorite example of a trade secret, however, is the Flaming Moe.

The Flaming Moe: The Life and Death of a Trade Secret

The "Flaming Moe" comes from a 1991 episode of *The Simpsons.* When Moe's Tavern runs out of beer one night, Homer tells Moe about a drink that he accidentally invented, called the "Flaming Homer." The drink is made up of many different types of liquor mixed together with a secret ingredient—Krusty's Non-Narkotik Kough Syrup—and set on fire before serving. The combination of the cough syrup and the fire makes the drink irresistible.

Moe steals Homer's recipe and begins serving it as the Flaming Moe. The drink is so popular that various restaurant chains attempt to obtain the secret recipe by stealing or reverse engineering the drink. When that doesn't work, the restaurants offer to purchase the secret recipe for one million dollars. Before Moe can sell the recipe, however, Homer tells everybody the secret of the drink. Within days, all the restaurants in Springfield are offering their own versions of the Flaming Moe, and Moe's Tavern has sunk back into obscurity.*

The story of the Flaming Moe has just about every essential element of trade secret law. We will walk through the story to illustrate the connection, pointing out differences or similarities with software development.

* For a longer summary, see Wikipedia's article at *http://en.wikipedia.org/wiki/Flaming_Moe's.* The story of the Flaming Moe may have been taken from the real-life case of *Mason v. Jack Daniel Distillery,* the "Lynchburg Lemonade" case, which raised a lot of the same issues. See *http://en.wikipedia.org/wiki/Lynchburg_Lemonade.*

Creating a Trade Secret

A trade secret is created when valuable business information is developed and then kept secret. Trade secrets do not require any registration or official recognition. As long as you realize a business advantage in the information and keep the information secret, you are covered by trade secret law.

It is debatable whether Homer ever had the Flaming Homer as a trade secret. On one hand, business plans and prospective business information are protected as trade secrets. If nothing else, Homer could have acted independently to sell the secret recipe, giving him an advantage. On the other hand, Homer wasn't in the drink business like Moe. Possession of the recipe wasn't valuable business information in Homer's work at the nuclear plant. (Although you can come up with scenarios in which Homer could have used the drink to increase his prospects in the nuclear power business, those scenarios all require more intelligence and imagination than Homer has.)

Even if Homer did have a trade secret, he didn't do what was necessary to keep his recipe. He spilled the whole thing after a couple of beers one night in the tavern—not exactly the way to maintain a valuable advantage.

Moe, on the other hand, *did* acquire a trade secret when Homer told him about the recipe. Moe was in the drink business and he immediately understood that holding the recipe for Flaming Homers would give him an advantage. It didn't matter that Homer also knew the recipe—it just made keeping the trade secret a little more difficult. Trade secrets don't require absolute secrecy. They just require that the sensitive information be kept away from potential commercial competitors through reasonable security precautions.

Trade Secrets Versus Copyrights and Patents

Trade secrets are one of the broadest forms of intellectual property. There are many things that can be protected by trade secret law that don't require inventive or creative activity, just work. Take lists of customer phone numbers, for example. The phone numbers are all public, but the work required to find the numbers associated with active business prospects is enough to make the resulting list protectable as a trade secret. That list of phone numbers cannot be copyrighted (it is a list of facts with no creative element) and it cannot be patented (it is not a technological advance).

Nevertheless, there is some overlap; some things that are eligible for copyright and patent protection can also be trade secrets. But patents and copyrights are oriented toward disclosure of information, not keeping things secret. Furthermore, patents and copyrights expire, which may limit the useful life of the information. Trade secrets will last forever if they are properly maintained.

For the Flaming Moe, the trade secret was the only type of protection available. While Homer could theoretically have patented the recipe at some point in the past, the one-year time frame available for patenting started running when he invented and served the drink to his houseguests. Further, Moe himself was barred from patenting the drink because he was not the inventor. Thus, the only way for Moe to keep the Flaming Moe for his exclusive use was to keep the recipe a secret.

The Elements of Trade Secret Protection

A trade secret has three essential elements: it is *secret*, it is *valuable*, and it *derives part of its value from being secret*. The Flaming Moe illustrates each part of this essential combination.

Secrecy

According to many state trade secret statutes, something can be considered a secret if it is not generally known or readily ascertainable. Unfortunately, "generally known" and "readily ascertainable" aren't exact concepts. Without going into all the different possible gradations of secrecy, I would say that something can be considered secret if it is not generally known or readily ascertainable *to those who have an interest in knowing the information.*

For example, the value of Planck's constant (6.626068×10^{-34} m^2 kg/s, in case you're curious) is not generally known among the population at large. It is well known among physicists, however, and the value is published in many places. If anyone can look up the information in a standard source, it's not a trade secret.

In similar fashion, not many people are able to read and understand code, so any knowledge published in source code form is not readily ascertainable to the general public. Nevertheless, publishing the source code is a secrecy-defeating disclosure to other programmers—those with an interest in knowing the information.

As the Flaming Moe illustrates, it is possible to establish a trade secret around a combination of elements, even if each of the elements is already known. However, combination-type trade secrets can be defeated if seeing the composition of elements automatically reveals the secret. For example, a new three-ingredient drink is not a trade secret if all three ingredients are revealed to anyone tasting the drink. Moe was able to maintain his trade secret recipe because the individual elements of the Flaming Moe were not immediately obvious to the patrons of his bar.

You can also reveal trade secrets in a product context. Having a "secret sauce" is practically a cliché, but it is much easier to uncover trade secrets embedded in products than to uncover trade secret processes. Therefore, trade secret-protected products probably constitute a minority of all trade secrets. Most trade secrets protect either pure information or processes—including the process for creating a non-trade secret product.

Valuable

To qualify for trade secret protection, the secret information must be valuable. Information that is not valuable is not a trade secret. It is easy to see how the Flaming Moe is valuable. Moe's Tavern was having difficulties before the introduction of the Flaming Moe. With the Flaming Moe, however, the tavern enjoyed record sales. In the episode, Aerosmith decided to make Moe's their official hangout; Moe's was elevated to a society hot spot, complete with its own theme song; and a complete line of "crappy merchandise" was branded as Moe's memorabilia. More directly, several restaurant chains approached Moe with an offer to buy the recipe for one million dollars.

Trade secrets do not have to be as valuable as the Flaming Moe recipe to qualify for trade secret protection. Scientific and technical ideas are classic trade secrets, but courts have also allowed trade secrets covering business plans, customer lists, and internal procedures. In many states, negative information (something that doesn't work) is also protectable as a trade secret. As long as the information has some business value, it can be part of a trade secret.

Derives value from being secret

The third characteristic of a trade secret is that the secret must derive some part of its value from being secret. Within the broad definition of secret information, it is hard to find any information of consequence that doesn't derive at least some value from being kept confidential within a business.

The Flaming Moe is a good example. As long as the recipe for the Flaming Moe was a secret, Moe's Tavern profited from being the only place where customers could buy one. As soon as Homer revealed the secret to everyone, however, the Flaming Moe wasn't exclusive to Moe's Tavern; Moe's sales and celebrity status both took a sharp downward turn.

It is worth noting that only *part* of the value of a trade secret need derive from its secrecy. For example, the Flaming Moe recipe was much more valuable to Moe's Tavern when it was a trade secret because it gave Moe's Tavern an exclusive advantage. Nevertheless, the Flaming Moe was still valuable as a drink even after the trade secret was destroyed.

Keeping a Trade Secret

In order to maintain trade secret status, the trade secret holders (and any people employed by them) must make reasonable efforts to keep the secret from being disclosed. That doesn't mean that nobody knows the trade secret; it just means that reasonable efforts have been made to guard the confidentiality of the trade secret information. If there is no effort, or at least no reasonable effort, to control business-confidential information, trade secret protection will not be granted.

Reasonable efforts

So what are reasonable efforts? The answer depends on the trade secret in question. The formula for Coca-Cola is fantastically valuable—for goodwill and mystique if nothing else—and so the reasonable efforts to control that secret are quite elaborate. The original copy of the formula is held in SunTrust bank's main vault in Atlanta. The official policy of the Coca-Cola company is that the formula is known to only two people at a time. (Evidence suggests that the formula is actually known by more than two people, but the exact recipe is still closely guarded.)

In ordinary circumstances, however, much less effort is required to maintain reasonable secrecy. For example, most companies maintain some sort of card-key system so that only current employees have access to the offices. In most cases, this is a reasonable effort to maintain the confidential information, allowing the businesses to maintain trade secret status for their internal documents and operations. Common business practices—such as password-protection on computers and intranet sites, locks on doors, permission-only access to sensitive documents—play similar roles. Although trade secrecy is not always the primary impetus for carrying out these practices, they do allow companies to claim trade secret status when needed.

In Moe's case, reasonable efforts included keeping the recipe to himself and lying about why he needed cases full of children's cough syrup. Moe also (apparently) didn't mix Flaming Moes in front of customers (as that would have revealed the secret). While Moe's commercial competitors were comically blind, not noticing the anomalous pallets of cough syrup being delivered all around Moe, the fact that Moe's competitors were not able to easily obtain the recipe is good evidence that Moe made reasonable efforts to keep the secret.

Trade Secret Misappropriation

Some trade secrets are incredibly valuable (like the formula for Coca-Cola or the recipe for Flaming Moes), but most trade secrets have a much lower value, and are therefore not as well guarded. For example, even though card-key systems do not provide absolute secrecy (they can be circumvented with modest effort), their use still constitutes a reasonable effort. In most cases, the purpose of the reasonable effort security is not to actually protect the business from all losses, as that would be very expensive. Companies spend money on security because reasonable effort security allows them to protect against *misappropriation* of the company trade secrets. Misappropriation basically comes in two forms: *improper means* and *breach of a confidential relationship*.

Improper means

Misappropriation by improper means is simply a way of saying that someone learned your trade secrets as a result of being underhanded or sneaky. When used by an outsider on an employee, this is the modern version of the *actio servi corrupti*; the bribery and intimidation targeted by that ancient law would be called "improper means" today.

Improper means is broader than intimidation or bribery of employees, however. Discovery of a trade secret as the result of illegal activity constitutes improper means. Further, any actions below the standard of commercial morality can be considered improper means, even if those actions are not otherwise illegal. In one famous case, some pilots were found guilty of using improper means when they flew over and photographed the construction of a manufacturing plant. Even though the flight was legal, the pilots should have known that it was unacceptable to defeat the manufacturing company's reasonable security measures.

The "standard of commercial morality" test is somewhat vague, but in practice it boils down to common sense: if you knew or should have known that anything illegal or unethical occurred anywhere in the chain that moved the trade secret information from the competitor's location to your hands, then you have used improper means.

This occasionally comes up in the software development realm if there has been a code leak onto the Internet. If a project incorporates code or know-how that came from a leak, then the code was obtained through improper means and the project or its maintainers can be the target of a lawsuit.

Occasionally, a software vendor claims that someone obtained proprietary code and contributed it to an open source software project without authorization. While it is possible that trade secret-protected code could be improperly donated by a developer, the transparent nature of open source development makes such impropriety unlikely. Open source code generally grows and is modified over time from many small contributions, each from a specific author. The author names and modification times are captured in source code control systems, and a large anomalous code check-in would be immediately noticed (and probably rejected for being too big!). Thus, the open source development process is resistant to the sort of trade secret code taint that could occur in closed-in and secret systems.

Breach of a confidential relationship

Courts most commonly find a breach of a confidential relationship in an employer-employee setting, but it can arise in other contractual and quasicontractual settings as well. If you enter into a confidential relationship and do not keep the related information secret, you are guilty of misappropriation.

Courts ask three basic questions to determine whether there exists a breach of a confidential relationship.

Was there a secret?
: To determine if there was a secret, the court relies primarily on evidence that reasonable efforts were made to maintain the secret.

Was there a confidential relationship?
: This question is more difficult to answer. Courts typically consider employer-employee status to imply a confidential relationship. However, other circumstances, such as contractor relationships, precontractual negotiations, and sales discussions may imply a

confidential relationship. non-disclosure agreements (NDAs) also create a confidential relationship, as do employee proprietary information agreements. These relationships are evaluated on a case-by-case basis. In general, the courts assume a confidential relationship when there is an implied limitation on the use of disclosed information or when there is fraud between the parties.

Was the secret used in violation of the relationship?

The court evaluates this question relative to the context of the relationship. In Moe's Tavern, for example, Moe hired an assistant bartender to help serve the customers their drinks. Moe's assistant knew about the secret recipe for Flaming Moes, but she didn't reveal the secret. If the bartender had made Flaming Moes outside of her work, however, then bringing the recipe outside of work could be a breach of a confidential relationship and trade secret misappropriation.

The question of whether there was a confidential relationship is the source of a lot of red tape and strange policies in many industries. For example, many large manufacturers refuse all product prototypes, returning them unopened. Hollywood studios respond to unsolicited scripts by replying with a form specifying that the submission is a free gift with no implied relationship. Companies are more concerned with avoiding confidential relationships (and possible trade secret lawsuits) than they are in receiving a new product idea or a new script.

For software developers, this issue arises most often during the search for venture capital funding. Venture capitalists review hundreds or thousands of business plans, and many of them have similar elements. To avoid liability for trade secret misappropriation, venture capitalists frequently refuse to sign confidentiality agreements and sometimes refuse unrequested business plans.

Another common situation involving a confidential relationship arises when a larger company is in talks to buy a smaller company. If the acquisition is unsuccessful, the smaller company will occasionally accuse the larger company of entering into negotiations in bad faith, learning the smaller company's trade secrets, and then going on to develop a competing product. In these situations, the smaller company may have an argument for the breach of a confidential relationship if it can prove that the larger company misrepresented its intentions in the acquisition negotiations. Proving misappropriation can be hard, though. It may not be enough to show that the larger company later created a competing product with similar (or sometimes identical) technology. Proving misappropriation frequently requires written evidence of bad faith or provable theft.

The doctrine of inevitable disclosure

One relatively recent addition to the world of trade secrets is the doctrine of inevitable disclosure. This doctrine states that if an employee who knows valuable trade secrets goes to work in a similar position for a competitor, that employee will "inevitably" let the knowledge of the secrets color his or her judgment. Ultimately, the secrets will be disclosed to the competitor, and the trade secret advantage will be lost.

In the case of the Flaming Moe, for example, imagine that Moe's new assistant bartender went to work as a bartender for another bar. Her knowledge of the secret recipe would "inevitably" leak out because the positions are so similar. If a court agreed that the secret recipe would inevitably leak out to the competitor, the court could grant an *injunction* preventing the assistant from working at the new bar.

The doctrine of inevitable disclosure is controversial, and is not accepted by some courts and some states. For example, California courts rejected the doctrine of inevitable disclosure because the doctrine created a *de facto covenant not to compete* that was contrary to the best interests of the citizens of California.

General knowledge versus trade secrets

One potential problem area in the software industry is defining the line between protectable trade secrets and general skills and knowledge. Employees are able to take their general knowledge with them, but not specific confidential information. Thus, information specific to a business, such as a customer list, stays with the employer.

Where this issue becomes difficult is when knowledge is embedded in a code toolbox—scripts, functions, classes, or algorithms that the developer has found useful across a number of projects. Developers argue that these tools are part of their general knowledge and do not constitute any particular code product belonging to the employer. Employers argue that any code written on their time is proprietary and is owned by the employer. Especially if parts of the code toolbox have been used to create products for the employer, the employer can argue the doctrine of inevitable disclosure—that use of the toolbox anywhere else will reveal trade secrets to competitors.

Unfortunately, there is no easy solution to this situation. Different courts have ruled different ways. The best advice is to communicate openly with your employer—in writing, and throughout your employment—concerning your ownership of independent pieces of code in your code toolbox. It is much less likely to be an issue if the status of the code is well communicated from the beginning.

Additionally, programmers starting a new job should always include a description of their code toolbox as an exclusion to any company proprietary information agreements required of new employees. For more about proprietary information agreements, see Chapter 9.

Destroying a Trade Secret

The only way to destroy a trade secret is to remove its secrecy. There are two classic ways in which this is done: reverse engineering and disclosure by the trade secret holder. Either way, as soon as the information in the trade secret is generally known or readily ascertainable, the trade secret protection is extinguished.

Reverse engineering

The classic response to a trade secret is reverse engineering. Courts have strongly supported reverse engineering as fundamentally good public policy. For example, the Flaming Moe was the subject of intense scrutiny by rival restaurateurs. They bought many of the drinks and broke them down in a gas chromatograph, but they were unable to correctly isolate the ingredient that set the Flaming Moe apart (the chromatograph identified the secret ingredient as "LOVE"). If the restaurant owners had been successful, they would have had no legal impediments to selling their own Flaming Moes.

Under current law, courts have routinely upheld the right to analyze and disassemble any product that has been legitimately *purchased*. For software developers, however, reverse engineering becomes trickier; software products are usually *licensed*, not purchased. There is no definitive legal opinion as to whether a seller can remove a buyer's reverse engineering right by contract, but the situation is murky enough that reverse engineering a licensed software product may be legally risky. This is one area where the law will probably develop further over time.

In spite of the legal risks, however, reverse engineering is one of the primary engines for competition in the software and technical worlds. Chapter 13 has an extensive discussion of reverse engineering, including a sample reverse engineering procedure.

Disclosure

The other way in which trade secrets can be destroyed is via disclosure. In *The Simpsons*, Homer destroyed the trade secret recipe when he shouted out the secret ingredient to everyone in Moe's Tavern. As frequently happens in *The Simpsons*, Homer couldn't have chosen a worse time; various industry leaders were assembled in the bar to formally purchase the recipe from Moe. Revealing the secret destroyed its value, and instantly, anyone who wanted to make a Flaming Moe could do so. Moe's rivals ripped up their million-dollar check and Moe's Tavern once again became nothing more than a regular corner bar. Other restaurants flourished because they could now serve "Flaming Maux" and other knockoff drinks.

In real life, trade secrets usually aren't revealed by crazy balding men seeking revenge, but rather by a trade secret holder. This can happen purposefully, but more often trade secrets are disclosed by accident.

One common method of disclosing trade secrets is when the secret-holder includes them in a patent application. Even if the trade secret is not the focus of the patent, trade secret information can be accidentally included in the patent specification. When the patent is published, the trade secret privilege is immediately destroyed and cannot be enforced against competitors.

Another place where trade secrets can be accidentally disclosed is in legal filings. Legal filings are usually open to the public, unless they are specifically *sealed* by a judge. Unsealed filings in cases involving technical details can therefore sometimes reveal trade secrets.

The best example of accidental disclosure via a legal filing comes from the DeCSS case, *Universal City Studios v. Reimerdes*, prohibiting the magazine *2600* from distributing code for reading encrypted DVDs. The president of the DVD Copy Control Association (DVD-CCA) included in his public testimony some anonymous C code that decrypted DVDs, revealing the trade secret method for everyone to see.

The rule about disclosure is very rigid. Knowledge, once allowed into the public domain, cannot be recaptured and forcibly kept from a competitor. If someone misappropriated your secret, you can prohibit that person from using the knowledge, but you typically cannot prevent others (even other competitors) from using your once-secret knowledge as they see fit.

Trade Secrets and Software Development

Trade secrets were the first form of intellectual property protection applied to software. Trade secrets fit early computing technology. Both the computers (and the programs) were kept within centralized glass rooms in data processing centers, and only a small number of qualified people were allowed to interact with the computer in any substantial way. The source code was very specialized and generally non-portable. There was little source or object code shared *anywhere*, inside or outside the company, and the few distributions of code were handled under individually negotiated agreements.

This was a perfect situation for the trade secret protection of software to develop. Secret information—the actual code—brought value to the businesses that used it. Keeping this information protected was relatively easy; very few people had access to the code or the computers that ran it, and the functioning of the programs was not usually immediately apparent to outside observers.

This trend continued through the heyday of the mainframe and minicomputers. Even when those computers were networked, users did not have "computers" on their desks. Instead, they had some sort of terminal device that showed only the green screen interface and did not reveal the underlying workings of the program. The centralization of the mainframe/minicomputer systems facilitated maintenance of trade secret protection.

The biggest blow to trade secret protection was the industry shift from centralized to distributed computing, also known as the rise of the personal computer. For the first time, the market required companies to have their programs installed on uncontrolled computers. The increasing standardization of computer languages and hardware has increased the feasibility and viability of reverse engineering by decompilation, making trade secret protection in software more fragile.

The Reemergence of Trade Secrets

Today, most software companies still attempt to maintain trade secret protection in their object code, mostly by including restrictions on reverse engineering and similar trade secret-defeating measures in contracts, EULAs (End User License Agreements), and *clickwrap* agreements. Nevertheless, trade secrets are no longer the dominant mode of protection for software. That distinction has fallen to copyright law, with patent law in second place.

Trade secrets may be on the rise, however. One aspect of today's software industry is the increasing emphasis on web services and web-delivered applications. While it would be very difficult to claim any sort of trade secret protection in the user interface delivered over the Web—it is, after all, just HTML and JavaScript, not even object code—the "secret sauce" is more and more frequently kept internal to the companies delivering the application. Web-delivered applications are well suited to trade secret protection because they display the same centralization as the mainframe and minicomputer applications from the 1970s and 1980s; the interface has just been updated.

The best example of this is Google, which has been fantastically successful in delivering web applications to millions of people. In Google's search engine, for example, there is no trade secret in the interface that Google delivers to its users. However, the essential technology behind Google's search results, PageRank, is maintained within Google as a trade secret. Nobody outside of Google knows the exact details of its search algorithms and, despite the best efforts of the search engine optimization crowd, nobody has been able to fully figure them out.

The trade secret protection afforded to PageRank is even more striking when the trade secret status is considered alongside Google's patent for PageRank, U.S. Patent No. 6,285,999. In theory, the full disclosure required of a patent applicant should make PageRank completely transparent. In practice, there are many aspects of Google's search technology that are not addressed by the patent and are therefore protectable as trade secrets. For example, there are considerable technical challenges associated with making the PageRank algorithm run well and run quickly on massive datasets; the solution to those challenges is a trade secret. A number of parameters can adjust the relative weight of pages, and the actual parameters used are a trade secret.

Finally, Google doesn't use just PageRank—it uses a number of other weighting algorithms in conjunction with PageRank and blends their results. That makes Google's ultimate weighting algorithm protectable under the same basis as the Flaming Moe. In Moe's case, the exact ingredients used (brandy, schnapps, gin, blackberry liqueur, strawberry juice, and cough syrup, according to About.com) were all publicly known or available, but the way that Moe combined them was a trade secret. For Google, even if every one of the weighting algorithms used by Google's search engine are known to the public, the exact selection of algorithms chosen by Google and the relative weights applied are trade secrets.

Trade Secrets and Open Source

There is a widespread misconception that open source software companies do not have any trade secrets. This is false. Open source code reduces the range of available trade secrets, but it does not eliminate them.

The Google search engine example illustrates why. Because Google chose to patent PageRank, the knowledge of that algorithm has moved out into the broader society. (Not everyone can use PageRank yet, but the knowledge of the algorithm is no longer a secret.) PageRank is the core technology used in Google's search engine, but the PageRank patent doesn't reveal *every* detail of how Google computes a search result. Similarly, source code is at the core of any computer application, but revealing the source code doesn't reveal everything about how the company uses, integrates, manages, builds, or supports the code.

Company X is one example of an open source company that keeps its trade secrets. Company X's products are open source and they make money through support and consulting around their products. As required by the license, it makes its product's source code available.

Company X is unusual, however, in refusing to make binaries of its products available without support contracts. Anybody can download the code and make a binary that resembles the official, supported product, but the company considers the product something more than the result of compiling the code.

Company X, despite being an open source company, has two areas of expertise protected by trade secrets. First, Company X is able to keep traditional business information as trade secrets —things such as customer lists, contract terms, and internal processes. Second, Company X also maintains trade secrets surrounding its open source code. The code may be open, but the flags and processes used to compile the code and make the code into the product are all protected.

Although other companies have re-created Company X's products, the *exact* mechanism used to build Company X's products is still unknown, and so it is still a trade secret. It may not be the most valuable secret kept in the software industry, but even the minimal secrecy maintained by Company X significantly helps advance their brand-based business strategy.

Trade Secrets, Businesses, and Consultants

Trade secrets are some of the basic building blocks of any intellectual property strategy for businesses. No matter how large, how small, or how open, each company has its own "secret sauce" that it uses to address new problems. Especially with the rise of software-as-a-service vendors, many companies are finding trade secret protection a valuable part of their intellectual property.

Most individuals, however, don't realize that trade secret protection can be used on a smaller scale as well. A programmer's code toolbox can be a trade secret, and so can personal development procedures and techniques. With the increasing use of developers as independent consultants, it is useful to keep trade secret law in mind as one tool that can enhance personal profitability.

CHAPTER SEVEN

Contracts and Licenses

It may seem strange to have a chapter on contracts and licenses in an intellectual property book. Contracts and licenses are not themselves intellectual property and are generally considered to be a distinct discipline, not part of the same area of law as intellectual property.

Nevertheless, contracts are essential to our system of intellectual property. They are the means by which you *share* intellectual property. Everything that we have talked about up to this point has been about how to keep intellectual property *inside* your organization.

The problem is that simply keeping knowledge to yourself is neither very profitable nor very socially constructive. Our economy runs on trading things, and in the intellectual property market that means *sharing*. Contracts and licenses are the means by which people let their intellectual property out in a controlled way.

Licenses and Firewalls

Security professionals usually recommend that firewalls be designed around the so-called German model: anything not expressly permitted is forbidden. An administrator usually starts by screening out all traffic in both directions. She then creates access rules that selectively allow in DNS traffic, web traffic, remote logins, and other allowed network uses. By using an appropriate set of rules, the administrator can have very fine-grained control over all traffic that goes across the network.

Intellectual property is similar. By default, users have (almost) no rights, so (almost) anything they do infringes on the rights granted to the intellectual property owner. Contracts and licenses provide access rules that allow other people to go through the legal firewall and use the intellectual property. By using the proper licenses, IP holders can have very fine-grained control over all uses of their work.

Why Contracts and Licenses Matter

It has to be acknowledged up front that "control" over intellectual property is a slippery concept. For example, movie producers relying on intellectual property laws invariably wish they had more control over the movies being shared via peer-to-peer networks. Network administrators can just drop "bad" packets at the router; intellectual property administrators have to write letters or sue people for not following their access rules.

While the proper *extent* of intellectual property control is hotly debated, however, the *mechanism* of control is widely accepted. The combination of the intellectual property firewall and contract access rules is enough to support the many thousands of businesses whose products are essentially intellectual property.

This is not surprising when you consider the essential role of contracts in our society generally. We live in a world of laws; everything from speeding tickets to subway signs are affected by or reflective of the laws governing our society. Despite our awareness of these laws, however, we don't interact with them very much. We (hopefully!) don't get speeding tickets very often. We aren't personally sued for product liability. Most people only go into court as a party once or twice in their entire lives. A lot of these laws are in a sense invisible to people following them.

That is not the case with contracts. Normal people interact with contracts on a daily basis. There are contracts for cell phone service, contracts for parking your car, and contracts for starting a job. Each time you pay with a credit card, you are entering a contract.

Contracts are also everywhere in the business world. Contracts are used to buy office supplies, arrange loans, sell assets, and enter partnerships. In one way of thinking, the only way for a corporation to interact with the world is through the language of contracts.

That is because contracts are just *agreements*. People sometimes think of "contracts" as something official, whereas "agreements" are something less. This is not the case. Any binding arrangement is a contract under law and will be subject to the legal system.

When dealing with intellectual property, we make agreements about how that IP can be used. These agreements, called *licenses* in this context, are contracts. You see these licenses all the time when you enter the world of software. For consumer-oriented or open source software, these licenses are usually standardized as *clickwrap* licenses on websites or in installers, *shrinkwrap* licenses on software boxes, or open source licenses on Sourceforge. Commercial software is licensed too, but the much larger amounts of money involved usually lead to custom-negotiated multipage licenses with provisions specific to the parties (and the software) involved.

Scopes and Roles of Contracts and Licenses

Although these license agreements are contracts, there is a subtle distinction between the law of contracts and the law of licenses. We discussed earlier that part of the power of intellectual property is its status as *property*. Property has certain legal privileges associated with it, in particular the right to seek a court order—an *injunction*—enforcing your control over that property.

In the context of intellectual property, control is usually defined by use. That means that intellectual property owners have the ability to ask a court to forbid anyone else's use of their patents, copyrights, or other IP. If someone else starts exercising control over (*using*) the intellectual property without permission, that use is said to *infringe* on the property owner's exclusive rights.

A *license* can be thought of as permission to use someone else's property. In a contract context, a license is an agreement in which one of the terms of the agreement is permission by the property holder to use the property. More precisely, in a contract license the property holder effectively promises not to sue someone else for actions that would ordinarily infringe the property holder's exclusive rights, often in exchange for money or something else of value.

Relative to intellectual property, this license has three practical effects:

- It gives people permission to use someone else's intellectual property.
- It allows intellectual property holders to put bounds and conditions on the use of their intellectual property. The most common of these conditions is "pay money," but other restrictions are also allowed. For example, many software licenses have restrictions on where and how the software is used and against reverse engineering.
- It allows intellectual property holders to exercise their property rights if the bounds and conditions on the license are not met.

Point number three is critical. All use of the intellectual property is explicitly *conditional*; using the IP outside the scope of the granted permission (the *license*) is an infringement on the IP holder's property rights.

This is important for two reasons. The first gets back to the injunctive power associated with property. The purpose of an injunction is to prevent the violation of a right, in this case, the exclusive rights associated with the use of intellectual property. By way of contrast, parties with ordinary broken contracts are usually only entitled to damages (i.e., money). In the case of intellectual property, the power to prevent someone from making, selling, or using an infringing product is a much more potent remedy than simple monetary damages. Damages can be written off as just an expense; an injunction stops all business operations cold if there isn't a suitable workaround.

The second reason has to do with the nature of the legal system in the United States. We have a bifurcated legal system, with parallel arrangements of laws (and courts) at the state and federal levels. Sometimes, being in one system or another has advantages, and that is the case with intellectual property.

Ordinary contracts are typically handled in state court, under state laws. Intellectual property enforcement, however, is almost exclusively dealt with at the federal level, under federal law. Because there are significant advantages for intellectual property holders in the federal courts, the ability to invoke federal intellectual property law can itself be an advantage.

CONTRACTS AND LICENSES: DIFFERING VIEWS

Authorities differ in their assessment of the relationship between contracts and licenses. The view I present in this chapter, that licenses are contracts, specialized for the specific subject matter of intellectual property, echoes that of Raymond Nimmer, one of the leading experts on copyright law. In his blog article titled "Licensing in the Absence of Intellectual Property Rights" (available at *http://www.ipinfoblog.com/archives/licensing-law-issues-licensing-in-the-absence-of-intellectual-property-rights.html*), Nimmer states:

> A "license" is a contract. It sets conditions on use of informational assets. When intellectual property rights are involved, part of the action of the license consists of a covenant not to sue for conduct that would be infringement if not within the license. But that is not an essential feature of an agreement that constitutes a license. The contractual agreement is the essential factor."

On the other hand, Eben Moglen, head of the Software Freedom Law Center, argues that, at least with regard to free and open source software, a license is something different entirely. The following is quoted by Pamela Jones in her article titled "The GPL Is a License, Not a Contract," available at *http://lwn.net/Articles/61292*:

> The word "license" has, and has had for hundreds of years, a specific technical meaning in the law of property. A license is a unilateral permission to use someone else's property. The traditional example given in the first-year law school Property course is an invitation to come to dinner at my house. If, when you cross my threshold, I sue you for trespass, you plead my "license," that is, my unilateral permission to enter on and use my property.
>
> A contract, on the other hand, is an exchange of obligations, either of promises for promises or of promises of future performance for present performance or payment. The idea that "license" to use patents or copyrights must be contracts is an artifact of twentieth-century practice, in which licensors offered an exchange of promises with users: "We will give you a copy of our copyrighted work," in essence, "if you pay us and promise to enter into certain obligations concerning the work." With respect to software, those obligations by users include promises not to decompile or reverse-engineer the software, and not to transfer the software.

Nevertheless, Mark Radcliffe, general counsel of the Open Source Initiative, thinks that it would be difficult to avoid a contract interpretation of many popular open source licenses. In his article titled "Software Freedom Law Center Files Second Round of Enforcement Actions for BusyBox Software" (available at *http://lawandlifesiliconvalley.blogspot.com/2007/11/software-freedom-law-center-files.html*), Radcliffe states:

> "Please note that the [Software Freedom Law Center] and the Free Software Foundation have consistently taken the position that the GPL is not a contract, but I believe that this position is difficult to defend."

The "pure license" interpretation favored by Eben Moglen makes the enforcement of the GPL much easier; there is no need to consider *offers*, or *acceptances*, or the other particulars of contract law discussed in this chapter. Unfortunately, it is impossible to say for certain if a particular agreement will be considered a license, a contract, or considered *both* a contract and a license. It is a tricky and case-specific question focused on whether the agreement includes a "restriction on the scope" of permissible action or whether it is simply a "covenant" to act in a certain way.

Contracts As Private Law

Contracts are a form of *private law*. Usually, we don't have private laws; the government is the only entity that is generally allowed to make laws. But contracts are promises that the law will enforce. That is the power of contract law; it allows *private parties* (i.e., anybody who is not the government) to make agreements that will then be recognized as official and binding by the courts.

To understand why this is important, think for a moment about the recent rise in distributed source code management systems (DSCMs). In the older-style centralized source code management systems, a person had to become a "committer" in order to affect the project. This had the benefit of allowing project-wide changes to propagate immediately; as soon as a change was committed to the centralized source code repository, it affected everybody. But this centralized model also had the disadvantage of a built-in bottleneck—for *any* code to go in, it had to go through a central committer.

In a DSCM, *everyone* is a committer, but only within a limited area. Each person can make changes that apply to his or her own repository only. Good changes can be optionally sent up to project leaders, but local situations and style rules can be addressed without having to coordinate with anybody else.

Contract law works like a DSCM. Contracts allow massive and decentralized lawmaking, addressing millions of individualized situations without having to go through a central authority. Also just like DSCMs, the private aspects of contract law apply only within a limited scope, typically, only to the entities who agree to the contract.

Contract Law Principles

Because the obligations of a contract only apply to the *contracting parties*, the people who sign or assent to the contract, the courts are very permissive regarding the allowable scope of contracts. Nevertheless, there are a few basic requirements for a contract to be considered valid.

The Purpose of Contracts

Contract law in its broadest sense is set up to ask (and answer) four basic questions about the entities associated with the contract (called *parties* to the contract):

- Did the parties make an agreement?
- How should the contract be interpreted? What did each party promise?
- Did one or both parties fail to keep a promise (called a *breach*)?
- If so, what compensation (*remedies*) should be given the non-breaching party?

In general, the role of contract law is not to punish wrongdoing. There aren't really "wrongs" in contract law, and contracts can be invalidated if the specific terms appear punitive. Rather than wrongdoing, there is only breach—failing to keep your promise. Enforcing a contract means that you are entitled to the benefit of your bargain, via *specific performance* (court-ordered follow-through on the contract), via damages (money), or both.

Some types of contracts, called *contracts against public policy*, cannot be enforced by the courts. These are contracts containing promises that, if fulfilled, would harm society in general. For example, contracts containing promises to do something illegal are against public policy, as are contracts designed to restrain competition in an industry, and marriage brokerage contracts.

It is noteworthy that contracts to pay gambling debts are against public policy in most places in the United States, and cannot be enforced in court. Therefore, people who loan money for use in gambling sometimes resort to other means to encourage payment.

Contracting Parties

The right to enter into a contract is one of the most basic economic rights; it is one of the essential aspects of becoming an adult in our society. As such, it is much easier to describe who *cannot* enter into a contract than to describe who can.

Minors (people under age 18) are generally not allowed to form enforceable contracts (there are some exceptions when the contract is for "necessities"). To discourage contracts with minors, any contracting minor has super contract powers; the contract can be cancelled upon request of the minor, but it is binding to the adult. That is why parents are always asked to sign contracts that involve minors—to provide a capable and independent party to the contract.

Age, and the associated ability to contract, can be a factor in open source development. In the proprietary software world, there is a central organizing company that directs development, so the age and legal status of each developer is known. In the widely distributed world of open source development, however, amazing contributions can come from developers who aren't even in high school. These young developers need parental consent to form a binding open source license or to sign a contributor license agreement.

Another instance where this can come up is when companies want to form contractual agreements with an open source project *as a whole*. For example, outside companies might sometimes want to sponsor the development of a particular feature in an open source project. If a project is organized as a non-profit corporation, then the non-profit has the power to enter into contracts by using a representative. Although the *representative* is the one that agrees to the contract, the *corporate entity* is responsible for the contract. For more about non-profit incorporation, see Chapter 14.

Making an Agreement

There are four basic elements that go into making a contract—an *offer, acceptance, mutual assent,* and *consideration.*

Offer

An offer is some indication of intent to enter into a contract with someone else. The law is generally ready to accept almost anything as an indication of intent, but this indication must be objectively verifiable by a reasonable third party. Therefore, certain types of communication are not considered offers or acceptances. For example, none of the following are offers:

- *Opinions,* including professional opinions
- *Statements of intention* (for example, the statement, "We intend to buy 300 copies of your software once the service pack is released," would not be enforceable as a contract).
- *Invitations to bid,* such as requests for proposals (RFPs)
- Most *price estimates*
- *Advertisements, catalogs,* and *mass mailings*

In all of these cases, it is impossible to objectively determine that the speaker wanted to enter into a specific contract with a specific person, so these sorts of communications are not considered offers in the contract sense.

The application of this rule can sometimes be counterintuitive. For example, if I put my vintage Transformers toy collection up on eBay, the terms of the deal (if there would be one) are unknown, so simply advertising my Transformers toys as available for sale is *not* an offer in contract terms. Instead, what I am doing is inviting other people to give *me* offers (like, "I will buy your toys for $100.00"). A contract is only formed when I *accept* the offer.

Acceptance

An acceptance is an indication that the offer has been received and approved. Just as the offer must be objectively verifiable, so too must its reception and acceptance. However, there are fewer restrictions on the acceptance. Some offers can be accepted simply through one party's promise to do something in the future; those are called *bilateral* contracts. They are called bilateral because both parties—both *sides* of the contract—are exchanging promises. For example, "I promise to pay you $100.00 if you promise to eat bananas every day for a year," is a bilateral contract.

Other contracts, called *unilateral* contracts, contain a promise only on the offering side. For example, "I promise to pay you $100.00 if you eat bananas every day for a year," is a unilateral contract. You accept the contract by performing some act (in this case, eating bananas).

The general rule is that the person making the offer can dictate how the offer must be accepted. If the offer specifies that people must accept by dancing on one foot and eating a sandwich, then that is the *only* way to accept. If the offer doesn't specify a method, however, the offer may be accepted by any reasonable means under the circumstances.

The most important exception to this rule is that an offer may not specify that a person accepts by *silence*. For example, I cannot make an offer that states, "I propose that you send me $5.00. In return, I will jump around like a monkey. If you do nothing, that will be considered an acceptance of this offer." The reason should be clear: not only is acceptance by silence not objectively verifiable, it also opens the door for contracts where one party doesn't actually have contractual intent. Another way of thinking about this issue is that contract formation must always be *opt-in*, and cannot be *opt-out*.

In the context of e-commerce, acceptance can be boiled down to a single click. The "I Agree" checkboxes that adorn almost every signup form are there to provide an objectively verifiable acceptance of each site's terms of use.

For those confused by the many commercials that state that "If you want to keep the service, simply do nothing and we will keep sending your beautiful *Moose-of-the-Month* calendar for only $14.99...," it is important to recognize that there are two parts to this agreement—the trial period (free) and the continuation service (not free). Contract law requires you to opt in to the *initial* service—to form the contractual relationship—but continued participation in a contractual relationship can be opt-out.

Mutual assent

To form a contract, both parties have to agree on the terms. Usually, this agreement is manifested by the offer (which gives the terms of the deal) and the acceptance (which shows approval of the terms). As described above, the law favors an objective view of the contract, that is, an objectively verifiable offer and acceptance. However, it is also important that the recipient of the offer has reasonably understood the deal; there should have been a meeting of the minds concerning the contract. Without such subjective intent, there is no contract.

The requirement of mutual assent is the basis of a number of arguments that can come up in a court case over a broken contract, *duress, mistake*, and *fraud* being the most significant. However, these arguments are difficult to make without very specific and convincing evidence that there was not a meeting of the minds concerning the contract. It is generally not enough for one party to assert that they did not understand the contract terms; the court must also find that the other party also knew there was no mutual assent, but went ahead with the contract anyway.

Consideration

Consideration is a legal term that just means *something of value*. The consideration is the reason why the parties enter into the contract. It is sometimes defined as the result of a "bargained-for exchange." Most often, the consideration for a contract is money, goods, or services. Other times, consideration can be simply a promise to do (or not do) something in the future. The consideration for a contract doesn't have to have any particular defined price; as long as it has some legally recognizable value, it is enough.

The existence of consideration distinguishes contracts from gifts. Gifts are voluntary transfers of value from one person to another, without anything of value being promised or given in return. If I promise to give you a gift, and then break my promise, it is not enforceable as a breach of contract because I was given no consideration for my promise. Gratitude, feelings of obligation, and undefined expectations of future benefit are not legally recognized as having value; if I promise to give you $100, your saying "thanks" is not enough consideration to turn that promise into a contract.

Consideration for modifying contracts

The issue of consideration also comes up when contracts are modified. Although there are provisions in the law for modifying contracts, under most circumstances the terms of a contract are frozen when the offer is accepted. Any subsequent unilateral changing of the terms is disallowed.

The reason is that each new set of terms is logically a new contract, and at least one party has not agreed to the new terms. Further, there has been no *current* exchange of consideration to induce the parties to accept the new contract. There was a previous exchange of consideration necessary to create the first contract, but *past* exchanges of value are not consideration for *current* or *future* actions.

One place where this issue has come up is in the use of shrinkwrap licenses. A shrinkwrap license is a contract, usually applied to commercial software, that is contained within the box and not visible at the time of sale. Because the terms of the contract are not clear at the time the bargain is made (when the product is bought), any new terms contained within the hidden license cannot technically be enforced without new consideration and agreement to the new terms. Some companies have tried to talk their way around the incompatibility of such licenses with established contract practice by arguing that the contract isn't formed until installation time (when the user clicks the I Agree button).

There were some early cases that called enforceability of shrinkwrap licenses into question, but courts have been increasingly friendly to these licenses as they have become more common in the industry. Frequently, software companies deal with this issue by summarizing essential contract terms on the outside of the box and putting the buyer on notice of the full contractual terms within.

Another place where this issue comes up is in contracts for the use of online services. The contract terms are technically frozen when you first agree to the use of the service, but periodically, providers of online services want to (and do) modify their terms of service.

Again, there isn't a definitive answer regarding the contractual soundness of this practice, but the courts have generally been friendly to it. The most common argument is that there isn't a *single* contract that covers all future use of the service; instead, there is a *series* of contracts, each one with possibly new terms, with each contract covering a single use of the service. Alternatively, the online service indicates in the initial terms of service that changes to the terms of service will occur. Because changing terms are part of the initial bargain, notice of the change and a chance to opt out of the service are usually considered sufficient.

Communication

One issue that comes up is the use of email to communicate offers or acceptances. Email is generally reliable, but mail delivery bugs and spam filters sometimes lead to dropped mail. Accordingly, people complain that important communications, like domain renewal notifications, were never received.

The general rule is that offers and acceptances can be made in any "commercially reasonable" manner. With the growing use of email for many business communications, courts generally accept that using email is "commercially reasonable" for almost all transactions. People are free to use methods of communication that deliver higher reliability, but it appears that the law will not generally force people to do so.

Oral versus written contracts

There is a common belief that all contracts must be in writing, but this is not true. Contracts can be oral, written, or have aspects that are both oral and written. Nevertheless, most contracts are in writing because the law favors written contracts.

For example, a set of laws called the *Statute of Frauds* requires certain types of contracts to be in writing (and signed) to be enforceable. The limitations of the Statute of Frauds apply if the value of the contract exceeds a certain dollar amount or if the *term* of the contract (the time over which the contractual work will occur) is longer than a year. In other words, an oral agreement to pay a million dollars to provide a service ten years down the road would probably be unenforceable (and, according to a common law school joke, not worth the paper it is written on).

The problem with oral contracts is that they are often ambiguous and the exact terms are hard to prove, especially if there are no independent witnesses. The parties themselves frequently will not recall the exact details to which they agreed. To maintain uniformity and to capture the advantages listed above, businesses (and lawyers) strongly prefer written contracts. These written contracts can be turned into standard "form contracts" that are applied to many situations and have standardized terms.

Of importance to software developers, contracts that assign copyright and patent rights must *always* be in writing. Most technical employers require all employees to sign proprietary information agreements that cover these issues (see Chapter 9). Without a written agreement, however, it is difficult for companies to claim ownership of outside employee projects and outside employee patents in the U.S.

Interpreting Contracts

Contract interpretation is very specific to facts and circumstances. Nevertheless, there are two basic modes of interpretation. The first mode is to look within the "four corners" of the document and seek to apply every term in the contract according to its generally accepted definition and without resorting to any outside information. The second mode of interpretation looks at the language of the contract in light of the intentions of the parties, their past dealings, and general business usage of important claim terms. While the first mode of interpretation is more common, both are used by the courts when evaluating contract cases.

Many common boilerplate clauses that show up in a variety of contracts have reasonably standard meanings. We'll look at a few in this section.

Merger and integration clause

A merger and integration clause prevents any of the parties from claiming that the written terms of the contract do not represent the entire agreement. As noted earlier, contracts can have both written and oral components. The merger and integration clause asserts that all components of the agreement have been "merged" or "integrated" into the single written agreement.

Choice of law clause

Different states have different laws with different rules of interpretation. The purpose of the choice of law clause is to fix the interpretation of the contract to the laws and rules of one particular state.

Term and time of performance

If the contract is for the delivery of some product or the provision of some service, it can be governed by a couple of common clauses. Some contracts will say that "time is of the essence," which means that the contract will be breached if the actions described in the contract are not performed according to a given time frame. Other contracts will say only that the work must be completed in a "reasonable" time, which gives more flexibility.

If a contract is only going to have effect for a certain period of time, there should be a defined term for the contract; otherwise, the contract may be too indefinite to enforce. In an intellectual property contract, as discussed further later section in this chapter, this clause may be used to provide a limitation on the use of the IP.

Severability clause

A severability clause states that each part of the contract is independent; even if some parts of the contract are declared unenforceable by a court, the rest of the contract should survive. In the absence of a severability clause, it is possible that the entire contract will be considered unenforceable if a single clause is rendered invalid.

Breach of Contract and Remedies

Just as every computer backup strategy requires a technique for restoring content, everyone who signs a contract should consider how to handle breaches. There are as many ways to breach a contract as there are contracts in the world; what constitutes a breach will vary from situation to situation. There are three specific points, though, that are common to the law of contract.

The necessity of performance

First, in order to have a breach of contract, at least one party to the contract has to have *performed* (carried out) his part under the contract. For example, if a person contracts to buy a laptop for $1,000, then he must pay the $1,000 to the computer seller before he is entitled to enforce the contract and compel the computer seller to hand over the goods. Until one or both parties have at least partially carried out their promises in the contract, the courts will not recognize a lawsuit for breach of contract.

One common question regarding performance and breach is the idea of *anticipatory repudiation*. This occurs when two parties have an agreement to do something at a future time, and one party tells the other that it will not carry out its part of the contract. For example, assume that you paid money to the computer seller for him to deliver a new laptop next week. A day or two after he receives your money, however, he tells you that he will not bring the laptop.

As strange as it may seem, there is no breach of contract in this scenario. The contract is not actually breached until a week goes by and the computer seller fails to bring the laptop. While there are a few exceptions where the courts will command future compliance with the contract, the general rule is that anticipatory repudiation is not something you can sue over.

Good faith

There is an implicit *good faith* term in all contracts. Contracts may be voided if one of the parties negotiated in bad faith, and may be breached if one of the parties starts acting in bad faith. There is no explicit definition of good faith, but it involves compliance with the generally accepted standards of decency and commercial morality, avoidance of deception, and a legitimate effort to fulfill any obligations entered into. For example, if the seller of a car knows that the car has serious hidden damage, but does not disclose that damage, the seller is not acting in good faith and will not be able to enforce the sales contract.

Damages and specific performance

There are two typical remedies for breach of contract: *damages* and *specific performance*. Both of these remedies are designed to give the non-breaching party the benefit of the bargain that he made initially. Note that federal law offers more remedies, as we will discuss later in the chapter.

Damages are just money—the amount of money that would have resulted from full observation of the contract. For example, assume Alice is going to sell some bracelets made by Bob. She expects to sell $1,000 worth of jewelry, but will only receive $100 of profit after expenses. If Bob breaches the contract by not providing the bracelets, Alice will be limited to recovering the expected benefit that she would have received by selling the bracelets: $100 in profit. She cannot enforce a claim against Bob for her $1,000 of lost revenue.

Real-life examples can get much more complicated as they take into account lost opportunities, expenses made while relying on the contract, and so forth, but the basic principle is the same —Alice will never get back more than the benefit she expected out of the bargain.

Specific performance is the name given to a court order to comply with the terms of the contract. It is applied when money damages will never be sufficient to give the non-breaching party the benefit of the bargain. For example, assume Ralph breaches a contract to sell the source code for his media player application to BuyCo. Although there are many other media player applications available, no other media player in the world is exactly like Ralph's, and so no other source code will do. Similarly, no amount of money will be a perfect substitute for Ralph's source code. In this case, a court may order specific performance: Ralph must comply with the contract and deliver the source code to BuyCo.

Intellectual Property Contracts

The essence of intellectual property law, like all property laws, is exclusion. Property can be arbitrarily used or sold because property holders can prevent others from using or intruding upon their property. Intellectual property holders generally use contracts to extract economic rent (profit) from the use of the property.

Assignments and Licenses

IP holders can make money from their intellectual property in two ways: they can sell all the rights to the property (an *assignment*) or grant limited rights to the property (a *license*).

Of these, intellectual property assignment is the most straightforward. As with physical property, an assignment hands complete ownership and control to the buyer (here called an *assignee*). Although there is specific legal language required to effectively assign a particular piece of intellectual property, assignment can be understood by analogy to the sale of a physical object like a car. While you own the car, you can do anything you want with it; but when you sell the car, you hand over both the car and all ability to use (i.e., drive, kick, wash, show off) the car.

Intellectual property assignment works the same way. Intellectual property has two aspects: the physical embodiment of the property and the associated rights. When you sell the IP, you hand over the physical embodiments of the property (such as the patent documents, copyright registration forms, software source code, etc.), as well as all rights to assign or license the intellectual property in the future.

Intellectual property licenses are trickier. Implicit in the ability to exclude *totally* is the ability to only exclude *partially*. An IP holder can use contract law to grant partial rights to many people at the same time.

To understand intellectual property licensing, think of a hotel. There is only a single building, but the owners have carved it up into many different pieces—the different rooms—that can be "sold" individually. Different rooms are reserved to different people each night, and each person may have paid a different price to rent the room. Different people may stay for different lengths of time. Regardless of how many people are staying in the hotel, however, the owners still maintain control over and ultimate ownership of the property.

Most of the time, intellectual property ownership is not as clear-cut as these examples. Assignments are rarely absolute; rather, assignments are made while still reserving some rights to the former owner. For example, imagine that the hotel was sold, but that the former owner included a clause in the contract that stated that he could stay at the hotel free of charge any time he wanted. This corresponds to the most common form of contract assignment in IP. A patent holder may assign the rights to a patent while reserving the right for his own company to make and sell products based on the patented technology (i.e., it retains a license back to the IP right).

Although patents and trademarks are the most common objects of negotiated intellectual property contracts, other types of IP can also be licensed. For example, copyright licenses are granted each time a piece of software is distributed. Technology know-how or trade secrets can be licensed in conjunction with patents or trademarks. For example, a cookie company may license trade secret recipes along with the contractual right to use the trademark to sell the cookies.

Making an IP Contract a License

The essential feature of a license that distinguishes it from a common contract is the inclusion of specific terms that allow one person to use another person's intellectual property. These are the *grant of a license*, *limitations* on the use of the intellectual property, and the *reservation of rights*.

ALL CAPS

YOU MAY NOTICE THAT LICENSES SOMETIMES SEEM TO BE SHOUTING AT YOU. That is on purpose. Certain license provisions—generally the ones that significantly restrict the legal rights of the contracting parties—are required by law to be in **bold**, *italic*, ALL CAPS, or otherwise distinguished from the text all around them.

So, if the license is shouting at you, pay attention. That means that you are probably giving up something significant.

Grant of the license

The first type of clause, the grant of the license, allows one party to use the other party's intellectual property. Intellectual property law itself makes very little or no provision for sharing, so without this clause, there would be no legal way to apply the intellectual property in a business context. A typical grant is below.

> *Grant of Copyright License.* Subject to the terms and conditions of this Agreement, [IP holding party] hereby grants to [the other party] a worldwide, non-exclusive, royalty-free copyright license to reproduce, prepare derivative works of, publicly display, publicly perform, sublicense, and distribute the work and associated derivative works.

Limitations on the scope of use

The second type of clause, the limitations on the use of the intellectual property, is essential to the application of federal intellectual property law to the license. The application of federal intellectual property law to a contract depends on its explicit inclusion of use limitations. If a contract simply states that one party can use another party's intellectual property, that contract may be considered a "mere covenant" and may therefore only be enforced under state contract law. That means that the only available remedies would be money damages and specific performance; the enhanced damages and injunctive power of federal law would not be applied. A typical limitations clause is below.

> *Limitations on Trademark License.* The Trademark License is limited to [party] and is revocable, non-transferable, and granted solely upon and in connection with [party] for use in the Licensed Territory during the specified Term. NO LICENSE IS GRANTED HEREUNDER FOR ANY USE OTHER THAN THAT SPECIFIED, AND NO LICENSE IS GRANTED HEREUNDER FOR ANY COMBINATION OF THE LICENSED MARKS WITH OTHER PRODUCTS, SERVICES OR MARKS WITHOUT PRIOR WRITTEN CONSENT OF LICENSOR WHICH SHALL NOT BE UNREASONABLY WITHHELD OR DELAYED.

Reservation of rights

The third type of clause, the reservation of rights, makes it clear that the intellectual property holder retains any rights that are not granted to the licensee. This prevents any of the rights being in legal limbo. The exercise of this clause means that all remaining rights are explicitly reserved. The clause explicitly reflects the principle described at the beginning of this chapter: anything not expressly permitted is forbidden.

The most common form of this clause is the simple phrase "all rights reserved" on some licensed use of intellectual property. A more extensive version of the clause follows.

> *Reservation of Rights.* All rights not expressly granted above are retained by [the IP holder]. Any use not expressly granted above is reserved. Further, this Agreement does not restrict or limit [IP Holder's] rights to utilize or license the works in any manner. Notwithstanding anything contained herein to the contrary, [IP Holder] shall have the unrestricted right to utilize (and to license another party to utilize) the works in other contexts.

These clauses are essential to intellectual property contracts because they tie the terms of the contract back into federal intellectual property law. Because IP licenses are contracts, courts may grant specific performance and money damages, just as in regular contract law. The inclusion of these clauses, however, allows the courts to also apply the increased damages of federal law.

Specific Limitations on Scope

A number of other clauses and terms are frequently used in intellectual property contracts to limit the scope of the license. One of the features of contract law is that any ambiguity in the license is *construed against the writer*. That means that given two interpretations, the interpretation less favorable to the party who wrote the contract will be chosen. Accordingly, a number of terms are used to specify the exact nature and terms of the grant.

Exclusivity
: An intellectual property license may be exclusive or non-exclusive. An exclusive license means that only one person is granted the ability to exercise a particular right associated with the IP. A non-exclusive license allows the IP holder to license the same right to many parties at the same time. For example, I gave O'Reilly the exclusive right to publish this book, so I can't make an extra buck by also offering it to a competitor to publish.

Sublicensing
: One particularly important right is the right to *sublicense* the intellectual property, in other words, to pass the received rights on to someone else. Even if somebody is a licensed user of intellectual property, passing on the IP without holding the right to sublicense induces infringement of the exclusive rights granted under the law.

Field of Use
: Intellectual property is frequently licensed for use only in particular technological areas. For example, a patent describing a water filtration system may be licensed to one manufacturer for industrial and chemical processing use and to another manufacturer for household water filtration. This restriction is most often applied to patent licenses, but it may occur in contracts licensing other forms of IP. For example, trademark licenses may have field of use restrictions. For example, the people who are licensed to make a Viagra-branded NASCAR racer aren't automatically allowed to also make Viagra-branded water.

Product
: Even more restrictive than a field of use is a product-based restriction. Product restrictions state that the licensed intellectual property may only be used in conjunction with a particular product.

Term
: Intellectual property is frequently licensed for a specific amount of time, such as five years. Because some forms of intellectual property, such as trademarks and trade secrets, have no built-in expiration date, the inclusion of a specific term can help to clarify the grant.

Territory
: Another common restriction is the limitation of the intellectual property use to a particular geographic area. Trademarks are frequently licensed with restrictions on the territory where they may be used. A good example is Cadbury Schweppes. You may not have heard of Cadbury Schweppes, but you have heard of its branded products: A&W Root Beer, Motts Apple Sauce, Bassett's candies, and Bubblicious gum, among many others. Cadbury Schweppes owns and manages these brands, and awards other companies, the *brand licensees*, the rights to make and sell products in association with the brand. However, the licensee bottling A&W Root Beer in Florida is not the same company that is bottling A&W Root Beer in Oregon. Each licensee is allowed to use the brand, but only within its defined geographic area.

Applying a License to Intellectual Property

When you create or invent something, you create new intellectual property. You can share that property by applying a license.

Because licenses are contracts, the number and variety of licenses is potentially infinite. However, intellectual property licensing law, like regular contract law, favors written contracts. And like regular contract law, certain types of contracts for intellectual property—notably assignments—must be *explicit* and *in writing* or they will not be enforceable.

If you are applying a license to some sort of software for commercial reasons, you should see an expert that can help you draft the exact license language you need to meet your business goals. Just as computer languages have a number of reserved words, so contract law has a number of reserved *terms of art*—particular phrases or sentences that have long-established legal meanings. Using the right keywords in a contract is just as important as using the right keywords in a computer program.

Open Source Licenses

One important option to consider is a license that open sources your software. Open source licenses are easier in the sense that they are not negotiated or drafted anew each time they are used, but are generally chosen from a list of standard open source licenses.

Applying an open source license to your code is relatively simple. The common method is to choose a license from the list at *http://opensource.org/* and include a copy of the license text in a file called *LICENSE.txt* in your repository. The license is applied to each file in the repository by including a short copyright notice in each file. For example, to apply the Apache Version 2.0 License to your code, you would include:

> Copyright [*year*] [*name of copyright owner*]
>
> Licensed under the Apache License, Version 2.0 (the "License"); you may not use this file except in compliance with the License. You may obtain a copy of the License at:
>
> *http://www.apache.org/licenses/LICENSE-2.0*
>
> Unless required by applicable law or agreed to in writing, software distributed under the License is distributed on an "AS IS" BASIS, WITHOUT WARRANTIES OR CONDITIONS OF ANY KIND, either express or implied.
>
> See the License for the specific language governing permissions and limitations under the License.

Many different contracts may be applied to the same piece of code. A good example is Mozilla, which is triple licensed (it has three different agreements attached to the same code). In a more commercial open source context, some companies wrap support and maintenance contracts around their source code. Even though the code may be licensed under an open source license like the GPL, these companies use contracts to say that, "You can't get to this code (or official binaries) unless you first buy a support contract."

Chapter 10 discusses some specific licenses and how they apply to different situations. Before addressing the specific provisions of those licenses, however, it is worth taking a step back and looking at what open source licensing is and how it works in context.

CHAPTER EIGHT

The Economic and Legal Foundations of Open Source Software

"Open source" is one of the most misunderstood concepts in the computing industry today. Most people in the industry, and even a number of people outside the industry, have heard of open source software. They may be able to name some of the most prominent open source projects, like Linux, Apache, and Firefox.

But what most people don't understand about open source software is *why it works.* Software released as open source costs money and time to make—it has value. To some people, especially those who are more business-minded, this sounds like a throwback to late-90s dot-com-era business plans: give your product away for free and make it up on volume. They see very few business models in that sort of thinking.

To others, open source sounds anti-commercial. This point of view was best illustrated by Steve Ballmer, CEO of Microsoft. "Linux is a cancer that attaches itself in an intellectual property sense to everything it touches," stated Ballmer in 2001. "The way the license is written, if you use any open source software, you have to make the rest of your software open source...open source is not available to commercial companies."

It is worth noting that Microsoft's own actions have since proved Ballmer wrong. Since Ballmer gave that quote, Microsoft has successfully released a number of open source products and certified two licenses as open source, all without making the rest of its software open source.

Nevertheless, the point remains that most people don't understand the basis of open source, even if they work with open source products. So that is where we begin: by addressing the general *why* and *what* of open source, before looking at the specifics of how open source licenses work.

ABOUT THIS CHAPTER

This chapter has one fairly narrow goal: to provide an economic and legal structure to help explain why open source works. Open source, like intellectual property in general, is really a legal and economic system rather than a simple collection of rules and licenses. In my opinion, understanding the big picture is just as important as understanding the language of a particular license. I hope that readers with many different backgrounds will be able to get a better grasp on the phenomenon of open source.

Like Chapter 1, this chapter is heavy on theory and light on practical application. For those interested in the more practical aspects of software licensing, Chapter 10 discusses the process of choosing a license and Chapter 12 discusses some of the particular issues surrounding the GPL.

For those interested in learning more about commons-based production, Professor Yochai Benkler has been doing some interesting work in this area. For example, see *The Wealth of Networks: How Social Production Transforms Markets and Freedom* (Yale Press 2006), and *Coase's Penguin, or Linux and the Nature of the Firm*, 112 Yale Law Journal 369 (2002). For a full list of Yochai Benkler's publications, see *http://www.benkler.org/*.

A Brief Digression into Terminology

First, a note about labels and semantics. One of the consistent debates in the free software community has been about labels. "Free software," "open source software," "free as in speech, not as in beer," and "*libre* software" have all been used to try to describe and put a label on the legal construct that I will discuss here as open source. By using the "open source" label, I am not trying to take a side in these debates.

For those involved in free software, I am aware of the important philosophical differences implied in the use of the term "free software" as opposed to "open source." Where applicable, I will use the correct term to describe how they are both socially and legally different. Nevertheless, because open source software is a strict superset of free software, I will generally use the more inclusive term when discussing legal elements common to both.

I also make a distinction between open source licenses as recognized by the Open Source Initiative (OSI) and other source-available open source licenses like the Microsoft Shared Source licenses. I will generally use the term "source-available" when discussing these licenses to distinguishing them from OSI- or FSF-approved licenses.

Understanding Open Source

Most people can't give a definition of open source, even those who work with open source projects on a day-to-day basis. Most people will say that it is about giving things away for free. Programmers will usually be more specific and talk about giving *source code* away for free. The savviest commenters will talk about freedom and the rights to modify the source code to a product.

It is true that open source software is frequently free (as in price), that source code is usually what is being provided for free, and that there are additional rights (or *freedoms*) given to those who receive the open source product. However, all of these are peripheral to the true nature of open source.

At its core, open source is *a legal construct for cooperation and trade in intellectual property.* People occasionally say that open source and intellectual property are opposites. This is not true. Open source software could not exist as we know it without intellectual property. So before I begin, I want to start outside the realm of software, and even outside the realm of intellectual property, to create a framework for understanding open source and how it applies in the market today.

Credit Unions and Open Source: An Analogy

To those not in the financial industry, banks and credit unions look about the same. They both accept deposits, give mortgages, and provide checking accounts. For a basic consumer of financial services, there isn't much difference in the day-to-day experience. However, the day-to-day experience is misleading; there are, in fact, substantial and important differences between these two outwardly similar institutions. These internal differences create very different incentives and lead to different results.

When looking at the software world, a similar division applies. Both traditional software and open source projects produce software, but like banks and credit unions, there are substantial differences between the two. While the analogy isn't exact, there are important similarities between what I will call *corporate model organizations* (like banks and traditional software companies) on one hand, and *cooperative model organizations* (like credit unions and open source projects) on the other.

Where necessary to help illustrate the difference, I will highlight examples from two roughly comparable software projects: the Apache HTTP Server and Microsoft Internet Information Services (IIS). These two software products address the same market, have roughly comparable functionality, and are, respectively, number one and number two in market share across the world. However, IIS is built in a corporate organization, and Apache is built in a cooperative organization.

Ownership

The first and most fundamental feature distinguishing corporate and cooperative organizations is *ownership*. Corporate organizations are owned by their shareholders, and cooperatives are owned by their members. This difference in ownership is fundamental because it changes the relationship between the directors of the organization and its customers. Each institution is set up primarily to serve the interests of its owners.

In a bank, the directors and executives have one mandate: to return profits to the owners (the shareholders) by making the bank profitable and successful overall. It works out that in the capitalist system, the standard way to make a profit for shareholders is to provide services desired by customers. If the interests of customers and shareholders ever diverge, however, it is the responsibility of the directors of the bank to make the choice that favors the shareholder/owners.

In contrast, credit unions are owned by their members; that is, their depositors. A credit union is a non-profit cooperative institution formed by the people who deposit money into the institution. While credit unions also have executives and a board of directors, the leaders of the credit union derive their authority from the vote or the consent of the members. The interests of the credit union owners and the credit union customers are fundamentally aligned because they are the same group of people.

Ownership and software development

Just like the financial institutions described here, the most fundamental difference between proprietary and open source software is *ownership*. In this case, ownership means control of the copyright and any necessary distribution rights.

Proprietary software companies own the copyrights to all the software they distribute (in some cases, there are portions of the code licensed from somebody else, but to the consumer, it all looks the same—the company owns the code). The licenses and purchase agreements surrounding the code all reflect this basic fact.

For example, Microsoft Technet specifies, "Standard Licensing specifies that you may not use the software [IIS] for 'commercial hosting'. So if you plan to sell the use of your IIS server like a web hosting provider does you are required to become a Microsoft Certified Partner and obtain proper licensing." Those who need more functionality are required to purchase a more expensive product. Microsoft exercises this control because that is how the company makes money; you are trading *your* money for the use of *their* code.

Open source projects, however, are owned by their communities, or more precisely, by their contributors. Just as depositors become part owners when they put their money into the credit union repository, coders become part owners when they put their code into the source code repository.

In a typical open source project, each contributor maintains copyright to the code he contributes to the project (some projects require copyright assignment to the project, but the contributor usually gets almost all rights granted back). By agreeing to share the code, the coder in turn receives the benefit of the code shared by everyone in the project.

As stated by the Apache Foundation FAQ: "Who owns the Apache code? All software developed within the Foundation belongs to the ASF, and therefore the members. The members own the code and the direction of it and the Foundation."

Just as with a credit union, the interests of the code owners and the code users (the "customers") are fundamentally aligned because they are the same group of people. Of course, the model presented here is incomplete; people can also join an open source project by becoming a user, without donating any code. Nevertheless, the overriding similarity remains: open source projects are fundamentally cooperative institutions because project contributors have refused to exercise the prerogatives of exclusive personal ownership. Instead, the privileges of ownership are shared. This principle of shared ownership manifests itself in many ways.

Involvement

The ownership issue can manifest as personal *involvement and investment in the institution.* In a bank, there is no necessary overlap between customers and shareholders. While the very largest investors may participate in the day-to-day functioning of the bank, most shareholders do not have any say in bank operations. The customers of the bank who are not stockholders are even further removed; they do not have any voice at all.

In credit unions, each customer is a shareholder in the institution. While some members of the credit union are more active in administration than others, each member is requested to vote on matters of importance to the cooperative at least once a year. The credit union membership (all the customers of the institution) have the incentive to stay interested and involved in both the health of their individual accounts and in the financial cooperative as a whole.

Involvement in software development

Similarly, one of the marked differences between proprietary software and open source software is the level of personal *involvement* and *investment* in the software community. The proprietary business model depends on ownership of the underlying code, so companies following that model must maintain control of all contributions. In practice, this usually means that only employees can contribute. Other users of the software (the customers) do not generally have a say in the development priorities or future directions of the software.

Under the open source model, each contributor has a say in the future direction of the project, speaking through his or her code, if in no other fashion. Those who are the most active in the community gain more influence over the project. As stated on the Apache Software Foundation's web site (*http://people.apache.org/~bayard/asf-index.html*), "Our membership consists of those individuals who have demonstrated a commitment to collaborative open-source software development through sustained participation and contributions within the Foundation's projects." The correlation of member involvement with project influence gives people the incentive to stay interested and involved with the project.

One of the ways in which this increased involvement manifests itself is through the creation of communities around the software. For example, a brief look at the home page of the Apache project reveals a hive of activity: more than fifty subprojects, conferences, a foundation, sponsors, and hundreds of individual foundation members.

It is also noteworthy that more than one third of the active members are listed as unaffiliated or independent, many of the members come from non-commercial entities, like universities, and the remainder of the members come from a range of commercial entities, including nominal competitors.

Furthermore, Apache Foundation members are only the most *active* members; there are over 2500 people with subversion commit privileges. The number of active community members is even larger.

It is true that a community can also develop around proprietary software. For example, Microsoft's IIS community site IIS.net has many users on its forums, and people are encouraged to post their questions and share their experiences with IIS. Even in a proprietary situation, there is substantial benefit to having a community, and Microsoft has done a good job of supporting and encouraging those who work with IIS.

Nevertheless, there is a vast difference in the scale of the two communities. Compared to the 2,500 developers with Apache commit privileges, there are 57 total people listed on the IIS team. Comparing total forum and newsgroup posts between the two communities, Apache generates more than an order of magnitude more discussion per day than the relatively well-done IIS community.

Profits, Rates, and Fees

Another distinguishing feature between corporate and cooperative organizations is the *profit motive*. The leaders of corporate organizations, like banks, have a duty to always act in the best interests of the shareholder/owners, and the best interests of the shareholders are generally measured by the shareholders' return on their investments. There is a profitability factor integrated into every business decision and into every financial product offered by the bank. If a decision or a product is not profitable, it will not be pursued.

It is important to understand the nature of this profit motive. In most cases, it is not enough that a product is profitable in the sense that it generates more money than it consumes. Banks are in competition with each other and with other industries for investors, and so the sum of all bank activities must provide a total risk-to-profit ratio in line with other similar investments.

Market pressure, therefore, dictates that certain profitable activities are disfavored if they are not making *enough* profit. There's not just a profit margin in the products offered by the bank, but the profit margin must also be commercially reasonable.

Credit unions, on the other hand, are non-profit institutions. While the financial services provided by the credit union are not free (after all, any losses would have to be borne by the credit union's member owners), there is no incentive to make every transaction profitable. Because there are no non-owner members, and no non-member owners, creating profits from member services and giving them right back to the members would be pointless. Instead, the members of the credit union generally enjoy lower interest rates, lower fees, and more favorable terms for financial services provided through the cooperative.

The profit motive in software development

Open source and proprietary software are also distinguished by the profit motive. Proprietary software companies are established to make a profit and, like the banking industry, the sum of all commercial activities must provide investors with a total risk-to-profit ratio in line with other investments.

Open source projects, however, are non-profit institutions by nature. Part of the *quid pro quo* inherent in open source is that you receive the benefit of other people's code at no charge, but only if you also provide the benefit of your code to them at no charge. It is this exchange that has led to the widespread idea that all open source code is free.

The idea that all open source code is free is difficult to discuss because it is both trivially true and essentially false. It is trivially true in the sense described above; open source involves a barter of value between the contributors. This barter offer is usually extended to users and potential contributors as well. Because there is no money involved, this transaction is "free."

However, there are costs associated with open source software. Most fundamentally, software costs time and money to develop. Open source software can be highly evolved and quite complex, making the development of such software actually quite expensive. One estimate pegged the redevelopment cost of the Linux kernel at $612 million U.S. (see "Linux Kernel 2.6: It's Worth More!" at *http://www.dwheeler.com/essays/linux-kernel-cost.html*).

Various commercial entities can and do sell packaged distributions of open source software. There is nothing that requires the distribution of a particular open source product free of charge. In fact, *all* open source licenses recognized by the OSI allow for paid distributions of software. Most open source software companies follow this model, selling a branded and tested version of otherwise available code.

Additionally, there are ancillary costs, such as service, support, and customization, that apply to all software, including open source software. Open source software sometimes increases these costs. Paraphrasing Internet pioneer Jamie Zawinsky, "[Open source software] is free only if your time has no value" (*http://www.jwz.org/doc/linux.html*).

To resolve this contradiction, look back at the example of the credit union. Credit unions are able to provide better interest rates and lower fees because they are *cooperative*. By pooling their resources and removing the profit motive, the depositors in the credit union are able to mutually serve each other at a lower cost than they would otherwise incur.

In similar fashion, the cooperative nature of open source software allows the users of the software to solve computing problems cooperatively. By pooling coding resources, the participants in the open source project receive the full benefits of the software product while only paying a fraction of the total cost.

FREE AS IN FREEDOM

An alternative common explanation of the "free" nature of open source software is that it is free as in freedom, not free as in cost. That is, the important aspect of free software is the additional rights that are provided, not the incidental cost of acquiring the code. As described by the FSF at *http://www.gnu.org/philosophy/free-sw.html*:

Free software is a matter of liberty, not price. To understand the concept, you should think of free as in free speech, not as in free beer.

Free software is a matter of the users' freedom to run, copy, distribute, study, change and improve the software. More precisely, it refers to four kinds of freedom, for the users of the software:

> The freedom to run the program, for any purpose (freedom 0).
>
> The freedom to redistribute copies so you can help your neighbor (freedom 2).
>
> The freedom to improve the program, and release your improvements to the public, so that the whole community benefits (freedom 3). Access to the source code is a precondition for this.
>
> A program is free software if users have all of these freedoms. Thus, you should be free to redistribute copies, either with or without modifications, either gratis or charging a fee for distribution, to anyone anywhere. Being free to do these things means (among other things) that you do not have to ask or pay for permission.

This rights-oriented approach to the "free" in free software hits upon an important point: a distinctive part of free and open source software development is the grant of additional rights.

These four freedoms by themselves, however, do not provide an explanation of why free and open source software projects have thrived. For example, public domain software has all of these features, but there isn't a "public domain software movement."

Instead, and as discussed in greater detail here, these rights—these *freedoms*—are part of the legal and social compact that allows people with different interests to cooperate and trust each other.

The Customer Relationship

Another difference between corporate and cooperative institutions is visible in the relationship between the organizations and their customers. For corporate organizations, a certain amount of cooperation is motivated by our economic system. Part of the genius of capitalism is that market forces usually conspire to align the interests of producers (in this case, the banks or proprietary software companies) and consumers (in this case, the institution customers). Speaking broadly, corporate organizations grow their market share and profits by providing products and services that customers want. The more customers, the more profit.

It doesn't take long, however, to start thinking of exceptions to this rule. Banks maintain some policies that customers hate because the policies generate billions of dollars a year in extra service charges and fees. For examples, see "When Banks Turn Evil" by finance columnist Liz Pulliam Weston at *http://articles.moneycentral.msn.com/Banking/BetterBanking/WhenBanksTurnEvil.aspx*.

Proprietary software and customer care

As with banks, the profit motive inherent in the proprietary business model puts software companies at odds with their customers in some very fundamental ways. Proprietary software companies make money by selling add-on services, upgrades, or new versions of the software —activities that sometimes have negative customer consequences.

End-of-life (EOL) policies are one example. EOL policies specify that after a certain date, the software companies will no longer support or recognize a particular product. In some cases, such as in Intuit's Quicken software, code implementing the EOL policy intentionally reduces the functionality of the product, making it less valuable. Such policies are adopted to reduce support costs for products that are no longer sufficiently profitable and to force customers to pay for new versions of the software products.

Another example is the inclusion of trial offers in software installers. For example, at one point during the 1990s, installing the AOL Instant Messenger product resulted in at least eight different shortcuts or programs being scattered all over your computer. These shortcuts and programs were added because they were profitable for AOL, not because customers wanted them.

A third example involves deliberate incompatibilities in software. For example, Microsoft released several new games, such as *Halo 2* and *Shadowrun*, as Windows Vista-only games. These games included code that prevented them from being installed or played on earlier versions of the Microsoft operating system. The unnecessary incompatibility of the games was demonstrated when they were subsequently (and *very* unofficially) patched to allow them to run on Windows XP.

Cooperative organizations and customers

The structure of cooperative institutions does not expose them to this same dynamic. Rather, the removal of the profit motive places the organization and its customers (its members) in a substantially different position.

For example, the members of a credit union have a direct financial interest in ensuring that it is successful, because the more successful the credit union is, the lower the cost will be for the services rendered by the credit union.

Similarly, is very difficult for open source software projects to act against the best interests of their users. As with credit unions, the group of open source owners and the group of users overlap. In most cases, there is no single person or small group of people that own all the code; rather, the code is a collective work depending upon the individually copyrighted contributions from many different programmers.

Market Profile

Another distinct difference has to do with the market profile of corporate and cooperative organizations. In general, the presence (or absence) of the profit motive leads to different target groups of customers and different market outcomes. These market profiles are driven by the extent to which the organization is serving a commodity market, with little differentiation between providers, or a specialty market, with substantial differentiation between providers. Of course, there is a sliding scale between pure commodity-oriented organizations and pure specialty-oriented organizations, but it is useful to look at the ends of the spectrum to better appreciate the differences.

Market profiles for banks and credit unions

Banks tend to have two common operational profiles. First are commodity-oriented banks. For these banks, the primary cost is customer acquisition. There are relatively high fixed costs associated with bringing in each new customer, but additional services can be provided relatively inexpensively (making the additional services more profitable). The more ways in which the bank interacts with the customer, the more ways the bank has to earn money.

The strategy for these institutions is to encourage customers to make the initial commitment to the bank and then to try to upsell the customer on additional services. For example, a bank may offer free checking accounts or discounted ATM fees to get new customers to sign up. Once a customer has already established a relationship with the bank, it is much more likely that the customer will get CDs, mortgages, or other financial products from the bank.

Second are specialty-oriented banks. These are banks serving markets where there is a substantial benefit to having a high degree of concentration in a particular area. For example, there are merchant banks, real estate banks, and investment banks, all of which provide very specialized services to smaller groups of customers. Major cost drivers include the expertise, capital, and connections needed to effectively deal with large, complex, and labor-intensive transactions.

Because the services provided by these specialized banks are so individualized, the banks charge very high fees. These high fees, in turn, restrict the market of potential customers to those who are pursuing very high-dollar-value transactions—transactions where the expertise offered by the bank lowers the transaction cost enough to justify the involvement of the specialty bank.

Credit unions also tend to have two operational profiles, corresponding to the same basic market profiles. Commodity-oriented credit unions operate in the broader market for relatively basic services. Deposits, checks, mortgages, and credit cards are all commodity services that can be provided to a large number of people in a relatively uniform fashion. For customers that don't need much sophistication in their financial services, credit unions may provide better rates, lower fees, or superior service.

The second operational profile for credit unions is in some ways similar to the second operational profile for banks; the target market is a smaller group of customers with common but unusual needs. Nevertheless, there is an important distinction. The removal of the profit motive allows lower-dollar-value needs to be addressed efficiently.

To give an illustration, it is generally accepted that teachers do not have high salaries, but they do have unique financial needs. For example, many teachers are not paid during the summer months. This income variability makes traditional mortgages inconvenient. Instead, it would be better to have special mortgage arrangements that allow payments to be made during the school year only.

Unfortunately, there isn't a First Teacher's Bank dedicated to solving these issues. For commodity-oriented banks, the specialty needs of the teachers make their accounts more expensive (and thus relatively less profitable) to administer. For specialty-oriented banks, the transaction volume and dollar amounts are too low to justify the focus on these transactions. Because this market is relatively less profitable, it is not well served.

Credit unions, on the other hand, don't have to worry about the profit motive, so the relative unprofitability of these specialty accounts is not an issue. In fact, there are hundreds of teacher-oriented credit unions available. By establishing a cooperative in the form of a credit union, teachers are able to receive the specialized services that they need without incurring the extra expenses associated with for-profit financial institutions. Speaking generally, the credit union is better suited to address a low-profitability specialty market than an equivalently positioned bank.

The difference—ownership

Ultimately, the difference between corporate and cooperative organizations comes down to ownership. Banks have a requirement to structure their businesses to satisfy the profit motives of their investor-owners, rather than their depositors. This profit motive has the beneficial effect of encouraging banks to offer a wide array of services, including highly complex services that would not otherwise be easy to provide. It also places the banks in opposition to their customers in some very fundamental ways.

On the other hand, credit unions are owned by their customer/members. Because there is no difference between the interests of the owners and the interests of the customers, credit unions are able to give better rates and better rights for roughly equivalent commodity products. Credit unions are also able to provide specialty services where there may not be sufficient profit to attract a commercial endeavor.

Market profiles and software development

Like banks and credit unions, proprietary and open source software also have distinct market profiles. And for similar reasons to those discussed relative to banks and credit unions, the difference is largely driven by the extent to which the software is serving a commodity or specialty market.

For proprietary software companies, there are two basic extremes. The first is mass-market software, in which the same software product is delivered to thousands or millions of customers. This is the most visible software market, covering most of what people normally think of as "software." Microsoft Windows, Intuit Quicken, Adobe Photoshop, the game *Halo*, and many more, are all commodity-market software. There is no difference between one instance of the product and another.

I noted that the strategy for commodity-oriented banks is to encourage customers to make the initial commitment to the bank, and then to try to upsell the customer on additional services. The business model for commodity-oriented proprietary software is similar—encourage customers to make an initial commitment to the software, and then try to sell additional services, upgrades, or new versions of the software. For example, Intuit's Quicken is configured to encourage Quicken-branded loans as well as affiliated brokerage and tax services. Microsoft's strategy of having differently labeled versions of its Vista operating system (from Starter Edition through Ultimate) is an explicit upsell tactic.

The specialty market for software is much less visible, but it is much bigger financially. Specialty software is customized for each installation or written for a specific company or specific situation. These software products can cost hundreds of thousands (or even millions) of dollars for each copy. Specialty software is the glue that ties together modern business practices.

There are a few well-known names in the specialty software business, such as SAP, Peoplesoft, and Lotus Domino, but most of the specialty software is invisible to people outside the business. Further, a substantial amount of this software is written internally or for a single client; it is never marketed as a distinct product.

The market for open source software

Open source software also has two traditional market profiles, again driven by the extent to which the software is aimed at commodity or specialty markets. Commodity-oriented open source software is generally standards-driven or infrastructural. For example, almost all of the networking code on the Internet, including the software running on proprietary platforms, is derived from or modeled on open source software. Most email delivery systems also run on open source software.

Firefox: A case study in commodity open source software

An even more instructive example is the open source browser, Firefox. Not too long ago, all significant web browsers were proprietary products. For those who remember downloading Netscape for free, only individuals could do that; businesses had to pay for licenses. The market for web browsers bore all the hallmarks of a commodity-oriented proprietary software business. For example, there were deliberate incompatibilities in the code (giving rise to "Best viewed in ______ browser" badges on some websites), free trial offers of associated products (such as dial-up Internet service), and unsolicited direct advertising (such as "push" channels).

In 1995, Microsoft entered the browser market to deal with the far-reaching competitive threat it saw in the Netscape web browser. Microsoft decided to drive the price for this particular piece of commodity software to zero by bundling its competitive browser for free with the Windows operating system. This aggressive market move "cut off Netscape's air supply" and eventually forced Netscape out of business.

In a last-ditch effort for market share, Netscape open sourced the code to its web browser in January of 1998. The web browser known today as Firefox is a product of the open source Mozilla organization created by Netscape to continue the development of its web browser software.

Over the long term, Netscape's open source derivatives, the Mozilla and Firefox browsers, have been able to compete against Microsoft and Microsoft's web browser, even when Netscape couldn't. This is because the Mozilla organization has had two advantages.

The first advantage is that the non-profit nature of open source development lowered the ongoing development costs sufficiently to continue development. From a systemic perspective, Microsoft's bundling of Internet Explorer made it commercially unreasonable for Netscape to continue with the development of Netscape Navigator; web browsers were no longer viable as a for-profit product. By open sourcing Navigator, however, Netscape moved the development of Navigator from a for-profit commodity market to a non-profit commodity market. This lowered the long-term cost enough that the Mozilla organization was able to regroup and effectively compete with a "free" competitor.

The second advantage of the Mozilla organization is that the move from for-profit to non-profit in the browser market has discouraged intentional incompatibility and strengthened the effect of web standards. With no one to fight with in the browser wars, Microsoft slowed development of its browser to a standstill, because it was economically inefficient to introduce new development costs into a money-losing product. On the other hand, the Mozilla organization was able to manage its development around the open standards set by the W3C. Although

Firefox has pioneered several enhancements to web browsing, Firefox's core mission is standards-driven—it must render web pages as accurately and quickly as possible.

One of the most interesting developments in this area has been the reemergence of web browser competition between Firefox and Internet Explorer. The introduction of an open source competitor in the market, however, has changed the ground significantly from the browser wars of the 1990s. Microsoft has greater total resources and is still leading in market share, but Firefox has a lower cost basis for ongoing development and has tilted market expectations toward standards-based browser implementations.

Linux: A case study in specialty-oriented open source software

As with credit unions, the operational profile for specialty open source software projects targets a smaller group of customers with common but unusual needs. Again, the removal of the profit motive allows lower-dollar-value needs to be addressed efficiently.

When Linux was first announced (version 0.02), it was a specialist project targeted at a small, unprofitable group of users with distinct needs. To quote from Linus Torvalds' newsgroup post "Free minix-like kernel sources for 386-AT":

> Do you pine for the nice days of minix-1.1, when men were men and wrote their own device drivers? Are you without a nice project and just dying to cut your teeth on a OS you can try to modify for your needs? Are you finding it frustrating when everything works on minix? No more all-nighters to get a nifty program working? Then this post might be just for you :-)
>
> As I mentioned a month(?) ago, I'm working on a free version of a minix-lookalike for AT-386 computers. It has finally reached the stage where it's even usable (though may not be depending on what you want), and I am willing to put out the sources for wider distribution. It is just version 0.02 (+1 (very small) patch already), but I've successfully run bash/gcc/gnu-make/gnu-sed/compress etc under it....
>
> I can (well, almost) hear you asking yourselves "why?". Hurd will be out in a year (or two, or next month, who knows), and I've already got minix. This is a program for hackers by a hacker. I've enjouyed *[sic]* doing it, and somebody might enjoy looking at it and even modifying it for their own needs. It is still small enough to understand, use and modify, and I'm looking forward to any comments you might have.

In announcing Linux, Linus identified and appealed to his core market—people who wanted a small, hackable, unfinished, hobbyist operating system with substantial drawbacks and a number of bugs. Unsurprisingly, this was an unprofitable market segment generally ignored by the commercial software vendors. Nevertheless, there were enough people interested in working on Linux that it was able to advance through the efforts of several thousand individual hackers.

Today, Linux inhabits several different markets. For some people (such as those at Canonical, who make the Ubuntu Linux distribution), Linux is a commodity desktop or server operating system product. For others (such as NASA, who make custom Linux-based supercomputers), Linux is still a specialty product—a software platform that can be adapted and hacked in response to specific and unusual needs.

Moving software from a specialty to a commodity product

The movement of Linux, at least in most cases, from a specialty to a commodity software product is representative of a number of open source projects. Many times open source projects are created because there is a perceived need that isn't being met by the market. This is sometimes called "scratching your own itch." All of these cases involve a small perceived market (sometimes as small as a single developer) that is apparently unprofitable for commercial vendors to target.

Sometimes, for example, this can be a desire for a better programming language (leading to the development of Perl, Python, and Ruby), the desire to make web applications easier to make (leading to the development of Ruby on Rails), or the desire to publish technical papers (leading to the creation of the World Wide Web).

All of these projects were once specialty open source projects with limited interest and very little commercial potential. Once these projects got off the ground, however, enough people started using and extending the new software that they evolved into projects with substantial commercial involvement.

The last example cited above is especially interesting. The set of technologies that we now know as the World Wide Web—HTML, HTTP, web servers, and web browsers—were originally designed in 1990 as specialty software products to scratch Tim Berners-Lee's itch for a better way to link physics documents at his research facility. By 1996, web browsers were commodity software products and the browser wars were in full swing. By 2004, when Firefox was released, web browsers were open source commodity products. As of this writing in 2008, web browsers are well on their way to becoming infrastructure for other applications.

Ownership, again

So why does open source work? It works, just as credit unions and other cooperative organizations do, because the common ownership of the codebase creates different incentives for those working on the software. No single person generally has control over the code, so the different interested parties are required to cooperate with each other. This cooperation allows development to proceed relatively quickly and at a lower cost compared with purely proprietary solutions.

In addition, there are new market niches opened each time a developer decides to scratch his own itch and create his own project. The shared ownership and involvement in open source allows some of these market niches to grow, becoming important across the industry.

Finally, the shared ownership and resulting lower development cost of open source software can drive adoption farther and faster than proprietary alternatives. In the cases where open source projects become central to some segment of the computing industry, they frequently lead to widespread commoditization and standardization of that segment.

The Role of Open Source Licenses

Open source software projects are driven by the commonly-owned, cooperative nature of development. The difficulty, however, is that the cooperative systems are unstable because there is a tendency for individuals to *free ride* on the work of others.

As discussed in Chapter 1, the free rider problem usually arises around public goods, which are costly and non-excludable. The situation with cooperative development is technically different; instead of being *intrinsically* non-excludable, open source developers make their code non-excludable by choice. Nevertheless, the result is the same. Once somebody has paid the cost of development, the incentive for all others is to use the free code without giving anything back. The role of open source licenses is to align the interests of the cooperating developers by providing the legal foundation for cooperation and trade in intellectual property.

Software Markets and Game Theory

To better understand the role of the law and open source licenses, it is useful to look for a moment at the field of *game theory*—the study of interactions leading to different cost and reward outcomes.

Zero-sum games

One of the fundamentals in game theory is the concept of the *zero-sum game*. A zero-sum game (ZSG) is any set of interactions conducted around a finite resource. Even an infinite resource has only 100% of market share, to be divided among competitors. A competition for market share is also a ZSG.

There are many different examples of ZSGs (markets, for example). If you track any fixed commodity (or fixed basket of commodities) over a period of time, some people will buy and some people will sell, but the collective gain by the winners in the transactions will be exactly equal to the collective loss by the losers.

Another ZSG is the share of advertising dollars spent on different advertising outlets. Over the past several years, the percentage of money spent on online advertising has gone up, by definition driving down the percentage of money spent on radio, television, newspaper, and other advertising. The competition for the pool of total advertising dollars is a ZSG.

It is true that even losers in a ZSG can do well if the total size of the market increases. For example, assume that the total amount of dollars spent on advertising is going up each year—the pie is growing. Even the percentage-share losers can do well (temporarily) in this situation. However, their revenue growth is constrained by another ZSG—the total amount of dollars spent by businesses.

These win-lose situations are fundamental to the structure of the commercial relationship established by proprietary software companies. In the case of software, the profit motive forces certain aspects of the relationship between the companies and their customers into a ZSG. The company cannot win (gain more profit) without the customer losing in some respect, and the customer cannot win (pay a lower price) without the company losing.

Non-zero-sum games

Open source projects are structured differently because they are *non-zero-sum games*. That means that for some particular set of interactions, the total value to all participants in the game will be greater than zero; all people in the game can end up better off than when they started.

Nevertheless, this win-win outcome is not guaranteed. In fact, win-win outcomes generally only occur if both sides cooperate in the face of risk. In this way, the structure of open source cooperation is somewhat similar to the famous game the *Prisoner's Dilemma*.

The Prisoner's Dilemma

In the classic *Prisoner's Dilemma* hypothetical, imagine two criminals arrested under the suspicion of having committed a crime together. Unfortunately, the police do not have sufficient proof to have them convicted. The two prisoners are isolated from each other and each is offered a deal: the one who offers evidence against the other one will be freed. If both of them are silent, they both get a small punishment because of the lack of proof. However, if one prisoner betrays the other by confessing to the police (called *defecting*), the defector will be freed; the prisoner who remains silent will receive the full punishment. If both prisoners confess to the police, they will both be punished, but less severely than if they had refused to talk.

The dilemma resides in the fact that the best outcome overall is reached when both prisoners cooperate. Without knowing what the other prisoner will do, however, the rational course for each prisoner is to defect, serving his own self-interest. Table 8-1 illustrates the consequences for each prisoner for each set of actions, with numbers included to better illustrate the relative payoff.

TABLE 8-1. The Prisoner's Dilemma payoff matrix

	Prisoner B cooperates	**Prisoner B defects**
Prisoner A cooperates	Prisoner A and Prisoner B: Small punishment (–1)	Prisoner A: Large punishment (–10) Prisoner B: No punishment (+1)
Prisoner A defects	Prisoner A: No punishment (+1) Prisoner B: Large punishment (-10)	Prisoner A and Prisoner B: Medium punishment (–6)

In the case of cooperative software development, a similar dynamic applies, which I will refer to as the *Programmer's Dilemma*. When valuable source code to an application is being offered, the rational and self-interested action is to defect by appropriating that source code and not sharing back. If both participants act cooperatively, however, the result is that they are both better off.

Specifically, if both programmers cooperate, they get a large reward (a working application) for a smaller cost (the cost of the contributed code alone). If both programmers defect (i.e., don't share their code), they still get a working application, but they must pay the full development costs. If one programmer defects and the other cooperates, the defector gets a large reward for a low cost, whereas the cooperative programmer pays the full cost for the application.

Table 8-2 shows the *Programmer's Dilemma* payoff matrix for Programmer A. Programmer B faces a similar decision matrix with the labels reversed.

TABLE 8-2. The Programmer's Dilemma: outcomes for Programmer A

	Programmer B cooperates	**Programmer B defects**
Programmer A cooperates	Contribution cost (–5), working application (+10): (+5) Overall	Contribution cost(–5): (–5) Overall
Programmer A defects	Appropriated code (+5): (+5) Overall	Full cost (–10) working application (+10): Zero Overall

Notice that in this model of cooperative software development, the fully cooperative set of choices is the only one that leads to a non-zero outcome when both players are taken into account. It is also interesting that the outcome in the lower right corner (when both defect) is equivalent to the ordinary proprietary development model. There's no cooperation, and therefore each programmer could just as well sit alone in a room and develop code without interacting with anybody.

The problem of suboptimization

The difficulty with the cooperative model, both in the *Prisoner's Dilemma* and in the *Programmer's Dilemma*, is that the cooperative, net positive outcome is unstable. The outcome is unstable because, given players (or programmers) A and B, player A's best choice is always to defect, no matter what player B chooses to do. So if both players are rational and looking to their immediate self-interest, they will not arrive at the non-zero-sum cooperative outcome. This problem is known generally as the problem of *suboptimization*.

Suboptimization occurs whenever solving each *part* of a problem optimally does not result in the best solution globally. This problem is familiar to any programmers who have worked with search strategies or evolutionary algorithms. These algorithms frequently return a suboptimal result when there is a local maximum in the output curve separate from the global maximum.

The rational, suboptimal solution for the people in the *Prisoner's Dilemma* (or the *Programmer's Dilemma*) is to defect and betray each other. If both players make the apparently "wrong" cooperative choice, however, they will both end up better off.

The role of licenses

Open source licenses are the solution to the *Programmer's Dilemma*. Although the classic model has each person making his or her own decisions, in the real world each programmer has a method of affecting the decisions of the other party, by putting a license on the code. Open source licenses serve two functions in a game-theoretic context. First, they allow programmers to signal their cooperative intentions to each other. By placing their code under a license that allows cooperation, programmers indicate to their peers that they are willing to participate in a cooperative solution.

Second, and more importantly, licenses are based in copyright law, which allows the original developer to dictate (to some extent) the users and uses of his code. The legal penalties associated with copyright violations change the decision matrix for other programmers, leading to a stable cooperative (and optimal) solution.

Specifically, the penalties built into copyright law only take effect when someone acts outside the scope of the license. In the case of open source software, the license is written so that a person acts outside the scope of the license when he or she defects, making defecting a less desirable option overall and encouraging the cooperative solution.

For game theorists: the model presented here is simplified and does not address every aspect of open source development. The key finding, however, is that open source licenses alter the payoff matrix in a *Prisoner's Dilemma*-type game, rendering it stable. The model presented here is also in some ways comparable to the findings described in the article "Escape from a Prisoners' Dilemma by Communication with a Trusted Third Party" by Shih-Hung Wu and Von-Wun Soo (*Proceedings, Tenth IEEE International Conference on Tools with Artificial Intelligence*, 1998), in that communication with a trusted third party can help solve the cooperation problems inherent in open source. In this case, however, the trusted third party is the *legal system* itself, as represented through the open source license.

Table 8-3 shows the *Programmer's Dilemma* payoff matrix for Programmer A as modified by the open source license and copyright law. Programmer B faces a similar decision matrix with the labels reversed.

TABLE 8-3. The Programmer's Dilemma, modified: outcomes for Programmer A

	Programmer B cooperates	**Programmer B defects**
Programmer A cooperates	Contribution cost (–5), working application (+10): (+5) Overall	Contribution cost(–5), Reimbursement for copyright violation(+7): (+2) Overall
Programmer A defects	Appropriated code (+5), Pay for copyright violation(–7): (–2) Overall	Full cost (–10) working application (+10): Zero Overall

To return briefly to the credit union example, credit unions have bylaws that allow the different depositors to trust each other and to cooperate in the context of the institution. In the case of open source software, projects have licenses that allow the different programmers to trust each other and to cooperate in the context of the group. In fact, there are two cooperation problems solved by open source. The first is defecting by taking other people's code. The second is a form of the free rider problem; letting others do the work and defecting by slacking off. This second cooperation problem is addressed partially by reducing the cost of contributing code, partially through non-legal community norms, and partially through other sources of motivation like reputation or altruism.

The Open Source Definition

Keeping in mind the cooperation-inducing function of open source licenses, it is interesting to look at the annotated open source definition on opensource.org (*http://www.opensource.org/docs/definition.php*):

> Open source doesn't just mean access to the source code. The distribution terms of open-source software must comply with the following criteria:
>
> 1. Free Redistribution
>
> The license shall not restrict any party from selling or giving away the software as a component of an aggregate software distribution containing programs from several different sources. The license shall not require a royalty or other fee for such sale.

> Rationale: By constraining the license to require free redistribution, we eliminate the temptation to throw away many long-term gains in order to make a few short-term sales dollars. If we didn't do this, there would be lots of pressure for cooperators to defect.

The open source definition is explicit about the purpose for requiring licenses to allow free redistribution: to encourage cooperation and discourage defection. This is the underlying motivation and economic rationale for open source licenses.

At first glance, this first principle of the open source definition is not too different from the FSF's freedom 2, "The freedom to redistribute copies so you can help your neighbor." Nevertheless, they are not equivalent.

The distinction between this part of the open source definition and the FSF's freedom 2 is that the open source definition is normative whereas freedom 2 is rights-oriented. Saying, "everyone should have the following rights," is not sufficient to create the necessary framework for cooperation. What is needed is the enforceable expectation of cooperative behavior, as provided by the second principle of the open source definition:

> 2. Source Code
>
> The program must include source code, and must allow distribution in source code as well as compiled form. Where some form of a product is not distributed with source code, there must be a well-publicized means of obtaining the source code for no more than a reasonable reproduction cost preferably, downloading via the Internet without charge. The source code must be the preferred form in which a programmer would modify the program. Deliberately obfuscated source code is not allowed. Intermediate forms such as the output of a preprocessor or translator are not allowed.
>
> Rationale: We require access to un-obfuscated source code because you can't evolve programs without modifying them. Since our purpose is to make evolution easy, we require that modification be made easy.

Principle 2 describes certain actions—such as providing only obfuscated source code—and makes it clear that this is considered uncooperative behavior. The power of setting such expectations as part of the open source definition is that these principles become part of the industry standard practices for open source. These industry standard practices are considered and given weight when courts interpret open source licenses, bringing the full policing power of copyright law behind otherwise amorphous ideals.

Principle 3 of the open source definition is as follows:

> 3. Derived Works
>
> The license must allow modifications and derived works, and must allow them to be distributed under the same terms as the license of the original software.

Rationale: The mere ability to read source isn't enough to support independent peer review and rapid evolutionary selection. For rapid evolution to happen, people need to be able to experiment with and redistribute modifications.

This further defines the scope of cooperation by making it explicit that others are allowed to modify the code *and* distribute their modifications. This principle is necessary because copyright law separates the right to make derived works from the right of distribution.

Principle 4 of the open source definition states:

4. Integrity of The Author's Source Code

The license may restrict source-code from being distributed in modified form only if the license allows the distribution of "patch files" with the source code for the purpose of modifying the program at build time. The license must explicitly permit distribution of software built from modified source code. The license may require derived works to carry a different name or version number from the original software.

Rationale: Encouraging lots of improvement is a good thing, but users have a right to know who is responsible for the software they are using. Authors and maintainers have reciprocal right to know what they're being asked to support and protect their reputations.

Accordingly, an open-source license must guarantee that source be readily available, but may require that it be distributed as pristine base sources plus patches. In this way, "unofficial" changes can be made available but readily distinguished from the base source.

Principle 4 pulls back somewhat from the unfettered model of cooperation, defining one form of source restriction as acceptable. This restriction may seem unusual, given the otherwise wide-open nature of the open source definition. Nevertheless, there are two facets of the software industry in which this provision can come into play.

First, code has both expressive and functional aspects, and there is a pride of authorship associated with a finished codebase. In one aspect, this provision recognizes that pride of authorship and recognizes a form of the author's moral rights; nobody else is allowed to distribute altered copies of the code.

Another way of looking at this is as an aspect of trademark protection. If someone has made his code an identifying aspect of the product or service they provide, he may use this provision to maintain his mark while still allowing open source cooperation.

For a hypothetical example, imagine a company that markets a product called AuditedBSD, where only code that has been audited by security experts is marketed under the AuditedBSD brand. Allowing other people to include patches and distribute them under the AuditedBSD brand would remove the distinctiveness of the mark. Therefore, the company could use this provision to allow cooperation while still maintaining their AuditedBSD mark.

Principles 5 and 6 of the open source definition exist to combat specific forms of uncooperative behavior:

> 5. No Discrimination Against Persons or Groups
>
> The license must not discriminate against any person or group of persons.
>
> Rationale: In order to get the maximum benefit from the process, the maximum diversity of persons and groups should be equally eligible to contribute to open sources. Therefore we forbid any open-source license from locking anybody out of the process.
>
> Some countries, including the United States, have export restrictions for certain types of software. An OSD-conformant license may warn licensees of applicable restrictions and remind them that they are obliged to obey the law; however, it may not incorporate such restrictions itself.
>
> 6. No Discrimination Against Fields of Endeavor
>
> The license must not restrict anyone from making use of the program in a specific field of endeavor. For example, it may not restrict the program from being used in a business, or from being used for genetic research.
>
> Rationale: The major intention of this clause is to prohibit license traps that prevent open source from being used commercially. We want commercial users to join our community, not feel excluded from it.

In particular, there is a tendency among some businesses to want to share code, but only if sharing doesn't help their competitors. These principles add clarity to the open source definition by forcing those licensing their code to make the hard choice: either cooperate or don't. Cooperation cannot be halfway.

Principles 7 and 8 state:

> 7. Distribution of License
>
> The rights attached to the program must apply to all to whom the program is redistributed without the need for execution of an additional license by those parties.
>
> Rationale: This clause is intended to forbid closing up software by indirect means such as requiring a non-disclosure agreement.
>
> 8. License Must Not Be Specific to a Product
>
> The rights attached to the program must not depend on the program's being part of a particular software distribution. If the program is extracted from that distribution and used or distributed within the terms of the program's license, all parties to whom the program is redistributed should have the same rights as those that are granted in conjunction with the original software distribution.
>
> Rationale: This clause forecloses yet another class of license traps.

The rationale for principles 7 and 8 is explicit—they are included to define other forms of uncooperative behavior and prohibit them. As the rationale for principle 8 states, these principles foreclose classes of license traps.

Principle 9 is as follows:

> 9. License Must Not Restrict Other Software
>
> The license must not place restrictions on other software that is distributed along with the licensed software. For example, the license must not insist that all other programs distributed on the same medium must be open-source software.
>
> Rationale: Distributors of open-source software have the right to make their own choices about their own software.

Principle 9 is based in the realization that there are many different aspects of the software market, some of which are very well served by proprietary software. This principle allows different market participants with different attitudes toward open source software to cooperate together.

The final principle (10) states:

> 10. License Must Be Technology-Neutral
>
> No provision of the license may be predicated on any individual technology or style of interface.
>
> Rationale: This provision is aimed specifically at licenses which require an explicit gesture of assent in order to establish a contract between licensor and licensee. Provisions mandating so-called "click-wrap" may conflict with important methods of software distribution such as FTP download, CD-ROM anthologies, and web mirroring; such provisions may also hinder code re-use. Conformant licenses must allow for the possibility that (a) redistribution of the software will take place over non-Web channels that do not support click-wrapping of the download, and that (b) the covered code (or re-used portions of covered code) may run in a non-GUI environment that cannot support popup dialogues.

Principle 10 has two effects. First, it has the operational effect stated in the rationale—to prevent those receiving the software from inadvertently violating the license because of some incidental aspect of their computing environment. However, it also has a second effect that is legally relevant. Because open source licenses cannot count on any particular clickwrap box or GUI dialog to get assent to their provisions, licenses must accept other forms of user assent, like downloading or running the software.

Different Types of Open Source Licenses

As described above, open source licenses have more commonalities than differences. Before leaving the abstract discussion of open source, however, there is one high-level difference in open source licenses that should be mentioned, and that is the difference between *academic* and *reciprocal* licenses.

Academic licenses receive their name from their historical context: most of them were originally developed and applied to code written in universities. These licenses allow unfettered use of the open source code, including the crucial aspect of embedding the open source code into proprietary applications.

Reciprocal licenses receive their name from the fact that they require each licensee of the code to reciprocally apply the same open source license to any code derived from the originally licensed code. Reciprocal licenses are sometimes called GPL-style licenses, after the most important reciprocal license, the GNU General Public License.

There are fervent advocates of both styles of licenses. Academic (BSD-style) license advocates argue that their licenses grant more "freedom" to the users of the code. GPL-style license advocates argue that the reciprocal nature of the license makes sure that the code *stays* free.

At the core, *both* sides are right. The essential difference between these two styles of licenses is the extent to which programmers are allowed to defect and act in an uncooperative manner. Academic licenses allow defection, while reciprocal licenses do not. Academic licenses thus allow programmers a wider array of licensing options while reciprocal licenses constrain the software to cooperative development only.

Academic Licenses and Instability

The primary concern with academic licenses is that they do not use the power of copyright to modify the Programmer's Dilemma payoff matrix in the same way that reciprocal licenses do. As a result, there is the temptation for individuals or businesses participating in development to defect.

There have been a number high-profile defections using academic-licensed code. For example, one of the most staunchly proprietary companies, Microsoft, ships code with its operating system that was originally licensed as open source under an academic license. Many other companies embed highly successful open source libraries for compression, database access, or XML handling into their proprietary products.

There are two possible responses to the question of instability as applied to academic-style licensed code. Both of these responses demonstrate that the game theory model does not capture all aspects of the situation.

First, there are many times when the code was written for a purpose other than for the use of the code itself. For example, many of the free Unix variants were written for research purposes, not because the writers wanted their own operating systems. By the time the code was completed, the writers of the code already received their rewards (and degrees) and there was nothing to be gained by putting a reciprocal license on the code.

A good example of this situation is the Mach operating system kernel. Mach was developed (and is still developed) at Carnegie Mellon University as an experimental operating system design. This computer science research did not require a long-term reciprocal license for the code, so it was licensed under the BSD license. The Mach kernel is now used as part of Apple's operating system, Mac OS X.

Second, people have the ability to forego short-term gains (such as the gains from defecting) in favor of a larger expected long-term gain (such as the gains from cooperating). Especially if there is already an expectation of cooperation, new participants in the software development process can make the rational long-term maximizing decision to cooperate. Repeated experience and reward for cooperative behavior reinforces that behavior. (Retreating a bit into game-theoretic terms, this models BSD-style licenses as an iterated prisoners dilemma.)

Once again, the Mach kernel is a good example. Although many parts of the Mac OS X operating system are proprietary, the Mach-derived kernel, called Darwin, is still open source. Apple has continued to support the open source development of Darwin and some of the other foundational parts of its operating system.

Choosing a Strategy for Open Source

Different licenses can be applied in different situations. There are costs and rewards associated with both proprietary and open source development; different situations may call for different strategies.

When choosing open source, the most fundamental decisions revolve around the risk of defection. Sometimes, for some projects, the risk of defection is less important than other considerations, such as growing the overall size of the community. In other situations, the risk-reducing nature of GPL-style licenses is preferred. We will look at some more specific situations and the associated specific license choices in Chapter 10.

CHAPTER NINE

So I Have an Idea...

Waking up one day, you have a flash of insight. You *know* your idea will take off—you have come up with the next Facebook or YouTube.

In the meantime, you help out with an open source project that allows people to automate their home stereos. You were recently made a core developer on the project, and it is just starting to get to the point where you know it will be successful.

Wait...you have a job?

You may already be in trouble.

Cautionary Tales

I know it sounds a little far-fetched that simply thinking of an idea or participating in an open source project while employed can get you into trouble. It almost sounds like the setup for a bad legal thriller. If merely thinking of an idea or sending in a patch could get you into trouble, people would be engaged in lawsuits all the time.

The more nuanced answer, which we will discuss further, is that it really depends on the specifics of what you do and the agreements you have already made with your employer. However, that doesn't mean that lawsuits over basic ideas don't happen.

DSC Communications Corp. v. Evan Brown

In 1994, Evan Brown approached his employer, DSC Communications, with a big idea: he had figured out an efficient way to decompile legacy binary code into high-level source code. DSC was initially interested, but negotiations between Brown and DSC soon broke down. Afraid that Brown would sell the idea to a competitor, DSC sued.

At the center of the case was DSC's proprietary information agreement (PIA). The PIA required employees to tell DSC about any new inventions developed or conceived while employed by DSC. It allowed employees to exclude any preexisting ideas or inventions, but any non-excluded inventions, including future inventions, were assigned to DSC as a condition of employment.

Brown insists that he came up with the initial concept in 1976, although he didn't declare the decompilation process on the PIA he signed when he joined DSC in 1987. From Brown's perspective, he hadn't completely figured out the decompilation process, so there was no "idea" to disclose. Further, the decompilation process was not related to Brown's job in DSC and Brown worked on the idea only at home.

From DSC's perspective, the PIA signed by Brown assigned all of the intellectual property developed by Brown during his employment to DSC. Their ownership could be justified by claiming that Brown's development of the process was suggested by the work and training he received on the job.

The difficulty was that when Evan Brown approached his employer, he hadn't written anything down—he had the concept only. Because he had not communicated the specifics of the decompilation process to anyone, Brown had not created any intellectual property as defined under the law. DSC had trouble invoking its standard assignment clause because legally, there was nothing to assign.

A district court judge agreed with DSC and ordered Brown to write the code implementing the decompilation process. Brown fought the decision, but when his final appeal was denied in 2004, DSC was awarded title to "The Solution"—the decompilation process that had only existed in Brown's head.

In the end, DSC spent $500,000 in legal fees to own the 400 pages of code eventually created by Brown. Brown lost his job and was driven into bankruptcy. And the breakthrough decompilation process? It didn't work.

DDB Tech v. MLB Advanced Media

David Barstow was an employee of Schlumberger, an oilfield services company, from the late 1980s until the mid-1990s. As part of his employment agreement, Barstow signed a PIA assigning to Schlumberger all rights to inventions relating to or resulting from Schlumberger's business.

When Barstow came up with an idea for a computer baseball simulator, Barstow's boss and the lawyers at Schlumberger agreed that the project didn't belong to Schlumberger. Schlumberger's lawyer stated at the time, "Dave [Barstow] came...and said this is what I'm doing. If there is any problem with this let me know...[we] discussed it and we don't see how it applies to Schlumberger's business."

David Barstow and his brother, Daniel, developed and patented the baseball simulator on their own time until 1994, when David left to go to DDB Tech, a company formed to commercialize the baseball simulator. Ten years after David Barstow left Schlumberger, DDB Tech sued Major League Baseball Advanced Media (MLB) for infringing the patent.

Before the case came to trial, MLB started negotiating with Schlumberger to buy any interest that Schlumberger had in the patents in suit. Presented with a willing buyer, Schlumberger asserted that it owned all the patents filed by the Barstows, including the patents filed after David Barstow left Schlumberger. Schlumberger assigned its ownership interest to MLB and granted MLB a patent license for the inventions. Based on this new information, the trial court dismissed DDB Tech's case against MLB.

This case is still ongoing. The trial court's decision was overturned in early 2008, and it will probably be several years before this case is finally settled.

Medsphere v. Shreeve

Medsphere is a healthcare software provider. Founded in 2002 by Scott and Steve Shreeve, its organizing mission was to build an open source medical information system for use by hospitals and doctors.

Medsphere's main product, OpenVistA (named for the VA—Veteran's Administration), is built around public domain code originally written by the government. Many different companies have taken the VA's code and created proprietary products with various extensions. According to Steve Shreeve in "Medsphere and Open Source" (*http://shreeve.blogspot.com/*), Medsphere wanted to use the cooperative nature of open source to remove "the stranglehold of 'vendor lock.'" Medsphere could keep the code open and make money by providing customized deployment and management services for hospitals.

In keeping with that strategy, Steve Shreeve, acting in his capacity as CTO of Medsphere, released a number of the company's internal projects on Sourceforge.net. Unfortunately, the code release was a little too open for Medsphere's CEO, who found it "an unwelcome and startling surprise." Quoting from Andis Robeznieks' web article "Medsphere Sues Company's Co-Founders":

> A $50 million, 12-count lawsuit charging misappropriation of trade secrets, breach of contract, breach of duty of loyalty, violations of the Racketeer Influenced and Corrupt Organization Act, commission of computer crimes, intentional interference with contract relations, unfair competition and other complaints has been filed by Aliso Viejo, Calif.-based Medsphere Systems Corp. against the company's co-founders, brothers Steve and Scott Shreeve.

Medsphere director Larry Augustin forced Sourceforge to remove the source code and the lawsuit was expanded to include a number of John Does—the unknown people who downloaded Medsphere's open source code.

Medsphere and the Shreeves settled about a year and a half later. Medsphere now manages a number of open source projects through Sourceforge and still bills itself as a "commercial open source healthcare software company," but the Shreeves were required to leave the company they founded.

Employees and Inventions

These cases are arguably overreaching, but the basic principle remains: if you are an employee, your employer *may* own the intellectual property created by your efforts. Thus, there may be legal difficulties with creating new code, either to use for your own business interests or to advance an open source project.

There are no bright-line rules here; instead, there are a number of interrelated legal issues. We will look at some of the legal doctrines that apply and then at a number of principles that can help keep you out of trouble.

Look At What You Sign

The first and most important principle is that if you have any expectation of participating in an independent project, *look at what you signed*. It is even better to do this before you do anything on your own, perhaps even before you sign the agreement! Employment is a contractual relationship between the employee and the employer. Accordingly, most aspects of what you can and can't do as an employee will be governed by the terms of your employment contract. Only in a few circumstances will other, overriding rights take precedence over the private agreement between you and the company.

Proprietary Information Agreements

If you have come up with an idea, the single most important document that you probably signed is a proprietary information agreement. In both the Brown and Barstow cases above, the PIA was the cornerstone of the company's case against the inventor. The employees had signed the agreement that granted their employers rights over their inventions.

Not all companies have PIAs, but most technically oriented companies will make you sign a PIA as a condition of employment. Companies usually include PIAs in the packet of papers to be signed by each new employee.

AN IMPORTANT CAVEAT

The law governing employment agreements varies from state to state, so there are no specific rules that will prove true in all circumstances. Also, even some of the general principles discussed here will have slightly different interpretations depending on where you are and where your employer is located.

Appendix A contains the full text of an example PIA. I will use text from this example agreement to illustrate some of the issues with PIAs generally, but be aware that individual aspects of this agreement may not apply in your state.

If you have a question about a particular employment contract or a particular PIA, it is worth the expense to have your own lawyer look at the individual circumstances and individual agreements that apply to you. This should be done before you sign a PIA or begin employment if you want the best chance of successfully modifying the terms.

Consideration

You will frequently see PIAs begin with language like, "In consideration of my employment with [Company],...[my salary, etc.]...I hereby agree to the following..." These words establish the PIA as a contract. As discussed in Chapter 7, contracts require *consideration*—something of legal value—to be exchanged to make a contract enforceable. In the case of a PIA, you agree to keep the company's secrets and assign your intellectual property rights (which are valuable to the company) in return for your salary (valuable to you).

Defining Proprietary Information

Because companies do not know what will be important in the future, they include terms that define *proprietary information* as broadly as possible. Proprietary information is the information that the employee officially recognizes as belonging to the company. The following definition is typical:

> The term "Proprietary Information" shall mean trade secrets, confidential knowledge, data, or any other proprietary information of, or acquired by, the Company and each of its subsidiaries or affiliated companies. By way of illustration but not limitation, "Proprietary Information" includes:
>
> (a) this Agreement;
>
> (b) inventions, trade secrets, ideas, processes, formulas, data, lists, programs, other works of authorship, know-how, improvements, discoveries, developments, designs, and techniques relating to the business or proposed business of the Company...

(c) information regarding plans for research, development, new products and services, marketing and selling, business plans, budgets and unpublished financial statements, licenses, prices and costs, suppliers, customer lists and customers ... [and]

(d) information regarding the skills and compensation of other employees of the Company.

Paragraphs (b) and (c) are the most important for software developers. Paragraph (b) covers knowledge as it comes into existence, whereas paragraph (c) protects company *plans* for the creation of knowledge in the future.

As shown by the example language above, almost anything can be defined as "proprietary information" for the exclusive use of the employer. For example, the definition of proprietary information in (b) is designed to encompass every type of intellectual property recognized by the law as well as a number of intellectual works not always recognizable or protectable as a specific form of property, such as "ideas" and "discoveries."

As a rule, employees should assume that any intellectual output they produce while employed will be considered proprietary information and subject to the company's PIA. It doesn't matter if the invention is in a completely different area of technology, or completely unconnected with your work; it still may be covered. The important issue is to see exactly what your particular PIA might say and explore whether any subject areas are excluded or any other limitations.

THE LAND GRAB

Engineers often complain that these kinds of PIAs are unfair; that the employer is trying to pull off some sort of intellectual property land grab. In my opinion, that is too anthropomorphic. Subjective fairness doesn't enter into the equation.

Companies draft overinclusive PIAs because there are significant incentives to write them this way. Expansive PIAs are more valuable to companies and there are no incentives to hold back.

First, there is very little cost associated with having a PIA that is highly favorable to the company. The relationship between employers and employees is typically asymmetric; offers of employment are presented on a "take it or leave it" basis with little or no negotiation about anything but compensation.

In theory, prospective employees could shop around for better terms in the PIA, but almost all tech companies use agreements with similar provisions. Accordingly, it hasn't become a differentiating factor between companies.

Second, expansive PIAs are a good hedge against uncertainty. Nobody knows what will be valuable in the future, so an inclusive PIA hedges the company's bets. For example, in the case of DDB Tech, Schlumberger didn't expect that Barstow's baseball simulator would be valuable 14 years later. When it did become valuable, though, Schlumberger was ready to claim the new market.

Third, there are no legal repercussions for overreaching when defining "proprietary information." Several states limit the application of PIAs when an author or inventor doesn't use company property or time to create the new work. However, even if state-imposed limits invalidate part of the PIA, other aspects of the agreement generally survive. Thus, an overinclusive PIA is better from the company's perspective because it receives the broadest protection allowed under the law. This limits the company's risk and increases the value it receives.

Assignment

The assignment clause is written to transfer the ownership of all "proprietary information" from the employee to the company. A typical assignment clause is below:

> I hereby assign to the Company all my right, title, and interest in and to any and all Inventions (and all Proprietary Rights with respect thereto), whether or not patentable or registrable under copyright or similar statutes, that were made or conceived or reduced to practice or learned by me, either alone or jointly with others, during the period of my employment with the Company.

Most assignment clauses, like this one, are written so that anything defined as "proprietary information" becomes the property of the employer. This claim survives even if the information is not protectable under intellectual property laws—note that the clause includes information "whether or not patentable or registrable under copyright or similar statutes."

This can have practical effects, as it did for Evan Brown. The particular PIA that he signed had an expansive definition of proprietary information, a definition that included ideas still in his head. Accordingly, the court found that Evan Brown's decompilation technique belonged to his employer, even though it had not yet become any sort of recognized intellectual property.

Present assignment and future assignment

One surprisingly slippery provision in the assignment is the simple phrase "I hereby assign." In contrast, some other PIAs include the phrase "I agree to assign" when discussing rights to any inventions.

The difference between these two provisions is that the "I hereby assign" language transfers (in the present) all rights to any inventions that may be created in the future. The "I agree to assign" language only creates a *promise* to assign inventions to the employer.

This apparently minor distinction is significant because it can control when company ownership of an invention begins. If an employee "hereby assigns" all inventions to the employer, the company owns the employee's ideas while they are still inside the employee's head, and there are no special steps required to transfer ownership to the employer. If an employee "agrees to assign" all rights to the employer, the employee must sign over each new invention or creative work as it is created.

This may seem like a very minor distinction, but it was important to both the Brown and DDB Tech cases. Without getting into too many specifics, there are time limits regarding how long a company can wait before claiming or enforcing intellectual property rights in a particular piece of creative output. If the employee "hereby assigns" the rights, however, then the company's claim on the employee's creative output applies immediately, and these time limits tend not to matter as much.

Cooperation with the company

A related PIA provision requires that the employee "assist the Company in every proper way to obtain and from time to time enforce United States and foreign Proprietary Rights relating to Company Inventions in any and all countries." This is sometimes called a cooperation or enforcement clause because it requires that the employee cooperate in pursuing and enforcing formal intellectual property rights.

The cooperation and enforcement clause is different from the assignment clause in that the assignment clause transfers ownership of all proprietary information to the company, while the cooperation clause requires the employee to help secure formal intellectual property rights for proprietary works. Most times, these cooperation and enforcement clauses continue to be enforced even after the job is over.

Restrictions on PIAs

Many states restrict the application of PIAs, so the provisions discussed here may not apply in any particular situation. For example, Delaware law states:

> Any provision in an employment agreement which provides that the employee shall assign or offer to assign any of the employee's rights in an invention to the employee's employer *shall not apply to an invention that the employee developed entirely on the employee's own time without using the employer's equipment, supplies, facility or trade secret information,* except for those inventions that; (i) relate to the employer's business or actual or demonstrably anticipated research or development, or (ii) result from any work performed by the employee for the employer. To the extent a provision in an employment agreement purports to apply to the type of invention described, it is against the public policy of this State and is unenforceable. An employer may not require a provision of an employment agreement made unenforceable under this section as a condition of employment or continued employment.*

This law says that regardless of any PIA signed by an employee, the company can require the assignment only of those inventions that directly relate to the company's business, result from company assignments, or were built with company resources. Anything that has been built

* 19 Del. 805 (emphasis added)

entirely on the employee's own time, is not related to the company's business, and does not use company resources is owned by the employee. It is true that exception (i), inventions that "relate to the employer's business or actual or demonstrably anticipated research or development, restricts the scope of what can be retained by the employee. Nevertheless, this policy provides a carve-out for employees to create and own their own works.

Other states have different policies. California, for example, puts similar limits on PIAs; Nevada and Texas both support more employer-friendly PIA policies.

The Employer-Employee Relationship

The second important principle is that *employers may have rights to employee works even if there isn't a contract.* Even when there isn't an explicit PIA governing what will and will not belong to the company, the company may still have some implicit rights to the intellectual property created by its employees.

Works for Hire

The first category of employer rights has to do with works for hire. A work for hire can be created when an *employee* creates the work *in the scope of his or her employment.* This is because the copyright act defines works for hire relative to the employer-employee relationship. Title 17, Section 101 of the United States Copyright Code defines *works made for hire* as "a work prepared by an employee within the scope of his or her employment."

To determine if this provision applies, the terms "employee" and "the scope of employment" must be analyzed.

Becoming an employee

An employer-employee relationship doesn't simply mean that you work for somebody (as with the common definition). Instead, employee status is determined under an area of law called *the common law of agency.* The common law of agency is used to describe a situation when one person is acting on behalf of another, or in other words, when a person is acting as an *agent.* Under the common law of agency, determination of employee status is generally made according to three factors:

- *The employer has control over the work.* If the company can control how the work is done, has all the work done at the company office, or provides the equipment and tools needed to create the work, the company may have control over the work.
- *The employer has control over the employee.* If the company sets the employee's schedule, controls the assignments given to the employee, and determines who will report to the employee, and to whom the employee will report, the company may have control over the employee.

- *The employer's dealings with the employee are consistent with employment.* This isn't as well-defined, but think of providing benefits, withholding taxes, and saying that the employee works for the company.

These factors are intentionally fuzzy, but traditional salaried or hourly employment almost always applies. Nevertheless, these rules have been applied in unexpected ways in some cases, so it is never safe to make assumptions.

For example, consider a software developer who telecommutes from home. If the developer uses his own computer to write the code, the company is not providing the tools used to create the work—strike one. If the developer works on his own schedule during the day, the company is not exercising control over the employee while he creates the work—strike two. In this case, the developer may be considered an independent contractor, retaining the copyright by default.

The scope of employment

If someone is found to be an employee, any copyrightable works will belong to the employer the works were created while if that person was acting in the scope of his or her employment. The scope of employment includes everything that the employee would reasonably be expected to do to perform the job.

For example, writing code would be within the scope of employment for a programmer and probably for most IT personnel. On the other hand, writing code would probably be outside the scope of employment for a human resources specialist or chef.

Also related are the normal business processes of the company. For example, creating a new copyrighted recipe might not be within the scope of employment for someone working at Microsoft, but it could be within the scope of employment for someone at AllRecipes. Microsoft is not in the business of creating new recipes to share, but Allrecipes could be.

Independent contractors

If a person does work for a firm without being an employee, he is an independent contractor. The default rule is that independent contractors keep the copyright on their own works unless some specific statutory requirements are met. According to the U.S. Copyright Code:

> [A work for hire is] (2) a work specially ordered or commissioned for use as a contribution to a collective work, as a part of a motion picture or other audiovisual work, as a translation, as a supplementary work, as a compilation, as an instructional text, as a test, as answer material for a test, or as an atlas, if the parties expressly agree in a written instrument signed by them that the work shall be considered a work made for hire.*

* 17 U.S.C. § 101

Breaking this down, there are really three requirements for a contractor's work to be considered a work for hire: first, a work must be "specially ordered or commissioned." Second, it must fit into one of the defined categories of works, and third, there must be a prior agreement in writing that the work will be a work for hire.

When the issue of work for hire comes up in a lawsuit, the requirement that something must be specially ordered or commissioned is usually not an issue. The normal process of asking someone to do a job is usually sufficient.

Statutory categories

The most difficult part of this statute is the second requirement. This element of copyright law hearkens back to earlier copyright statutes that allowed copyright protection only for certain types of works. If someone's new creation didn't exactly fit into the statutory guidelines, it could not be protected under copyright.

The current work for hire doctrine for a non-employee is similarly rigid. There are only nine allowed categories:

- A contribution to a collective work
- A motion picture or other audiovisual work
- A translation
- A supplementary work
- A compilation
- An instructional text
- A test
- Answer material for a test
- An atlas

Some cases try to blur the lines around what is a collective work or an audiovisual work, but other cases interpret those categories very strictly.

As a result, many works by independent contractors cannot be considered works for hire. In particular, software and graphic design aren't in the specified categories, although some courts might consider them part of a collective or audiovisual work.

Written agreement

Even if a work is specially ordered or commissioned and fits within the statutory categories, it still cannot be considered a work for hire unless the author of the work agrees in writing, in advance, that the work will be considered a work for hire.

This is different from being hired to create the work; the contract must actually contain the magic phrase "work for hire" or "work made for hire." This language is frequently included in a PIA as part of the assignment clause. For example:

> I acknowledge that all original works of authorship that are made by me (solely or jointly with others) during the term of my employment with the Company and that are within the scope of my employment and protectable by copyright are "works made for hire," as that term is defined in the United States Copyright Act.

When the development of software is outsourced, each contract must similarly include the provision that any resulting works are "works made for hire."

Applying the rules

The logic underlying these rules is that the fundamental creative effort is the conception of something new. After someone conceives a work, it doesn't matter as much whether she creates the new work or directs someone else to create a work.

On the other hand, if there is very little oversight and direction concerning the creation of the work, simply asking or suggesting that something be done is not enough of a creative input to justify copyright ownership. I must stress again, though, it is never safe to make assumptions. Sometimes the courts decide that the two people were joint authors, both with creative input into the work. In that case, each joint owner has full rights to license or sell the work.

Either way, any work, including those not eligible to be works for hire, can be assigned as part of a contract. This is normally done in the assignment portion of a PIA or as part of a negotiated contract.

LAWYERS AND FAILURE CONDITIONS

When programming, one of the most important things you do is deciding how to deal with and recover from failures. One common technique for doing that is called *defensive programming*. A programmer using defensive programming techniques never assumes that function calls will succeed; instead, each call is bracketed by code attempting to handle possible error states.

Law isn't much different. The following is a commonly used full assignment clause in a PIA:

3.1) I hereby assign to the Company all my right, title, and interest in and to any and all Inventions...whether or not patentable or registrable under copyright...

3.2) I acknowledge that all original works of authorship that are made by me (solely or jointly with others) during the term of my employment with the Company and that are within the scope of my employment and protectable by copyright are "works made for hire," as that term is defined in the United States Copyright Act.

The assignment clause here is a good example of defensive lawyering. There are three different ways in which a copyrightable work will be assigned to the company under this agreement.

In the common case, the person signing the PIA is *probably* an employee, so software written by that person is *probably* a work for hire.

If the definition of "employee" leads to unexpected results, the PIA incorporates the second method of creating a work for hire. The language of paragraph 3.2 provides the necessary written agreement so that any "specially ordered or commissioned" works created will be considered works for hire. If the work done by the contractor can be included in one of the nine categories eligible to be works for hire, this paragraph will automatically transfer ownership of the copyright to the company.

Even if both of these methods fail, paragraph 3.1 provides a third method for transferring ownership of the work to the company. Anything created by an independent contractor was almost certainly "made, conceived, reduced to practice, or learned" during the term of employment. This fallback provision also assigns all rights to the company.

Trademarks and other forms of non-patent IP

The doctrine of works for hire applies only to copyrighted works, but the effective result of the assignment described in the "Lawyers and Failure Conditions" sidebar is to assign most non-patent intellectual property of any sort to the employer. For example, think about a trademarked logo; before the logo is ever used in commerce (creating trademark rights), the logo is protected as a copyrighted piece of art. Thus, the copyright assignment is necessary (and sufficient) to control the rights to the trademarked logo. Further, trademarks gain protection when they are associated in the marketplace with particular goods and services. If a trademarked logo is associated only with a company, the trademark rights can belong only to that company, regardless of who originally created the logo.

Patents—Being Hired to Invent

Another situation important to developers and engineers concerns the output of employees who have been *hired to invent*. An employee is hired to invent when the purpose of the job is to solve particular problems associated with the employer's business. For example, a developer working on a highly available web application may discover unique solutions to scaling problems. If an employee is assigned the responsibility of solving a particular problem and does so, the employee is obligated to transfer all patent rights associated with that solution to the employer. This is true no matter where or how the invention is made.

Under normal circumstances, the employee's PIA will require the assignment of the invention regardless. In the absence of a PIA, however, the company still owns all patent rights in the specific solutions created by employees hired to invent. This obligation applies only to problems specifically related to the employer's business; in the absence of a PIA, any inventions created on the employee's own time, with the employee's own resources, and outside the scope of employment are generally owned by the employee.

Prior inventions

One difficult issue that can come up is timing—*when* the employee creates the invention. Inventions that were created by the employee before the job starts do not become the property of the company as a result of employment.

This timing issue was the central problem in the Brown case. Evan Brown argued that he came up with his decompilation process in 1976. DSC argued that he came up with the process in 1996, when he approached them. DSC won the case in part because Brown did not have the documentation to support his argument that he had been considering his idea for 20 years.

When an invention is "made" is still an open issue, but most courts have decided that an invention takes place when it has been both conceived and reduced to practice. This is the same standard used in the patent statute, which requires the inventor to both think of an idea and build it or describe how to make it work in sufficient detail. By this standard, Evan Brown arguably never invented anything because he was never able to get his decompiler to work. (See Chapter 2 and Chapter 3 for discussions of inventorship.)

Invention declarations

The most common way to deal with this issue is an *invention declaration*. This declaration, usually attached to the PIA, asks the new employee to list all previously existing inventions. Anything listed as a prior invention will be excluded from the PIA. This paragraph is typical:

> Prior Inventions. Inventions, if any, patented or unpatented, that I made prior to the commencement of my employment with the Company are excluded from the scope of this Agreement. To preclude any possible uncertainty, I have set forth on Exhibit A attached hereto a complete list of all Inventions that I have, alone or jointly with others, conceived, developed, or reduced to practice or caused to be conceived, developed, or reduced to practice prior to commencement of my employment with the Company, that I consider to be my property or the property of third parties and that I wish to have excluded from the scope of this Agreement. If disclosure of any such Invention on Exhibit A would cause me to violate any prior confidentiality Agreement, I understand that I am not to list such Inventions in Exhibit A but am to inform the Company that all Inventions have not been listed for that reason.

Attached to the PIA will be a sheet giving space to list any inventions. This is one of the most important documents that home inventors and open source contributors can fill out. By specifying projects, even those that are still in the thought stage, new employees will be able to continue their personal activities and retain their rights while employed. There is much more protection for ideas listed on an invention declaration. For example, it was highly significant in the Brown case that Evan Brown put "None" on his invention declaration. Later ideas have a much higher probability of being owned by the company.

Later inventions

A related issue is what happens after the job has ended. Ending the employer-employee relationship does not end any of the rights that were established during employment. In the DDB case, for example, Schlumberger was able to make a claim on David Barstow's patents because their PIA "hereby assigned" all patent rights to Schlumberger. Accordingly, Schlumberger was able to argue that their ownership of the patents started during Barstow's term of employment.

Some PIAs require employees leaving the job to continue assigning the rights to their inventions back the company for a set time period, usually a year. Courts have been generally unfriendly to these provisions, however, often finding reasons why they do not apply or holding them invalid for being against public policy.

Fiduciary Duties

A unique situation can arise when entrepreneurs are employees that hold positions of authority in the company. If someone is an *officer* or *director* of a corporation, she has a *fiduciary duty* to act in good faith and in the best interests of the corporation and the stockholders. This duty obligates her to assign to the company any patent rights related to the corporation's business if the invention was made while the employee worked at the company.

This is true even if the employee/CEO is a major stockholder in the corporation; as long as the employee is acting in the name of the corporation, she has the responsibility to act in the corporation's best interests.

Tell the Company

The third principle to keep in mind is to *always communicate with your employer—in writing*. Both the "communicate" and the "in writing" parts are important.

For developers, the easy and *wrong* approach is to ignore this principle. While at first it may seem easier to ask forgiveness than permission, such a strategy is risky. Assume for a moment that you have a great idea, but you decide not to tell your employer. What happens?

If your idea turns out not to be successful, maybe nothing will happen. Your efforts will attract no attention, no funding, and no lawsuits. This is the best-case scenario.

If your idea is a success it will likely attract attention. In many cases, your employer will then start wondering about the success of your project and why you are not making *their* products successful instead. Perhaps you will be fired. If your project is a substantial financial success, your employer may in fact be obligated to sue you. From the employer's perspective, you may have profited from intellectual property that was, in fact, owned by the company. Your employer's duties to the company and to the shareholders may require him to recover the profits and code that (in his opinion) should have belonged to the company. This lawsuit won't necessarily be successful, but it won't be fun to go through, even if you win.

Communication and the PIA

Communication with the company is important enough that most PIAs include a paragraph requiring that employees must keep their companies informed of any new ideas, inventions, or advances. The following paragraph is typical:

> During the period of my employment, I will promptly disclose to the Company fully and in writing and will hold in trust for the sole right and benefit of the Company any and all Inventions. In addition, I will disclose all patent applications filed by me during the three (3) years after termination of my employment with the Company.

The company includes this provision so that it will have the chance to enforce the other contract rights included in the PIA, in particular, the obligation to assign any new intellectual property to the employer.

Communication Gone Wrong

Of course, it is possible for efforts to tell the company to go awry. Two examples are the Brown and Barstow cases. In the Brown case, Evan Brown approached DSC with his idea as soon as it was fully formed; the company sued and forced him to write out the code.

The problem with the Brown case is that Evan Brown did not tell the company soon enough. If he had told the company up front on his invention declaration, he would have had a clear right to his ideas. Before negotiations broke down, DSC was interested in paying up to two million dollars for Brown's idea. Whether or not the idea worked, this would have been a much better outcome for Brown than losing his job and being sued.

The Barstow case is harder because David Barstow did most of the right things. He talked to his supervisor *and* the legal team at Schlumberger, both of whom signed off on his baseball simulator. Nevertheless, the trial court decided that Schlumberger owned the patents.

In spite of appearances, the Barstow case is the exception that proves the rule. The trial court judge was overruled because he did not give David Barstow the chance to demonstrate how much he told Schlumberger about his project. Quoting from the court of appeals:

> Schlumberger's view that the agreement did not apply (and its silence) would only be significant if Schlumberger had been aware of the nature of Barstow's project. *The crucial question thus was the extent of Schlumberger's knowledge of the project* at

the time that the company's officers concluded that the project was not within the scope of the agreement. The problem is that DDB was [not allowed to proceed] on this central issue" (emphasis added).*

The Barstow case is currently being reexamined by the trial court. If the Barstows are able to prove that they told Schlumberger about their work, they will be able to keep their patents and any patent earnings from MLB.

What Do You Do?

The chapter so far can be summarized pretty easily: if you have a job, your company may own your code and you may get into trouble if you try to start a business or contribute to an open source project. In particular, watch what you sign, because your employment agreements will control what you can and can't do.

So, what can you do? Nothing is a silver bullet, but there are a number of principles that will help keep you out of trouble.

First, Read What You Sign

There are a number of documents that you sign, and they affect what you can do with the things you create. If you have questions about your particular PIA or employment agreements, refuse the temptation to guess about what they mean; see a lawyer. The laws vary so much from state to state that seemingly clear paragraphs may not mean what you think they mean.

Tell Your Employer About Your Project

The most important thing you can do is to be open with your employer about what you want to do. When cases come to court, the most troublesome evidence comes when the inventors tried to keep secrets from their companies. The secrecy *itself* opens the door to the lawsuit and provides evidence of wrongdoing.

Tell Your Employer About Your Project Early

The reason why some developers try to keep secrets is because they are afraid that they won't be able to pursue their ideas. That is why inventors and developers should talk to their employers before they start to do *anything*. Preemptive permission is the most effective.

The key is to approach your employer before you have created any intellectual property at all. For example, imagine that your company makes voice recognition software. If you approach

* *DDB Techs., L.L.C. v. MLB Advanced Media, L.P.*, No. 2007–1211, 2008 U.S. App. LEXIS 3086 (Fed. Cir. Feb. 13, 2008).

your company and get permission to start playing with web applications on the side, they will likely say yes, because that is not directly related to any company products, and it will increase your skills as a developer. If you later approach them saying that you would like to create an application for serving homemade videos over the web, they will again likely say yes. After all, they have already given permission to create web applications in general. If your site then turns out to be the next YouTube, you will have a much better chance at keeping control over your IP because you were open about it.

One very effective time to tell your employer about your ideas is right when you are starting. Most technical companies will have you sign a prior invention disclosure form (as discussed above). Make sure that you include any side projects on that form, even if those projects are in rudimentary form. Excluding projects via the prior invention disclosure form gives the broadest breathing space for development because there is no question about where they came from.

Some companies will allow you to add projects to the list of excluded inventions as they come up, as long as you have told the employer what you want to do. If your company allows this, it is a good habit to get into.

Tell Your Employer About Your Open Source Projects

This same reasoning applies to open source contributions. There is value for employers in letting developers participate in open source projects; the developer stays happy and improves his coding skills at the same time. Therefore, approaching your employer before contributing any code is a positive value proposition for the company.

Getting clearance before you have contributed any code is also important for open source projects. Having clear permissions from each contributor helps ensure that projects are not put into legal trouble later due to intellectual property issues. For this reason alone, the Apache project requires a signed agreement from employers before their employees can become committers on an Apache project. See *http://www.apache.org/licenses/cla-corporate.txt*.

Finally, Tell Your Employer in Writing

Perhaps you shared everything with your manager and corporate lawyer and got their approval for your independent project. However, people move, change jobs, and change their minds. The safest thing is to tell your employer in writing and get a written acknowledgment back. Email is fine; the important thing is to create a record.

CHAPTER TEN

Choosing a License

The following is a typical exchange from an Internet discussion about software licensing issues:

> Person #1: I posted my code under the [license] license.
>
> Person #2: You should have used the [LICENSE] license. It is the only license that is free.
>
> Person #1: I chose the [license] because only [license] really is free!
>
> Person #2: You chose wrong.
>
> Person #1: You only think I chose wrong! You fool! You fell victim to one of the classic blunders! The most famous of which is never choose emacs over vi, but only slightly less well-known is this: never ever license your code under [LICENSE]! Ha ha ha ha ha ha ha! Ha ha ha ha ha ha ha! Ha ha ha....

There have been many hours and pages dedicated to analyzing the difference between different software licenses. Software licensing can be a headache—one of the unfortunate costs that the intellectual property system imposes on society. Nevertheless, we spend the time because it is vital to get these issues handled correctly.

Why Do I Need a License?

Intellectual property (and copyright in particular, which covers source code) is oriented toward preventing use of copyrighted material. Speaking generally, if you don't license your code, it can't be used (legally) by other people.

More specifically, software licensing is about setting boundaries on what other people can do with your code. The complexity of licensing comes from defining and explaining those boundaries in legal, enforceable terms.

Licenses and Communities

The most important thing to keep in mind is that software licenses are social contracts just as much as they are legal documents. When you choose a license, what you are really doing is charting a course for the future, and often you are establishing a relationship to a larger community. A few questions to consider might be:

- Are you interested in commercial, proprietary companies being part of your community?
- Are you morally opposed to proprietary software?
- Why are you distributing the code?
- Are you joining an existing community?
- Are you trying to start a business, and if so, what is your business model?
- What are your expectations for the code and the people using the code?

These questions, while not usually talked about, are at the core of software licensing. If licensing were purely about mechanical and legal choices, licensing discussions would not be so interesting and would not invite such strong feelings. Especially because licenses (and business models and community expectations) can be difficult to change later, it is worthwhile spending the time to understand these questions up front.

No License Required

Under our current copyright law, copyrighted intellectual property comes into existence as soon as someone creates a tangible work. In the absence of any licensing declarations, the default provisions of copyright law are applied, which do not allow any uses other than *fair use*. Therefore, *some* sort of declaration is necessary to allow greater sharing (or greater control).

One option, however, is to declare that no license is required to use the work. This is sometimes referred to as putting works *in the public domain*, but it can also technically be considered a license of its own under property law principles. As described in Chapter 7, one meaning of the word "license" is a unilateral permission to use someone else's property. An author may give others *license* (permission) to use copyrighted materials however they might like.

Some people are surprised that this would be considered, but for others this may be the most attractive "licensing" option of all. Writers write, musicians play, and developers code, even in the absence of financial rewards. The essence of this philosophy was captured by Woody

Guthrie in the late 1930s when he was distributed a songbook to listeners of his L.A. radio show *Woody and Lefty Lou* who wanted the words to his recordings:

> This song is Copyrighted in U.S., under Seal of Copyright #154085, for a period of 28 years, and anybody caught singin' it without our permission, will be mighty good friends of ourn, cause we don't give a dern. Publish it. Write it. Sing it. Swing to it. Yodel it. We wrote it, that's all we wanted to do.

For some artists, the psychic rewards of seeing others enjoy their work may be more valuable than the financial rewards associated with copyright.

Even for those with more commercial purposes in mind, releasing control over code is a good way to encourage other people to use the code. For example, the embeddable database SQLite has seen wide usage in a number of systems, from Apple's CoreData system to Mozilla's new bookmarks database, in part because of its public domain license declaration. Further, SQLite's author has achieved *personal* commercial success as a consultant, being paid to extend SQLite and roll new functionality into the core SQLite distribution. Similarly, web standards guru Tantek Çelik recently started requiring all additions to the microformats.org list of microformats to be licensed under a public domain declaration, with the explicit purpose of achieving maximum possible reuse.

Public Domain Dedications

If this is how you would like to license your work, the easiest way to handle it is to place a public domain dedication on your work. In a file named *COPYING* (by convention, familiar from many other projects), place a copy of the sample public domain dedication (included in Appendix E). At the top of each file, place a public domain declaration:

> The contents of this file are dedicated to the public domain. To the extent that dedication to the public domain is not available, everyone is granted a worldwide, perpetual, royalty-free, non-exclusive license to exercise all rights associated with the contents of this file for any purpose whatsoever. No rights are reserved.

For websites, writings, photos, and other artistic content, the Creative Commons website (*http://www.creativecommons.org/*) has a licensing wizard that will register your public domain dedication and provide links to an easily understandable explanation of public domain licensing.

Moral Rights

An alternative to a public domain declaration is a *moral rights declaration*. A moral rights declaration doesn't have any legal force (in the United States, at least), but it expresses the author's hope that downstream uses will recognize the author's contribution and the integrity of the work. One example is Russell Nelson's tongue-in-cheek moral rights public dedication (MRPD), found in the web article "(Too-)Simple Licenses" (*http://opensource.org/node/239*):

> I am not going to rely on the use of the legal system to enforce the below restrictions on the distribution of this code, therefore I am putting this code into the public domain. However, that does not mean that you are free to do anything you want. I assert a moral right to require you to give credit to myself whenever you take credit for the work you have combined my work with. If you fail to do this, I will tell your mother, your wife, your girlfriend, your mistress, and your religious leader.

More seriously, most countries outside the United States already respect moral rights in authors' works, specifically the right of attribution, the right to prevent false attribution, and the right of integrity. These moral rights are granted above and in addition to the "economic rights" obtained through traditional copyright.

One difficulty with international moral rights concerns the right of integrity. The right of integrity gives authors the right to prevent alterations or mutilations of their work that are prejudicial to their reputation or honor. In some countries, the right to prevent alterations can prevent the creation of derivative works. This can undermine the development of code based upon a public domain contribution. In that case, the moral right of integrity may have to be waived or otherwise restricted.

Proprietary Commercial Licensing

A second licensing option is to exercise tight control over all downstream use of your work. The best example of tight control is traditional proprietary software licensing. The number of different possible tight-control licenses is almost infinite, because the rights granted under copyright can be partitioned arbitrarily.

In the simplest case, the person receiving the software is usually granted only the rights to install a single copy and run the software on a single computer. In these licenses, there are so few rights granted to downstream users that it is relatively easy for the license to specify the few allowed uses. Most shrink-wrapped software, like games, is licensed along this model.

More complex are time-based, seat-based, or other "flexible" proprietary licensing schemes. These licenses try to *partition the market*, charging different users different licensing fees according to their specific needs and ability to pay. The licensing programs for Microsoft Server and Oracle are examples of this model.

There are also some proprietary licenses that allow redistribution of some closed source components. For example, many applications are written in Visual Basic, a proprietary language owned and controlled by Microsoft. These applications require the Visual Basic interpreter to run, so Microsoft has licensed portions of the Visual Basic runtime so that application developers can include it free of charge with their applications, but there are restrictions on what is available as a "redistributable" and which other applications can be linked with the final application.

Any particular application can be licensed in a number of ways, and licensed to many different users under different license agreements. If this is how you would like to license your work, it is worth consulting with a lawyer to create a license that will match your business needs.

Open Source Licensing

The third important option is licensing code under an open source license. This forms a middle ground between public domain and proprietary licensing, and can most accurately be thought of as a spectrum of licensing options. The various open source licenses should be considered in terms of the control that you would like to exercise later over your software.

Academic Licenses

The simplest licenses make very few demands on downstream users, reserving only the rights of attribution (essentially, keeping names and copyright notices intact). These licenses are typically short because it is relatively easy to specify the few restrictions imposed on use. These are sometimes called *academic licenses* because they were originally written for and popularized by universities. The MIT and BSD *2-clause* licenses are examples of this type.

Permissive Licenses

Moving slightly up the scale in control and complexity are licenses that grant substantial rights to downstream users, but include patent, trademark, or public recognition provisions. Works created under these licenses are available for almost all downstream uses, including use in proprietary closed source products.

Although most downstream *uses* of the code are allowed, there are some restrictions on ancillary or peripheral rights granted to users downstream. Most of these restrictions center on things that downstream users might do to legally challenge the authors of a program.

License clauses discussing patent and trademark provisions are common (and important) in this context. Quoting from the Apache License version 2.0:

> 3. *Grant of Patent License*. Subject to the terms and conditions of this License, each Contributor hereby grants to You a perpetual, worldwide, non-exclusive, no-charge, royalty-free, irrevocable (except as stated in this section) patent license to make, have made, use, offer to sell, sell, import, and otherwise transfer the Work, where such license applies only to those patent claims licensable by such Contributor that are necessarily infringed by their Contribution(s) alone or by combination of their Contribution(s) with the Work to which such Contribution(s) was submitted. If You institute patent litigation against any entity (including a cross-claim or counterclaim in a lawsuit) alleging that the Work or a Contribution incorporated within the Work constitutes direct or contributory patent infringement, then any patent licenses

> granted to You under this License for that Work shall terminate as of the date such litigation is filed.

This paragraph has two purposes. First, for the users of Apache v2.0-licensed software, it reduces the uncertainty over software patents generally—but especially over *submarine* software patents. Submarine patents are patents that apply to a certain technology, but are hidden—unpublished or unasserted—during the development of that technology. Once the market matures and the patented technology is in wide use, the submarine patent surfaces and the company owning the patent tries to claim patent royalties from across the industry. In some cases, the companies owning the submarine patents have encouraged the adoption of their technologies by standards groups. One example is Rambus, the makers of RDRAM memory. The Rambus patents are currently in litigation because Rambus allegedly encouraged the standardization of its technology without telling anyone about its patents.

Even in the normal course of patenting, there is an 18-month delay between when a patent is filed and when it is published. Typical computer-related inventions may not be issued as patents for three or four years (or more) after filing. That can be a long time, considering the speed of change in the computer industry.

Many open source software projects, such as the various Apache projects, are in wide use in many industries and across the Internet. The patent license provision helps protect both end users and the Apache projects themselves from Rambus-like surprises.

The Apache License v2.0 states:

> 6. *Trademarks.* This License does not grant permission to use the trade names, trademarks, service marks, or product names of the Licensor, except as required for reasonable and customary use in describing the origin of the Work and reproducing the content of the NOTICE file.

Open source projects gain trademark rights the same way that businesses do: by using their names and logos in commerce and by creating an association in the minds of the public. For example, being accepted as an Apache project creates expectations among developers and users who might adopt the project. These user and developer expectations are technically known as *goodwill* and are an asset of the Apache Software Foundation.

The Apache Software Foundation is required to maintain its trademarks to maintain that goodwill. One of the rules of trademark law is that marks can be lost if they are not protected. The trademark clause of the Apache License v2.0 helps protect and maintain the Foundation's trademark-related IP.

Partially Closable Licenses

The next step up in control (and complexity) are licenses that allow the creation of proprietary, closed source systems using the code while still mandating some code sharing. Good examples of *partially closable licenses* are the MPL (Mozilla Public License) and the LGPL (originally the "Library" GNU Public License, now the "Lesser" GNU Public License).

A key driver of open source is the ability to integrate improvements and modifications made by many different people. Nevertheless, both the academic and permissive license families allow products derived from open source code to be modified and redistributed in a closed source fashion. In practice, closed-source redistribution is frequently not an issue; it is cheaper and easier to integrate improvements with the main line of the project, so the lower costs of sharing the code are usually enough to encourage cooperation. Allowing closed source development also allows commercially oriented businesses to base closed source products on the open source code, leading to a larger community around the code.

Sometimes, though, the initial developers (or the community) decide to require that certain parts of the code be shared. In general, partially closable licenses divide the code into two pieces. All code associated with the first piece must remain open source. The second piece can be distributed without sharing back the source code. Because there is a required separation between the open and closable parts of the application, partially closable licenses usually show up in two areas: libraries and extensible applications.

When a partially closable license (usually the LGPL) is applied to a library, proprietary applications can use an unmodified version of the library in a closed source, proprietary-licensed product. If there are any changes to the LGPLed code, though, the modified source code corresponding to the LGPLed library must be distributed along with the binary application, but the application itself can remain closed source as a whole. Passing changes upstream to the library maintainers is not required, although it is usually done as a courtesy. The goal is to make sure that the functionality embedded in the library is always available to the community under an open source license.

Partially closable licenses thus apply two simultaneous policies to the same code. They allow proprietary coders to reuse generalized library code in a proprietary application without applying open source licensing to the application as a whole. In this case, the value of the application is maintained in the proprietary code. If the proprietary coder treats the library as a thing of value in itself, and modifies it, reciprocal code sharing rules apply.

Extensible applications are usually the mirror image of the library situation. Instead of an open source library with closed source applications, partially closable applications usually have an open source core and allow proprietary extensions. A good example is Mozilla. Mozilla's licensing ensures that the core code will always be available under an open source license, but closed source plug-ins (such as Firefox extensions) and proprietary builds (such as Activestate's Komodo IDE) are allowed.

Reciprocal Licenses

The final stop on the scale of control are *reciprocal licenses*. Reciprocal licenses require that each binary distribution of the code also include full source code to the application. The moment that people or organizations incorporate any reciprocally licensed code into an application, they must release the application's full source code.

Additionally, the people releasing code under a reciprocal license must allow others to freely modify and redistribute their source code under the same reciprocal license. Code is not considered open merely because it is published; it must also be modifiable and distributable.

These licenses are sometimes called *viral* licenses because there is no artificial separation between the open and closed parts of an application, as with the partially closable licenses. If reciprocally licensed code is incorporated into an application, then the application is "infected" —the source code to the entire application must be made available.

Because there is so much confusion around this point, it must be stressed that if someone incorporates reciprocally licensed code into code that is either reserved for personal use or used only within an organization, that individual has no responsibility to release the code. The source code only has to be made open if the resulting program is distributed (in binary or source form).

The best-known reciprocal license is the GNU GPL (General Public License), but there are many others.

License Compatibility

One of the issues to consider when choosing an open source license is *license compatibility*. License compatibility is like blood type compatibility. Two blood types are compatible if donations from two different people can be used together. Two licenses are compatible if code with two different licenses can be used together.

The compatibility of two different licenses is determined by comparing the restrictions imposed by a first license with the restrictions imposed by a second license (usually the GPL). If the restrictions imposed by the first license are a strict subset of the restrictions imposed by the GPL, the licenses are compatible; a person distributing code under the stricter GPL will automatically be in compliance with the less restrictive compatible license.

Appendix D contains a table showing compatibility between the GPL and a number of other open source licenses. When comparing licenses other than the GPL for compatibility, the rule is that code can only move up the chain of control, from academic to permissive, permissive to partially closable, and so on.

Why You Should Not Write Your Own License

Do not write your own license. You would think this principle would be obvious, but it apparently isn't. Many hundreds of people have attempted to write their own open source licenses over the years, and many thousands more have tried to write their own proprietary licenses. Appendix D includes a table of the open source licenses applied to packages in a typical Linux distribution—there are over two hundred.

Some people think they can do it better, clearer, shorter, or with a different arrangement of rights; they can't. Others think it might be thrilling to have their names associated with a new license; it isn't. It is essentially *never* a good idea to write your own license. *Don't do it.* These sections explain why.

You Limit Your Community

The first reason why you should not write your own license goes back to the idea of picking a community by picking a license. Widely used licenses allow projects to tap into broader development communities. They bring in developers and arouse interest just as a function of the license. Of course, applying a widely accepted license to your code is not enough to guarantee success. Many other things are also important, such as code quality and the usefulness of a project. Nevertheless, license issues can present a substantial initial barrier to participation. Many developers will not even *look* at a project unless the license is widely known and widely accepted.

On the other hand, creating and using your own license also puts you in a different community —a community of one. Just as using a widely accepted license creates the opportunity for code sharing and development from a broader group of developers, using your own license confines the possible collaborators for your project to the people willing to work with your license.

Your Code Will Not be Open Source (or Free Software)

A number of years ago, "open source" and "free software" were concepts only. People were free to come up with their own licenses focusing on the principles of source availability and modification rights. These licenses were "free software" (and later "open source") because of their ideological perspective only.

Since the late 1990s, however, there has been an important shift in the terminology associated with free and open source software. Free Software and Open Source Software have essentially become trademarked terms, and they cannot and should not be used by anybody who has not received the approval of either the FSF or the OSI. You may create a *source-available* license, but it will not be an official free software or open source license.

You Will Probably Get it Wrong

Writing a license can be tricky. In Chapter 3, we discussed why it is a bad idea to file your own patent: the law has its own syntax and idioms that need to be respected for patents to be legally effective. Licenses are no different. Without an understanding of applicable law, it is remarkably easy to create a license that doesn't do what you want it to, and can actually prove harmful to the broader community of software developers.

The Artistic License and JMRI

One of Larry Wall's rules for language design is TMTOWTDI (there's more than one way to do it). This rule is applicable throughout Perl, a famously expressive and idiosyncratic language. There is such expressiveness in Perl that valid Perl programs can be written that are *also* valid C, valid Unix shell, or valid Java. There is a price to be paid for this expressiveness, however; many observers complain that Perl is very hard to read and that any particular section of Perl code can be ambiguous unless you understand the entire context around the code.

When Larry Wall decided to license Perl, he decided to follow this same philosophy. He found that a number of people were uncomfortable with the GPL, so he decided to give people a choice. Wall licensed Perl under the GPL *and* under the Artistic License, a license that he wrote himself.

Unfortunately, there are bugs in the Artistic License. In particular, it is legally ambiguous about *exactly* what can and cannot be done with the code. Other projects that have used the Artistic License inherited these same ambiguities.

One project that adopted the Artistic License was JMRI (the Java Model Railroad Interface project). Three years ago, the founders of the JMRI project got into a lawsuit with KAM, a proprietary company that took the Artistic-Licensed project files and integrated them into its own proprietary software product. The problem was not the use of the Artistic-Licensed files in a proprietary product, but that the company took the copyright notices off the files and represented the files as its own work.

When the JMRI case came to court, the ambiguity of the Artistic License took its toll. Key to the court's decision were two phrases in the Artistic License allowing others "the right to use and distribute the Package in a more-or-less customary fashion, plus the right to make reasonable modifications," and the right to "distribute this Package in aggregate with other (possibly commercial) programs as part of a larger (possibly commercial) software distribution."* Based on these provisions, the judge decided that the Artistic License should only be interpreted as a contract, not as a copyright license.

As discussed in Chapter 7, the judge's decision had two legal effects. First, the authors of the JMRI project could not get an injunction; they could not ask the court to order KAM to stop distributing the software. Second, they were not eligible for the higher minimum penalties provided by the copyright statute; they could go after KAM only for their actual damages. Since JMRI was an open source project, these were quite low.

The judge's decision rendered the Artistic License mostly toothless. Beyond the difficulties for the JMRI project, the text of the decision called into question the applicability of copyright remedies for any open source license, potentially affecting the entire spectrum of open source licenses. For further discussion on the JMRI case, see Mark Radcliffe's blog post at *http://*

* *Jacobsen v. Katzer*, U.S.D.C. N.D. Cal., Case no. C 06-CV-1905, decided August 17, 2007.

lawandlifesiliconvalley.blogspot.com/2007/08/new-open-source-legal-decision-jacobsen.html.

This decision is currently being appealed. The Linux Foundation, the OSI, the Software Freedom Law Center, The Perl Foundation, and the Wikimedia Foundation all filed a *friend of the court* (*amicus curiae*) brief with the appeals court, pointing out the problems with the trial judge's interpretation of open source in general.*

The appeal on the JMRI case will be argued after this book goes to press. In the meantime, the JMRI project has switched to the GPL.

ON THE SAME TERMS AS PERL ITSELF...

One reason why the Artistic License is so troublesome as a license is because it is attached to a very successful open source project: Perl. Other people contributing Perl code therefore chose the same license combination as Perl for their contributions. For many modules on CPAN, this was done by including the text, "you can distribute this software under the same terms as Perl itself."

As is the rule with Perl, there's more than one way to do that. Without knowing the entire context of the code, "the same terms as Perl itself" can mean many different things:

- An unspecified semi-open source license written by Larry Wall (Perl 1 and Perl 2).
- The GPL only (Perl 3).
- Dual-licensed under the GPL and "any version" of the Artistic License (Perl 4 and Perl 5, including the current 5.10 version).
- Perl 6 does not yet (fully) exist, but Parrot (the official in-progress virtual machine for Perl 6) is licensed under the Artistic License 2.0, and Pugs (another in-progress virtual machine) is dual-licensed under the GPL and the Artistic License v2.0, and under some circumstances is available under the MIT license.

Choosing an Open Source License

Choosing a license can be both easy and difficult. A number of factors enter into the choice, the most important of which are the hard decisions about the business and community expectations you have for your software. After that initial decision, however, the remaining decisions can be broken down into a relatively easy series of steps.

* The amicus brief itself is available at *http://jmri.sourceforge.net/k/docket/cafc-pi-1/ccc_brf.pdf.*

Joining an Existing Community

The first decision is whether your code is intended for use with an existing open source project. If your work will be shared with an existing community, particularly a large existing community, you should consider using the predominant license.

For example, contributors to the Linux kernel should use the GPL version 2 (GPL2). Contributors to the Eclipse IDE should use the Eclipse Public License. Contributors to OpenSolaris should use the Sun Common Development and Distribution License (CDDL), and so on.

The exception to this rule is when the community is using a license that is either proven legally deficient (such as the Artistic License) or is obscure enough that it is not recognized as either free software by the FSF or open source by the OSI. In that case, you can participate in the community by licensing your code under an academic or permissive license: the BSD License, the Academic Free License (AFL) or the Apache License (AL). Other developers will still be able to use your code, and you will be able to use theirs.

Licensing Your Own Work

When licensing your own work, there are hundreds of licenses available to choose from: Appendix B includes a list of approved open source licenses, Appendix C includes a list of approved free software licenses, and Appendix D includes a list of licenses used in the Fedora Linux distribution.

In fact, there are far too many licenses. A number of other books discuss and analyze open source licensing, including Andrew St. Laurent's *Understanding Open Source and Free Software Licensing* (O'Reilly) and Lawrence Rosen's *Open Source Licensing: Software Freedom and Intellectual Property Law* (Prentice Hall). Both of those works go into more detail about the specifics of each license.

Recommended licenses

Unless you are confronted with very special circumstances, there are only a few licenses you should consider for your own work. Those licenses are:

- The 2-clause BSD license
- The Apache License version 2.0
- The Mozilla Public License
- The Lesser/Library GPL, version 2 or 3
- The GNU GPL, version 2 or 3
- The Open Software License version 3.0

These licenses cover the range from very permissive to fully reciprocal. One of these licenses should be appropriate for almost any purpose. Copies of all these licenses are included in Appendixes F-M.

The BSD License

The BSD License is an academic license, and the shortest and simplest of all the recommended licenses. It has relatively few restrictions and as such is generally compatible with every other license, including various proprietary licenses.

One advantage of the BSD license is that it is relatively easy for BSD-licensed code to be brought into corporate products or established as part of a standard. For example, the KAME project was started in 1998 as a joint effort between a number of Japanese networking and electronics companies to develop a free, high-performance IPv6 networking stack.

In part because of its BSD licensing, the KAME reference implementation was integrated into a number of commercial products, including the FreeBSD, OpenBSD, NetBSD, and Mac OS X operating systems, Hitachi and Fujitsu routers, Extreme and ALAXALA switches, CEC camera servers, and Ricoh printers. The leaders of the KAME project were also brought into the IETF (Internet Engineering Task Force) committee on IPv6 and significantly affected the implementation of IPv6 around the world.

The Apache License v2.0 (Apache)

The Apache License version 2.0 and later is a permissive license and a good default choice if no other licenses seem to fit. The Apache License allows a wide variety of downstream uses in both the closed and open source worlds. Apache-licensed code is compatible with both proprietary software *and* the GPL version 3.0 (although not within the same application—compatibility with proprietary licenses or the GPL is strictly one-way).

The Apache License includes a number of provisions that make it particularly useful for open source projects. As previously noted, the Apache License includes trademark and patent provisions, which protect open source projects as they gain more users.

The same trademark and patent provisions that help open source projects also help fee-for-support open source business models. Even though the code is open source, the Apache License does not grant any downstream control over the trademarks associated with the code—the marks must be licensed in association with the product. Several companies have followed this model, including Stronghold and Red Hat.

It is also useful that the Apache License includes provisions governing the *submission* of new code contributions. Although it is best to have an explicit contributor agreement (as discussed in Chapter 11), open source projects can start out just accepting contributions under the Apache License and still be confident that they have the necessary IP rights to advance the project.

The Mozilla Public License (MPL)

The MPL is one of the most important and successful licenses to be developed in the last 10 years. It successfully straddles the line between the laissez-faire of the academic licenses and the significant restrictions inherent in the reciprocal licenses. By developing this middle ground, the MPL has established itself as the most business-friendly free software license that also requires some reciprocal sharing of code.

There are three key elements to the MPL. First, the MPL includes a clear model of how open source projects are established and grow over time. There is an *initial developer* who releases *original code*. As allowed under copyright law, the initial developer has a number of special rights, including the express right to apply multiple licenses to the original code. Subsequent contributors make *modifications* to the original code. As these modifications grow, covered code (defined as either original code from the initial developer or modifications to the original code) is maintained with reciprocal license obligations. This embedded logical model of open source development strengthens the license and allows for a clear understanding of each party's roles and obligations.

Second, the MPL is a reciprocal license that only applies to *files*, not projects. This is a subtle distinction, as the GPL also applies to individual files within larger projects. The GPL's provisions, however, are all designed to apply to the program and the distribution or modification of the program; smaller units of code (such as files) are considered part of the program.

In contrast, the MPL does not concern itself with any entity higher than the file. The basic entity of the MPL is *covered code*. The MPL allows the covered code and other code to be used to create a *larger work*, but the license is carefully constructed to apply only to the Mozilla-licensed code, and not to any other code that might be in the larger work. The effect of this provision is that a company can create a core product that is covered under the MPL and use that product as an open source base for proprietary innovation, while the underlying source remains free software.

Third, the MPL has a much more thorough treatment of patents than the other licenses recommended here. The MPL contains both patent licensing and patent defense provisions. Relative to patent licensing, code covered under the MPL is accompanied by a patent grant to exercise any patent rights associated with the Mozilla-licensed code only. Subsequent contributors must also grant reciprocal patent rights that cover just their modifications. This arrangement of patent grants draws a line of patent protection around the Mozilla-licensed code while still allowing the use and sale of patented technology in other contexts. Further, it *sometimes* allows patented code licensed from a third party to be used in an open source context. This is a unique and useful aspect of the MPL.

Relative to patent defense, the MPL contains the equivalent of an intellectual property *poison pill*. A poison pill is a business tactic used to defend companies against hostile takeovers. If a hostile company attempts to take control, poison pill provisions in the company bylaws automatically take effect, drastically increasing the cost or difficulty of completing the acquisition.

The MPL's intellectual property poison pill takes effect if a hostile party sues for patent infringement in court. Immediately upon filing the suit, *all* patent licenses under *all* Mozilla-licensed code are terminated, even for code not associated with the lawsuit. This deters patent infringement suits by drastically increasing the costs and dangers of the lawsuit. This intellectual property poison pill has a downside—some commercial contributors may be put off by the broad scope of the patent termination clause. In that case, Sun's CDDL is very similar to the MPL version 1.1, but scales back this provision.

There are a number of other provisions to the MPL. Discussion of each provision is not necessary here, except to note that the MPL does a good job of dealing with a number of real-world legal issues that can otherwise cause problems. See *Understanding Open Source and Free Software Licensing* (O'Reilly, 2004) and *Open Source Licensing: Software Freedom and Intellectual Property Law* (Prentice Hall, 2004) for substantive legal analysis of the MPL. The careful wording and excellent legal work that went into the MPL make it a good choice for open source licensing in a corporate context.

The Lesser/Library GPL (LGPL)

In the world of open source licensing, the LGPL occupies the same ecological niche as the MPL. Like the MPL, it allows reciprocally licensed code to be used in the context of a proprietary software application, while still maintaining the licensed code as free software. In fact, the LGPL and the MPL are similar enough that the MPL could be seamlessly substituted for the LGPL in almost every circumstance.

In practice, the MPL is most often used for larger platform or infrastructural projects, whereas the LGPL is used for libraries and small pieces of well-defined accessory code. However, there are a few large projects that use the LGPL to maintain critical pieces of infrastructure. For example, the Wine project (a Microsoft Windows compatibility layer for Unix) has successfully used the LGPL over the past five years to maintain its user and developer base.

The one solid advantage of the LGPL is the size and vitality of the community associated with the license. The Wine project provides a good example of this benefit. Early Wine releases were under the MIT license, an academic-style license with few restrictions. Although commercial support for Wine was always a goal, the project switched to the LGPL in 2003 over concern that improvements to the core Wine code were not being contributed back to the community.

When Jeremy White (one of the core contributors to Wine) was asked about the effects of the license change, he noted the effect of the LGPL license change on the Wine community (*http://interviews.slashdot.org/article.pl?sid=04/05/17/0057241*):

> [A] number of people seem to prefer the LGPL; we seemed to get an influx of new blood to the project as a result of the change. Further, our cooperation with other

xGPL projects like ReactOS improved, and so we got some further energy from there as well.

If community development is the highest priority for your project, or if your code has to interact with other GNU-licensed projects, the LGPL may be a good choice. In considering the differences between the LGPLv2 and the LGPLv3, the best answer is probably dual licensing under both version 2 and version 3 as discussed relative to the GPL below.

The GNU GPL

The GPL was the original reciprocal license and it remains the most popular free and open source license today. The *copyleft* concept embodied in the GPL was a revolutionary new way of thinking about intellectual property, and is still vital and important today. It is unlikely that open source and free software as we know them today would have developed without the GPL.

At its core, the GPL is a very simple license; if I share my code with you, you should share your code with me. The GPL imposes downstream restrictions on later uses of the code to prevent anyone from taking away the benefits of the shared code. Within the world of the GPL, code shared once is code shared forever.

It is important to note that the GPL requires this sharing at the level of the program, which is defined very generally (in the GPL version 2) as, "either the Program or any derivative work under copyright law: that is to say, a work containing the Program or a portion of it, either verbatim or with modifications."

This definition of "program" is noteworthy because it captures both the strength and the weakness of the GPL as a license.

One strength is that this definition of the program gives the GPL its "viral" nature. As noted earlier, if GPL-licensed code is incorporated into an application, then the entire application is infected—the source code to the entire application must be made available. This is because the GPL doesn't really recognize any licensed units smaller than the program.

A good analogy is the use of significant digits in engineering applications. For example, imagine an equation with solutions that can be guaranteed only within a range of values. Because of the rules about significant digits, the specific numbers used within the equation (like 5.65831 versus 6.24897 versus 6) don't matter. Having values *anywhere* within the allowed range results in an overall correct answer.

Using GPL-licensed code works in a similar fashion. Because of the rules in the GPL, it doesn't matter how many specific lines of GPL-licensed code are used within a work. If there are a sufficient number of GPL-licensed lines *anywhere* within the code base, the program must be licensed under the GPL. When considered from Richard Stallman's perspective that sharing is a moral right, this is a brilliant way to spread the sharing of code.

A weakness of the GNU GPL is that the definition of "program" highlights the fact that the GPLv2 has a number of legal ambiguities. These ambiguities create uncertainty about the GPL (all versions) and discourage some people and companies from using GPL-licensed code.

For example, this definition of a program commits one of the basic sins of legal writing—defining a term twice. Quoting the GPLv2 again, the license applies to "either the *Program or any derivative work under copyright law*: that is to say, *a work containing the Program or a portion of it, either verbatim or with modifications*" (emphasis added). This language suggests that "a derivative work under copyright law" is equivalent to "a work containing the Program or a portion of it, either verbatim or with modifications." This is not the case.

A similar issue arises with the interpretation of the GPL as a whole. Is the GPL a "bare license," giving conditional permission for others to use the covered intellectual property, or is it a contract, which includes an intellectual property license as a provision? Nobody knows. Lawyers debate this issue, but until a *court* looks at the GPL, it is a sort of Schrödinger's license, existing as both simultaneously.

Fortunately, the GPLv2 is one of the most highly analyzed licenses in the world. The wealth of excellent analyses of the GPLv2 and its various provisions help the situation. Nevertheless, the existence of these legal ambiguities is a serious flaw in the GPLv2 because nobody really knows exactly how far the GPL applies. Given that copyright law imposes significant damages for copyright infringement, nobody is especially eager to find out.

The GPL raises some very complex issues, discussed in much more depth in Chapter 12. Ultimately, however, the greatest strength of the GPLv2 is the strong community of developers that have accepted and embraced it for their projects. The GPL has created a large community of interoperable software—interoperable at the source and the sharing level. If wide community participation and the morality of sharing are important to you, the GPL may be a good choice.

The GPL version 3 (GPLv3)

The GPLv3 was released in 2007 after a lengthy public comment period and several drafts. The GPLv3 was drafted to eliminate some of the legal ambiguity associated with the GPLv2, as well as to forestall abuses that the drafters perceived possible when analyzing license issues in the computer field.

As a result, the GPLv3 is a significantly stronger license. It has been internationalized in its terms and brought up to date with patent provisions. The GPLv3 is thus a better and surer foundation for future development than the GPLv2.

Nevertheless, the GPLv3 still has some drawbacks. There are a number of provisions in the GPLv3, such as the "anti-Tivoization" and anti-Digital Rights Management provisions that may make the GPLv3 unworkable in some contexts. The GPLv3 continues its Schrödinger's license existence as license versus contract, and there is still uncertainty regarding the GPL and how it interacts with the copyright concept of derivative works. Finally, the GPLv3 is incompatible with the GPLv2, and doesn't have as large a community of projects associated with it right now.

If you decide to choose the GPL (or the LGPL) for your project, it may make sense to dual-license your code under the GPLv2 and the GPLv3, allowing downstream users to choose the version they prefer.

The Open Software License (OSL)

The OSL is a copyleft-style reciprocal license. It has the same practical effects as the GNU licenses and is essentially interchangeable with the GPL. Nevertheless, the OSL makes the list of recommended licenses because it is legally sound. Noted open source lawyer Lawrence Rosen wrote the OSL with the intent of reducing the legal ambiguity surrounding the GPL.

The OSL is a good choice in situations where GPL-style free software licensing is desired but the GPL itself is legally, socially, or economically unviable.

CHAPTER ELEVEN

Accepting Patches and Contributions

Imagine that you are a developer with a new open source project. You got permission from your employer (Chapter 9), you chose a license (Chapter 10), and you released version 0.01 on the Web. The next day, you received a bug report and a patch.

Great, but who owns the bug report? Who owns the patch? Can you use them?

Most people would answer that of course they can use the patch—after all, that is why the contributor sent it in. Unfortunately, that is not the whole story. Open source is a great mechanism for sharing code and sharing ideas, but it relies upon copyright to function smoothly. Therefore, proper copyright licensing has to be respected.

Back to (Copyright) Basics

Copyright is sometimes called the "metaphysics of the law" because it can get so theoretical about the interplay of ideas, expressions, and works. It should not be surprising, then, that the first item to be determined is whether a patch is a "work" that is eligible for copyright protection.

Rules for Works

Unfortunately, courts have not established a clear, easily applicable standard regarding whether or not something is a copyrightable work, especially in the software realm. Nevertheless, there are a number of good rules of thumb that can help you make this determination.

Patch length

The first thing to look at is the length of the patch. While there is no set length for determining whether something is a copyrightable work or not, many courts have found that very short contributions are not considered works for purposes of the copyright law. This could be because very short contributions can fall under the words and phrases doctrine. If a particular expression is so short that there are only a few ways to express it, then the expression is not copyrightable and is not a "work" that has to be analyzed under the copyright law.

Of course, "very short" isn't a very exact definition, but the courts have not given a specific number of characters or lines that qualify as "very short." The GNU projects consider anything under 15–20 lines to be very short and do not require any additional paperwork; other projects go up to 25 or 50 lines.

Patch context

Another aspect to look at is the context of the patch. A patch that implements a particularly tricky function or has an elegant expression of an algorithm is more likely to be considered a "work" than a patch that deals with more mundane aspects of the code.

In a similar vein, it can be helpful to look at anything that might be considered expressive. Comments and non-requisite functions are much more likely to contain copyrightable expression. On the other hand, even large patches that are just mechanical (like patches that fix code indentation or globally rename a particular function) are unlikely to contain any copyrightable expression at all.

Code ideas

A final factor to consider is whether patches and bug reports just contain *ideas* for code or whether they contain the final code itself. For example, imagine a bug report or feature request that contains extensive documentation about some piece of functionality in the program. The bug report itself may be a work, but if there are no elements from the bug report that will go directly into the codebase, then there is no "work" to be integrated with the code. However, if some of the bug report text is integrated into the code, perhaps as a comment, then there may be a copyrightable work to consider.

Owner of a Lonely Patch

If a particular bug report or patch contains copyrightable content, then it is important to note that the owner of the patch is the *author*. One mistake that developers sometimes make is to assume that any patch submissions grant copyright ownership of the patch to the project maintainer. This is not so.

Federal law says that copyrights (like many other forms of intellectual property) can only be transferred with an *explicit* assignment *signed* by the author. Any other sorts of transfers (such as sending in a patch) are sufficient to give some rights to the receiver, but are not enough to transfer ownership.

In fact, although an author may have sent a copy of a patch to a software developer, the software developer has very few (if any) rights to the creative work embedded in the patch. For example, imagine that a musician sent a copy of her newest CD to the same developer. There would be no question that the musician retained copyright over her music. By the same token, the author of a patch retains all rights over the patch.

Assuming that the submission is just a bare patch, the project maintainer doesn't really have many rights at all. There is an implied license from the patch owner to apply the patch to the project sources (and perhaps to copy, publish, and distribute the patch), but the key thing to note is that this is an *implied* right based upon the implications of receiving a patch. There are no explicit grants at all and the default copyright rules grant very little latitude for unlicensed use. Any use beyond the scope of the implied license is not authorized and is therefore a violation of the copyright—a situation that could conceivably become very difficult if someone decided that he didn't want his patch to be part of a particular project.

The open source amalgam

If a copyrightable patch is applied to an open source project, the ownership structure of the project changes. The new code tree is a derivative work of the original code and the patch together. The original author has superior rights, including the ability to prohibit any downstream publication or distribution of the derivative work in combination with the underlying work. However, both the original author's and the patch author's continuing agreements are necessary to maintain distribution of the complete project.

Further, suppose that a second patch is submitted to the project. In that case, both the original author and the author of the first patch would be upstream "original" authors, relative to the author of the second patch. The result is that any active open source project can create a very complex chain of ownership in a very short period of time. Because all the authors of the various works need to agree on licensing and distribution arrangements for the combined project, licensing open source projects can become unwieldy.

Three Solutions

It is probably becoming obvious that creating open source projects with unregulated contributions can quickly become unworkable. In fact, one of the fastest ways to doom a promising project is to create an active project with no copyright licensing and assignment policies. Just at the time such a project acquires enough momentum and enough contributors to succeed, there may be too much copyright inertia (or uncertainty) to allow many other potential developers—including businesses—to participate.

Developers contributing code to open source projects, therefore, should make sure that there are explicit policies governing the receipt and licensing of outside patches and contributions. Without such an agreement, it is possible, or even likely, that any contributed code will end up in an unproductive legal limbo.

From a project maintainer's perspective, though, the set of choices is a little more complex. There are three different ways of dealing with the licensing of open source projects, and it may make sense to transition from one choice to another over the lifetime of the project.

Open Source Licensed Contributions

The first method of dealing with open source copyright issues is to require that all new contributions be licensed under a preferred existing open source license. Requiring an open source license for all contributions helps confirm that all users—the project maintainer as well as all downstream users—have sufficient rights to run and distribute the code.

One particularly easy way to handle this issue is to cover the entire project under a license that has a contributions clause, such as the one included in the Apache License, version 2.0:

> *Submission of Contributions.* Unless You explicitly state otherwise, any Contribution intentionally submitted for inclusion in the Work by You to the Licensor shall be under the terms and conditions of this License, without any additional terms or conditions. Notwithstanding the above, nothing herein shall supersede or modify the terms of any separate license agreement you may have executed with Licensor regarding such Contributions.

By using a license with this specific provision, projects are empowered to accept contributions. This is a very powerful and easy way to handle the copyright assignment issue, because it doesn't matter whether a particular contribution is a copyrightable work or not—if something can be copyrighted, then the contributions provision of the license applies.

This method of dealing with contributions is the most appropriate for small, just-starting projects. It keeps the barrier to participation in the project very low—all sorts of people can easily participate without having to carry out specific individual registration.

Contributor License Agreements

A slightly more sophisticated solution for open source project licensing is an explicit *contributor license agreement* (CLA). Any project that has grown beyond 10 contributors should start using explicit CLAs.

A CLA is an explicit grant that covers all contributions of code. First, the CLA requires that all contributors document their contributions as their own private work, and second, it requires all contributors to promise that they are indeed allowed to contribute their work. Finally, the CLA grants all applicable copyright and patent licenses needed to use the code. The requirements of the CLA lead to clear expectations for the code and protect the project and its participating contributors. They also allow companies to reduce or remove their exposure to the risks involved in dealing with and distributing open source code.

Although some very small projects can get by with something like the Apache license, any project that has corporate or foundation backing should use a CLA. For example, contributors to the Google App Engine project are required to sign the Google CLA, contributors to Python are required to sign the Python Software Foundation CLA, and contributors to MySQL are required to sign the MySQL CLA.

Corporate Contributor License Agreements

In Chapter 9, we talked about employer ownership of code. Under most proprietary information agreements, the employer owns all ideas and code developed by the employee, regardless (in most cases) of whether that code was developed on company time or on the employee's own time.

As a result, any employees that participate in open source development during off hours can be putting the projects they contribute to at risk. Just as open source projects cannot afford to have individual claims on parts of the code, they similarly cannot handle having parts of the code encumbered by trade secret, copyright, or patent claims.

The solution for open source projects—as for personal projects—is full disclosure. Most projects that require a personal CLA also require a corporate CLA for all employed contributors.

The requirements for corporate CLAs provide a good model for the type of corporate disclosure normally required for individual developers:

- Corporate CLAs are required before any code is checked into the project, before any real development has taken place (as described in Chapter 9).
- Corporate CLAs must clearly communicate which open source activities the developers are going to contribute. Most corporate CLAs require that an officer of the contributor's company (usually a VP or higher) sign the CLA on behalf of the company, indicating his or her title.

Corporate CLAs can usually be signed to cover individual developers, particular groups of people, or blanket contributions to particular projects.

Copyright Assignment Forms

If you require more sophistication than a CLA can provide, you might consider using a *copyright assignment form*. The difference between copyright assignment forms and CLAs is that with a copyright assignment form, each contributor is required to assign partial or complete copyright ownership to the project maintainer. The project maintainer then grants the contributor a license to exercise all rights associated with the contribution (a *grantback* license).

Copyright assignment forms are stronger than simple license agreements, so they only tend to be used on the oldest, largest, most centralized projects. For example, the FSF collects copyright assignment forms for any projects established as part of the GNU system. Similarly, Sun has a copyright assignment form for its projects.

Copyright assignment forms are drafted to provide some of the same guarantees and promises for the project as CLAs. In general, these assignment agreements:

- Grant copyrights to the project controller.
- License any patents bearing on the contributions.
- Affirm that the contributions are original works.
- State that there are no other restrictions on the code (like patents or employer's rights).

Unified legal control

There are several reasons to use copyright assignment with a grantback license, as opposed to using ordinary licenses or CLAs. First, copyright assignment allows a single entity to act as a legal control point to handle any licensing disputes or copyright enforcement actions. In order to represent a code base against legal challenges, a single entity must have copyright ownership of all the code in that project.

A good example of this is the BusyBox project. The BusyBox project is a collection of common shell utilities in a single tiny binary. BusyBox has been used in a number of systems, particularly in embedded systems that require small and efficient code. When people found out that BusyBox was being distributed in proprietary products without adherence to the license restrictions, the Software Freedom Law Center (SFLC) was able to file suit on behalf of the project because tthere were only two people that owned all the copyrighted code. The same legal action would have been more difficult and expensive if ownership of the code had been distributed among a number of different parties.

Simplified relicensing

If a project's copyrights are consolidated under a single individual or party, it is much easier to relicense the project when necessary. Usually, the initial choice of licenses is intended to be permanent, but the opportunity to relicense code has become increasingly important. One reason that code may have to be relicensed is if the existing licenses change. For example, the GPL recently underwent a revision from version 2 to version 3. The Perl community is still working out how to change the Artistic License, and the Apache License went from version 1.1 to 2.0.

If a project's copyrights are consolidated under one holder, it is possible to adjust to changing conditions by simply relicensing the whole code base as necessary. Conversely, if control of the copyrights is fragmented, a license change means that each contributor must be contacted in an attempt to secure his or her permission for the change. For example, the Linux kernel has famously fractured ownership. Because of that fractured ownership it would be very difficult to re-license the kernel from its current GPL2.

Commercial licensing

Another benefit of copyright assignment in commercially backed open source projects is that it allows a commercial holder of open source code to create proprietary distributions of the code. From an individual contributor's perspective, this may not seem like much of a benefit, but there are currently a number of companies that don't allow any GPL-licensed or open source-licensed code in their products. For example, the open source company Funambol uses its ability to provide commercial licenses for open source risk-averse companies to create market opportunities in the short term and ultimately increase support for free and open source software.

Administrative Issues

License agreements come with a number of administrative issues that can make the difference between a project that is viable for the long term and one that is not. These administrative tasks are a cost imposed by the system. Choosing good practices for handling these issues, though, can substantially reduce such costs (and any associated risks).

Keep Track of Contributors

One of the easiest and most important things that code maintainers can do is to make sure that there is a record of all contributors. This information can be integrated with the project's source code control system. Just about every source code repository allows administrators to keep track of who made which check-ins. Some repository systems also allow comments to be included at check-in time. If a developer has been granted repository commit privileges, then her username will be associated with her contributions. If someone is doing a commit on behalf of another user, the comment field can be used to record the original author of the contribution. Without these records, reconstructing the correct commit history of a project can be very difficult.

Require Agreements Before Giving Commit Privileges

One best practice that all open source projects should adopt is to require a signed contributor agreement or copyright assignment before giving commit privileges to a new developer. The completed license agreements or copyright assignments should be recorded in the source code repository. By keeping the agreements close to the code, you make it easier to correlate particular contributions with particular agreements.

When people are just trying to get in their first patch, it is too easy to let licensing documentation slide. Nevertheless, if you make contributor agreements part of the initial setup procedure—just like exchanging SSH keys and setting up user accounts—you are less likely to overlook them.

Make Sure Agreements Are Signed

Federal law requires that a number of important documents—including any intellectual property assignments—be completed in writing and signed. When a developer needs to sign a CLA or an assignment agreement, it is necessary to have someone ready to receive the agreement via mail, fax, or email.

One thing that may be useful for many projects is the use of electronic signatures. An electronic signature is defined more broadly than a digital signature (which usually implies encryption). According to the U.S. ESIGN Act (see 15 U.S.C. § 7001), an electronic signature is just "an electronic sound, symbol, or process, attached to or logically associated with a record and executed or adopted by a person with the intent to sign the record." It is probably a good idea to use cryptographic signatures to increase the security of the electronically signed agreements, but any "symbols" made with the intent to sign the document will be honored.

CHAPTER TWELVE

Working with the GPL

A lot of the most difficult questions in free and open source software revolve around the GPL. The GPL has a lot of things going for it: it is the single most common open source software license, it has brought together a large and vibrant community of developers, and it is a brilliant hack, socially and legally.

At the same time, there is no single license that is more mistrusted or reviled than the GPL. Many open source developers refuse to accept or release code under the GPL because it imposes restrictions at the same time that it grants freedoms. I know from personal experience that the GPL gives most lawyers fits.

In short, very few people have a balanced or nuanced view of the GPL—they either love it or hate it. Speaking in broad generalizations, though, I think that these strong emotional reactions arise from two core issues.

The first issue is the philosophy of free software. More than any other single document, the GPL has come to embody the free software movement, so people's reactions to the GPL mirror their opinions of free software as a moral imperative. Supporters see the Free Software Foundation (FSF) and the GPL as an ethical vanguard, paving the way for a better society. Detractors feel imposed upon because they see the FSF mixing its morality with its code. Many companies don't like the GPL because they have a hard time seeing the business models that accompany free software. They only see that *their* business models are threatened.

These social issues are interesting, but beyond the scope of this book.

The second issue, though, is quite appropriate to our discussion: legal ambiguity. There is basically no argument that the GPL is a valid and enforceable license. There is, however, a lot of confusion about when and where the GPL applies. In some ways, the GPL is treated like HIV/AIDS in the early 1980s; a lot of people weren't sure how you get infected, so there was a lot of hyperbole and misinformation.

By way of comparison, there is a current controversy in the Python language community about setuptools, a packaging system that puts Python code into packages known as "eggs." Like the GPL, some people love setuptools, and some people hate it. After a long discussion with a number of detractors, the setuptools author wrote a post titled, "Wow, I Think I Actually *Get* It Now!" (*http://mail.python.org/pipermail/python-dev/2008-March/077964.html*):

> [T]his information is VERY helpful. It makes it blindingly obvious to me now that the difference between loving and hating setuptools is whether you're *intentionally* using it, or whether it shows up in your ecosystem uninvited....
>
> This makes total sense to me now. I don't have any *solutions* to the problem, mind you, but at least now I understand what before seemed like some sort of bizarre anomaly where literally thousands of people use setuptools and many dozens actually express their happiness with or even love for the system, and then others hate it like they hate Microsoft, or worse. ;-)
>
> Meanwhile, from the "outsiders" point of view, setuptools looks like the Matrix or the Borg, happily assimilating the masses, who then start coming to you and say, "But you'll be so much happier once you join us..." ...and off in the distance, you hear a quiet rumbling of zombies chanting "eeeeggs...eeeeggggs...mussst havve eggggssss!

The controversy over the GPL is similar. As Lawrence Rosen put it, there is "an unreasonable fear of infection" associated with GPL-licensed code because the legal ambiguity of the licenses makes people unsure about whether or not the GPL will show up in their ecosystem uninvited. This uncertainty makes some people afraid or unwilling to use the GPL and amplifies their social and philosophical concerns about free software.

Daily Life with the GPL

Before continuing, it is important to point out that there is wide agreement on a number of the issues that have traditionally surrounded the GPL. In day-to-day use, people don't usually encounter the difficult situations that we will discuss throughout this chapter. Accordingly, a lot of frequently asked GPL-related questions have easy answers.

The Usual Suspects

There are four common situations involving the GPL: distributing GPL-licensed code, avoiding GPL-licensed code, running GPL-licensed code, and creating a larger distribution of independent programs, some of which are licensed under the GPL.

Distributing GPL-licensed code

When someone distributes GPL-licensed code, the terms of the GPL apply. Full GPL-licensed source code (or at least an offer of full source code) must accompany the distribution of any binary applications. It doesn't matter if the GPL-licensed program has been modified or not; if source code comes into a company licensed under the GPL, then it must leave the company licensed under the GPL. Any modifications to the program must also be licensed under the GPL.

The few times that the GPL has been an issue in court, GPL enforcers have generally won because there have been obvious violations of the license conditions—a GPL-licensed program was being distributed with "no source nor offer." (Technically, the cases have not continued to the point where the court issued a final ruling, but the GPL enforcers settled on favorable terms).

Avoiding GPL-licensed code

If people don't want to deal with the GPL, they usually completely avoid it. In a corporate setting, this is usually manifested by creating a corporate policy against using any GPL-licensed code.

In most cases, corporate policies against GPL-licensed code are limited to developers. Sometimes, however, corporate managers have the incorrect impression that *any* use of GPL-licensed applications requires the company to release all of the company source code under the GPL. This unreasonable fear of GPL infection leads people to ban *all* GPL-licensed applications from corporate computers.

Running GPL-licensed code

The GPL gives *unlimited* permission for end users to copy, run, and modify GPL-licensed software for their own private use. As long as there is no distribution of the software outside the company, *anything* can be done with GPL-licensed software—even combining GPL-licensed and proprietary-licensed software.

For example, a company using an embedded Linux system to control its manufacturing operations can compile proprietary source code into the Linux kernel and use the resulting binary without permission and without violating the GPL. As long as the company doesn't distribute its modified kernel, the GPL just doesn't apply.

Distributions of independent programs

A good example of the final situation—GPL-licensed code as part of a larger software distribution—is a Linux distribution containing both GPL-licensed and non-GPL-licensed code. In this case, the programs side by side on the same disk (a *mere aggregation* in the language of the GPLv2) are separate works with separate copyrights. The distribution, as a whole, is a collective work under copyright law.

This situation doesn't change when the programs are run. Multiple programs loaded into RAM are still separate works with separate copyrights, regardless of the licenses governing use of the various programs. It also doesn't matter if the programs communicate. Separate processes using inter-process communication are all separate works.

Persistent Questions

Nevertheless, there is a persistent issue that won't go away—whether linking programs together creates a derivative work. If linking creates a derivative work, the GPL applies to the linked program; otherwise, the GPL doesn't apply.

The FSF recognized this problem early and created the LGPL license to help deal with this issue. The LGPL (originally called the *library* GPL because of its intended use with linked libraries) explicitly grants permission to make links between LGPL-licensed code and proprietary applications. Creating the LGPL didn't resolve the question of linking between GPL- and non-GPL-licensed programs, however; it merely reduced the array of programs facing the problem. With the growing importance of plug-in architectures (and the FSF's public shift away from the LGPL—see Richard Stallman's essay "Why You Shouldn't Use the Lesser GPL for Your Next Library," at *http://www.gnu.org/philosophy/why-not-lgpl.html*), the problems of linking and licensing have again moved to center stage.

In legal practice, this arises as a common concern of clients just getting into open source. This question is usually phrased as either, "Can I load and use a GPL-licensed library without applying the GPL to my application?" or, "Do I have to apply the GPL to my plug-in for a particular program if that program is licensed under the GPL?" The latter question is particularly important for computer hardware makers; the answer to this question determines whether proprietary modules can be loaded into the Linux kernel.

I won't keep you in suspense; the short answer is that we don't know. For a longer, perhaps more satisfying answer you can skip to the end of the chapter, but this is a very complicated question.

Understanding the Terms of the Debate

Before analyzing the debate over linking and the GPL, we need to define a couple of essential terms more explicitly: *derivative works*, *collective works*, and *functional language*.

Derivative Works

As discussed in Chapter 4, the copyright statute defines a derivative work as "a work based upon one or more preexisting works." On one hand, basing a work "upon one or more preexisting works" usually means that there is some sort of transformation or adaptation of the original. Otherwise the combination would simply be a compilation under copyright law.

No transformation or adaptation takes place during the linking of program code (the code is transformed in the compilation step, but linking just resolves references). On the other hand, the statute also allows a derivative work to be created when the original work is accompanied by "annotations, elaborations, or other modifications, which, as a whole, represent an original work of authorship." In other words, a work *may* be considered a derivative work if it layers additional creative expression on top of an underlying original work, even if there are no changes to the underlying work.

Creating a derivative work is one of the specific property rights granted under copyright law, so the owner of the original work has the right to impose restrictions on derivative works. In the case of the GPL, this means that the author of the original program has the right to require any derivative works to also be licensed under the GPL.

Collective Works

The copyright statute states that a collective work (or compilation) is created when a person brings together "preexisting materials or...data...in such a way that the resulting work as a whole constitutes an original work of authorship." In a software context, you can create a collective work when you combine different pieces of software without making changes to the individual pieces, like in a Linux distribution. In GPLv2 language, a collective work is a mere aggregation of software.

Under the law, the copyrights on the individual parts of a collective work are independent of each other and are also independent of the copyright on the collective work itself. For example, in a Linux distribution, the copyright and licensing applied to GCC is completely separate from the copyright and licensing of qmail. Furthermore, the copyright and licensing of GCC and qmail are completely separate from the copyright and licensing of the Linux distribution as a whole.

This is also true in reverse. While it is *theoretically* possible to create a proprietary Linux distribution, the only thing proprietary about it would be the specific selection of packages. Anyone could take GCC and qmail from the proprietary distribution and use them to create his or her own selection of packages. Again, the copyrights on each independent piece and on the collection as a whole *are all independent.*

Relative to the GPL, this means that the author of an original program that is subsequently used in a collective work cannot require any other program in the collective work to be licensed under the GPL.

Functional Language

Section 102(b) of the copyright statute explicitly excludes from protection "any idea, procedure, process, system, method of operation, concept, principle, or discovery." These are known as *functional works,* and they are not protectable, regardless of whether they are expressed in English or another language, like a computer language. Instead, protection for these works is limited to what can be covered under the patent laws. When there are both creative and functional aspects to a work, as with software, copyright is limited to those parts of the work that display the author's *creative* expression.

Because copyright does not extend to functional language, copying purely functional language from a GPL-licensed program into another program does not create a derivative work. The difficulty, however, is distinguishing between what is "functional" and what is "creative."

Linking and Licensing

There are a number of reasons for concern over the issue of linking and licensing. We already explored one reason: how the uncertainty surrounding this issue magnifies the social concerns around the GPL. Even people who would like to work with GPL-licensed code are worried that it will show up uninvited in their ecosystem. Corporate policies prohibiting the GPL are just the most benign manifestation of this concern. On a deeper level, comments comparing free software to communism or to cancer are expressions of this underlying uncertainty—as logically incoherent and factually incorrect as those comments might be.

The more fundamental problem is that the arguments over linking and licensing are really arguments over the scope of copyright...and regardless of your opinion about what should and should not be copyrighted, winning this argument is a losing proposition. This issue was brought into relief by an April 10, 2008 blog post from Bradley Kuhn (FOSS Community Liaison for the Software Freedom Law Center) titled, "The GPL is a Tool to Encourage Freedom, Not an End in Itself" (*http://www.softwarefreedom.org/technology/blog/2008/apr/10/gpl-not-end-in-itself/*):

> I was amazed to be involved in yet another discussion recently regarding the old debate about the scope of the GPL under copyright law. The debate itself isn't amazing —these debates have happened somewhere every six months, almost on cue, since around 1994 or so...
>
> I'm disturbed by the notion that some believe the goal of the GPL is to expand copyrightability and the inclusiveness of derivative works. It seems that so many forget (or maybe they never even knew) that copyleft was invented to hack copyright —to turn its typical applications to software inside out. [...]
>
> It's unfortunate that the entrenched interests outside of software are (more or less) inadvertently strengthening software copyright, too. Thus, in the meantime, we must hold steadfast to the GPL going as far as is legally permitted under this ridiculously expansive copyright system we have.

Military leaders sometimes talk about the difference between *strategy* and *tactics*. Strategies are long-term goals, whereas tactics are short-term actions designed to carry out the strategy. Sometimes, however, short-term tactical decisions can be at odds with the long-term strategic objective. Because the scope of the GPL is intrinsically tied to the scope of copyright, a short-term tactic of strong GPL enforcement may result in the long-term strategic problem of stronger copyrights overall. For proprietary software makers, the short-term tactic of limiting the applicability of the GPL may result in a long-term strategic reduction in copyright protection.

Copyright Confusion

With these terms in mind, let's turn our attention to the strategy and tactics surrounding the GPL. The GPLv2 makes an explicit tie between derivative works under copyright and the reach of the GPL; the GPL applies to "either the *Program or any derivative work under copyright law*: that is to say, *a work containing the Program or a portion of it, either verbatim or with modifications*" (emphasis added). The GPLv3 similarly ties its interpretation to copyright law.

Strategically, the FSF has stated that it is opposed to strong software copyrights in general. Copyright law must be interpreted to determine what constitutes derivative work; the GPL intends to go only as far as copyright law does.

The problem is that in a number of public statements from the FSF, the tactical decision has been to take an expansive view of copyright, applying the GPL in the broadest range of situations possible. In the words of Bradley Kuhn, there has been a decision to "hold steadfast to the GPL going as far as is legally permitted under this ridiculously expansive copyright system we have." The result is uncertainty and a perception, fed by the FSF itself, that the GPL is more infective than the license and the law may support.

THE SECRET CONTROVERSY

The relationship between linking, derivative works, and the scope of the GPL is one of the secret controversies of free and open source software. Despite its importance, this issue isn't on the radar for most free and open source software developers.

To understand why, think of the old controversy between vi and emacs. People can argue for either editor, but the arguments are mostly technical and can really only be appreciated by those with the proper background. Those outside the programming tradition, particularly outside the Unix programming tradition, are largely unaware of the controversy.

The controversy over linking and licensing is similar. As you can see in this chapter, this is a complex technical and legal issue, and the arguments on each side are hard to appreciate without having the proper background. Like the vi and emacs "holy war," this isn't an issue that is easily resolved. There are arguments and prominent open source experts on both sides of the divide. For example, Eben Moglen (attorney for the FSF and founder of the Software Freedom Conservancy) and Lawrence Rosen (former general counsel and director of the OSI) disagree on the scope of linking and licensing.

Even within the FSF there isn't always agreement. In the paper, "A Funny Thing Happened on the Way to the Market,"* Matt Asay quotes Richard Stallman and Eben Moglen's responses to questions about linking, and comes to the conclusion:

> [I]t is telling how widely their responses diverge—there appear to be no definitive answers to the question of what constitutes a derivative work under the GPL, not even from the holders of the licenses in question. This uncertainty may well be the most nettlesome issue inhibiting the widespread adoption of Linux by computer makers.

It is impossible to say that the FSF is *wrong* about its interpretation of the GPL and the GPL's interaction with copyright law. The real problem is that the FSF's interpretation just isn't *right*. Copyright law, especially as applied to computer software, is a difficult subject. Until a court rules on the exact terms of the GPL in exactly these circumstances, we just don't know how the law deals with the issue of linking and derivative works.

From the FAQ

Representative of the short-term tactical language presented by the FSF is the GPL Frequently Asked Questions (FAQ) list, available at *http://www.gnu.org/licenses/gpl-faq.html*. For example:

> If the program *dynamically links* plug-ins, and they make function calls to each other and share data structures, we believe they form a single program, which must be treated as an extension of both the main program and the plug-ins." (Emphasis added)

This statement asserts that dynamically linked programs are "a single program" and "must be treated as an extension of both the main program and the plug-ins." The GPL FAQ was written for programmers, not for lawyers, but this sounds like a layman's description of the copyright term "derivative work." Translating this text into lawyer-speak, the GPL FAQ says that, "dynamically linked programs are derivative works." Based upon this interpretation, the FAQ concludes that the GPL applies to the combination:

> This means [in the dynamic linking case] the plug-ins must be released under the GPL or a GPL-compatible free software license, and that the terms of the GPL must be followed when those plug-ins are distributed.

The GPL FAQ also asserts that static linking creates a derivative work. From the FAQ:

* Asay, Matt. "A Funny Thing Happened on the Way to the Market: Linux, the General Public License, and a New Model for Software Innovation," April 2002. Available at *http://www.linuxdevices.com/files/misc/asay-paper.pdf*.

> Linking ABC statically or dynamically with other modules is making a combined work based on ABC. Thus, the terms and conditions of the GNU General Public License cover the whole combination.

Static linking is a close issue, and as discussed shortly, arguments can be made on both sides. Finally, though, and most amazingly, the FAQ asserts that communication through shared memory is sufficient to create a derivative work:

> Using shared memory to communicate with complex data structures is pretty much equivalent to dynamic linking.

This statement does not agree with the common understanding of current copyright law. It is also inconsistent with the statement that multiple processes are separate works. For example, many high-performance multiprocessing programs use shared memory for communication. Under the GPL FAQ, it is unclear if they are one program (under the GPL) or separate programs (under separate licenses).

The Darth Vader Scale of Derivative Works

To understand the FSF's position on the applicability of the GPL, it is useful to view the interaction between programs on a scale from "mere aggregation" of differently licensed work to wholesale incorporation of code into a modified GPL-licensed binary. Figure 12-1 summarizes the FSF's view of the situation; anything more than "mere aggregation" moves a user toward violating the GPL.

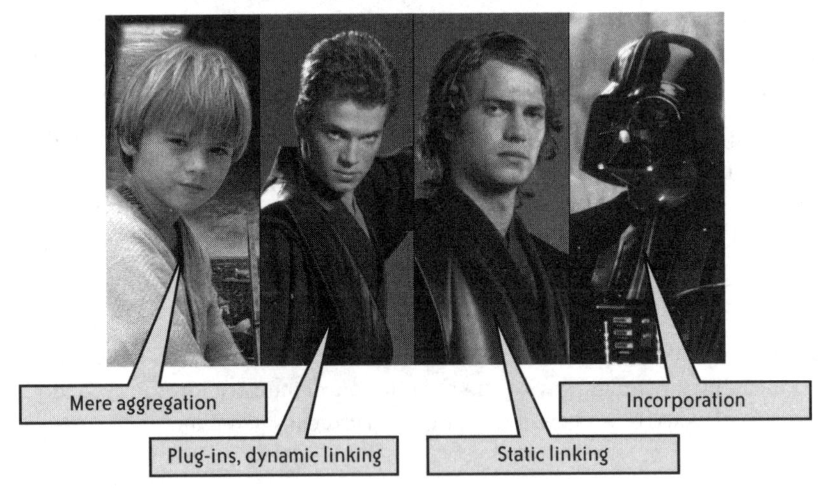

FIGURE 12-1. The Darth Vader scale of derivative works

Thinking About Derivative Works

The key issue is whether linking creates a derivative work. Because of the intricacies of both copyright law and computer software, this is a complex and difficult question. For example, the standard definition of a derivative work usually requires some transformation of the original work, but not always.

Sometimes, a dynamically linked work could just include annotations and elaborations on a base binary. Consider the Linux kernel. Are kernel modules annotations or elaborations upon the base expression of the kernel? Perhaps—so *maybe* they are derivative works under the law.

Another argument is that linking creates a collective work, not a derivative work. Collective works are treated differently under the law (and under the GPL). In support of this argument, there is no real difference between having two binary images on disk and having two binary images in memory. Some systems, in fact, may not have separate disks or memory, but just a single area for both storage and working memory. In that case, the distinction between a link and an aggregation is unclear.

A counter-argument is that while collective works are usually different from derivative works, it is *possible* for something to be a collective work and a derivative work *at the same time*. Courts sometimes look at the Congressional Record to figure out the meaning of a law. When discussing the Copyright Act, one representative said:

> Between them the terms "compilations" and "derivative works" which are defined in section 101, comprehend every copyrightable work that employs preexisting material or data of any kind. *There is necessarily some overlapping between the two*, but they basically represent different concepts. (emphasis added)*

If the courts recognize any overlap between the worlds of collective and derivative works, then the results of software linking might be one of the few types of works that inhabit that space. If so, the GPL might apply to linked software that is a collective-derivative work hybrid.

Another wrinkle is the relationship between copyright licensing and contract law. As discussed in Chapter 10, it is an open question as to whether a court would consider the GPL under copyright or contract law. This is important because there is a contract law principle called the *usage of trade*. Usage of trade means that certain words and phrases can have accepted meanings within an industry, and any industry contract using those phrases is assumed to incorporate those industry-specific meanings.

For example, "long" cotton has a length between 28 and 34 mm. Unless the contract itself specifies a meaning for "long," any contract in the cotton industry for "long" cotton uses the industry standard usage of trade when defining what is considered long.

* H.R. Rep. No. 94-1476 at 57.

The FSF has been talking about linking, licensing, and derivative works for a long time. Many people have accepted the FSF's definitions of the terms. Arguably, the FSF has set the usage of trade in this area.

If the GPL is considered as a contract, the FSF's definition of "derivative work" might apply because of the principle of the usage of trade. In this scenario, distribution of a linked work may be outside the scope of the GPL, and thus an infringement on the copyright.

Header Files

Another aspect of this issue is the use of header files. The use of header files for compilation is at least one hook upon which the FSF sometimes bases its "dynamic linking is a derivative work" position.

To summarize very briefly, there are two steps to creating a program: compilation and linking. Compilation is the part that takes source code and turns it into object code. Linking takes different pieces of object code, loads them into memory, and resolves *references* between the different code objects.

References are symbolic names that refer to different parts of the program. In order for a computer to run the program, those names have to be mapped to the address of the code in memory. By way of analogy, the names are something like "Jane's house." During linking, "Jane's house" is replaced by "234 Some St, Anytown, PA, USA." Using this information, the computer knows where to go when the program needs to interact with a function defined in an outside library.

These references are the issue. When you are building your non-GPL program, the compiler must be instructed on which functions and names will be provided by the library when the library and your program are ultimately linked together. Therefore, libraries generally provide header files to indicate the functions and names that are exported by the library.

To continue the analogy, assume that you have a set of directions (your source code) that include one instruction to "go to Jane's house." You cannot follow your directions from start to finish unless at some point somebody tells you where Jane's house is located. The header file is like a letter that says, "I will tell you the address of Jane's house right before you start actually following the directions. Until then, just accept that you will go to Jane's house during your trip."

The problem is that this header file is wholly incorporated into your program during compilation. Therefore, even if your program dynamically links with a GPL-licensed library, you still have to have incorporated a part of the GPL-licensed code (the header file) into your own program. The incorporation of this code may create a derivative work, causing the GPL to apply.

Other Types of Linking

We haven't exhausted the issues raised by header files; there are situations that don't fit the situation laid out in the previous section. For example, there is COM-style linking, which is designed to allow linking without the explicit inclusion of header files. In this case, the interface is "discoverable" at runtime.

Also, consider foreign function interfaces, which assume prior knowledge on the part of the programmer. There is no compilation step and no real linking step. Instead, the programmer knows ahead of time what functions are available in the library and resolves all references on the fly.

Another type of linking occurs when the GPL-licensed library is not standalone, but rather is designed for use in conjunction with another program. A good example of this is a library that is designed for use with a dynamic language like Python or Perl, or as a runtime loadable module by the Apache HTTP server. In this situation, linking as described above *does* take place, but the dynamic between linker and linkee is subtly changed.

Specifically, if I create a GPL-licensed library to be used with Apache, the Apache server doesn't include my header file. Rather, I include *Apache's* header file when creating my library. This is because Apache does not change in order to interoperate with my library; instead, I have to make a special effort to make my library interoperable with Apache.

This is a very difficult situation. It is possible that the GPL might apply to a dynamically linked work when a programmer has made special provision to use a GPL-licensed library by incorporating its header file into the project. When the GPL-licensed library has conformed itself to an outside plug-in architecture, however, the situation seems different.

Even if the in-memory running program could be considered a derivative work of the GPL-licensed library, it is the end user who actually creates the derivative work. The programmer distributes something much closer to a mere aggregation of programs on the same disk.

Functional and Expressive Language

Another aspect to consider is the distinction between functional and expressive language. When programs are linked together, the linking strips out the comments or most of the expressive elements in the source. What is left seems more like an "idea, procedure, process, system, method of operation," which isn't covered by copyright. More generally, the compilation of code may remove some (but not all) of the copyrightable creative elements.

For example, the core machine-code construct in the original lisp interpreter was the *goto*; all lisp code was expanded out to machine-native stack instructions and gotos between different sections of the code. A high-level lisp *REPL* construct may be *expressive*, but it may be difficult to consider the machine-level version as anything more than *functional*.

On the other hand, an individual name or symbol may not be copyrighted or copyrightable, but a particular selection of symbols may be. The selection of symbols to be exported is inherent to API design, which may be a copyrightable creative work.

Further, just looking at the header file, fairly substantial macro programs can be implemented solely in the headers. These require creativity and originality to write, bringing them under the copyright law; it may not matter that some of the expression is stripped out by the linking process.

Questions and Answers

Unfortunately, there are no clear and definitive answers for the questions raised here. Nevertheless, the purpose of this chapter is to give guidelines, not headaches. Keeping in mind the difficulty of these issues, here are some questions and answers about GPL, linking, and copyright.

Can I link a GPL-licensed program to and from other software under different licenses?
: The short answer is, "Maybe." It depends on whether the linking is for your own private use and whether you create a derivative work of the GPL-licensed program. Also note that code may be covered by more than one type of intellectual property protection, and each type of intellectual property protection has to be considered individually. For example, the functional parts of your code may be subject to patents. The use of patented program functionality requires the agreement of the patent owner.

Does the GPL apply to merely compiling or running a GPL-licensed program?
: No, the GPL does not apply to just compiling and running the program for private use. The GPLv2 excludes "activities other than copying, distribution and modification" of the program and "the act of running the Program" is specifically not restricted. The GPLv3 states that, "You may make, run and propagate covered works that you do not convey, without conditions so long as your license otherwise remains in force."

Does the GPL apply to compiling a GPL-licensed program by itself and distributing it to someone else?
: Yes. The compiled program may or may not be a derivative work, but distribution is the key; the GPL always applies. Under the terms of the GPL, the developer must distribute the source code for the program along with the binary copy. To ease this burden for embedded systems, the GPL frees the developer from including the source code with the device; instead, the developer can provide it online (or by mail order) and provide documentation pointing to it.

Does the GPL apply to compiling a GPL-licensed program, linking it to a non-GPL-licensed program or library, and distributing it to someone else?
: This question is too broad to be answered definitively. This issue is at the boundaries of copyright law, and has not been directly examined by a court. Until the law is clarified on this issue, the best we can do is apply the general principles of the law. If you need advice about your specific situation, you should call a lawyer. Note that the LGPL allows the

linking and distribution of LGPL-licensed and non-LGPL-licensed code under all circumstances.

*OK, does the GPL apply when I compile an **unchanged** GPL-licensed program, statically link it to a non-GPL-licensed program or library, and distribute the resulting binary to someone else?*

Maybe. This is the primary area of disagreement. There are two basic views on this issue:

- View number 1: The GPL does not apply to the resulting binary. The GPL only applies to the copyrightable *creative* expression in the code; purely *functional* aggregation of two blobs of binary code, even within the same program or memory space, does not receive copyright protection and so does not implicate the GPL.

  At most, static linking creates a compilation under copyright law, which is governed by different rules. Distribution of GPL-licensed code in a compilation with non-GPL-licensed code is allowed.

- View number 2: The GPL applies to the resulting binary. The GPL applies to derivative works, and a derivative work can be created when the original work is accompanied by annotations or elaborations that build upon an original copyrighted work. A combined work consisting of annotations or elaborations may be both a compilation and a derivative work under copyright law.

  Further, we don't know right now whether the courts will treat the GPL as a license (governed only by copyright law) or as a contract (governed also by contract law). If the GPL is interpreted as a contract, then the language of the GPL itself—not copyright law—might be used to define what falls within the bounds of the GPL. The text of the GPLv2 says that it considers a "derivative work" to include "a work containing the Program or a portion of it." The GPLv3 is similar. A statically linked binary "contains the Program or a portion of it," so the GPL should apply.

This is a difficult question to answer, and the two views presented above are oversimplified. Until a court rules on this issue, it is safest to assume that the GPL applies to a statically linked binary containing unchanged GPL code. Note, however, that this view is not necessarily correct. Many experts believe that regardless of the functional method, linking by itself doesn't create a derivative work. For example, Stanford legal professor Mark Lemley was quoted in an April 21, 2008 post on the Open Bar legal mailing list: "Modifying open source programs may create a derivative work, though even then fair use might mean there is no need for a license. But linking surely isn't copyright infringement."

Does the GPL apply when I compile an unchanged GPL-licensed program, dynamically link it to a non-GPL-licensed program or library, and distribute the binaries to someone else?

Probably not. The GPL does not apply to binaries that are not distributed as a single program, and the GPL places no restrictions on the end user's ability to combine the GPL-licensed and non-GPL-licensed programs into a single binary at runtime. Particularly if the GPL-licensed and non-GPL-licensed programs come from different people or in different packages, it seems unlikely that dynamically bringing the two programs together would violate the GPL. A good example is the readline library distributed under the GPL.

A non-GPL-licensed program does not become a GPL-covered derivative work if it is designed to optionally use readline if the latter is installed. On the other hand, using dynamic linking as an obvious dodge around the GPL would probably not be upheld by a court. If a proprietary program and a GPL-licensed library were shipped together and advertised as a single program, then a judge might apply the GPL to the combination.

That is different than the official GPL FAQ! Why?

The GPL FAQ was written in inexact language, and gives the impression that the rules regarding derivative works may have greater reach than current copyright law allows. The FSF has repeatedly stated, however, that they believe in copyright minimalism and that the GPL should not be interpreted to extend beyond the reach of copyright.

Does the GPL apply to a program where a GPL-licensed process or thread communicates with another process or thread only via shared memory?

The GPL applies to the GPL-licensed portion; the GPL should not apply to the program as a whole. Communication between two cooperating processes or threads does not create a derivative work under copyright law, the section of the GPL FAQ concerning shared memory notwithstanding.

Does the GPL apply if I have to modify the GPL-licensed program to make it link to my software?

Modification of a software program creates a derivative work, so the GPL applies.

Can I depend on the answers in this Q&A to keep me out of trouble?

No. This is our best understanding of copyright law as it stands right now, but it could change tomorrow—and *nobody* really knows until these questions are resolved in a court of law.

Norms and Law

Ultimately, we need to acknowledge the commercial force of social expectations. Open source licenses act like social contracts just as much as they act as legal documents. While a strict legal interpretation may allow a certain range of activity, community expectations may dictate otherwise.

One of the classic computer movies of the 1980s was *WarGames*—the story of an unlikely friendship between a teenage computer hacker and an artificially intelligent computer. After running through the tactics available for a global thermonuclear war, the computer eventually learned that the only winning strategy was not to play.

As I discussed in this chapter, the uncertainty surrounding the GPL can and has dissuaded people from using and adopting free and open source software. Further, no matter who "wins" the argument about linking and the GPL, both sides lose. From my perspective, the best resolution to this issue would be to adopt a standard interpretation of what will and will not be considered a derivative work for purposes of free and open source software. While there are no guarantees, a widely accepted standard would reduce the possibilities for lawsuits and defuse a lot of the tension over the GPL. Getting rid of the "unreasonable fear of infection" would benefit both the free/open source software communities and proprietary companies by encouraging better and broader use of open source software.

CHAPTER THIRTEEN

Reverse Engineering

One of the themes of this book is the growing strength of intellectual property protections like fortresses on the intellectual landscape. Like medieval castles, many different types of protection can be placed around a particular piece of intellectual turf. There are patent walls, copyright towers, and trade secret battlements that can only be accessed through licensing gates.

When medieval armies attacked, they had two ways to overcome castle defenses: by siege and by assault. During a siege, attackers would try to wait out the defenders of the castle, letting time do the work of removing the castle defenses. An assault, on the other hand, would attack the castle protections head-on to defeat them.

Both of these tactics are applicable to modern intellectual property defenses. Some sorts of protection, notably patent protection, can just be waited out. For example, the entire generic drugs industry exists because the patent protections around certain drugs have expired.

Reverse engineering, on the other hand, is more like a direct assault; the intellectual property protections are carefully surmounted or avoided to capture the prize within. Like medieval assaults, reverse engineering is risky, expensive, and complicated, but when it works, it provides a way inside the intellectual property fortress.

Storming the Castle

Reverse engineering is one of the most celebrated traditions of our legal system. It isn't often that the dry world of intellectual property produces a good story, but reverse engineering has been at the center of some of the best stories in the history of computer engineering.

Understanding important reverse engineering cases is also essential to new reverse engineering projects. Part of what makes reverse engineering risky is that there is no law that clearly lays out the requirements for acceptable reverse engineering. There is only a selection of incidents where courts have looked at specific cases of reverse engineering and either accepted the result as acceptable or not. By seeing what courts have accepted in the past, general guidelines for reverse engineering have been developed.

IBM and the PC BIOS

One of the most famous instances of reverse engineering was the creation of a compatible PC BIOS in the early 1980s. In the early days of the personal computer revolution, IBM decided that it needed some sort of computer to compete with the increasingly successful Apple II. IBM's Data Systems Division, however, was afraid that a too-powerful entry-level computer would cannibalize sales of the more profitable IBM DisplayWriter. Ideally, IBM wanted the PC as a low-power, low-quality product that could blunt the effect of Apple's sales, allowing IBM to keep control of the computer industry while still retaining the ability to up-sell serious computer users on the mainframes and minicomputers that were IBM's primary products.

So instead of using custom designed, high quality IBM components, the IBM PC used commodity hardware components from different vendors. IBM intended to keep control of the architecture by retaining copyright control over just one component, the ROM-BIOS.

Against IBM's own expectations, however, the PC was very successful. It very quickly created a market for IBM PC-compatible computers, which a number of computer makers attempted to address.

Poisoning the well

IBM's initial efforts to keep PC clones out of the market were fairly successful. One of the key aspects of the IBM case was that the PC BIOS was not kept as a trade secret. The full specification of the BIOS, *including source code*, was published in every PC repair manual. The publication of this information was a deliberate effort by IBM to *poison the well* of available engineers; that is, to contaminate engineers with knowledge of IBM's copyrighted BIOS code. If anyone tried to reverse engineer the BIOS after seeing the source code, IBM could claim in court that the contaminated engineers would have necessarily incorporated IBM's copyrighted code into the new BIOS.

Two companies in particular were able to successfully reverse engineer the PC BIOS: Compaq and Phoenix. Compaq was first, hiring a team of "virgin" engineers who could prove that they had never been exposed to IBM's copyrighted code. Compaq set up a clean-room reverse engineering team, with the "dirty" team creating a specification from IBM's code and the "clean" team creating new code to implement the specification. The effort took many months and one million dollars, but Compaq was able to create the first completely IBM PC-compatible computer. Compaq sales skyrocketed.

However, Compaq decided to keep its BIOS as a trade secret—it was a competitive advantage over other computer makers—so another company had to duplicate the work and create a second IBM-compatible implementation.

The second company to successfully clone the PC BIOS was Phoenix. Like Compaq, Phoenix was careful to recruit engineers that had never seen or worked on the 8088/8086 chips used in the IBM PC. That alone might not have stopped a lawsuit by IBM, but Phoenix also took the unusual step of getting a legal insurance policy through Lloyd's of London. This legal insurance policy gave Phoenix the legal resources of a company many times its size—enough to fight and survive through a long legal battle. Ultimately, IBM was unwilling to fight a company armed with both a reverse engineered BIOS and an insurance-funded war chest. Phoenix decided to sell copies of its BIOS instead of keeping it a proprietary secret, thus creating the massive clone PC market of the 1980s.

Atari v. Nintendo

Nintendo's Nintendo Entertainment System (NES) was one of the most successful game consoles of the 1980s. Nintendo only granted limited licenses to software developers developing for the NES, and maintained strict controls over the number and types of games that could be released for the system. Nintendo prevented the system from playing unlicensed cartridges via a console "lock" and cartridge "key" system called the 10NES. Although Atari had a license to create games for the NES, the company didn't want to be limited by Nintendo's license, so it decided to create its own cartridge key.

Atari tried a couple of times to reverse engineer Nintendo's key. In Atari's first attempt, the engineers tried to figure out the workings of the key by watching the communications between the console and cartridge. When that did not work, the Atari engineers deconstructed the 10NES chips and looked at the embedded object code, which they then decompiled into source code.*

Fair and unfair use

When Atari's second attempt didn't allow the creation of new games, Atari decided to take a shortcut; it illegally acquired a copy of the 10NES program from the Copyright Office and used it to replicate the 10NES source code. Armed with Nintendo's code, Atari developed its own system (called Rabbit) to act as a key to the 10NES.

When Nintendo sued Atari, the court decided that reverse engineering object code to discern the unprotectable ideas in a computer program *was* fair use. The Atari court reasoned that the "Copyright Act permits an individual in rightful possession of a copy of a work to undertake necessary efforts to understand the work's ideas, processes, and methods of operation." However, Atari's illegal possession of Nintendo's code from the Copyright Office disallowed a

* *Atari Games Corp. v. Nintendo of America Inc.*, 975 F.2d 832 (Fed. Cir. 1992)

finding of fair use. Further, Rabbit included many non-functional elements of 10NES, such as unnecessary instructions, which indicated produced *substantial similarity* in the code.

Although Atari lost this legal battle, the decision in this case established two important principles. First, reverse engineering of object code, including decompilation, is a fair use. A "dirty" specification team may be able to decompile programs to help create specifications if no other sources of information are available. Second, there is a difference between bug-compatible reverse engineering, where certain bugs are necessary for the correct functioning of programs, and the unnecessary inclusion of extra code (including error code) in a reverse engineered product. To protect against a finding of substantial similarity (and thus copyright infringement), the specification team and the evaluation team must remove all expression, including seemingly functional elements that are actually expressive.

Sega v. Accolade

The Sega case is probably the single most important reverse engineering case. It is outwardly similar to the *Atari v. Nintendo* case, but Accolade, the company doing the reverse engineering, was successful.*

Sega manufactured the Genesis game system and granted limited licenses to software developers to manufacture compatible games. As with Nintendo, a security feature on the Genesis console prevented the system from playing unlicensed cartridges via a console "lock" and cartridge "key" system. Accolade wanted to create games for the Genesis, but did not want to be limited by a license, so it tried to replicate the "key" portion of cartridges.

Clean room procedures

Accolade's clean room procedure included two steps. First, Accolade had a "dirty" team that deconstructed the Genesis chips and decompiled the code, creating a copy of Sega's code in the process. Using the copied code, Accolade created a development manual containing functional descriptions of the interface requirements. According to Accolade employees who created the manual, the manual contained only functional descriptions of the interface requirements and did not include any of Sega's code. Second, Accolade's clean room team developed games for the Genesis, relying only on the information concerning interface specifications for the Genesis contained in the manual.

In the decompiling process, Accolade discovered a piece of code without a function. Correctly guessing that future Genesis versions would require the code to properly power up, Accolade directly copied the code to the development manual to be used in all games. Although the code was directly copied, the court decided that there was no copyright infringement. According to the Sega court, the code was functional expression only, performing the function of "unlocking" the console, and therefore not protectable under copyright: "When specific

* *Sega Enterprises Ltd. v. Accolade, Inc.*, 977 F.2d 1510 (9th Cir. 1992).

instructions, even though previously copyrighted, are the only and essential means of accomplishing a given task, their later use by another will not amount to infringement." Additionally, the court noted that the copying of the "key" code could be excused because the copied code was so minimal—only 20 bytes out of about 500,000—and so was unprotectable under the words and short phrases doctrine.

The court also allowed Accolade's decompilation and transcription of Sega's code from the chips to paper. The court decided that the transcription was necessary to discover the functional specifications. According to the Sega court, preventing reverse engineering that produced a copy would allow copyright holders to gain a de facto monopoly over the functional aspects of the work because those functional elements are not discoverable without the reverse engineering: "[W]here disassembly is the only way to gain access to the ideas and functional elements embodied in a copyrighted computer program and where there is a legitimate reason for seeking such access, disassembly is a fair use of the copyrighted work, as a matter of law."

Cadence v. Avant!

Several employees left Cadence to work for Avant!, a competitor in the field of place and route software. Cadence sued Avant! for copyright infringement, alleging that the employees copied portions of Cadence's software. In response, Avant! followed a clean room process to remove the allegedly infringing portions of code.*

Avant! hired an independent expert, acting as the specification team, to create specifications based on the Cadence code. Other Avant! programmers, acting as the development team (without access to the Cadence code), created new code based on those specifications. Nevertheless, the court found that Avant!'s software still infringed Cadence's copyright. The court didn't think there was sufficient isolation between the independent expert (as the dirty team) and Avant!'s clean room programming team. In particular, the clean room team included a number of former Cadence employees, who were able to take advantage of their knowledge of the basic structure of the Cadence code.

In Chapter 6, we discussed the *doctrine of inevitable disclosure*. The doctrine of inevitable disclosure is based on the notion that no matter how good an employee's intentions, it is impossible for people to compartmentalize the knowledge or experience gained from prior employment. Thus, former employees will "inevitably" disclose trade secrets if they do the same or similar work for a new employer.

The doctrine of inevitable disclosure has been limited by many states, but it still has substantial force when it is applied in a reverse engineering context. In this case, for example, Avant! hired former Cadence employees for the express purpose of replicating Cadence software, leading to substantial non-functional similarities between the two products. When reverse engineering

* *Cadence Design Sys., Inc. v. Avant! Corp.*, 125 F.3d 824 (9th Cir. 1997).

products where team members have some prior product knowledge, teams must make an extra effort to be *different* from the product being reverse engineered.

NEC v. Intel

NEC v. Intel is a good example of acceptable reverse engineering using a team with prior product knowledge. NEC used microcode found on Intel's chips to create its own microprocessors. Like Atari, and Avant!, NEC's developers admitted having access to Intel's code. However, this case provides guideposts about how courts might look at clean room procedures.*

In particular, one NEC employee on the development team had performed a complete disassembly of Intel's microprocessor as a student before joining NEC. Although the student was not a former Intel employee, his disassembly of Intel's product gave him substantial familiarity with the original program. Nevertheless, the court found that even if NEC's code was originally copied from Intel's code, the code was changed enough to not be infringing.

Minor changes and thin copyrights

As discussed in Chapter 4 (on copyright) and Chapter 12 (on the GPL), software code is sometimes only protected by *thin* copyrights, meaning that there is only a little bit of copyrightable creative expression mixed into a larger functional (or otherwise uncopyrightable) work. One result of thin copyrights is that even minimal changes to the copyrightable creative expression can be enough to overcome charges of copyright infringement.

In the NEC case, the court stated that "a defendant may legitimately avoid infringement by intentionally making sufficient changes in a work which would otherwise be regarded as substantially similar to that of the plaintiff's." The court looked only at whether the final version of NEC's program contained any of Intel's expression. Upon determining that there was none, the court found no infringement.

In looking for substantial similarity in the creative copyrightable parts of the two programs, the court noted that none of NEC's subroutines were identical to Intel's. Further, any subroutines that were similar were short and functional, while the long subroutines were quite different. Rather than parsing the code, the court looked at the program as a whole and held that an ordinary observer would not recognize NEC's code as having been taken from Intel's code.

* *NEC Corp. v. Intel Corp.*, 10 U.S.P.Q.2d (BNA) 1177 (N.D. Cal. 1989).

Bug compatibility

Intel's code contained a bug, and NEC's code for one processor included a solution to that bug. However, the correction was in response to a *functional* definition of NEC's hardware, which was similar to Intel's hardware. Thus, being "bug-compatible" with the Intel code was considered part of the functional definition of the program. This was in contrast to the Atari case, where the copied errors were not connected with the functionality of the game.

Recordkeeping and overall similarity

Finally, the court looked at each company's selection and arrangement of the elements of the code. This was a complex aspect to the case, because the internal order of NEC's code matched Intel's. Nevertheless, the court found that there were outside factors other than copying that could result in the similarity, such as similar broad visions of the program, industry conventions, or efficiency optimizations. Key to the court's decision was the fact that earlier versions of NEC's code contained a different sequence than Intel's code, but the two became closer in later revisions. NEC's recordkeeping was essential during litigation in proving that code was not copied.

A Sample Reverse Engineering Procedure

In both the open source and commercial contexts, reverse engineering is an essential part of the software ecosystem, but it is especially important in the world of open source. Many of the most commercially important and widely used open source products are reverse engineered clones of proprietary products.

For example, the Samba project started out as an effort to reverse engineer Microsoft's proprietary Server Message Block (SMB) disk-sharing protocol, which has now expanded into an effort to replicate the server-side file sharing, printing, and domain administration functions of Microsoft Windows servers. Samba was (and is) developed using reverse engineering processes because most of the necessary specifications do not exist or are not published outside of Microsoft.

The Wine Project is another reverse engineering project addressing compatibility with Microsoft Windows, but does so in a more ambitious fashion. The Wine project aims to provide a complete reimplementation of the Windows API. OpenOffice.org and Abiword are word processors that have implemented reverse engineered compatibility with some Microsoft Office file formats. Mono is a reimplementation of the .NET runtime.

Reverse engineering is also important to the Linux kernel. Some companies do not release drivers for Linux, so a number of hardware drivers have been reverse engineered from the available hardware.

When open source projects re-create proprietary software, proper reverse engineering procedure is necessary to protect the integrity of the projects. In the few cases where proper procedures have not been followed, there have been substantial negative repercussions, from the removal of code to the shutting down of entire projects.

Legal Definition

A clean room procedure is a method of software development that intends to produce new code functionally similar to a competitor's copyrighted code without infringing the competitor's copyright. The difference from the traditional development procedure is that the specification is not created from scratch, but is instead based on the competitor's product.

Reverse engineering (without copying) works legally because copyright law only protects expression, not functionality. To prove copyright infringement, an accused infringer must both create material that is substantially similar to the original code and have had access to the original code for copying purposes. Adhering to well-designed clean room procedures is one way to avoid the "access" prong of the infringement test.

White box and black box reverse engineering

To be precise, there are two forms of reverse engineering: *white box* reverse engineering and *black box* reverse engineering. White box reverse engineering allows the author of the code to "look inside" the original software by studying or decompiling it. White box reverse engineering is most often used in a research context only. The results of white box reverse engineering are not "clean" and cannot be used in open source or commercial products; with access to the underlying program, there is a presumption that similar functionality has been copied.

Black box reverse engineering is an extension of the white box method. Instead of code, the white box (dirty) team creates a specification, and the black box (implementation) team creates code that successfully interoperates using the specification only.

Methodology

Formal clean room procedures can be divided into a number of steps. Some of these steps can be burdensome or just annoying, but this extra effort in reverse engineering is required to prove that new functionality has been created from scratch and not copied except in purely functional aspects.

At each point in the reverse engineering procedure, project members should maintain written records to document the proper completion of each step. Under normal circumstances, normal open source development procedures will be enough; communication through archived public mailing lists and code check-ins to public source repositories should probably suffice.

Step 1: Creating Teams

The first step is to form four teams:

Specification team
: Responsible for extracting the desired functionality from the original software and creating the technical specification.

Evaluation team
: Responsible for analyzing the technical specification and cleansing the technical specification of any lingering protected expression.

Development team
: Responsible for developing the new software based upon the technical specification.

Testing team
: Responsible for testing the new software to determine whether it operates as required by the specification.

The separate evaluation and testing teams are optional, but should be used when the software being reverse engineered is particularly sensitive. Many times, the testing function can be assigned to outside users of the project.

Reverse engineering is one case where the typical geographic separation of open source teams is particularly helpful. The specification and development teams must be strictly segregated with no contact permitted (professional, social, casual, or otherwise). Separate locations, preferably over large geographic distances, are ideal.

Step 2: Creating a Specification

The first task in the actual reverse engineering process is creating a specification. In this step, the specification team:

1. Obtains original existing software to use as a guide in developing new software
2. Reviews the license agreement for the original software to ensure compliance with the license agreement
3. Determines the functionality of the original software by methods that include examining its operation, studying users manuals, and/or developing a code flow chart
4. Develops a technical specification that describes the functionality of the original software
5. Sends the technical specification to the evaluation team

Using public documentation

In some cases, the specification has already been created. For example, there may be public documentation of interfaces, or ISO/ECMA standardized implementation notes. In a reverse engineering context, information taken from ECMA or ISO specifications is preferred. Creating code for the purpose of interoperability with a standard will almost always be counted as fair use by a court. Further, code whose structure is dictated by standard documents will always be functional, not creative expression, and will thus not be copyrightable.

Publicly available documentation from the original vendor is also another source of information, but it is important not to duplicate non-functional elements of the original software. Public function signatures and interfaces will always be purely functional, but deeper inspection of the code should be avoided by anybody but the "dirty" specification team.

The problem with using standards, of course, is that most implementations deviate from the standard. If developers really want to interoperate with a popular product, they probably have to go through some additional reverse engineering steps.

Decompiling software

It may also be necessary sometimes to create the specification directly from the "target" software product. In that case, the target product should always be legally obtained, because illegally obtained software will never support a finding of fair use.

Many products contain end user license agreements (EULAs) that prohibit reverse engineering. The enforceability of these anti-reverse engineering provisions is up in the air right now. Reverse engineering is a recognized right under federal law, but it is impossible to say how a specific EULA provision will be interpreted in a court case. Where possible, it is preferable to obtain legal copies of the software from resale markets so that members of the team creating the specification do not themselves agree to the license.

Keeping the development team "clean" is especially important if there have been public releases of source code from the original vendor. In the IBM case, for example, Compaq and Phoenix had to make sure that their clean room engineers had never seen the published IBM source code. In a more recent example, the Mono team currently refuses code contributions from anyone who has seen the source code of Rotor, the source-available .NET implementation for FreeBSD.

Keeping the specification clean

When the specification has been created, it is important not to include any creative expression. For example, the specification should not include comments, initials, security descriptions, or irrelevant code put in place to catch copyright infringers. Instead, the specification should be high-level and contain no expression.

Step 3: Reviewing the Specification

If the product being reverse engineered is especially sensitive, it may be useful to incorporate an optional review step before the reverse engineered specification is sent to the clean room development team. If an evaluation team has been created, the evaluators review the technical specification for any protected copyrightable expression from the original program. As an additional precaution, outside experts who have no working knowledge of the original software could be used to review the technical specification. After this review, the specification is sent to the development team.

Step 4: Developing New Code

In this step, the development team develops the new software based upon the functional specification. The development team should have no contact with either the specification team or with the original software. Also, members of the development team should not be former employees of the company that created the original software. If they are former employees, it is important to ensure that they did not work on the original software and that they did not have access to related trade secrets.

In cases where the product being reverse engineered is very sensitive, it is also important to filter communications between the development team and the specification team. One way to do this is to have the evaluation team act as a communication channel between the development team and the specification team, filtering communications as needed. The evaluation team may also communicate administrative details such as the schedule, the type of programming language to use, and the type of computer to use.

Step 5: Testing the New Software

The job of the testing team is to test the software to determine whether it operates as required. If it does not, the testing team notifies the specification team of where the problem is, but not how to fix it. Based upon the results of the testing, either the specification or the code may have to be modified. All communications between the testing team and the specification team and the development team should be documented and reviewed by the evaluation team.

As with the development team, the testing team should not have access to the original software, and members of the testing team should not be former employees of the company that created the original software. If they are former employees, ensure that they did not work on the original software and that they did not have access to related trade secrets.

Step 6: Evaluating the New Software

When the reverse engineered product is sensitive, it may make sense to have the evaluation team evaluate the final software to make sure it contains no copyrighted material. The evaluation team should also provide a double check that proper procedures were followed. In particular the evaluation team should ensure that:

- Any decompiled programs were acquired legally
- If possible, end user license agreements were not accepted by the "dirty" specification team

- All expression was removed from the specification (leaving in some very minimal or purely functional language might be permitted)
- Elements have been rearranged where possible, as the selection and arrangement of unprotectable functional code may be protected
- Intentional errors, useless code, and unique nomenclature have been removed, except where removal creates functional incompatibility (i.e., the code has to be "bug-compatible" with the original)
- No one with access to the original program, especially former employees that created the program, is on the development or testing teams
- Proper records have been kept

Reverse engineering poses a precarious legal situation, so developers starting on a reverse engineering project should check with their lawyer. Although these procedures are designed to keep people out of trouble, they do not guarantee the legal outcome, and they don't guarantee that the reverse engineering project won't be challenged in court. (Or at least it helps in the defense when the company that created the original software comes suing.)

Test-Driven Development

One new (and particularly effective) way of reverse engineering is by adhering to a rigorous system of test-driven development. Test-driven development (TDD) is an iterative software development technique wherein test cases covering the desired improvement or new functionality are written *first*. Code is only developed to pass previously written test suites.

In test-driven reverse engineering, the specification team provides test suites to the development team instead of written specifications. The development team writes code to pass the test suites. There is no separate evaluation or testing team; evaluation of the produced software is performed automatically through the running of the tests.

Rigorous test-driven development is effective for reverse engineering for three reasons. First, tests are intentionally opaque—they are designed to test functions for proper inputs and outputs only, and are not dependent upon the internal structure of the code *except where that internal structure has a functional aspect*. This is on purpose; one frequently cited benefit of test-driven development is the ability to refactor the code (incidentally removing copyrightable similarity) without affecting the functionality of the code. Therefore, test-driven development suites effectively screen all copyrightable expression from the development team.

Second, test-driven development provides an easily verifiable "clean" communication and evaluation channel between the clean and dirty teams. Having a traditional outside evaluation team absorbs limited resources. With test-driven reverse engineering, however, the test-running software itself acts as the neutral evaluation team. The tests themselves are in functional language and must be unambiguously interpreted by the test runner. The functional nature of the tests themselves acts to clean all communications between the teams; specifications can't be passed unless they are expressible in functional, testable terms.

Third, test-driven reverse engineering provides a tighter testing loop. Outside testers aren't needed to verify that the newly written code works the same way as the existing product; the tests themselves provide instant feedback because they can be run against both the old and the new code.

The Digital Millennium Copyright Act

The Digital Millennium Copyright Act, or DMCA, is a relatively new extension to the copyright statute that can restrict reverse engineering. Ironically, the DMCA was one of the first copyright acts to explicitly recognize the value of reverse engineered interoperability, and contains explicit protections for reverse engineering. Specifically, Section 1201(f) of the DMCA allows software developers to circumvent technological protection measures of a lawfully obtained computer program in order to identify and analyze those "elements necessary to achieve interoperability of an independently created computer program with other programs."

In spite of the official protection for reverse engineering, however, the creation of specific reverse engineering requirements has had the effect of reducing the scope of the reverse engineering rights. For example, developers can only reverse engineer software if there are no other means available to achieve interoperability, if the reverse engineering is otherwise allowed under the fair use provisions of copyright law, and if the developer asks permission to reverse engineer the software first. The difficulties imposed by these requirements, particularly the "permission" requirement, are obvious.

The DMCA and Digital Rights Management

The DMCA is also noted for its "trafficking" provisions. Under the DMCA, it is illegal to "traffic" "in any technology, product, service, device, component, or part thereof, that is primarily designed or produced for the purpose of circumventing protection afforded by a technological measure that effectively protects a right of a copyright owner under this title in a work or a portion thereof." This portion of the DMCA is designed to protect digital rights management (DRM) technologies.

Digital rights management is an umbrella term given to technologies that attempt to prevent unlicensed or unauthorized uses of copyrighted material. For example, CSS (Content Scrambling System) on DVDs, FairPlay on iTunes songs, and SecuROM on many game discs are all examples of DRM.

In theory, DRM allows the owners of copyrighted content to technologically control the uses of their copyrighted material to the full extent granted by the law. In practice, however, DRM systems are generally ineffective. Theoretical work has proven that it is impossible to allow some uses of the material and completely disallow other unapproved uses. Not surprisingly, therefore, DRM restrictions have turned into arms races with reverse engineering enthusiasts on one side and content producers on the other.

In particular, the DMCA anti-trafficking provisions make it illegal to share any circumvention technologies, which are generally defined as any decryption technologies that allow access to copyrighted works, even if the use of those circumvention technologies would be fair use under the law.

The unusual consequences of this law can be seen in the Dmitry Skylarov case. Dmitri Skylarov created a tool that removes DRM protections from Adobe eBook files. The actual *removal* of the DRM protections was legal both in the Russia, where Skylarov worked, as well as in the United States, where the tool was distributed. Nevertheless, *providing a tool* that could remove the DRM protections was prohibited under the DMCA's anti-trafficking provisions. When Skylarov came to the United States for a conference, he was arrested and held in jail for several months.

The DMCA and Reverse Engineering

When reverse engineering a file format or technical standard that allows users to access underlying functionality, it is important to note that reverse engineering for *data* interoperability is not protected or allowed under the DMCA, but reverse engineering for *program* interoperability is allowed. Therefore, reverse engineering a product to allow copyrighted works to be accessed in any way not already provided for by the copyright owner is prohibited. For example, this means that carrying out reverse engineering in order to view digitally formatted works, including music, movies, and video games, is explicitly prohibited.

One worrisome aspect of the DMCA is that these restrictions on reverse engineering are considered by some to extend the long terms of copyright control into the domain of physical, functional works. For example, recent cases have tried to use the DMCA to prevent reverse engineering of printer cartridges and garage door openers.

So far, most courts have not allowed the DMCA anti-circumvention provisions to create patent-like control over a product unless there has been an underlying creative and copyrighted work, but the future applicability of the DMCA to similar cases is still unclear.

CHAPTER FOURTEEN

Incorporating As a Non-Profit

You have a successful project. Everybody from the U.S. Government to Google is using your code and loving it. Companies want to donate time and resources to your project. So what are you going to do now?

~~You're going to Disneyland!~~ You're going to incorporate as a non-profit entity.

I realize that incorporating as a non-profit entity is not nearly as exciting as going to Disneyland. But if you are in this situation, incorporating as a non-profit entity may be one of the best things that you can do for your project.

Why Incorporate Your Project?

Incorporating your project is a fairly substantial step, one that imposes substantial additional burdens on the developers involved. Nevertheless, most projects that get to a certain size or achieve a certain amount of distribution choose to incorporate. Why? In a word, scalability.

Imagine a new web application. It contains a stack of individual components, such as the typical LAMP (Linux/Apache/MySQL/PHP) setup, that communicate only vertically. Although Linux, Apache, and MySQL all tolerate a certain amount of concurrency, all requests ultimately trickle down to the database layer, which handles the requests coming in from the processes.

This setup works great—up to a certain point. When faced with overwhelming traffic, the database becomes a bottleneck. It can't keep up with the flood of requests, and the web application falls over.

That is why companies handling billions of hits each day don't have a single database; they have a distributed system that hands off queries to a large number of different backend database machines. Concurrency between the many backend databases is handled by some sort of distributed locking system. The distributed lock imposes a layer of overhead on the entire application, but the overhead is necessary to coordinate the large numbers of machines needed for massive-scale web serving.

Open source projects work the same way. At the start, you set up an account with Sourceforge or Google Code, a simple web page with documentation, and away you go. Contributors come and fit themselves into your project.

As projects get larger, however, coordinating the work of the many volunteers becomes more difficult. At a certain point, project administration becomes more effort than the coding itself.

This scenario should be familiar, even if you don't participate in a project that has entered the heavy administration phase. It is a classic computer science coordination problem, applied to people. The project maintainer acts like a big lock at the center of the project, and if there are too many volunteers, the project starts to suffer from lock contention. Unfortunately, the most important work on the project—the code—can get pushed aside.

Creating a non-profit entity is like using a distributed locking system to organize people's efforts. The non-profit entity can scale much more easily than a single person while still providing the necessary coordination.

This metaphor is also appropriate in that adding a distributed locking system imposes overhead on your application, just as incorporating as a non-profit adds overhead to your project. For this reason, most projects don't incorporate until necessary. However, adding additional overhead is sometimes the only way to break through a bottleneck in the system.

It so happens, however, that when you need scalability, there are usually other difficult issues knocking at the door—issues of money, control, and continuity. Incorporation not only helps with scalability, it also provides solution for some of these other challenges.

WARNING: LEAKY ABSTRACTIONS AHEAD

Programmers frequently talk about *leaky abstractions*, when hidden underlying complexity bleeds into the cleaner high-level description of a system. While programmers may sometimes abstract away important details, it is essential to be aware that there is more complexity under the hood.

This chapter is full of leaky abstractions. It is a very *high-level* look at some of the issues surrounding recognition of non-profit status under IRS code 501(c)(3), but there are many other issues under the hood that are not discussed. There are also many other types of non-profit organizations with completely separate rules. Further, non-profit status with a state is a completely separate issue that is not addressed here.

The purpose here is not to give a how-to manual for incorporation as a non-profit. That book would be much, *much* larger than this one. Instead, I hope this helps explain the issues so that you can recognize when the advantages of non-profit incorporation might apply to your situation.

Accepting Corporate Help

One concern that can come up in a successful project is how to accept corporate help. If a successful project is used by major corporations, those corporations will often be interested in funding and ensuring the stability of a project that is helpful or essential to their infrastructures.

However, special coordination problems arise when money is involved. How should the money be spent? How should the money be allocated between the developers, since most successful open source projects have more than one developer donating time? What assurances are there that the money provided will actually be used to benefit the project?

Further, corporations have special rules that prevent their resources from being misused, and one of the most basic rules is that they cannot just cut checks to individual developers without sufficient justification. Unfortunately, "works on an open source project" is not a sufficient justification.

On the other hand, supporting a non-profit entity *is* a sufficient justification for spending money. The non-profit entity gives corporate supporters a coordination point for donations of time and code, and through the magic of tax law, may make those donations tax-deductible.

Additionally, non-profit entities can optionally be structured to give corporate users of open source projects a voice in the direction and goals of the project.

Holding Intellectual Property

Considering that this book is about intellectual property, it is probably unsurprising that there are significant intellectual property benefits to be gained by using a non-profit corporation. These benefits generally come from the ability of a non-profit to centralize control over the intellectual property.

In particular, one of the most significant pieces of intellectual property associated with an open source project is its name and logo—its trademarks. In the absence of a non-profit entity, who owns the trademarks? Who approves their usage? The lack of centralized control can put a project's goodwill—its trademarks—at risk.

For example, "Linux" is a United States registered trademark owned by Linus Torvalds, but this wasn't always so. The United States trademark on "Linux" was originally filed in 1994 by William R. Della Croce, Jr. As soon as the trademark was granted, Della Croce saw an opportunity to capitalize on the growing popularity of Linux by demanding royalties from various Linux distributors. Linus Torvalds was forced to sue in order to have the trademark assigned to him. Largely because of this incident, one of the first and largest tasks of the Linux Foundation was to register the Linux trademark in countries around the world.

Non-profit incorporation can also help handle project copyrights, as discussed in Chapter 11. Open source projects should use contributor license agreements or contributor assignment agreements. Without a central non-profit, who actually receives these license agreements? If a corporate contributor agreement is required, who are the parties on each side of the agreement?

Another important and frequently overlooked element of intellectual property is the definition of the project itself—the ability to define your own future course of action. This point is subtle, but it can be seen relative to the Python language. Python has several compatible implementations: the original Python interpreter itself, sometimes called cPython; IronPython, running on Microsoft's Common Language Runtime (the .NET platform); Jython, running on the Java Virtual Machine; PyPy, an implementation of Python in Python; and clPython, an implementation of Python in common lisp.

With all of these different implementations, it is easy to see how there might be some confusion as to what the "Python language" entails. Who defines Python? Guido van Rossum, the creator of Python and lead on cPython development? Microsoft's IronPython team? The Jython maintainers?

To avert this issue, the Python Software Foundation (the non-profit corporation set up to hold Python's intellectual property) has the power to define a compatibility standard that the various Python implementations must adhere to so that they can be called "Python-compatible." Although a "Python-compatible" standard has not yet been needed to maintain compatibility, trademark law gives the Python Software Foundation the power to define itself and its own future.

This technique is not limited to non-profits. Sun maintains its control over Java on the same basis, even though most of the Java runtime and library is now licensed under the GPL.

Legal Protection

One of the primary benefits of incorporation is legal protection for the participants in the project. When project participants form a non-profit corporation, the non-profit is the entity that is primarily liable in the case of a lawsuit. Even though lawsuits over open source projects are rare, they do happen.

For example, America Online sued the Gaim project for infringing on its trademark (this problem was discussed in Chapter 5). More specifically, America Online sued individual contributors to the Gaim project. Each person targeted by a lawsuit was forced to go to the expense and trouble of finding a lawyer and responding to the suit. This effectively brought Gaim development to a halt for a couple years.

The solution for the Gaim project was to organize under a non-profit foundation. The non-profit could negotiate for all of the Gaim project members at once, and more importantly, the individual developers were all protected from individual liability.

Project Continuity and Transfer of Ownership

Another difficult issue to overcome is project continuity. What do you do when the original developers can't contribute as much time? How do you keep projects alive from maintainer to maintainer? non-profit organizations provide a resolution to all of these issues. Usually, the non-profit is made the "owner" of the project, and individual contributors are "members" or "directors" of the project. Even when one member or director stops contributing, the legal structure continues operating. This structure makes it easy to maintain a project over the long term.

Creating a Non-Profit Entity

The laws for creating a non-profit entity vary from state to state, so there is no single magic formula to create a non-profit foundation for your project. The following principles are representative, however, and they give an idea of the types of strictures and structures that you may have in your state.

Choosing a State

Speaking of states, the first thing to do is to choose a state in which to incorporate. Although some states may have advantages over others, such as lower fees or fewer required reports, the best course of action is usually to incorporate in the state where one or more members of the project will establish the *principal place of business*—the official address for the new non-profit and its legal home. The problem is that the principle place of business for an open source project can be somewhat nebulous, as projects can have contributors from all over the globe. In that case, other considerations, such as convenience or well-developed non-profit law might apply.

About Delaware

Despite the general rule above, there is one state that must be mentioned in particular. Many non-profits (like many corporations) choose to register in Delaware. This is for three reasons.

First, it is easy to create a Delaware corporation. As of this writing, the state requires only an $89 filing fee and no yearly franchise fee. Delaware even has expedited filing rules that allow you to create your non-profit in a day. The convenience also extends to corporate formalities; Delaware requires fewer directors and fewer meetings than many other states.

Second, Delaware has a long history of business law. Court cases are decided on *precedent*—on what has been decided before. Delaware has an advantage because its long history of business cases has given it the most extensive and well-defined body of corporate law in the United States. This makes it is easy for lawyers and courts to find the right answers for basic issues and makes business decisions more predictable, both of which may lower legal costs.

Third, Delaware business rules allow lawyers outside of Delaware to provide opinions to Delaware-incorporated entities. If you're incorporated in another state, it is possible that only a lawyer admitted to that state can provide a formal opinion on some matters.

However, the convenience of filing for incorporation in Delaware may be more than offset by a greater inconvenience if you do most of your business in another state. Some states have requirements for corporations (including non-profit corporations) formed elsewhere to register as "foreign businesses" subject to extra requirements and fees. Some states have additional registration requirements for non-profit entities soliciting funds within the state.

Further, unless an organizing project member lives in the state of incorporation, the state may require the project to appoint an *agent for service of process* within the state. This agent is somebody who can be contacted for official business regarding the non-profit. There are businesses that will perform this function for a fee, but that imposes another burden on the project.

As a side note, Delaware may also be a good place to incorporate if you are bent on world domination. For example, KAOS, the terrorist organization in the *Get Smart!* TV show of the 1960s, was incorporated in Delaware.

Formation Documents

When you are compiling open source software, the process normally involves three types of input files: the *source file*, *make*, and *configure*. Even though the source file contains all the code for the eventual binary, *configure* and *make* are necessary to direct the compilation of the code into binary form. *Make* directs the compiler to create the binary, and *configure* specifies the options that will be used.

Similarly, forming a non-profit usually requires three inputs: the people on the project, the articles of incorporation, and the bylaws. The people on the project are like the source code; they do the work year after year and provide the reason for the non-profit entity to exist. The *articles of incorporation* are like *make*, directing the state to create the non-profit, and the *bylaws* are like *configure* in that they specify the "options" and procedures that will be used to run the non-profit.

Articles of incorporation

Articles of incorporation (also called by other names, like the *Certificate of Incorporation*, the *Corporate Charter*, or the *Certificate of Formation*) are contained in a single document filed with the state government, usually the Secretary of State.

The articles of incorporation usually contain just the bare minimum of information necessary to create the non-profit entity, specifically, the fundamental *identifying* and *operating* characteristics of the non-profit. This document (there are multiple articles contained in the single document) actually creates the non-profit. Once the document containing the articles is filed with and approved by the state, your new non-profit legally exists.

The articles of incorporation generally contain:

The entity name
: The entity name must be unique in your jurisdiction (basically, your state). In computing terms, your entity name is a unique pointer that people can use to identify your non-profit. In some jurisdictions, the name must include a designation of the entity's legal status as a corporation by including a word such as "incorporated," "limited," "corporation," or their respective abbreviations. The name must also be chosen so that it isn't deceptive and doesn't imply that the non-profit has governmental authority (like "State Police"). This type of restriction can apply in other circumstances. For example, Texas limits the use of terms that would imply that the entity is a bank or financial institution.

The address
: This is the location of the non-profit's registered office, the place where the organization can be reached if necessary. If you think of the entity name as a pointer to a const object, this is the address referred to by the pointer.

The organizers
: The articles must include the name of the person or persons organizing the non-profit. This is often the same group that will be on the initial board of directors, although the directors can be named separately.

The entity's purpose
: For for-profit corporations, the purpose of the organization is usually described as "any legal purpose." For a non-profit open source organization, the articles would usually specify that the non-profit is organized "exclusively for educational and scientific purposes." The tax code may specify other necessary language.

The duration
: Some entities are created only for a specific period of time, while others can exist indefinitely. For most non-profits, the specified duration would be "perpetual," although this may be limited by state law.

MUTUAL BENEFIT SAMPLE

ARTICLES OF INCORPORATION

I

The name of the corporation is *[NAME OF CORPORATION]*.

II

A. This corporation is a nonprofit **Mutual Benefit Corporation** organized under the Nonprofit Mutual Benefit Corporation Law. The purpose of this corporation is to engage in any lawful act or activity, other than credit union business, for which a corporation may be organized under such law.

B. The specific purpose of this corporation is to ______________________________
______________________________.

III

The name and address in the State of California of this corporation's initial agent for service of process is:

Name ______________________________

Address ______________________________

City ______________________________ State **CALIFORNIA** Zip Code __________

IV

Notwithstanding any of the above statements of purposes and powers, this corporation shall not, except to an insubstantial degree, engage in any activities or exercise any powers that are not in furtherance of the specific purposes of this corporation.

[Signature of Incorporator]
____
[Typed Name of Incorporator], Incorporator

If an individual is designated as the initial agent for service of process, include the agent's business or residential street address in California (a P.O. Box address is not acceptable). If another corporation is designated as the initial agent for service of process, do not include the address of the designated corporation.

This sample is provided to be used as a guideline ONLY in the preparation of the original document for filing with the Secretary of State.

Secretary of State **Sample**
ARTS-MU (REV 01/2008)

FIGURE 14-1. California non-profit articles of incorporation (sample only)

Tax statements

Non-profit organizations must include specific wording stating that none of the assets of the corporation will be used to benefit the members. Additional statements may be required by the IRS or state law.

Many states offer sample forms for articles of incorporation. Figure 14-1 shows a sample of non-profit articles of incorporation provided by the state of California. Be aware, however, that each situation is unique and using random forms found on a search engine will usually lead to poor results.

Bylaws

Bylaws can be a bit more complicated than the articles of incorporation. They are the "instruction manual" for running and operating the non-profit. They are not usually filed with the state, but instead are kept as part of the non-profit's official paperwork. Typical bylaws may include information about:

Directors
: The bylaws specify the number of directors, how they are elected, their terms of office, and what they are allowed to do. The directors are usually the people who ultimately control and are responsible for the non-profit.

Officers
: Officers are different from directors. Directors supervise the overall functioning of the organization, whereas officers are responsible for the day-to-day handling of events that come up. Not all non-profits have officers; the bylaws specify which positions and roles will be officially supported by the non-profit, as well as how those roles will be filled. State law may dictate which officers are required.

Members
: Not all non-profit organizations have members, but open source foundations usually do. If there are members, the bylaws specify how they are chosen, their rights, and how (and when) those rights can be exercised. Members can sometimes control the organization instead of directors, depending on state law.

Meetings
: The bylaws normally include the time and place for meetings of officers, directors, and members, as well as the number of people necessary to conduct the business of the non-profit.

Financial information
: Broad-brush financial rules are frequently included in the bylaws. For example, the bylaws may contain rules for the budgeting procedures and the fiscal year of the non-profit, as well as for approval of contracts, checks, and donations.

Operating procedures
: The procedures typically spell out the method of voting, requirements for record-keeping, and rules for inspection of the records. One important procedure is the procedure for changing the bylaws, so that the non-profit can adapt to changing circumstances.

Open source non-profit foundations generally have the flexibility to adopt rules that work for their projects. Most times, bylaws will be adopted to reflect the existing internal workings of the community. If there is a democratic process for problem resolution, similar processes can be adopted in the bylaws. Other "benevolent dictator"-style projects may choose to give the officers and directors of the non-profit greater discretion.

Many of the open source projects that have started non-profit foundations make their formation documents available on the Web. For example, you can see the Apache Foundation's bylaws at *http://apache.org/foundation/bylaws.html*.

Tax-Exempt Status

Charitable non-profit organizations must apply to the Internal Revenue Service (IRS) to establish a tax-exempt status for federal income tax purposes. Without recognition from the IRS of 501(c)(3) tax-exempt status, contributions to the organization will generally not be deductible by donors as charitable contributions. They may, however, be deductible by businesses as "business expenses."

The application for tax-exempt status (Form 1023) should usually be filed with the IRS within 27 months after the creation of the organization. Form 1023 is quite lengthy, but it is basically designed to demonstrate four points:

- The foundation is organized and operated only to forward a recognized "exempt" purpose. In most cases, open source non-profits will be organized with the charitable and scientific purposes of promoting the use and development of their open source software.
- None of the net earnings of the non-profit will go toward the benefit of private shareholders or individuals.
- The non-profit will not attempt to influence legislation or participate in political campaigns.
- The non-profit is not organized or operated for the benefit of private interests, such as those of the founder, the founder's family, or the members of the foundation.

Most open source foundations should be able to meet these requirements. If the IRS approves the application, it will issue a *determination letter* to the foundation, which states that the foundation is exempt from federal income tax under section 501(c)(3) of the Internal Revenue Code. You should keep that letter, as it provides evidence to potential donors that yours is an organization to which some deductible charitable contributions can be made and identifies the type of organization recognized under the tax code.

Getting Registered

Another piece of preliminary business is registering with the IRS for an Employer Identification Number (EIN). An EIN is like a social security number, but is granted to a corporation (or a non-profit). Even if you don't anticipate ever having any employees, the EIN is still required for filing various tax documents and interacting with other companies. For example, the EIN is necessary to apply to the IRS for tax-exempt status and will probably be necessary to open a bank account.

To apply for an EIN you have to file a Form SS-4. You can do this online or via the IRS's toll-free number. If needed, detailed instructions are available at the IRS's web site at *http://www.irs.gov/*.

It is also possible that you will need the equivalent of the EIN for your state. The IRS has a collection of links to state government web sites on its small business portal. You can also ask your state for a copy of the new business guide. Most states provide these guides for free.

Operating a Non-Profit Organization

As I mentioned earlier, there are drawbacks to having a non-profit organization. They have reporting and fundraising requirements, and must adhere to certain formalities. These requirements must be observed, and that takes time.

However, the first and most important thing to remember about incorporated non-profit organizations is that the people associated with them must always remember to *respect the existence of the organization*. This almost sounds ridiculous, but it is the single biggest problem that people encounter.

To understand why this is a problem, think again about the analogy of a distributed locking system for an application. Assume for a moment that you implemented such a system, but instead of using it, you allowed certain threads or processes to directly manipulate protected shared resources.

Crazy, right? The application is already paying for the overhead of the locking system. Completely ignoring the locks means that you get none of the protection that the locking system is supposed to provide, and the application is going to blow up sooner or later when it turns out that two processes have done the wrong thing at the wrong time.

This is exactly analogous to ignoring the corporate formalities required for your non-profit entity. If you have already paid for the overhead of incorporating a non-profit organization, why ignore it? Just like in the distributed locking system, ignoring your non-profit means that the legal protections (and tax-exempt status) provided by the corporate form may not protect you, and your project may blow up when someone does the wrong thing at the wrong time.

Thankfully, the operating requirements for a non-profit are very manageable. They basically boil down to rules about doing your best, holding meetings, keeping notes, receiving money, spending money, and providing reports.

Doing Your Best

The people involved in a non-profit cannot and are not expected to be perfect. We can't make the right decisions all the time. However, those who have been entrusted to act for a non-profit organization are required to do their best to advance the interests of the non-profit and to not let their own interests get in the way.

More specifically, the principal members of a non-profit should make sure they take care of their duties in good faith, with ordinary care, and in a manner that they reasonably believe to be in the best interests of the organization. As long as these three requirements are met, the directors can avoid being held individually liable for any mistakes they make as directors.

Good faith refers to putting forth legitimate and honest efforts to meet the obligations of the office. *Ordinary care* is usually described as the same level of care that a reasonably prudent person would use under the same circumstances. *Reasonable belief regarding the best interests of the organization* is self-explanatory. Notice, however, that all beliefs and actions must be *reasonable* to an ordinary person.

Officers and directors may generally have fiduciary duties to the non-profit in certain circumstances. A *fiduciary* is someone who has been placed in a position of trust, frequently relative to some property owned by another person. In the case of an open source organization, this could refer both to the money brought in to support the project and to the project itself. A person placed in that position of trust is expected to be extremely loyal to those that expressed that trust (the *duty of loyalty*) and he must be prudent with the objects of that trust (the *duty of care*). In practical terms, this means that the people in charge of a non-profit must not put their personal interests before their work for the organization, and they must not receive any unwarranted compensation or profit from their work in the organization.

Holding Meetings

Non-profits must comply with the *corporate formalities* required by their state in order to maintain their status as a non-profit organization. The most significant of these formalities is holding an annual Board of Directors meeting. At these annual meetings, directors should, among other things, elect the incoming directors and officers of the foundation and adopt resolutions concerning some of the foundation's more significant activities. The time and place of these annual meetings may be determined by the Board of Directors, and the general rules for these meetings are usually described in the bylaws. In the case of open source organizations, these meetings are frequently held in conjunction with a major conference to facilitate and encourage attendance.

The exact requirements may vary from state to state, but the general rule is that the Board of Directors will take an action if a *quorum* (minimum number) of directors are present, and if a majority of the directors present at the meeting vote for the action. The bylaws may specify, for example, that a majority of all directors constitutes a quorum. Directors can usually vote in person, by telephone conference, via signed email, or by unanimous written consent, although specifics vary depending on state law and the organization's organizational documents.

Part of the duty of reasonable care includes holding meetings as necessary. The exact timing and frequency of these additional meetings (outside of the required yearly meeting) can be set in the bylaws or otherwise arranged by the Board of Directors.

Keeping Notes

An organization has two kinds of actions: making decisions and spending money. In order to make sure that the people in charge of the organization are doing the right things, organizations are required to keep notes of all that they do.

This is especially important for non-profit organizations. A non-profit should not engage in non-exempt activities. The only way to prove to the government that your organization deserves to maintain its tax-exempt status is to keep the necessary notes and report back as necessary. Specifically, this means keeping *minutes* and *financial records*.

Minutes

Non-profit organizations act by making decisions. The exact method for making decisions is laid out in the bylaws, but the usual method is that decisions are made based on a majority vote of the directors of the organization. A non-profit should keep minutes of any meetings of the Board of Directors (as well as of any committees having the authority of the Board of Directors). If decisions can be made in any other contexts, appropriate minutes should be kept there as well.

Minutes are simply records of what went on in the meetings where decisions were made—who was there, which topics were discussed, which votes were taken, and which conclusions were reached. These minutes should be prepared for each meeting and kept in storage.

Financial records

Non-profits must maintain correct and complete books and records of all financial transactions. To properly document its activities, the non-profit should keep detailed records showing:

- The names and addresses of all parties who received *distributions* (money)
- The amount of each distribution
- The purpose of each distribution
- The relationship between persons receiving distributions and the foundation's officers, grantors, or substantial contributors (as well as their families and the corporations controlled by them)

The IRS requires that tax-exempt non-profits keep permanent books setting forth contributions, gross income, deductions, credit, or other matters that are required in any return that the organization is required to file.

Receiving Money

There are two broad categories of 501(c)(3) non-profit organizations: *private foundations* and *public charities*. (The categories are sometimes called "private foundations" and "other than private foundations," showing an unusual mastery of Venn diagrams.) The status of any particular organization is determined by source of its funds. It is useful to be a public charity because donors to public charities get better tax treatment than donors to private foundations, and private foundations are subject to more IRS restrictions than public charities.

The public support test

The difference between private foundations and public charities is public support, as measured by a "public support test." An organization will generally be treated as a publicly supported organization if the total amount of support normally received by the organization (as measured by a government formula) from the general public, other charities, or the government, is at least one third of the total support normally received by the organization.

Alternatively, the non-profit may be considered publicly supported if it receives at least 10% of its financial support from the sources described above and the "facts and circumstances" around the non-profit show the public nature of the organization. Documenting the necessary facts and circumstances, however, involves many pages of supporting detail, exceptions, and rules. It is usually necessary to have an accountant to help set up the books.

Most open source organizations should be able to set themselves up so that their non-profit organizations are considered public charities.

Related and unrelated income

While generally exempt from federal income tax, non-profits may be subject to tax on any *unrelated* income. Income is considered unrelated when it comes from an activity that does not promote the recognized educational, scientific, or charitable purpose of the non-profit organization.

Specific activities are considered on a "duck typing" principle; a particular activity will be scrutinized if the non-profit carries out that activity in a manner comparable to a taxable organization. If the activity contributes substantially to one of the non-profit organization's recognized exempt purposes, then it may be considered *related* income. All other income is unrelated. Note that simply generating income that will be used to pursue an exempt purpose does not make that income related.

As an oversimplified example, one open source non-profit may declare its purpose to be "educating people about the advantages of Linux in the computing industry." In that case, the revenue from selling "Linux has more uptime!" t-shirts may be related income, as it could further the educational purposes described in the non-profit's charter.

On the other hand, another open source non-profit may declare its purpose to be "providing a free interoperable IPv6 stack for use across platforms." In this case, the revenue from "Linux has more uptime!" T-shirts would not necessarily further the scientific purposes described in the charter.

If a non-profit receives more than $500 in unrelated income, that income will be taxed. Unrelated business income also affects the income calculations used for the public support test, so more donations will be needed to maintain its status as a public charity. Consult an accountant about the application of these rules in particular circumstances.

Commingling funds

Regardless of how a non-profit receives money, project maintainers should *never* commingle organization funds with their own money.

What is commingling? Well, imagine you receive $100 for your non-profit from a donor. You have separate books for your non-profit, of course, because you are keeping notes about each financial transaction. You methodically update the books to reflect the new total and then carefully deposit it in your private bank account, making sure that the total in the bank account exactly matches the sum from your books and the organization's books.

Bzzzt!

You just commingled funds. Commingling just means, "putting in the same bank account," and again, you should never do it. Always put the funds in the *organization's* bank account.

Spending Money

In order to retain its tax-exempt status, a non-profit must be operated exclusively for tax-exempt purposes. Somewhat tautologically, a non-profit is exempt from taxes unless any substantial part of its activities is directed toward a non-exempt purpose. Because spending money is one primary way in which organizations operate and affect the outside world, a non-profit must spend its money on things related to its tax-exempt purposes. If a non-profit is found to violate this requirement, it may lose its exempt status or be subject to other penalties.

Lobbying prohibited

Generally, political lobbying may not be a substantial part of organizational activities, and non-profits may not participate in political campaigns for or against any candidate for public office. Open source organizations should avoid doing anything that could be considered political lobbying or involvement in a political campaign.

Excess benefits

One of the benefits given to public charities is that they are not generally subject to additional *excise taxes*, which may apply to private foundations. Nevertheless, 501(c)(3) public charities and those closely associated with them may become subject to excise taxes under Code Section 4958 if there are *excess benefit transactions*.

An excess benefit transaction exists if an economic benefit that is provided by a non-profit organization to a disqualified person in the organization, where the value of the economic benefit exceeds the value received in return by the organization.

Disqualified persons generally include:

- Substantial contributors to the foundation
- Foundation managers
- An owner of a substantial percentage of a corporation, partnership, trust, or unincorporated enterprise that is a substantial contributor to the foundation
- A family member of any disqualified person
- Another legal entity in which disqualified persons hold more than a 35% interest (these are generally organization insiders)

To restate the issue, the non-profit organization cannot give any unearned money or benefits to organization insiders. This doesn't prevent the non-profit from paying people for services rendered. Even insiders may receive reasonable compensation for their services to the organization and reimbursement of expenses. Any excess benefits, however, may be taxed.

Providing Reports

One of the benefits of receiving recognition from the IRS as a 501(c)(3) organization is the ability of project donors to potentially receive tax deductions for their contributions. Non-profit organizations must provide receipts for any contributions made to the non-profit.

In addition, 501(c)(3) non-profits are required to file a form (Form 990, 990-EZ, or 990-PF) each year, describing the source of non-profit funds, contributions made during the year, substantial contributors, and the recipients of *disbursements* (payouts) for the year. Individual states also have filing rules and reporting requirements that must be maintained. Check the rules established by your state. Providing these reports should be relatively easy, however, if you have kept good financial notes as described above.

Umbrella Organizations As an Alternative

One growing alternative to the incorporation of individual projects is to join an *umbrella organization*. An umbrella organization is a single non-profit organization that is designed to provide infrastructure and support to many related or unrelated subprojects. This single umbrella organization acts as the fiscal sponsor and corporate parent for the projects, allowing them to receive the benefits of non-profit incorporation while sharing some of the burdens.

In particular, projects organized under the umbrella organization receive the benefits described above, without actually having to form and maintain their own organizations. Another benefit is that the only Board of Directors is at the level of the umbrella organization, so open source projects coming in under an umbrella organization can usually keep the same organizational structure they had as a decentralized project. This single professionalized organization can provide support to many separate associated projects.

If your project already has substantial corporate involvement, in may make sense to form your own non-profit organization. If your project needs the infrastructure provided by a non-profit, but is relatively new or growing, it may make sense to apply for membership in an umbrella organization. As these organizations are presently constituted, the option remains to form your own dedicated non-profit organization later.

The three most prominent umbrella organizations for free and open source software are the Free Software Foundation (*http://www.fsf.org/*), the Apache Software Foundation, (*http://www.apache.org/foundation/*), and the Software Freedom Conservancy (*http://conservancy.softwarefreedom.org/*). It would probably be best to try the Software Freedom Conservancy first, as that organization handles the broadest range of projects.

APPENDIX A

Sample Proprietary Information Agreement (PIA)

Proprietary Information and Inventions Assignment Agreement

[NAME OF COMPANY]

In consideration of my employment with ______________________ (the "*Company*"), the Company's promise to disclose to me its confidential and proprietary information (as defined below), the compensation now and hereafter paid to me, and for other good and valuable consideration, the receipt and sufficiency of which is hereby acknowledged, I hereby agree with the Company as follows:

1. **Recognition of Company's Rights; Nondisclosure.** At all times during the term of my employment and thereafter, I will hold in strictest confidence and will not disclose, use, lecture upon, or publish any of the Company's Proprietary Information (defined below), except as such disclosure, use, or publication may be required in connection with my work for the Company, or unless the President or the Board of Directors of the Company expressly authorizes such in writing. I hereby assign to the Company any rights I may have or acquire in such Proprietary Information and recognize that all Proprietary Information shall be the sole property of the Company and its assigns and that the Company and its assigns shall be the sole owner of all patent rights, copyrights, trade secret rights, and all other rights throughout the world (collectively, "*Proprietary Rights*") in connection therewith.

The term *"Proprietary Information"* shall mean trade secrets, confidential knowledge, data, or any other proprietary information of, or acquired by, the Company and each of its subsidiaries or affiliated companies. By way of illustration but not limitation, *"Proprietary Information"* includes:

a. this Agreement;

b. inventions, trade secrets, ideas, processes, formulas, data, lists, programs, other works of authorship, know-how, improvements, discoveries, developments, designs, and techniques relating to the business or proposed business of the Company and that were learned or discovered by me during the term of my employment with the Company, except as expressly permitted by the Board of Directors of the Company during the term of my employment, at the time of my termination, or subsequent to my termination (hereinafter, included Proprietary Information is collectively referred to as *"Inventions"*);

c. information regarding plans for research, development, new products and services, marketing and selling, business plans, budgets and unpublished financial statements, licenses, prices and costs, suppliers, customer lists, and customers that were learned or discovered by me during the term of my employment with the Company, except as expressly permitted by the Board of Directors of the Company during the term of my employment, at the time of my termination, or subsequent to my termination; and

d. information regarding the skills and compensation of other employees of the Company. The Company hereby promises to disclose to you its confidential and Proprietary Information.

2. **Third Party Information**. I understand, in addition, that the Company may from time to time receive from third parties confidential or proprietary information (*"Third Party Information"*) subject to a duty on the Company's part to maintain the confidentiality of such information and to use it only for certain limited purposes. During the term of my employment and thereafter, I will hold Third Party Information in the strictest confidence and will not disclose (to anyone other than Company personnel who need to know such information in connection with their work for the Company) or use, except in connection with my work for the Company, Third Party Information unless expressly authorized by an executive officer of the Company in writing.

3. **Assignment of Inventions.**

   1. I hereby assign to the Company all my right, title, and interest in and to any and all Inventions (and all Proprietary Rights with respect thereto), whether or not patentable or registrable under copyright or similar statutes, that were made or conceived or reduced to practice or learned by me, either alone or jointly with others, during the period of my employment with the Company.

   2. I acknowledge that all original works of authorship that are made by me (solely or jointly with others) during the term of my employment with the Company and that are within the scope of my employment and protectable by copyright are "works made

for hire," as that term is defined in the United States Copyright Act (17 U.S.C. § 101). Inventions assigned to the Company by this paragraph 3 are hereinafter referred to as "*Company Inventions.*"

4. **Enforcement of Proprietary Rights.** I will assist the Company in every proper way to obtain and from time to time enforce United States and foreign Proprietary Rights relating to Company Inventions in any and all countries. To that end I will execute, verify, and deliver such documents and perform such other acts (including appearances as a witness) as the Company may reasonably request for use in applying for, obtaining, perfecting, evidencing, sustaining, and enforcing such Proprietary Rights and the assignment thereof. In addition, I will execute, verify, and deliver assignments of such Proprietary Rights to the Company or its designee. My obligation to assist the Company with respect to Proprietary Rights relating to such Company Inventions in any and all countries shall continue beyond the termination of my employment, but the Company shall compensate me at a reasonable rate after my termination for the time actually spent by me at the Company's request on such assistance.

   In the event the Company is unable for any reason, after reasonable effort, to secure my signature on any document needed in connection with the actions specified in the preceding paragraph, I hereby irrevocably designate and appoint the Company and its duly authorized officers and agents as my agent and attorney in fact, to act for and in my behalf to execute, verify, and file any such documents and to do all other lawfully permitted acts to further the purposes of the preceding paragraph thereon with the same legal force and effect as if executed by me. I hereby waive and quitclaim to the Company any and all claims, of any nature whatsoever, that I now or may hereafter have for infringement of any Proprietary Rights assigned hereunder to the Company.

5. **Obligation to Keep Company Informed.** During the period of my employment, I will promptly disclose to the Company fully and in writing and will hold in trust for the sole right and benefit of the Company any and all Inventions. In addition, I will disclose all patent applications filed by me during the three (3) years after termination of my employment with the Company.

6. **Prior Inventions.** Inventions, if any, patented or unpatented, that I made prior to the commencement of my employment with the Company are excluded from the scope of this Agreement. To preclude any possible uncertainty, I have set forth on Exhibit A attached hereto a complete list of all Inventions that I have, alone or jointly with others, conceived, developed, or reduced to practice or caused to be conceived, developed, or reduced to practice prior to commencement of my employment with the Company, that I consider to be my property or the property of third parties and that I wish to have excluded from the scope of this Agreement. If disclosure of any such Invention on Exhibit A would cause me to violate any prior confidentiality Agreement, I understand that I am not to list such Inventions in Exhibit A but am to inform the Company that all Inventions have not been listed for that reason.

7. **Other Activities; Non-Competition; Non-Solicitation; Inevitable Disclosure.**

    1. During the term of my employment with the Company, I will not, directly or indirectly, participate in the ownership, management, operation, financing or control of, or be employed by or consult for or otherwise render services to, any person, corporation, firm, or other entity that competes in the State of [State], or in any other state in the United States, or in any country in the world with the Company in the conduct of the business of the Company as conducted or as proposed to be conducted, nor shall I engage in any other activities that conflict with my obligations to the Company.

    2. In consideration of the promises hereof and in further consideration of the Company's promise to disclose to me confidential and proprietary information and trade secrets of the Company and the Company's promise to provide me with immediate specialized training, and the experience I will gain throughout my employment with the Company, and for other good and valuable consideration, the receipt and sufficiency of which is hereby acknowledged, I hereby agree that for a period of one (1) year after the date that my employment with the Company is terminated, for any reason, I will not, directly or indirectly,

        1. compete in the state of [State], or in any other State of the United States, or in any other country in the world where the Company engages in business, or proposes to engage in business, on the date of the termination of my employment with the Company, or

        2. participate in the ownership, management, operation, financing, or control of, or be employed by or consult for or otherwise render services to, any person, corporation, firm, or other entity that competes in the state of [State], or in any other State of the United States, or in any other country in the world with the Company in the conduct of the business of the Company as conducted and as proposed to be conducted on the date of termination of my employment. Notwithstanding the foregoing, I am permitted to own up to 5% of any class of securities of any corporation that is traded on a national securities exchange or through Nasdaq.

    3. During the term of my employment and for a period of one (1) year after my employment with the Company is terminated for any reason, I will not, directly or indirectly, individually or on behalf of any other person, firm, partnership, corporation, or business entity of any type, hire, solicit, assist or in any way encourage any current employee or consultant of the Company or any subsidiary of the Company to terminate his or her employment relationship or consulting relationship with the Company or subsidiary nor will I hire or solicit the employment services of any former employee of the Company or any subsidiary of the Company whose employment has been terminated for less than six (6) months.

4. For a period of one (1) year after my employment with the Company is terminated for any reason, I will not, directly or indirectly, individually or on behalf of any other person, firm, partnership, corporation, or business entity of any type, solicit, contact, call upon, communicate with, or attempt to communicate with, any Customer of the Company if such solicitation, contact, call or communication could be deemed by the Company to be competitive with the business of the Company as conducted or as proposed to be conducted. For purposes of this section, "*Customer*" shall mean any company or business entity that the Company sells goods or services to and that I had contact with or performed services for during the last year of my employment with the Company.

5. In consideration of the promises hereof and in further consideration of the Company's promise to disclose to me confidential and proprietary information and trade secrets of the Company and the Company's promise to provide me with immediate specialized training, and the experience I will gain throughout my employment with the Company, and for other good and valuable consideration, the receipt and sufficiency of which is hereby acknowledged, I hereby agree that in the event that I am employed by, consult for or otherwise render services to, any person, corporation, firm, or other entity that is a competitor of the Company, in the same or comparable position as my position in the Company, I agree that my services for that competitor would result in the inevitable disclosure of the Company's confidential information, proprietary information and/or trade-secrets. In addition, I agree to provide the Company with at least five (5) days prior written notice before I begin any employment with any third party within one (1) year after the termination of my employment with the Company.

8. **No Improper Use of Materials**. I understand that I shall not use the proprietary or confidential information or trade secrets of any former employer or any other person or entity in connection with my employment with the Company. During my employment by the Company, I will not improperly use or disclose any proprietary or confidential information or trade secrets, if any, of any former employer or any other person or entity to whom I have an obligation of confidentiality, and I will not bring onto the premises of the Company any unpublished documents or any property belonging to any former employer or any other person or entity to whom I have an obligation of confidentiality unless consented to in writing by that former employer, person, or entity.

9. **No Conflicting Obligation**. I represent that my performance of all the terms of this Agreement and as an employee of the Company does not and will not breach any agreement between me and any other employer, person, or entity. I have not entered into, and I agree I will not enter into, any agreement either written or oral in conflict herewith.

10. **Return of Company Documents**. When I leave the employ of the Company, I will deliver to the Company all drawings, notes, memoranda, specifications, devices, formulas, and

documents, together with all copies thereof, and any other material containing or disclosing any Company Inventions, Third Party Information, or Proprietary Information of the Company. I further agree that any property situated on the Company's premises and owned by the Company, including disks and other storage media, filing cabinets or other work areas, is subject to inspection by Company personnel at any time with or without notice.

11. **Legal and Equitable Remedies**. Because my services are personal and unique and because I may have access to and become acquainted with the Proprietary Information of the Company, the Company shall have the right to enforce this Agreement and any of its provisions by injunction, specific performance, or other equitable relief, without bond and without prejudice to any other rights and remedies that the Company may have for a breach of this Agreement.
12. **Authorization to Notify New Employer**. I hereby authorize the Company to notify my new employer about my rights and obligations under this Agreement following the termination of my employment with the Company.
13. **Notices**. Any notices required or permitted hereunder shall be given to me at the address specified on the signature herein, and to the Company, at its principal executive office. Such notice shall be deemed given upon personal delivery to the appropriate address or if sent by certified or registered mail, three days after the date of mailing.
14. **General Provisions.**
    1. <u>Governing Law</u>. This Agreement will be governed by and construed according to the laws of the State of [State] without regard to conflicts of law principles.
    2. <u>Exclusive Forum</u>. I hereby irrevocably agree that the exclusive forum for any suit, action, or other proceeding arising out of or in any way related to this Agreement shall be in the state or federal courts in [State], and I agree to the exclusive personal jurisdiction and venue of any court in [Location].
    3. <u>Entire Agreement</u>. This Agreement sets forth the entire agreement and understanding between the Company and myself relating to the subject matter hereof and supercedes and merges all prior discussions between us. No modification of or amendment to this Agreement, nor any waiver of any rights under this Agreement, will be effective unless in writing signed by the party to be charged. Any subsequent change or changes in my duties, salary, or compensation will not affect the validity or scope of this Agreement. As used in this Agreement, the period of my employment includes any time during which I may be retained by the Company as a consultant.
    4. <u>Severability</u>.
        a. I acknowledge and agree that each agreement and covenant set forth herein constitutes a separate agreement independently supported by good and adequate consideration and that each such agreement shall be severable from the other provisions of this Agreement and shall survive this Agreement.

b. I understand and agree that Section 7 of this Agreement is to be enforced to the fullest extent permitted by law. Accordingly, if a court of competent jurisdiction determines that the scope and/or operation of Section 7 is too broad to be enforced as written, the Company and I intend that the court should reform such provision to such narrow scope and/or operation as it determines to be enforceable, provided, however, that such reformation applies only with respect to the operation of such provision in the particular jurisdiction with respect to which such determination was made. If, however, Section 7 is held to be illegal, invalid, or unenforceable under present or future law, and not subject to reformation, then

   1. such provision shall be fully severable,
   2. this Agreement shall be construed and enforced as if such provision was never a part of this Agreement, and
   3. the remaining provisions of this Agreement shall remain in full force and effect and shall not be affected by the illegal, invalid, or unenforceable provision or by its severance.

5. Successors and Assigns. This Agreement will be binding upon my heirs, executors, administrators, and other legal representatives and will be for the benefit of the Company, its successors and assigns.
6. Survival. The provisions of this Agreement shall survive the termination of my employment for any reason and the assignment of this Agreement by the Company to any successor in interest or other assignee.
7. Employment. I agree and understand that my employment with the Company is at will, which means that either I or the Company may terminate the employment relationship at any time, with or without prior notice and with or without cause. I further agree and understand that nothing in this Agreement shall confer any right with respect to continuation of employment by the Company, nor shall it interfere in any way with my right or the Company's right to terminate my employment at any time, with or without cause.
8. Waiver. No waiver by the Company of any breach of this Agreement shall be a waiver of any preceding or succeeding breach. No waiver by the Company of any right under this Agreement shall be construed as a waiver of any other right. The Company shall not be required to give notice to enforce strict adherence to all terms of this Agreement.
9. Headings. The headings to each section or paragraph of this Agreement are provided for convenience or reference only and shall have no legal effect in the interpretation of the terms hereof.

* * * * *

I HAVE READ THIS CONFIDENTIALITY, PROPRIETARY INFORMATION AND INVENTIONS AGREEMENT CAREFULLY AND UNDERSTAND ITS TERMS. I HAVE COMPLETELY FILLED OUT EXHIBIT A TO THIS AGREEMENT.

This Agreement shall be effective as of the first day of my employment with the Company, namely: ___________________, 20__.

I UNDERSTAND THAT THIS AGREEMENT AFFECTS MY RIGHTS TO INVENTIONS I MAKE DURING MY EMPLOYMENT, RESTRICTS MY RIGHT TO DISCLOSE OR USE THE COMPANY'S CONFIDENTIAL AND PROPRIETARY INFORMATION DURING OR SUBSEQUENT TO MY EMPLOYMENT, AND PROHIBITS ME FROM COMPETING WITH THE COMPANY AND/OR FROM SOLICITING EMPLOYEES AND CUSTOMERS OF THE COMPANY FOR TWO (2) YEARS AFTER MY EMPLOYMENT WITH THE COMPANY IS TERMINATED FOR ANY REASON.

Dated: ___________________, 20__

____

Signature of Employee

____

Print Name of Employee

Address:

____

____

ACCEPTED AND AGREED TO:

[Name of Company]

By: ______________________

Name: __________________

Title: ___________________

EXHIBIT A

The following is a complete list of all inventions or improvements relevant to the subject matter of my employment with ____________________ (the *"Company"*) that have been made or conceived or first reduced to practice by me alone or jointly with others prior to my employment by the Company that I desire to remove from the operation of the Company's Proprietary Information and Inventions Assignment Agreement.

_____ No inventions or improvements.

_____ See below:

_____ Additional sheets attached.

I propose to bring to my employment the following materials and documents of a former employer:

_____ No materials or documents. See below:

Signature ____

Date ____

INVENTION DISCLOSURE

Invention Disclosure #

Inventors:

1. ______________________________

2. ______________________________

3. ______________________________

Title of Invention: ____________________________________

Problem solved by invention: ___________________________

Invention Description: _______________________________

Add additional signed, witnessed, and dated sheets and drawings if necessary.

Has this invention been disclosed outside of the Company? Yes No

Inventor Signature: _________________ Date: _________________

Witness Signature: __________________ Date: _________________

APPENDIX B

Open Source License List

Open Source Licenses

The following licenses* have been certified as Open Source by the Open Source Initiative. The license categories are from the Open Source Initiative's License Proliferation Committee report.

For a list of current licenses, see the following sites:

http://opensource.org/licenses/category

http:// opensource.org/licenses/alphabetical

Licenses That Are Popular and Widely Used or with Strong Communities

We used statistics obtained from public sources to determine which licenses are widely used. We believed that there were a few licenses that, while not the most popular, were widely used within their communities and that these also belonged in this group.

Apache License, 2.0
New and Simplified BSD licenses
GNU General Public License (GPL)(version 2)
GNU Library or "Lesser" General Public License (LGPL) (version 2)
MIT license
Mozilla Public License 1.1 (MPL)

* From "Open Source Licenses By Category," *http://opensource.org/licenses/category*. Used under CC-BY license.

Common Development and Distribution License
Common Public License 1.0
Eclipse Public License

Special Purpose Licenses

Certain licensors, such as schools and the U.S. government, have specialized concerns, such as specialized rules for government copyrights. Licenses that were identified as meeting a special need were placed in this group.

Educational Community License
NASA Open Source Agreement 1.3
Open Group Test Suite License

Other/Miscellaneous Licenses

Adaptive Public License
Artistic License 2.0
Open Software License
Qt Public License (QPL)
zlib/libpng License

Licenses That Are Redundant with More Popular Licenses

Several licenses in this group are excellent licenses and have their own followings. The committee struggled with this group, but ultimately decided that if we were to attack the license proliferation problem, we had to prune licenses. Thus, licenses that were perceived as completely or partially redundant with existing licenses were placed in this group.

Academic Free License
Attribution Assurance Licenses
Eiffel Forum License version 2.0
Fair License
Historical Permission Notice and Disclaimer
Lucent Public License version 1.02
University of Illinois/NCSA Open Source License
X.Net License

Non-reusable Licenses

Licenses in this group are specific to their authors and cannot be reused by others. Many, but not all, of these licenses fall into the category of vanity licenses.

Apple Public Source License
Computer Associates Trusted Open Source License 1.1
CUA Office Public License version 1.0
EU DataGrid Software License
Entessa Public License

Frameworx License
IBM Public License
Motosoto License
Multics License
Naumen Public License
Nethack General Public License
Nokia Open Source License
OCLC Research Public License 2.0
PHP License
Python license (CNRI Python License)
Python Software Foundation License
RealNetworks Public Source License version 1.0
Reciprocal Public License
Ricoh Source Code Public License
Sleepycat License
Sun Public License
Sybase Open Watcom Public License 1.0
Vovida Software License version 1.0
W3C License
wxWindows Library License
Zope Public License

Superseded Licenses

Licenses in this category have been superseded by newer versions. No one should use these licenses going forward, although we assume that licensors may or may not choose to continue to use them.

Apache Software License 1.0
Artistic license 1.0
Eiffel Forum License (version 1)
Lucent Public License (Plan9)
Mozilla Public License 1.0 (MPL)

Licenses That Have Been Voluntarily Retired

Intel Open Source License
Jabber Open Source License
MITRE Collaborative Virtual Workspace License (CVW License)
Sun Industry Standards Source License (SISSL)

Uncategorized Licenses

Affero GNU Public License
Boost Software License (BSL1.0)
Common Public Attribution License 1.0 (CPAL)
GNU General Public License version 3.0 (GPLv3)
GNU Library or "Lesser" General Public License version 3.0 (LGPLv3)

ISC License
Microsoft Public License (Ms-PL)
Microsoft Reciprocal License (Ms-RL)
NTP License
Reciprocal Public License 1.5 (RPL1.5)
Simple Public License 2.0.

APPENDIX C

Free Software License List

Free Software Licenses

These licenses have been certified as Free Software Licenses by the Free Software Foundation. For discussion of these licenses, see "Various Licenses and Comments about Them," at *http://www.gnu.org/licenses/license-list.html*.

The GPL-Compatible Free Software Licenses

GNU General Public License (GPL) version 3
GNU General Public License (GPL) version 2
GNU Lesser General Public License (LGPL) version 3
GNU Lesser General Public License (LGPL) version 2.1
GNU Affero General Public License (AGPL) version 3
Apache License, version 2.0
Artistic License 2.0
Clarified Artistic License
Berkeley Database License (a.k.a. the Sleepycat Software Product License)
Boost Software License
Modified BSD license
CeCILL version 2
Cryptix General License
eCos license version 2.0
Eiffel Forum License, version 2
EU DataGrid Software License
Expat License

FreeBSD license
License of the iMatix Standard Function Library
Intel Open Source License
Microsoft Public License (Ms-PL)
NCSA/University of Illinois Open Source License
License of Netscape Javascript
OpenLDAP License, Version 2.7
License of Perl 5 and below
Public Domain
License of Python 2.0.1, 2.1.1, and newer versions
License of Python 1.6a2 and earlier versions
License of Ruby
Standard ML of New Jersey Copyright License
License of Vim, version 6.1 or later
W3C Software Notice and License
X11 License
XFree86 1.1 License
License of Zlib
Zope Public License, versions 2.0 and 2.1

GPL-Incompatible Free Software Licenses

The following licenses are free software licenses, but are not compatible with the GNU GPL.

Affero General Public License version 1
Academic Free License, all versions through 3.0
Apache License, version 1.1
Apache License, version 1.0
Apple Public Source License (APSL), version 2
Original BSD license
Common Development and Distribution License (CDDL)
Common Public License version 1.0
Condor Public License
Eclipse Public License version 1.0
IBM Public License, version 1.0
Interbase Public License, version 1.0
Jabber Open Source License, version 1.0
LaTeX Project Public License 1.3a
LaTeX Project Public License 1.2
Lucent Public License version 1.02 (Plan 9 license)
Microsoft Reciprocal License (Ms-RL)
Mozilla Public License (MPL)
Netizen Open Source License (NOSL), version 1.0
Netscape Public License (NPL), versions 1.0 and 1.1
Nokia Open Source License
Old OpenLDAP License, version 2.3
Open Software License, all versions through 3.0
OpenSSL license
Phorum License, version 2.0

PHP License, version 3.01
License of Python 1.6b1 through 2.0 and 2.1
Q Public License (QPL), version 1.0
RealNetworks Public Source License (RPSL), version 1.0
Sun Industry Standards Source License 1.0
Sun Public License
License of xinetd
Zend License, version 2.0
Zope Public License version 1

APPENDIX D

Fedora License List and GPL Compatibility

Licenses Approved for Use with Fedora

Table D-1 shows the licenses that are approved for use with the Fedora project.* This is for software only; documentation and other content have different licenses. For the current list, see the licensing page on the Fedora wiki: *http://fedoraproject.org/wiki/Licensing*.

TABLE D-1. Fedora-approved licenses

Full name	Short name	FSF free?	GPLv2 compat?	GPLv3 compat?
3dfxGlide License	Glide	Yes	NO	NO
Academic Free License	AFL	Yes	NO	
Academy of Motion Picture Arts and Sciences BSD	AMPAS BSD	Yes	NO	NO
Adobe Systems Incorporated Source Code License Agreement	Adobe	Yes	Yes	Yes
Affero General Public License 1.0	AGPLv1	Yes	NO	
Affero General Public License 3.0	AGPLv3	Yes	NO	Yes—special exception

* Taken from the Licensing page on the Fedora wiki, maintained by Tom "spot" Calloway. Used by permission.

Full name	Short name	FSF free?	GPLv2 compat?	GPLv3 compat?
Amazon Digital Services License	ADSL	Yes	Yes	Yes
Apache Software License 1.0	ASL 1.0	Yes	NO	NO
Apache Software License 1.1	ASL 1.1	Yes	NO	NO
Apache Software License 2.0	ASL 2.0	Yes	NO	Yes
Apple Public Source License 2.0	APSL 2.0	Yes	NO	
Artistic (clarified)	Artistic clarified	Yes	Yes	Yes
Artistic 2.0	Artistic 2.0	Yes	Yes	Yes
Aspell-ru License	ARL	Yes	NO	NO
BitTorrent License	BitTorrent	Yes	NO	NO
Boost Software License	Boost	Yes	Yes	Yes
BSD License (original)	BSD with advertising	Yes	NO	NO
BSD License (no advertising)	BSD	Yes	Yes	Yes
BSD License (two clause)	BSD	Yes	Yes	Yes
CeCILL License v2	CeCILL	Yes	Yes	
CMU License (BSD like)	MIT	Yes	Yes	Yes
Common Development Distribution License	CDDL	Yes	NO	
Common Public License	CPL	Yes	NO	
Condor Public License	Condor	Yes	NO	
Copyright Attribution Only	Copyright only	Yes	Yes	Yes
CPAL License 1.0	CPAL	Yes	NO	NO
Cryptix General License	Cryptix	Yes	NO	
Crystal Stacker License	Crystal Stacker	Yes	Yes	Yes
Do What The F*ck You Want To Public License	WTFPL	Yes	Yes	Yes
DOC License	DOC	Yes	Yes	Yes
Eclipse Public License 1.0	EPL	Yes	NO	
eCos License v2.0	eCos	Yes	Yes	
enna License	MIT	Yes	Yes	Yes
Eiffel Forum License 2.0	EFL 2.0	Yes	Yes	

Full name	Short name	FSF free?	GPLv2 compat?	GPLv3 compat?
Enlightenment License (e16)	MIT with advertising	Yes	NO	NO
EU Datagrid Software License	EU Datagrid	Yes	Yes	
Fedora Directory Server License	GPLv2 with exceptions	Yes	Yes	Yes
Fair License	Fair	Yes	Yes	Yes
feh License	MIT	Yes	Yes	Yes
FLTK License	LGPLv2 with exceptions	Yes	Yes	
FreeImage Public License	MPLv1.0	Yes	NO	
Freetype License	FTL	Yes	NO	Yes
Giftware License	Giftware	Yes	Yes	Yes
GNU General Public License (no version)	GPL+	Yes	Yes	
GNU General Public License v2.0 only	GPLv2	Yes	See Matrix	See Matrix
GNU General Public License v2.0 only, with font embedding exception	GPLv2 with exceptions	Yes	See Matrix	See Matrix
GNU General Public License v2.0 or later	GPLv2+	Yes	N/A	See Matrix
GNU General Public License v2.0 or later, with font embedding exception	GPLv2+ with exceptions	Yes	N/A	See Matrix
GNU General Public License v3.0 only	GPLv3	Yes	See Matrix	N/A
GNU General Public License v3.0 only, with font embedding exception	GPLv3 with exceptions	Yes	See Matrix	N/A
GNU General Public License v3.0 or later	GPLv3+	Yes	See Matrix	N/A
GNU General Public License v3.0 or later, with font embedding exception	GPLv3+ with exceptions	Yes	See Matrix	N/A

Full name	Short name	FSF free?	GPLv2 compat?	GPLv3 compat?
GNU Lesser General Public License (no version)	LGPLv2+	Yes	Yes	
GNU Lesser General Public License v2 (or 2.1) only	LGPLv2	Yes	See Matrix	See Matrix
GNU Lesser General Public License v2 (or 2.1), with exceptions	LGPLv2 with exceptions	Yes	See Matrix	See Matrix
GNU Lesser General Public License v2 (or 2.1) or later	LGPLv2+	Yes	See Matrix	See Matrix
GNU Lesser General Public License v2 (or 2.1) or later, with exceptions	LGPLv2+ with exceptions	Yes	See Matrix	See Matrix
GNU Lesser General Public License v3.0 only	LGPLv3	Yes	See Matrix	See Matrix
GNU Lesser General Public License v3.0 only, with exceptions	LGPLv3 with exceptions	Yes	See Matrix	See Matrix
GNU Lesser General Public License v3.0 or later	LGPLv3+	Yes	See Matrix	See Matrix
GNU Lesser General Public License v3.0 or later, with exceptions	LGPLv3+ with exceptions	Yes	See Matrix	See Matrix
gnuplot License	gnuplot	Yes	NO	NO
IBM Public License	IBM	Yes	NO	
iMatix Standard Function Library Agreement	iMatix	Yes	Yes	
ImageMagick License	ImageMagick	Yes	Yes	Yes
Imlib2 License	Imlib2	Yes	Yes	Yes
Independent JPEG Group License	IJG	Yes	Yes	Yes
Intel ACPI Software License Agreement	Intel ACPI	Yes	Yes	
Interbase Public License	Interbase	Yes	NO	
ISC License (Bind, DHCP Server)	ISC	Yes	Yes	Yes
Jabber Open Source License	Jabber	Yes	NO	
JasPer License	JasPer	Yes	Yes	Yes
LaTeX Project Public License	LPPL	Yes	NO	

Full name	Short name	FSF free?	GPLv2 compat?	GPLv3 compat?
Lawrence Berkeley National Labs BSD variant license	LBNL BSD	Yes	Yes	Yes
libtiff License	libtiff	Yes	Yes	Yes
Lucent Public License (Plan9)	LPL	Yes	NO	
mecab-ipadic license	mecab-ipadic	Yes	?	
MIT license (also X11)	MIT	Yes	Yes	Yes
Mozilla Public License v1.0	MPLv1.0	Yes	NO	
Mozilla Public License v1.1	MPLv1.1	Yes	Compatible if dual licensed with GPL, otherwise Incompatible	
mpich2 License	MIT	Yes	Yes	Yes
MySQL License	GPLv2 with exceptions	Yes	?	
Naumen Public License	Naumen	Yes	Yes	Yes
NCSA/University of Illinois Open Source License	NCSA	Yes	Yes	
Neotonic Clearsilver License	ASL 1.1	Yes	NO	NO
NetCDF license	NetCDF	Yes	Yes	Yes
Nethack General Public License	NGPL	Yes	NO	
Netizen Open Source License	NOSL	Yes	NO	
Netscape Public License	Netscape	Yes	NO	
Nokia Open Source License	Nokia	Yes	NO	
NRL License	BSD with advertising	Yes	NO	
OpenLDAP License	OpenLDAP	Yes	Yes	
OpenPBS License	OpenPBS	Yes	NO	NO
Open Software License 1.0	OSL 1.0	Yes	NO	NO
Open Software License 1.1	OSL 1.1	Yes	NO	NO
Open Software License 2.0	OSL 2.0	Yes	NO	NO
Open Software License 3.0	OSL 3.0	Yes	NO	NO
OpenSSL License	OpenSSL	Yes	NO	

Full name	Short name	FSF free?	GPLv2 compat?	GPLv3 compat?
O'Reilly License	O'Reilly	Yes	NO	NO
Perl License	GPL+ or Artistic	Yes	Yes	Yes
Perl License (variant)	GPLv2+ or Artistic	Yes	Yes	Yes
Phorum License	Phorum	Yes	NO	
PHP License v3.0	PHP	Yes	NO	
Public Domain	Public Domain	Yes	Yes	
Python License	Python	Yes	Yes	
Q Public License	QPL	Yes	NO	
RealNetworks Public Source License v1.0	RPSL	Yes	NO	
Ruby License	Ruby	Yes	Compatible if dual licensed with GPL, otherwise Incompatible	
Sendmail License	Sendmail	Yes	Compatible if Eric Allman, Sendmail Inc. or the University of California is the copyright holder	Compatible if Eric Allman, Sendmail Inc. or the University of California is the copyright holder
Sleepycat Software Product License	Sleepycat	Yes	Yes	
SLIB License	SLIB	Yes	Yes	Yes
Standard ML of New Jersey License	MIT	Yes	Yes	
Sun Industry Standards Source License	SISSL	Yes	NO	
Sun Public License	SPL	Yes	NO	
TCL/TK License	TCL	Yes	Yes	Yes
Unicode Character Database Terms Of Use	UCD	Yes	Yes	Yes
Vim License	Vim	Yes	Yes	
Vita Nuova Liberal Source License	VNLSL	Yes	NO	

Full name	Short name	FSF free?	GPLv2 compat?	GPLv3 compat?
VOSTROM Public License for Open Source	VOSTROM	Yes	NO	NO
Vovida Software License v1.0	VSL	Yes	NO	
W3C Software Notice and License	W3C	Yes	Yes	
wxWidgets Library License	wxWidgets	Yes	Yes	
xinetd License	xinetd	Yes	NO	
Xerox License	Xerox	Yes	NO	NO
Zend License v2.0	Zend	Yes	NO	
Zope Public License v1.0	ZPLv1.0	Yes	NO	NO
Zope Public License v2.0	ZPLv2.0	Yes	Yes	Yes
Zope Public License v2.1	ZPLv2.1	Yes	Yes	Yes
zlib/libpng License	zlib	Yes	Yes	
zlib/libpng License with Acknowledgement	zlib with acknowledgement	Yes	NO	NO

GPL Compatibility Matrix

In Table D-2, the labels across the top of the columns show the license under which you want to release your project, whereas the labels down the left side of the rows show the license of the code you want to copy into your project.

TABLE D-2. Including source code in your project

		GPLv2 only	GPLv2 or later	GPLv3 or later	LGPLv2.1 only	LGPLv2.1 or later	LGPLv3 or later
	GPLv2 only	OK	OK [a]	NO	OK if you convert to GPLv2 [b]	OK if you convert to GPLv2 [b] [a]	NO
	GPLv2 or later	OK [c]	OK	OK	OK if you convert to GPL [b]	OK if you convert to GPL [b]	OK if you convert to GPLv3 [d]
	GPLv3	NO	OK if you upgrade to GPLv3 [e]	OK	OK if you convert to GPLv3 [b]	OK if you convert to GPLv3 [b] [e]	OK if you convert to GPLv3 [d]

		GPLv2 only	GPLv2 or later	GPLv3 or later	LGPLv2.1 only	LGPLv2.1 or later	LGPLv3 or later
	LGPLv2.1 only	OK if you convert to GPLv2 [b]	OK if you convert to GPL [b] [a]	OK if you convert to GPLv3 [b]	OK	OK [f]	OK if you convert to GPLv3 [b] [d]
	LGPLv2.1 or later	OK if you convert to GPLv2 [b] [g]	OK if you convert to GPL [b]	OK if you convert to GPLv3 [b]	OK [h]	OK	OK
	LGPLv3	NO	OK if you upgrade and convert to GPLv3 [d] [e]	OK if you convert to GPLv3 [d]	OK if you convert to GPLv3 [d]	OK if you upgrade to LGPLv3 [i]	OK

a If you do this, as long as the project contains the code released under GPLv2 only, you will not be able to upgrade the project's license to GPLv3 or later.

b LGPLv2.1 gives you permission to relicense the code under any version of the GPL since GPLv2. If you can switch the LGPLed code in this case to using an appropriate version of the GPL instead (as noted in the table), you can make this combination.

c You must follow the terms of GPLv2 when incorporating the code in this case. You cannot take advantage of terms in later versions of the GPL.

d LGPLv3 gives you permission to relicense the code under GPLv3. In these cases, you can combine the code if you convert the LGPLed code to GPLv3.

e If you have the ability to release the project under GPLv2 or any later version, you can choose to release it under GPLv3 or any later version—and once you do that, you'll be able to incorporate the code released under GPLv3.

f If you do this, as long as the project contains the code released under LGPLv2.1 only, you will not be able to upgrade the project's license to LGPLv3 or later.

g You must follow the terms of GPLv2 when incorporating the code in this case. You cannot take advantage of terms in later versions of the GPL.

h You must follow the terms of LGPLv2.1 when incorporating the code in this case. You cannot take advantage of terms in later versions of the LGPL.

i If you have the ability to release the project under LGPLv2.1 or any later version, you can choose to release it under LGPLv3 or any later version—and once you do that, you'll be able to incorporate the code released under LGPLv3.

In Table D-3, the labels across the top of the columns show the license under which you want to release your project, whereas the labels down the left side of the rows show the license of the code you want to copy into your project.

TABLE D-3. Linking libraries with your project

		GPLv2 only	GPLv2 or later	GPLv3 or later	LGPLv2.1 only	LGPLv2.1 or later	LGPLv3 or later
	GPLv2 only	OK	OK [a]	NO	OK if you convert to GPLv2 [b]	OK if you convert to GPLv2 [b] [a]	NO

	GPLv2 only	GPLv2 or later	GPLv3 or later	LGPLv2.1 only	LGPLv2.1 or later	LGPLv3 or later
GPLv2 or later	OK [c]	OK	OK	OK if you convert to GPL [b] [c]	OK if you convert to GPL [b]	OK if you convert to GPLv3 [c]
GPLv3	NO	OK if you upgrade to GPLv3 [d]	OK	OK if you convert to GPLv3 [b]	OK if you convert to GPLv3 [b] [d]	OK if you convert to GPLv3 [c]
LGPLv2.1 only	OK	OK	OK	OK	OK	OK
LGPLv2.1 or later	OK	OK	OK	OK	OK	OK
LGPLv3	NO	OK	OK	OK	OK	OK

a If you do this, as long as the project contains the code released under GPLv2 only, you will not be able to upgrade the project's license to GPLv3 or later.

b LGPLv2.1 gives you permission to relicense the code under any version of the GPL since GPLv2. If you can switch the LGPLed code in this case to using an appropriate version of the GPL instead (as noted in the table), you can make this combination.

c LGPLv3 gives you permission to relicense the code under GPLv3. In these cases, you can combine the code if you convert the LGPLed code to GPLv3.

d If you have the ability to release the project under GPLv2 or any later version, you can choose to release it under GPLv3 or any later version—and once you do that, you'll be able to incorporate the code released under GPLv3.

APPENDIX E

Public Domain Declaration

Copyright-Only Dedication (based on United States law) or Public Domain Certification[*]

The person or persons who have associated work with this document (the "Dedicator" or "Certifier") hereby either (a) certifies that, to the best of his knowledge, the work of authorship identified is in the public domain of the country from which the work is published, or (b) hereby dedicates whatever copyright the dedicators holds in the work of authorship identified below (the "Work") to the public domain. A certifier, moreover, dedicates any copyright interest he may have in the associated work, and for these purposes, is described as a "dedicator" below.

A certifier has taken reasonable steps to verify the copyright status of this work. Certifier recognizes that his good faith efforts may not shield him from liability if in fact the work certified is not in the public domain.

Dedicator makes this dedication for the benefit of the public at large and to the detriment of the Dedicator's heirs and successors. Dedicator intends this dedication to be an overt act of relinquishment in perpetuity of all present and future rights under copyright law, whether vested or contingent, in the Work. Dedicator understands that such relinquishment of all rights includes the relinquishment of all rights to enforce (by lawsuit or otherwise) those copyrights in the Work.

* Taken from Creative Commons, *http://creativecommons.org/licenses/publicdomain.*

Dedicator recognizes that, once placed in the public domain, the Work may be freely reproduced, distributed, transmitted, used, modified, built upon, or otherwise exploited by anyone for any purpose, commercial or non-commercial, and in any way, including by methods that have not yet been invented or conceived.

APPENDIX F

The Simplified BSD License

The following is a BSD license template. To generate your own license, change the values of OWNER, ORGANIZATION, and YEAR from their original values as given here, and substitute your own.

There is also a third optional clause, shown in brackets below.

The BSD License

Copyright (c) <YEAR>, <OWNER>

All rights reserved.

Redistribution and use in source and binary forms, with or without modification, are permitted provided that the following conditions are met:

- Redistributions of source code must retain the above copyright notice, this list of conditions and the following disclaimer.
- Redistributions in binary form must reproduce the above copyright notice, this list of conditions and the following disclaimer in the documentation and/or other materials provided with the distribution.
- [OPTIONAL] Neither the name of the <ORGANIZATION> nor the names of its contributors may be used to endorse or promote products derived from this software without specific prior written permission.

APPENDIX G

The Apache License, Version 2.0

Apache License,

Version 2.0,

January 2004

http://www.apache.org/licenses/

TERMS AND CONDITIONS FOR USE, REPRODUCTION, AND DISTRIBUTION

1. **Definitions.**

   "License" shall mean the terms and conditions for use, reproduction, and distribution as defined by Sections 1 through 9 of this document.

   "Licensor" shall mean the copyright owner or entity authorized by the copyright owner that is granting the License.

   "Legal Entity" shall mean the union of the acting entity and all other entities that control, are controlled by, or are under common control with that entity. For the purposes of this definition, "control" means (i) the power, direct or indirect, to cause the direction or management of such entity, whether by contract or otherwise, or (ii) ownership of fifty percent (50%) or more of the outstanding shares, or (iii) beneficial ownership of such entity.

   "You" (or "Your") shall mean an individual or Legal Entity exercising permissions granted by this License.

   "Source" form shall mean the preferred form for making modifications, including but not limited to software source code, documentation source, and configuration files.

"Object" form shall mean any form resulting from mechanical transformation or translation of a Source form, including but not limited to compiled object code, generated documentation, and conversions to other media types.

"Work" shall mean the work of authorship, whether in Source or Object form, made available under the License, as indicated by a copyright notice that is included in or attached to the work (an example is provided in the Appendix below).

"Derivative Works" shall mean any work, whether in Source or Object form, that is based on (or derived from) the Work and for which the editorial revisions, annotations, elaborations, or other modifications represent, as a whole, an original work of authorship. For the purposes of this License, Derivative Works shall not include works that remain separable from, or merely link (or bind by name) to the interfaces of, the Work and Derivative Works thereof.

"Contribution" shall mean any work of authorship, including the original version of the Work and any modifications or additions to that Work or Derivative Works thereof, that is intentionally submitted to Licensor for inclusion in the Work by the copyright owner or by an individual or Legal Entity authorized to submit on behalf of the copyright owner. For the purposes of this definition, "submitted" means any form of electronic, verbal, or written communication sent to the Licensor or its representatives, including but not limited to communication on electronic mailing lists, source code control systems, and issue tracking systems that are managed by, or on behalf of, the Licensor for the purpose of discussing and improving the Work, but excluding communication that is conspicuously marked or otherwise designated in writing by the copyright owner as "Not a Contribution."

"Contributor" shall mean Licensor and any individual or Legal Entity on behalf of whom a Contribution has been received by Licensor and subsequently incorporated within the Work.

2. **Grant of Copyright License**. Subject to the terms and conditions of this License, each Contributor hereby grants to You a perpetual, worldwide, non-exclusive, no-charge, royalty-free, irrevocable copyright license to reproduce, prepare Derivative Works of, publicly display, publicly perform, sublicense, and distribute the Work and such Derivative Works in Source or Object form.

3. **Grant of Patent License**. Subject to the terms and conditions of this License, each Contributor hereby grants to You a perpetual, worldwide, non-exclusive, no-charge, royalty-free, irrevocable (except as stated in this section) patent license to make, have made, use, offer to sell, sell, import, and otherwise transfer the Work, where such license applies only to those patent claims licensable by such Contributor that are necessarily infringed by their Contribution(s) alone or by combination of their Contribution(s) with the Work to which such Contribution(s) was submitted. If You institute patent litigation against any entity (including a cross-claim or counterclaim in a lawsuit) alleging that the Work or a Contribution incorporated within the Work constitutes direct or contributory

patent infringement, then any patent licenses granted to You under this License for that Work shall terminate as of the date such litigation is filed.

4. **Redistribution**. You may reproduce and distribute copies of the Work or Derivative Works thereof in any medium, with or without modifications, and in Source or Object form, provided that You meet the following conditions:

    1. You must give any other recipients of the Work or Derivative Works a copy of this License; and

    2. You must cause any modified files to carry prominent notices stating that You changed the files; and

    3. You must retain, in the Source form of any Derivative Works that You distribute, all copyright, patent, trademark, and attribution notices from the Source form of the Work, excluding those notices that do not pertain to any part of the Derivative Works; and

    4. If the Work includes a "NOTICE" text file as part of its distribution, then any Derivative Works that You distribute must include a readable copy of the attribution notices contained within such NOTICE file, excluding those notices that do not pertain to any part of the Derivative Works, in at least one of the following places: within a NOTICE text file distributed as part of the Derivative Works; within the Source form or documentation, if provided along with the Derivative Works; or, within a display generated by the Derivative Works, if and wherever such third-party notices normally appear. The contents of the NOTICE file are for informational purposes only and do not modify the License. You may add Your own attribution notices within Derivative Works that You distribute, alongside or as an addendum to the NOTICE text from the Work, provided that such additional attribution notices cannot be construed as modifying the License.

    You may add Your own copyright statement to Your modifications and may provide additional or different license terms and conditions for use, reproduction, or distribution of Your modifications, or for any such Derivative Works as a whole, provided Your use, reproduction, and distribution of the Work otherwise complies with the conditions stated in this License.

5. **Submission of Contributions**. Unless You explicitly state otherwise, any Contribution intentionally submitted for inclusion in the Work by You to the Licensor shall be under the terms and conditions of this License, without any additional terms or conditions. Notwithstanding the above, nothing herein shall supersede or modify the terms of any separate license agreement you may have executed with Licensor regarding such Contributions.

6. **Trademarks**. This License does not grant permission to use the trade names, trademarks, service marks, or product names of the Licensor, except as required for reasonable and customary use in describing the origin of the Work and reproducing the content of the NOTICE file.

7. **Disclaimer of Warranty**. Unless required by applicable law or agreed to in writing, Licensor provides the Work (and each Contributor provides its Contributions) on an "AS IS" BASIS, WITHOUT WARRANTIES OR CONDITIONS OF ANY KIND, either express or implied, including, without limitation, any warranties or conditions of TITLE, NON-INFRINGEMENT, MERCHANTABILITY, or FITNESS FOR A PARTICULAR PURPOSE. You are solely responsible for determining the appropriateness of using or redistributing the Work and assume any risks associated with Your exercise of permissions under this License.
8. **Limitation of Liability**. In no event and under no legal theory, whether in tort (including negligence), contract, or otherwise, unless required by applicable law (such as deliberate and grossly negligent acts) or agreed to in writing, shall any Contributor be liable to You for damages, including any direct, indirect, special, incidental, or consequential damages of any character arising as a result of this License or out of the use or inability to use the Work (including but not limited to damages for loss of goodwill, work stoppage, computer failure or malfunction, or any and all other commercial damages or losses), even if such Contributor has been advised of the possibility of such damages.
9. **Accepting Warranty or Additional Liability**. While redistributing the Work or Derivative Works thereof, You may choose to offer, and charge a fee for, acceptance of support, warranty, indemnity, or other liability obligations and/or rights consistent with this License. However, in accepting such obligations, You may act only on Your own behalf and on Your sole responsibility, not on behalf of any other Contributor, and only if You agree to indemnify, defend, and hold each Contributor harmless for any liability incurred by, or claims asserted against, such Contributor by reason of your accepting any such warranty or additional liability.

END OF TERMS AND CONDITIONS

APPENDIX: How to apply the Apache License to your work

To apply the Apache License to your work, attach the following boilerplate notice, with the fields enclosed by brackets "[ ]" replaced with your own identifying information. (Don't include the brackets!) The text should be enclosed in the appropriate comment syntax for the file format. We also recommend that a file or class name and description of purpose be included on the same "printed page" as the copyright notice for easier identification within third-party archives. Copyright [yyyy] [name of copyright owner] Licensed under the Apache License, Version 2.0 (the "License"); you may not use this file except in compliance with the License.

You may obtain a copy of the License at:

http://www.apache.org/licenses/LICENSE-2.0

APPENDIX H

The Mozilla Public License, Version 1.1

1. Definitions

1.0.1. "Commercial Use" means distribution or otherwise making the Covered Code available to a third party.

"Contributor" means each entity that creates or contributes to the creation of Modifications.

1.2. "Contributor Version" means the combination of the Original Code, prior Modifications used by a Contributor, and the Modifications made by that particular Contributor.

1.3. "Covered Code" means the Original Code or Modifications or the combination of the Original Code and Modifications, in each case including portions thereof.

1.4. "Electronic Distribution Mechanism" means a mechanism generally accepted in the software development community for the electronic transfer of data.

1.5. "Executable" means Covered Code in any form other than Source Code.

1.6. "Initial Developer" means the individual or entity identified as the Initial Developer in the Source Code notice required by Exhibit A.

1.7. "Larger Work" means a work which combines Covered Code or portions thereof with code not governed by the terms of this License.

1.8.1. "Licensable" means having the right to grant, to the maximum extent possible, whether at the time of the initial grant or subsequently acquired, any and all of the rights conveyed herein.

1.9. "Modifications" means any addition to or deletion from the substance or structure of either the Original Code or any previous Modifications. When Covered Code is released as a series of files, a Modification is:

a. Any addition to or deletion from the contents of a file containing Original Code or previous Modifications.

b. Any new file that contains any part of the Original Code or previous Modifications.

1.10. "Original Code" means Source Code of computer software code which is described in the Source Code notice required by Exhibit A as Original Code, and which, at the time of its release under this License is not already Covered Code governed by this License.

1.10.1. "Patent Claims" means any patent claim(s), now owned or hereafter acquired, including without limitation, method, process, and apparatus claims, in any patent Licensable by grantor.

1.11. "Source Code" means the preferred form of the Covered Code for making modifications to it, including all modules it contains, plus any associated interface definition files, scripts used to control compilation and installation of an Executable, or source code differential comparisons against either the Original Code or another well known, available Covered Code of the Contributor's choice. The Source Code can be in a compressed or archival form, provided the appropriate decompression or de-archiving software is widely available for no charge.

1.12. "You" (or "Your") means an individual or a legal entity exercising rights under, and complying with all of the terms of, this License or a future version of this License issued under Section 6.1. For legal entities, "You" includes any entity which controls, is controlled by, or is under common control with You. For purposes of this definition, "control" means (a) the power, direct or indirect, to cause the directionor management of such entity, whether by contract or otherwise, or (b) ownership of more than fifty percent (50%) of the outstanding shares or beneficial ownership of such entity.

2. Source Code License

2.1. The Initial Developer Grant

The Initial Developer hereby grants You a world-wide, royalty-free, non-exclusive license, subject to third party intellectual property claims:

a. under intellectual property rights (other than patent or trademark) Licensable by Initial Developer to use, reproduce, modify, display, perform, sublicense and distribute the Original Code (or portions thereof) with or without Modifications, and/or as part of a Larger Work; and

b. under Patents Claims infringed by the making, using or selling of Original Code, to make, have made, use, practice, sell, and offer for sale, and/or otherwise dispose of the Original Code (or portions thereof).

c. the licenses granted in this Section 2.1(a) and (b) are effective on the date Initial Developer first distributes Original Code under the terms of this License.

d. Notwithstanding Section 2.1(b) above, no patent license is granted:

   1. for code that You delete from the Original Code;
   2. separate from the Original Code; or
   3. for infringements caused by:
      1. the modification of the Original Code or
      2. the combination of the Original Code with other software or devices.

2.2. Contributor Grant

Subject to third party intellectual property claims, each Contributor hereby grants You a world-wide, royalty-free, non-exclusive license

a. under intellectual property rights (other than patent or trademark) Licensable by Contributor, to use, reproduce, modify, display, perform, sublicense and distribute the Modifications created by such Contributor (or portions thereof) either on an unmodified basis, with other Modifications, as Covered Code and/or as part of a Larger Work; and

b. under Patent Claims infringed by the making, using, or selling of Modifications made by that Contributor either alone and/or in combination with its Contributor Version (or portions of such combination), to make, use, sell, offer for sale, have made, and/or otherwise dispose of:

   1. Modifications made by that Contributor (or portions thereof); and
   2. the combination of Modifications made by that Contributor with its Contributor Version (or portions of such combination).

c. the licenses granted in Sections 2.2(a) and 2.2(b) are effective on the date Contributor first makes Commercial Use of the Covered Code.

d. Notwithstanding Section 2.2(b) above, no patent license is granted:

   1. for any code that Contributor has deleted from the Contributor Version;
   2. separate from the Contributor Version;
   3. for infringements caused by:
      1. third party modifications of Contributor Version or
      2. the combination of Modifications made by that Contributor with other software (except as part of the Contributor Version) or other devices; or

4. under Patent Claims infringed by Covered Code in the absence of Modifications made by that Contributor.

3. Distribution Obligations

3.1. Application of License

The Modifications which You create or to which You contribute are governed by the terms of this License, including without limitation Section 2.2. The Source Code version of Covered Code may be distributed only under the terms of this License or a future version of this License released under Section 6.1, and You must include a copy of this License with every copy of the Source Code You distribute. You may not offer or impose any terms on any Source Code version that alters or restricts the applicable version of this License or the recipients' rights hereunder. However, You may include an additional document offering the additional rights described in Section 3.5.

3.2. Availability of Source Code

Any Modification which You create or to which You contribute must be made available in Source Code form under the terms of this License either on the same media as an Executable version or via an accepted Electronic Distribution Mechanism to anyone to whom you made an Executable version available; and if made available via Electronic Distribution Mechanism, must remain available for at least twelve (12) months after the date it initially became available, or at least six (6) months after a subsequent version of that particular Modification has been made available to such recipients. You are responsible for ensuring that the Source Code version remains available even if the Electronic Distribution Mechanism is maintained by a third party.

3.3. Description of Modifications

You must cause all Covered Code to which You contribute to contain a file documenting the changes You made to create that Covered Code and the date of any change. You must include a prominent statement that the Modification is derived, directly or indirectly, from Original Code provided by the Initial Developer and including the name of the Initial Developer in (a) the Source Code, and (b) in any notice in an Executable version or related documentation in which You describe the origin or ownership of the Covered Code.

3.4. Intellectual Property Matters

a. Third Party Claims.

   If Contributor has knowledge that a license under a third party's intellectual property rights is required to exercise the rights granted by such Contributor under Sections 2.1 or 2.2, Contributor must include a text file with the Source Code distribution titled "LEGAL" which describes the claim and the party making the claim in sufficient detail that a recipient will know whom to contact. If Contributor obtains such knowledge after the Modification is made available as described in Section 3.2, Contributor shall promptly modify the LEGAL file in all copies Contributor makes available thereafter and shall take other steps (such as notifying appropriate mailing lists or newsgroups) reasonably calculated to inform those who received the Covered Code that new knowledge has been obtained.

b. Contributor APIs.

   If Contributor's Modifications include an application programming interface and Contributor has knowledge of patent licenses which are reasonably necessary to implement that API, Contributor must also include this information in the LEGAL file.

c. Representations.

   Contributor represents that, except as disclosed pursuant to Section 3.4(a) above, Contributor believes that Contributor's Modifications are Contributor's original creation(s) and/or Contributor has sufficient rights to grant the rights conveyed by this License.

3.5. Required Notices

You must duplicate the notice in Exhibit A in each file of the Source Code. If it is not possible to put such notice in a particular Source Code file due to its structure, then You must include such notice in a location (such as a relevant directory) where a user would be likely to look for such a notice. If You created one or more Modification(s) You may add your name as a Contributor to the notice described in Exhibit A. You must also duplicate this License in any documentation for the Source Code where You describe recipients' rights or ownership rights relating to Covered Code. You may choose to offer, and to charge a fee for, warranty, support, indemnity or liability obligations to one or more recipients of Covered Code. However, You may do so only on Your own behalf, and not on behalf of the Initial Developer or any Contributor.

You must make it absolutely clear than any such warranty, support, indemnity or liability obligation is offered by You alone, and You hereby agree to indemnify the Initial Developer and every Contributor for any liability incurred by the Initial Developer or such Contributor as a result of warranty, support, indemnity or liability terms You offer.

3.6. Distribution of Executable Versions

You may distribute Covered Code in Executable form only if the requirements of Section 3.1–3.5 have been met for that Covered Code, and if You include a notice stating that the Source Code version of the Covered Code is available under the terms of this License, including a description of how and where You have fulfilled the obligations of Section 3.2. The notice must be conspicuously included in any notice in an Executable version, related documentation or collateral in which You describe recipients' rights relating to the Covered Code. You may distribute the Executable version of Covered Code or ownership rights under a license of Your choice, which may contain terms different from this License, provided that You are in compliance with the terms of this License and that the license for the Executable version does not attempt to limit or alter the recipient's rights in the Source Code version from the rights set forth in this License. If You distribute the Executable version under a different license You must make it absolutely clear that any terms which differ from this License are offered by You alone, not by the Initial Developer or any Contributor. You hereby agree to indemnify the Initial Developer and every Contributor for any liability incurred by the Initial Developer or such Contributor as a result of any such terms You offer.

3.7. Larger Works

You may create a Larger Work by combining Covered Code with other code not governed by the terms of this License and distribute the Larger Work as a single product. In such a case, You must make sure the requirements of this License are fulfilled for the Covered Code.

4. Inability to Comply Due to Statute or Regulation

If it is impossible for You to comply with any of the terms of this License with respect to some or all of the Covered Code due to statute, judicial order, or regulation then You must: (a) comply with the terms of this License to the maximum extent possible; and (b) describe the limitations and the code they affect. Such description must be included in the LEGAL file described in Section 3.4 and must be included with all distributions of the Source Code. Except to the extent prohibited by statute or regulation, such description must be sufficiently detailed for a recipient of ordinary skill to be able to understand it.

5. Application of this License

This License applies to code to which the Initial Developer has attached the notice in Exhibit A and to related Covered Code.

6. Versions of the License

6.1. New Versions

Netscape Communications Corporation ("Netscape") may publish revised and/or new versions of the License from time to time. Each version will be given a distinguishing version number.

6.2. Effect of New Versions

Once Covered Code has been published under a particular version of the License, You may always continue to use it under the terms of that version. You may also choose to use such Covered Code under the terms of any subsequent version of the License published by Netscape. No one other than Netscape has the right to modify the terms applicable to Covered Code created under this License.

6.3. Derivative Works

If You create or use a modified version of this License (which you may only do in order to apply it to code which is not already Covered Code governed by this License), You must (a) rename Your license so that the phrases "Mozilla", "MOZILLAPL", "MOZPL", "Netscape", "MPL", "NPL" or any confusingly similar phrase do not appear in your license (except to note that your license differs from this License) and (b) otherwise make it clear that Your version of the license contains terms which differ from the Mozilla Public License and Netscape Public License. (Filling in the name of the Initial Developer, Original Code or Contributor in the notice described in Exhibit A shall not of themselves be deemed to be modifications of this License.)

7. DISCLAIMER OF WARRANTY

COVERED CODE IS PROVIDED UNDER THIS LICENSE ON AN "AS IS" BASIS, WITHOUT WARRANTY OF ANY KIND, EITHER EXPRESSED OR IMPLIED, INCLUDING, WITHOUT LIMITATION, WARRANTIES THAT THE COVERED CODE IS FREE OF DEFECTS, MERCHANTABLE, FIT FOR A PARTICULAR PURPOSE OR NON-INFRINGING. THE ENTIRE RISK AS TO THE QUALITY AND PERFORMANCE OF THE COVERED CODE IS WITH YOU. SHOULD ANY COVERED CODE PROVE DEFECTIVE IN ANY RESPECT, YOU (NOT THE INITIAL DEVELOPER OR ANY OTHER CONTRIBUTOR) ASSUME THE COST OF ANY NECESSARY SERVICING, REPAIR OR CORRECTION. THIS DISCLAIMER OF WARRANTY CONSTITUTES AN ESSENTIAL PART OF THIS LICENSE. NO USE OF ANY COVERED CODE IS AUTHORIZED HEREUNDER EXCEPT UNDER THIS DISCLAIMER.

8. Termination

8.1. This License and the rights granted hereunder will terminate automatically if You fail to comply with terms herein and fail to cure such breach within 30 days of becoming aware of the breach. All sublicenses to the Covered Code which are properly granted shall survive any termination of this License. Provisions which, by their nature, must remain in effect beyond the termination of this License shall survive.

8.2. If You initiate litigation by asserting a patent infringement claim (excluding declaratory judgment actions) against Initial Developer or a Contributor (the Initial Developer or Contributor against whom You file such action is referred to as "Participant") alleging that:

a. such Participant's Contributor Version directly or indirectly infringes any patent, then any and all rights granted by such Participant to You under Sections 2.1 and/or 2.2 of this License shall, upon 60 days notice from Participant terminate prospectively, unless if within 60 days after receipt of notice You either:

   1. agree in writing to pay Participant a mutually agreeable reasonable royalty for Your past and future use of Modifications made by such Participant, or
   2. withdraw Your litigation claim with respect to the Contributor Version against such Participant.

   If within 60 days of notice, a reasonable royalty and payment arrangement are not mutually agreed upon in writing by the parties or the litigation claim is not withdrawn, the rights granted by Participant to You under Sections 2.1 and/or 2.2 automatically terminate at the expiration of the 60 day notice period specified above.

b. any software, hardware, or device, other than such Participant's Contributor Version, directly or indirectly infringes any patent, then any rights granted to You by such Participant under Sections 2.1(b) and 2.2(b) are revoked effective as of the date You first made, used, sold, distributed, or had made, Modifications made by that Participant.

8.3. If You assert a patent infringement claim against Participant alleging that such Participant's Contributor Version directly or indirectly infringes any patent where such claim is resolved (such as by license or settlement) prior to the initiation of patent infringement litigation, then the reasonable value of the licenses granted by such Participant under Sections 2.1 or 2.2 shall be taken into account in determining the amount or value of any payment or license.

8.4. In the event of termination under Sections 8.1 or 8.2 above, all end user license agreements (excluding distributors and resellers) which have been validly granted by You or any distributor hereunder prior to termination shall survive termination.

9. LIMITATION OF LIABILITY

UNDER NO CIRCUMSTANCES AND UNDER NO LEGAL THEORY, WHETHER TORT (INCLUDING NEGLIGENCE), CONTRACT, OR OTHERWISE, SHALL YOU, THE INITIAL

DEVELOPER, ANY OTHER CONTRIBUTOR, OR ANY DISTRIBUTOR OF COVERED CODE, OR ANY SUPPLIER OF ANY OF SUCH PARTIES, BE LIABLE TO ANY PERSON FOR ANY INDIRECT, SPECIAL, INCIDENTAL, OR CONSEQUENTIAL DAMAGES OF ANY CHARACTER INCLUDING, WITHOUT LIMITATION, DAMAGES FOR LOSS OF GOODWILL, WORK STOPPAGE, COMPUTER FAILURE OR MALFUNCTION, OR ANY AND ALL OTHER COMMERCIAL DAMAGES OR LOSSES, EVEN IF SUCH PARTY SHALL HAVE BEEN INFORMED OF THE POSSIBILITY OF SUCH DAMAGES. THIS LIMITATION OF LIABILITY SHALL NOT APPLY TO LIABILITY FOR DEATH OR PERSONAL INJURY RESULTING FROM SUCH PARTY'S NEGLIGENCE TO THE EXTENT APPLICABLE LAW PROHIBITS SUCH LIMITATION. SOME JURISDICTIONS DO NOT ALLOW THE EXCLUSION OR LIMITATION OF INCIDENTAL OR CONSEQUENTIAL DAMAGES, SO THIS EXCLUSION AND LIMITATION MAY NOT APPLY TO YOU.

10. U.S. Government End Users

The Covered Code is a "commercial item," as that term is defined in 48 C.F.R. 2.101 (Oct. 1995), consisting of "commercial computer software" and "commercial computer software documentation," as such terms are used in 48 C.F.R. 12.212 (Sept. 1995). Consistent with 48 C.F.R. 12.212 and 48 C.F.R. 227.7202-1 through 227.7202-4 (June 1995), all U.S. Government End Users acquire Covered Code with only those rights set forth herein.

11. MISCELLANEOUS

This License represents the complete agreement concerning subject matter hereof. If any provision of this License is held to be unenforceable, such provision shall be reformed only to the extent necessary to make it enforceable. This License shall be governed by California law provisions (except to the extent applicable law, if any, provides otherwise), excluding its conflict-of-law provisions. With respect to disputes in which at least one party is a citizen of, or an entity chartered or registered to do business in the United States of America, any litigation relating to this License shall be subject to the jurisdiction of the Federal Courts of the Northern District of California, with venue lying in Santa Clara County, California, with the losing party responsible for costs, including without limitation, court costs and reasonable attorneys' fees and expenses. The application of the United Nations Convention on Contracts for the International Sale of Goods is expressly excluded. Any law or regulation which provides that the language of a contract shall be construed against the drafter shall not apply to this License.

12. Responsibility for Claims

As between Initial Developer and the Contributors, each party is responsible for claims and damages arising, directly or indirectly, out of its utilization of rights under this License and You agree to work with Initial Developer and Contributors to distribute such responsibility on an equitable basis. Nothing herein is intended or shall be deemed to constitute any admission of liability.

14. Multiple-Licensed Code

Initial Developer may designate portions of the Covered Code as Multiple-Licensed. Multiple-Licensed means that the Initial Developer permits you to utilize portions of the Covered Code under Your choice of the MPL or the alternative licenses, if any, specified by the Initial Developer in the file described in Exhibit A.

Applying the Mozilla Public License

To apply the Mozilla Public License to your code, include the following information at the top of your file:

> The contents of this file are subject to the Mozilla Public License Version 1.1 (the "License"); you may not use this file except in compliance with the License. You may obtain a copy of the License at *http://www.mozilla.org/MPL/*
>
> Software distributed under the License is distributed on an "AS IS" basis, WITHOUT WARRANTY OF ANY KIND, either express or implied. See the License for the specific language governing rights and limitations under the License.
>
> The Original Code is ______________________________________.
>
> The Initial Developer of the Original Code is ________________________.
>
> Portions created by ______________________ are Copyright (C) ______ ______________________.
>
> All Rights Reserved.
>
> Contributor(s): ______________________________________.
>
> Alternatively, the contents of this file may be used under the terms of the _____ license (the [___] License), in which case the provisions of [______] License are applicable instead of those above. If you wish to allow use of your version of this file only under the terms of the [____] License and not to allow others to use your version of this file under the MPL, indicate your decision by deleting the provisions above and replace them with the notice and other provisions required by the [___] License. If you do not delete the provisions above, a recipient may use your version of this file under either the MPL or the [___] License.

APPENDIX I

The GNU Lesser General Public License, Version 2.1

The GNU Lesser General Public License (LGPL), Version 2.1

Version 2.1, February 1999

Copyright (C) 1991, 1999 Free Software Foundation, Inc.

51 Franklin Street, Fifth Floor, Boston, MA 02110-1301 USA

Everyone is permitted to copy and distribute verbatim copies of this license document, but changing it is not allowed.

[This is the first released version of the Lesser GPL. It also counts as the successor of the GNU Library Public License, version 2, hence the version number 2.1.]

Preamble

The licenses for most software are designed to take away your freedom to share and change it. By contrast, the GNU General Public Licenses are intended to guarantee your freedom to share and change free software—to make sure the software is free for all its users.

This license, the Lesser General Public License, applies to some specially designated software packages—typically libraries—of the Free Software Foundation and other authors who decide to use it. You can use it too, but we suggest you first think carefully about whether this license or the ordinary General Public License is the better strategy to use in any particular case, based on the explanations below.

When we speak of free software, we are referring to freedom of use, not price. Our General Public Licenses are designed to make sure that you have the freedom to distribute copies of free software (and charge for this service if you wish); that you receive source code or can get it if you want it; that you can change the software and use pieces of it in new free programs; and that you are informed that you can do these things.

To protect your rights, we need to make restrictions that forbid distributors to deny you these rights or to ask you to surrender these rights. These restrictions translate to certain responsibilities for you if you distribute copies of the library or if you modify it.

For example, if you distribute copies of the library, whether gratis or for a fee, you must give the recipients all the rights that we gave you. You must make sure that they, too, receive or can get the source code. If you link other code with the library, you must provide complete object files to the recipients, so that they can relink them with the library after making changes to the library and recompiling it. And you must show them these terms so they know their rights.

We protect your rights with a two-step method: (1) we copyright the library, and (2) we offer you this license, which gives you legal permission to copy, distribute and/or modify the library.

To protect each distributor, we want to make it very clear that there is no warranty for the free library. Also, if the library is modified by someone else and passed on, the recipients should know that what they have is not the original version, so that the original author's reputation will not be affected by problems that might be introduced by others.

Finally, software patents pose a constant threat to the existence of any free program. We wish to make sure that a company cannot effectively restrict the users of a free program by obtaining a restrictive license from a patent holder. Therefore, we insist that any patent license obtained for a version of the library must be consistent with the full freedom of use specified in this license.

Most GNU software, including some libraries, is covered by the ordinary GNU General Public License. This license, the GNU Lesser General Public License, applies to certain designated libraries, and is quite different from the ordinary General Public License. We use this license for certain libraries in order to permit linking those libraries into non-free programs.

When a program is linked with a library, whether statically or using a shared library, the combination of the two is legally speaking a combined work, a derivative of the original library. The ordinary General Public License therefore permits such linking only if the entire combination fits its criteria of freedom. The Lesser General Public License permits more lax criteria for linking other code with the library.

We call this license the "Lesser" General Public License because it does Less to protect the user's freedom than the ordinary General Public License. It also provides other free software developers Less of an advantage over competing non-free programs. These disadvantages are the reason we use the ordinary General Public License for many libraries. However, the Lesser license provides advantages in certain special circumstances.

For example, on rare occasions, there may be a special need to encourage the widest possible use of a certain library, so that it becomes a de-facto standard. To achieve this, non-free programs must be allowed to use the library. A more frequent case is that a free library does the same job as widely used non-free libraries. In this case, there is little to gain by limiting the free library to free software only, so we use the Lesser General Public License.

In other cases, permission to use a particular library in non-free programs enables a greater number of people to use a large body of free software. For example, permission to use the GNU C Library in non-free programs enables many more people to use the whole GNU operating system, as well as its variant, the GNU/Linux operating system.

Although the Lesser General Public License is Less protective of the users' freedom, it does ensure that the user of a program that is linked with the Library has the freedom and the wherewithal to run that program using a modified version of the Library.

The precise terms and conditions for copying, distribution and modification follow. Pay close attention to the difference between a "work based on the library" and a "work that uses the library". The former contains code derived from the library, whereas the latter must be combined with the library in order to run.

TERMS AND CONDITIONS FOR COPYING, DISTRIBUTION AND MODIFICATION

0. This License Agreement applies to any software library or other program which contains a notice placed by the copyright holder or other authorized party saying it may be distributed under the terms of this Lesser General Public License (also called "this License"). Each licensee is addressed as "you".

   A "library" means a collection of software functions and/or data prepared so as to be conveniently linked with application programs (which use some of those functions and data) to form executables.

   The "Library", below, refers to any such software library or work which has been distributed under these terms. A "work based on the Library" means either the Library or any derivative work under copyright law: that is to say, a work containing the Library or a portion of it, either verbatim or with modifications and/or translated straightforwardly into another language. (Hereinafter, translation is included without limitation in the term "modification".)

   "Source code" for a work means the preferred form of the work for making modifications to it. For a library, complete source code means all the source code for all modules it contains, plus any associated interface definition files, plus the scripts used to control compilation and installation of the library.

Activities other than copying, distribution and modification are not covered by this License; they are outside its scope. The act of running a program using the Library is not restricted, and output from such a program is covered only if its contents constitute a work based on the Library (independent of the use of the Library in a tool for writing it). Whether that is true depends on what the Library does and what the program that uses the Library does.

1. You may copy and distribute verbatim copies of the Library's complete source code as you receive it, in any medium, provided that you conspicuously and appropriately publish on each copy an appropriate copyright notice and disclaimer of warranty; keep intact all the notices that refer to this License and to the absence of any warranty; and distribute a copy of this License along with the Library.

   You may charge a fee for the physical act of transferring a copy, and you may at your option offer warranty protection in exchange for a fee.

2. You may modify your copy or copies of the Library or any portion of it, thus forming a work based on the Library, and copy and distribute such modifications or work under the terms of Section 1 above, provided that you also meet all of these conditions:

   a. The modified work must itself be a software library.

   b. You must cause the files modified to carry prominent notices stating that you changed the files and the date of any change.

   c. You must cause the whole of the work to be licensed at no charge to all third parties under the terms of this License.

   d. If a facility in the modified Library refers to a function or a table of data to be supplied by an application program that uses the facility, other than as an argument passed when the facility is invoked, then you must make a good faith effort to ensure that, in the event an application does not supply such function or table, the facility still operates, and performs whatever part of its purpose remains meaningful.

      (For example, a function in a library to compute square roots has a purpose that is entirely well-defined independent of the application. Therefore, Subsection 2d requires that any application-supplied function or table used by this function must be optional: if the application does not supply it, the square root function must still compute square roots.)

      These requirements apply to the modified work as a whole. If identifiable sections of that work are not derived from the Library, and can be reasonably considered independent and separate works in themselves, then this License, and its terms, do not apply to those sections when you distribute them as separate works. But when you distribute the same sections as part of a whole which is a work based on the Library, the distribution of the whole must be on the terms of this License, whose permissions for other licensees extend to the entire whole, and thus to each and every part regardless of who wrote it.

Thus, it is not the intent of this section to claim rights or contest your rights to work written entirely by you; rather, the intent is to exercise the right to control the distribution of derivative or collective works based on the Library.

In addition, mere aggregation of another work not based on the Library with the Library (or with a work based on the Library) on a volume of a storage or distribution medium does not bring the other work under the scope of this License.

3. You may opt to apply the terms of the ordinary GNU General Public License instead of this License to a given copy of the Library. To do this, you must alter all the notices that refer to this License, so that they refer to the ordinary GNU General Public License, version 2, instead of to this License. (If a newer version than version 2 of the ordinary GNU General Public License has appeared, then you can specify that version instead if you wish.) Do not make any other change in these notices.

   Once this change is made in a given copy, it is irreversible for that copy, so the ordinary GNU General Public License applies to all subsequent copies and derivative works made from that copy.

   This option is useful when you wish to copy part of the code of the Library into a program that is not a library.

4. You may copy and distribute the Library (or a portion or derivative of it, under Section 2) in object code or executable form under the terms of Sections 1 and 2 above provided that you accompany it with the complete corresponding machine-readable source code, which must be distributed under the terms of Sections 1 and 2 above on a medium customarily used for software interchange.

   If distribution of object code is made by offering access to copy from a designated place, then offering equivalent access to copy the source code from the same place satisfies the requirement to distribute the source code, even though third parties are not compelled to copy the source along with the object code

5. A program that contains no derivative of any portion of the Library, but is designed to work with the Library by being compiled or linked with it, is called a "work that uses the Library". Such a work, in isolation, is not a derivative work of the Library, and therefore falls outside the scope of this License.

   However, linking a "work that uses the Library" with the Library creates an executable that is a derivative of the Library (because it contains portions of the Library), rather than a "work that uses the library". The executable is therefore covered by this License. Section 6 states terms for distribution of such executables.

   When a "work that uses the Library" uses material from a header file that is part of the Library, the object code for the work may be a derivative work of the Library even though the source code is not. Whether this is true is especially significant if the work can be linked without the Library, or if the work is itself a library. The threshold for this to be true is not precisely defined by law.

If such an object file uses only numerical parameters, data structure layouts and accessors, and small macros and small inline functions (ten lines or less in length), then the use of the object file is unrestricted, regardless of whether it is legally a derivative work. (Executables containing this object code plus portions of the Library will still fall under Section 6.)

Otherwise, if the work is a derivative of the Library, you may distribute the object code for the work under the terms of Section 6. Any executables containing that work also fall under Section 6, whether or not they are linked directly with the Library itself.

6. As an exception to the Sections above, you may also combine or link a "work that uses the Library" with the Library to produce a work containing portions of the Library, and distribute that work under terms of your choice, provided that the terms permit modification of the work for the customer's own use and reverse engineering for debugging such modifications.

   You must give prominent notice with each copy of the work that the Library is used in it and that the Library and its use are covered by this License. You must supply a copy of this License. If the work during execution displays copyright notices, you must include the copyright notice for the Library among them, as well as a reference directing the user to the copy of this License. Also, you must do one of these things:

   a. Accompany the work with the complete corresponding machine-readable source code for the Library including whatever changes were used in the work (which must be distributed under Sections 1 and 2 above); and, if the work is an executable linked with the Library, with the complete machine-readable "work that uses the Library", as object code and/or source code, so that the user can modify the Library and then relink to produce a modified executable containing the modified Library. (It is understood that the user who changes the contents of definitions files in the Library will not necessarily be able to recompile the application to use the modified definitions.),

   b. Use a suitable shared library mechanism for linking with the Library. A suitable mechanism is one that (1) uses at run time a copy of the library already present on the user's computer system, rather than copying library functions into the executable, and (2) will operate properly with a modified version of the library, if the user installs one, as long as the modified version is interface-compatible with the version that the work was made with,

   c. Accompany the work with a written offer, valid for at least three years, to give the same user the materials specified in Subsection 6a, above, for a charge no more than the cost of performing this distribution.

   d. If distribution of the work is made by offering access to copy from a designated place, offer equivalent access to copy the above specified materials from the same place.

   e. Verify that the user has already received a copy of these materials or that you have already sent this user a copy.

For an executable, the required form of the "work that uses the Library" must include any data and utility programs needed for reproducing the executable from it. However, as a special exception, the materials to be distributed need not include anything that is normally distributed (in either source or binary form) with the major components (compiler, kernel, and so on) of the operating system on which the executable runs, unless that component itself accompanies the executable.

It may happen that this requirement contradicts the license restrictions of other proprietary libraries that do not normally accompany the operating system. Such a contradiction means you cannot use both them and the Library together in an executable that you distribute.

7. You may place library facilities that are a work based on the Library side-by-side in a single library together with other library facilities not covered by this License, and distribute such a combined library, provided that the separate distribution of the work based on the Library and of the other library facilities is otherwise permitted, and provided that you do these two things:

    a. Accompany the combined library with a copy of the same work based on the Library, uncombined with any other library facilities. This must be distributed under the terms of the Sections above.

    b. Give prominent notice with the combined library of the fact that part of it is a work based on the Library, and explaining where to find the accompanying uncombined form of the same work.

8. You may not copy, modify, sublicense, link with, or distribute the Library except as expressly provided under this License. Any attempt otherwise to copy, modify, sublicense, link with, or distribute the Library is void, and will automatically terminate your rights under this License. However, parties who have received copies, or rights, from you under this License will not have their licenses terminated so long as such parties remain in full compliance.

9. You are not required to accept this License, since you have not signed it. However, nothing else grants you permission to modify or distribute the Library or its derivative works. These actions are prohibited by law if you do not accept this License. Therefore, by modifying or distributing the Library (or any work based on the Library), you indicate your acceptance of this License to do so, and all its terms and conditions for copying, distributing or modifying the Library or works based on it.

10. Each time you redistribute the Library (or any work based on the Library), the recipient automatically receives a license from the original licensor to copy, distribute, link with or modify the Library subject to these terms and conditions. You may not impose any further restrictions on the recipients' exercise of the rights granted herein. You are not responsible for enforcing compliance by third parties with this License.

11. If, as a consequence of a court judgment or allegation of patent infringement or for any other reason (not limited to patent issues), conditions are imposed on you (whether by

court order, agreement or otherwise) that contradict the conditions of this License, they do not excuse you from the conditions of this License. If you cannot distribute so as to satisfy simultaneously your obligations under this License and any other pertinent obligations, then as a consequence you may not distribute the Library at all. For example, if a patent license would not permit royalty-free redistribution of the Library by all those who receive copies directly or indirectly through you, then the only way you could satisfy both it and this License would be to refrain entirely from distribution of the Library.

If any portion of this section is held invalid or unenforceable under any particular circumstance, the balance of the section is intended to apply, and the section as a whole is intended to apply in other circumstances.

It is not the purpose of this section to induce you to infringe any patents or other property right claims or to contest validity of any such claims; this section has the sole purpose of protecting the integrity of the free software distribution system which is implemented by public license practices. Many people have made generous contributions to the wide range of software distributed through that system in reliance on consistent application of that system; it is up to the author/donor to decide if he or she is willing to distribute software through any other system and a licensee cannot impose that choice.

This section is intended to make thoroughly clear what is believed to be a consequence of the rest of this License.

It is not the purpose of this section to induce you to infringe any patents or other property right claims or to contest validity of any such claims; this section has the sole purpose of protecting the integrity of the free software distribution system, which is implemented by public license practices. Many people have made generous contributions to the wide range of software distributed through that system in reliance on consistent application of that system; it is up to the author/donor to decide if he or she is willing to distribute software through any other system and a licensee cannot impose that choice.

This section is intended to make thoroughly clear what is believed to be a consequence of the rest of this License.

12. If the distribution and/or use of the Library is restricted in certain countries either by patents or by copyrighted interfaces, the original copyright holder who places the Library under this License may add an explicit geographical distribution limitation excluding those countries, so that distribution is permitted only in or among countries not thus excluded. In such case, this License incorporates the limitation as if written in the body of this License.

13. The Free Software Foundation may publish revised and/or new versions of the Lesser General Public License from time to time. Such new versions will be similar in spirit to the present version, but may differ in detail to address new problems or concerns.

    Each version is given a distinguishing version number. If the Library specifies a version number of this License which applies to it and "any later version", you have the option of following the terms and conditions either of that version or of any later version published by the Free Software Foundation. If the Library does not specify a license version number, you may choose any version ever published by the Free Software Foundation.

14. I f you wish to incorporate parts of the Library into other free programs whose distribution conditions are incompatible with these, write to the author to ask for permission. For software which is copyrighted by the Free Software Foundation, write to the Free Software Foundation; we sometimes make exceptions for this. Our decision will be guided by the two goals of preserving the free status of all derivatives of our free software and of promoting the sharing and reuse of software generally.

NO WARRANTY

15. BECAUSE THE LIBRARY IS LICENSED FREE OF CHARGE, THERE IS NO WARRANTY FOR THE LIBRARY, TO THE EXTENT PERMITTED BY APPLICABLE LAW. EXCEPT WHEN OTHERWISE STATED IN WRITING THE COPYRIGHT HOLDERS AND/OR OTHER PARTIES PROVIDE THE LIBRARY "AS IS" WITHOUT WARRANTY OF ANY KIND, EITHER EXPRESSED OR IMPLIED, INCLUDING, BUT NOT LIMITED TO, THE IMPLIED WARRANTIES OF MERCHANTABILITY AND FITNESS FOR A PARTICULAR PURPOSE. THE ENTIRE RISK AS TO THE QUALITY AND PERFORMANCE OF THE LIBRARY IS WITH YOU. SHOULD THE LIBRARY PROVE DEFECTIVE, YOU ASSUME THE COST OF ALL NECESSARY SERVICING, REPAIR OR CORRECTION.

16. IN NO EVENT UNLESS REQUIRED BY APPLICABLE LAW OR AGREED TO IN WRITING WILL ANY COPYRIGHT HOLDER, OR ANY OTHER PARTY WHO MAY MODIFY AND/OR REDISTRIBUTE THE LIBRARY AS PERMITTED ABOVE, BE LIABLE TO YOU FOR DAMAGES, INCLUDING ANY GENERAL, SPECIAL, INCIDENTAL OR CONSEQUENTIAL DAMAGES ARISING OUT OF THE USE OR INABILITY TO USE THE LIBRARY (INCLUDING BUT NOT LIMITED TO LOSS OF DATA OR DATA BEING RENDERED INACCURATE OR LOSSES SUSTAINED BY YOU OR THIRD PARTIES OR A FAILURE OF THE LIBRARY TO OPERATE WITH ANY OTHER SOFTWARE), EVEN IF SUCH HOLDER OR OTHER PARTY HAS BEEN ADVISED OF THE POSSIBILITY OF SUCH DAMAGES.

END OF TERMS AND CONDITIONS

How to Apply These Terms to Your New Libraries

If you develop a new library, and you want it to be of the greatest possible use to the public, we recommend making it free software that everyone can redistribute and change. You can do so by permitting redistribution under these terms (or, alternatively, under the terms of the ordinary General Public License).

To apply these terms, attach the following notices to the library. It is safest to attach them to the start of each source file to most effectively convey the exclusion of warranty; and each file should have at least the "copyright" line and a pointer to where the full notice is found.

> *One line to give the program's name and a brief idea of what it does.*
>
> Copyright (C) <year> <name of author>
>
> This program is free software; you can redistribute it and/or modify it under the terms of the GNU Lesser General Public License as published by the Free Software Foundation; either version 2.1 of the License, or (at your option) any later version.
>
> This program is distributed in the hope that it will be useful, but WITHOUT ANY WARRANTY; without even the implied warranty of MERCHANTABILITY or FITNESS FOR A PARTICULAR PURPOSE. See the GNU Lesser General Public License for more details.
>
> You should have received a copy of the GNU General Public License along with this library; if not, write to the Free Software Foundation, Inc., 51 Franklin Street, Fifth Floor, Boston, MA 02110-1301 USA

Also add information on how to contact you by electronic and paper mail.

You should also get your employer (if you work as a programmer) or your school, if any, to sign a "copyright disclaimer" for the library, if necessary. Here is a sample; alter the names:

> Yoyodyne, Inc., hereby disclaims all copyright interest in the library `Frob' (a library for tweaking knobs) written by James Random Hacker.
>
> signature of Ty Coon, 1 April 1990
>
> Ty Coon, President of Vice

APPENDIX J

The GNU Lesser General Public License, Version 3

The GNU Lesser General Public License (LGPL), Version 3

Copyright (C) 2007 Free Software Foundation, Inc. *<http://fsf.org/>*

Everyone is permitted to copy and distribute verbatim copies of this license document, but changing it is not allowed.

This version of the GNU Lesser General Public License incorporates the terms and conditions of version 3 of the GNU General Public License, supplemented by the additional permissions listed below.

0. Additional Definitions

As used herein, "this License" refers to version 3 of the GNU Lesser General Public License, and the "GNU GPL" refers to version 3 of the GNU General Public License.

"The Library" refers to a covered work governed by this License, other than an Application or a Combined Work as defined below.

An "Application" is any work that makes use of an interface provided by the Library, but which is not otherwise based on the Library. Defining a subclass of a class defined by the Library is deemed a mode of using an interface provided by the Library.

A "Combined Work" is a work produced by combining or linking an Application with the Library. The particular version of the Library with which the Combined Work was made is also called the "Linked Version".

The "Minimal Corresponding Source" for a Combined Work means the Corresponding Source for the Combined Work, excluding any source code for portions of the Combined Work that, considered in isolation, are based on the Application, and not on the Linked Version.

The "Corresponding Application Code" for a Combined Work means the object code and/or source code for the Application, including any data and utility programs needed for reproducing the Combined Work from the Application, but excluding the System Libraries of the Combined Work.

1. Exception to Section 3 of the GNU GPL

You may convey a covered work under sections 3 and 4 of this License without being bound by section 3 of the GNU GPL.

2. Conveying Modified Versions

If you modify a copy of the Library, and, in your modifications, a facility refers to a function or data to be supplied by an Application that uses the facility (other than as an argument passed when the facility is invoked), then you may convey a copy of the modified version:

a. under this License, provided that you make a good faith effort to ensure that, in the event an Application does not supply the function or data, the facility still operates, and performs whatever part of its purpose remains meaningful, or

b. under the GNU GPL, with none of the additional permissions of this License applicable to that copy.

3. Object Code Incorporating Material from Library Header Files

The object code form of an Application may incorporate material from a header file that is part of the Library. You may convey such object code under terms of your choice, provided that, if the incorporated material is not limited to numerical parameters, data structure layouts and accessors, or small macros, inline functions and templates (ten or fewer lines in length), you do both of the following:

a. Give prominent notice with each copy of the Combined Work that the Library is used in it and that the Library and its use are covered by this License.

b. Accompany the Combined Work with a copy of the GNU GPL and this license document

4. Combined Works

You may convey a Combined Work under terms of your choice that, taken together, effectively do not restrict modification of the portions of the Library contained in the Combined Work and reverse engineering for debugging such modifications, if you also do each of the following:

a. Give prominent notice with each copy of the Combined Work that the Library is used in it and that the Library and its use are covered by this License.

b. Accompany the Combined Work with a copy of the GNU GPL and this license document.

c. For a Combined Work that displays copyright notices during execution, include the copyright notice for the Library among these notices, as well as a reference directing the user to the copies of the GNU GPL and this license document.

d. Do one of the following:

   1. Convey the Minimal Corresponding Source under the terms of this License, and the Corresponding Application Code in a form suitable for, and under terms that permit, the user to recombine or relink the Application with a modified version of the Linked Version to produce a modified Combined Work, in the manner specified by section 6 of the GNU GPL for conveying Corresponding Source.

   2. 1) Use a suitable shared library mechanism for linking with the Library. A suitable mechanism is one that (a) uses at run time a copy of the Library already present on the user's computer system, and (b) will operate properly with a modified version of the Library that is interface-compatible with the Linked Version.

e. Provide Installation Information, but only if you would otherwise be required to provide such information under section 6 of the GNU GPL, and only to the extent that such information is necessary to install and execute a modified version of the Combined Work produced by recombining or relinking the Application with a modified version of the Linked Version. (If you use option 4d0, the Installation Information must accompany the Minimal Corresponding Source and Corresponding Application Code. If you use option 4d1, you must provide the Installation Information in the manner specified by section 6 of the GNU GPL for conveying Corresponding Source.)

5. Combined Libraries

You may place library facilities that are a work based on the Library side by side in a single library together with other library facilities that are not Applications and are not covered by this License, and convey such a combined library under terms of your choice, if you do both of the following:

a. Accompany the combined library with a copy of the same work based on the Library, uncombined with any other library facilities, conveyed under the terms of this License.

b. Give prominent notice with the combined library that part of it is a work based on the Library, and explaining where to find the accompanying uncombined form of the same work.

6. Revised Versions of the GNU Lesser General Public License

The Free Software Foundation may publish revised and/or new versions of the GNU Lesser General Public License from time to time. Such new versions will be similar in spirit to the present version, but may differ in detail to address new problems or concerns.

Each version is given a distinguishing version number. If the Library as you received it specifies that a certain numbered version of the GNU Lesser General Public License "or any later version" applies to it, you have the option of following the terms and conditions either of that published version or of any later version published by the Free Software Foundation. If the Library as you received it does not specify a version number of the GNU Lesser General Public License, you may choose any version of the GNU Lesser General Public License ever published by the Free Software Foundation.

If the Library as you received it specifies that a proxy can decide whether future versions of the GNU Lesser General Public License shall apply, that proxy's public statement of acceptance of any version is permanent authorization for you to choose that version for the Library.

APPENDIX K

The GNU General Public License, Version 2, June 1991

The GNU General Public License (GPL), Version 2

Preamble

The licenses for most software are designed to take away your freedom to share and change it. By contrast, the GNU General Public License is intended to guarantee your freedom to share and change free software—to make sure the software is free for all its users. This General Public License applies to most of the Free Software Foundation's software and to any other program whose authors commit to using it. (Some other Free Software Foundation software is covered by the GNU Library General Public License instead.) You can apply it to your programs, too.

When we speak of free software, we are referring to freedom, not price. Our General Public Licenses are designed to make sure that you have the freedom to distribute copies of free software (and charge for this service if you wish), that you receive source code or can get it if you want it, that you can change the software or use pieces of it in new free programs; and that you know you can do these things.

To protect your rights, we need to make restrictions that forbid anyone to deny you these rights or to ask you to surrender the rights. These restrictions translate to certain responsibilities for you if you distribute copies of the software, or if you modify it.

For example, if you distribute copies of such a program, whether gratis or for a fee, you must give the recipients all the rights that you have. You must make sure that they, too, receive or can get the source code. And you must show them these terms so they know their rights.

We protect your rights with two steps: (1) copyright the software, and (2) offer you this license which gives you legal permission to copy, distribute and/or modify the software.

Also, for each author's protection and ours, we want to make certain that everyone understands that there is no warranty for this free software. If the software is modified by someone else and passed on, we want its recipients to know that what they have is not the original, so that any problems introduced by others will not reflect on the original authors' reputations.

Finally, any free program is threatened constantly by software patents. We wish to avoid the danger that redistributors of a free program will individually obtain patent licenses, in effect making the program proprietary. To prevent this, we have made it clear that any patent must be licensed for everyone's free use or not licensed at all.

The precise terms and conditions for copying, distribution and modification follow.

TERMS AND CONDITIONS

0. This License applies to any program or other work which contains a notice placed by the copyright holder saying it may be distributed under the terms of this General Public License. The "Program", below, refers to any such program or work, and a "work based on the Program" means either the Program or any derivative work under copyright law: that is to say, a work containing the Program or a portion of it, either verbatim or with modifications and/or translated into another language. (Hereinafter, translation is included without limitation in the term "modification".) Each licensee is addressed as "you".

   Activities other than copying, distribution and modification are not covered by this License; they are outside its scope. The act of running the Program is not restricted, and the output from the Program is covered only if its contents constitute a work based on the Program (independent of having been made by running the Program). Whether that is true depends on what the Program does.

1. You may copy and distribute verbatim copies of the Program's source code as you receive it, in any medium, provided that you conspicuously and appropriately publish on each copy an appropriate copyright notice and disclaimer of warranty; keep intact all the notices that refer to this License and to the absence of any warranty; and give any other recipients of the Program a copy of this License along with the Program.

You may charge a fee for the physical act of transferring a copy, and you may at your option offer warranty protection in exchange for a fee.

2. You may modify your copy or copies of the Program or any portion of it, thus forming a work based on the Program, and copy and distribute such modifications or work under the terms of Section 1 above, provided that you also meet all of these conditions:

    a. You must cause the modified files to carry prominent notices stating that you changed the files and the date of any change.

    b. You must cause any work that you distribute or publish, that in whole or in part contains or is derived from the Program or any part thereof, to be licensed as a whole at no charge to all third parties under the terms of this License.

    c. If the modified program normally reads commands interactively when run, you must cause it, when started running for such interactive use in the most ordinary way, to print or display an announcement including an appropriate copyright notice and a notice that there is no warranty (or else, saying that you provide a warranty) and that users may redistribute the program under these conditions, and telling the user how to view a copy of this License. (Exception: if the Program itself is interactive but does not normally print such an announcement, your work based on the Program is not required to print an announcement.)

    These requirements apply to the modified work as a whole. If identifiable sections of that work are not derived from the Program, and can be reasonably considered independent and separate works in themselves, then this License, and its terms, do not apply to those sections when you distribute them as separate works. But when you distribute the same sections as part of a whole which is a work based on the Program, the distribution of the whole must be on the terms of this License, whose permissions for other licensees extend to the entire whole, and thus to each and every part regardless of who wrote it.

    Thus, it is not the intent of this section to claim rights or contest your rights to work written entirely by you; rather, the intent is to exercise the right to control the distribution of derivative or collective works based on the Program.

    In addition, mere aggregation of another work not based on the Program with the Program (or with a work based on the Program) on a volume of a storage or distribution medium does not bring the other work under the scope of this License.

3. You may copy and distribute the Program (or a work based on it, under Section 2) in object code or executable form under the terms of Sections 1 and 2 above provided that you also do one of the following:

    a. Accompany it with the complete corresponding machine-readable source code, which must be distributed under the terms of Sections 1 and 2 above on a medium customarily used for software interchange; or,

b. Accompany it with a written offer, valid for at least three years, to give any third party, for a charge no more than your cost of physically performing source distribution, a complete machine-readable copy of the corresponding source code, to be distributed under the terms of Sections 1 and 2 above on a medium customarily used for software interchange; or,

c. Accompany it with the information you received as to the offer to distribute corresponding source code. (This alternative is allowed only for noncommercial distribution and only if you received the program in object code or executable form with such an offer, in accord with Subsection b above.)

The source code for a work means the preferred form of the work for making modifications to it. For an executable work, complete source code means all the source code for all modules it contains, plus any associated interface definition files, plus the scripts used to control compilation and installation of the executable. However, as a special exception, the source code distributed need not include anything that is normally distributed (in either source or binary form) with the major components (compiler, kernel, and so on) of the operating system on which the executable runs, unless that component itself accompanies the executable.

If distribution of executable or object code is made by offering access to copy from a designated place, then offering equivalent access to copy the source code from the same place counts as distribution of the source code, even though third parties are not compelled to copy the source along with the object code.

4. You may not copy, modify, sublicense, or distribute the Program except as expressly provided under this License. Any attempt otherwise to copy, modify, sublicense or distribute the Program is void, and will automatically terminate your rights under this License. However, parties who have received copies, or rights, from you under this License will not have their licenses terminated so long as such parties remain in full compliance.

5. You are not required to accept this License, since you have not signed it. However, nothing else grants you permission to modify or distribute the Program or its derivative works. These actions are prohibited by law if you do not accept this License. Therefore, by modifying or distributing the Program (or any work based on the Program), you indicate your acceptance of this License to do so, and all its terms and conditions for copying, distributing or modifying the Program or works based on it.

6. Each time you redistribute the Program (or any work based on the Program), the recipient automatically receives a license from the original licensor to copy, distribute or modify the Program subject to these terms and conditions. You may not impose any further restrictions on the recipients' exercise of the rights granted herein. You are not responsible for enforcing compliance by third parties to this License.

7. If, as a consequence of a court judgment or allegation of patent infringement or for any other reason (not limited to patent issues), conditions are imposed on you (whether by court order, agreement or otherwise) that contradict the conditions of this License, they

do not excuse you from the conditions of this License. If you cannot distribute so as to satisfy simultaneously your obligations under this License and any other pertinent obligations, then as a consequence you may not distribute the Program at all. For example, if a patent license would not permit royalty-free redistribution of the Program by all those who receive copies directly or indirectly through you, then the only way you could satisfy both it and this License would be to refrain entirely from distribution of the Program.

If any portion of this section is held invalid or unenforceable under any particular circumstance, the balance of the section is intended to apply and the section as a whole is intended to apply in other circumstances.

It is not the purpose of this section to induce you to infringe any patents or other property right claims or to contest validity of any such claims; this section has the sole purpose of protecting the integrity of the free software distribution system, which is implemented by public license practices. Many people have made generous contributions to the wide range of software distributed through that system in reliance on consistent application of that system; it is up to the author/donor to decide if he or she is willing to distribute software through any other system and a licensee cannot impose that choice.

This section is intended to make thoroughly clear what is believed to be a consequence of the rest of this License.

8. If the distribution and/or use of the Program is restricted in certain countries either by patents or by copyrighted interfaces, the original copyright holder who places the Program under this License may add an explicit geographical distribution limitation excluding those countries, so that distribution is permitted only in or among countries not thus excluded. In such case, this License incorporates the limitation as if written in the body of this License.

9. The Free Software Foundation may publish revised and/or new versions of the General Public License from time to time. Such new versions will be similar in spirit to the present version, but may differ in detail to address new problems or concerns.

   Each version is given a distinguishing version number. If the Program specifies a version number of this License which applies to it and "any later version", you have the option of following the terms and conditions either of that version or of any later version published by the Free Software Foundation. If the Program does not specify a version number of this License, you may choose any version ever published by the Free Software Foundation.

10. If you wish to incorporate parts of the Program into other free programs whose distribution conditions are different, write to the author to ask for permission. For software which is copyrighted by the Free Software Foundation, write to the Free Software Foundation; we sometimes make exceptions for this. Our decision will be guided by the two goals of preserving the free status of all derivatives of our free software and of promoting the sharing and reuse of software generally.

NO WARRANTY

11. BECAUSE THE PROGRAM IS LICENSED FREE OF CHARGE, THERE IS NO WARRANTY FOR THE PROGRAM, TO THE EXTENT PERMITTED BY APPLICABLE LAW. EXCEPT WHEN OTHERWISE STATED IN WRITING THE COPYRIGHT HOLDERS AND/OR OTHER PARTIES PROVIDE THE PROGRAM "AS IS" WITHOUT WARRANTY OF ANY KIND, EITHER EXPRESSED OR IMPLIED, INCLUDING, BUT NOT LIMITED TO, THE IMPLIED WARRANTIES OF MERCHANTABILITY AND FITNESS FOR A PARTICULAR PURPOSE. THE ENTIRE RISK AS TO THE QUALITY AND PERFORMANCE OF THE PROGRAM IS WITH YOU. SHOULD THE PROGRAM PROVE DEFECTIVE, YOU ASSUME THE COST OF ALL NECESSARY SERVICING, REPAIR OR CORRECTION.
12. IN NO EVENT UNLESS REQUIRED BY APPLICABLE LAW OR AGREED TO IN WRITING WILL ANY COPYRIGHT HOLDER, OR ANY OTHER PARTY WHO MAY MODIFY AND/OR REDISTRIBUTE THE PROGRAM AS PERMITTED ABOVE, BE LIABLE TO YOU FOR DAMAGES, INCLUDING ANY GENERAL, SPECIAL, INCIDENTAL OR CONSEQUENTIAL DAMAGES ARISING OUT OF THE USE OR INABILITY TO USE THE PROGRAM (INCLUDING BUT NOT LIMITED TO LOSS OF DATA OR DATA BEING RENDERED INACCURATE OR LOSSES SUSTAINED BY YOU OR THIRD PARTIES OR A FAILURE OF THE PROGRAM TO OPERATE WITH ANY OTHER PROGRAMS), EVEN IF SUCH HOLDER OR OTHER PARTY HAS BEEN ADVISED OF THE POSSIBILITY OF SUCH DAMAGES.

END OF TERMS AND CONDITIONS

How to Apply These Terms to Your New Programs

If you develop a new program, and you want it to be of the greatest possible use to the public, the best way to achieve this is to make it free software which everyone can redistribute and change under these terms.

To do so, attach the following notices to the program. It is safest to attach them to the start of each source file to most effectively convey the exclusion of warranty; and each file should have at least the "copyright" line and a pointer to where the full notice is found.

> *One line to give the program's name and a brief idea of what it does.*
>
> Copyright (C) <year> <name of author>
>
> This program is free software; you can redistribute it and/or modify it under the terms of the GNU General Public License as published by the Free Software Foundation; either version 2 of the License, or (at your option) any later version.
>
> This program is distributed in the hope that it will be useful, but WITHOUT ANY WARRANTY; without even the implied warranty of MERCHANTABILITY or FITNESS FOR A PARTICULAR PURPOSE. See the GNU General Public License for more details.

You should have received a copy of the GNU General Public License along with this program; if not, write to the Free Software Foundation, Inc., 59 Temple Place, Suite 330, Boston, MA 02111-1307 USA

Also add information on how to contact you by electronic and paper mail.

If the program is interactive, make it output a short notice like this when it starts in an interactive mode:

Gnomovision version 69, Copyright (C) <year> <name of author>

Gnomovision comes with ABSOLUTELY NO WARRANTY; for details type `show w'. This is free software, and you are welcome to redistribute it under certain conditions; type `show c' for details.

The hypothetical commands `show w' and `show c' should show the appropriate parts of the General Public License. Of course, the commands you use may be called something other than `show w' and `show c'; they could even be mouse-clicks or menu items - whatever suits your program.

You should also get your employer (if you work as a programmer) or your school, if any, to sign a "copyright disclaimer" for the program, if necessary. Here is a sample; alter the names:

Yoyodyne, Inc., hereby disclaims all copyright interest in the program `Gnomovision' (which makes passes at compilers) written by James Hacker.

signature of Ty Coon, 1 April 1989

Ty Coon, President of Vice

This General Public License does not permit incorporating your program into proprietary programs. If your program is a subroutine library, you may consider it more useful to permit linking proprietary applications with the library. If this is what you want to do, use the GNU Library General Public License instead of this License.

APPENDIX L

The GNU General Public License, Version 3, June 2007

The GNU General Public License (GPL), Version 3

Preamble

The licenses for most software and other practical works are designed to take away your freedom to share and change the works. By contrast, the GNU General Public License is intended to guarantee your freedom to share and change all versions of a program—to make sure it remains free software for all its users. We, the Free Software Foundation, use the GNU General Public License for most of our software; it applies also to any other work released this way by its authors. You can apply it to your programs, too.

When we speak of free software, we are referring to freedom, not price. Our General Public Licenses are designed to make sure that you have the freedom to distribute copies of free software (and charge for them if you wish), that you receive source code or can get it if you want it, that you can change the software or use pieces of it in new free programs, and that you know you can do these things.

To protect your rights, we need to prevent others from denying you these rights or asking you to surrender the rights. Therefore, you have certain responsibilities if you distribute copies of the software, or if you modify it: responsibilities to respect the freedom of others.

For example, if you distribute copies of such a program, whether gratis or for a fee, you must pass on to the recipients the same freedoms that you received. You must make sure that they, too, receive or can get the source code. And you must show them these terms so they know their rights.

Developers that use the GNU GPL protect your rights with two steps: (1) assert copyright on the software, and (2) offer you this License giving you legal permission to copy, distribute and/or modify it.

For the developers' and authors' protection, the GPL clearly explains that there is no warranty for this free software. For both users' and authors' sake, the GPL requires that modified versions be marked as changed, so that their problems will not be attributed erroneously to authors of previous versions.

Some devices are designed to deny users access to install or run modified versions of the software inside them, although the manufacturer can do so. This is fundamentally incompatible with the aim of protecting users' freedom to change the software. The systematic pattern of such abuse occurs in the area of products for individuals to use, which is precisely where it is most unacceptable. Therefore, we have designed this version of the GPL to prohibit the practice for those products. If such problems arise substantially in other domains, we stand ready to extend this provision to those domains in future versions of the GPL, as needed to protect the freedom of users.

Finally, every program is threatened constantly by software patents. States should not allow patents to restrict development and use of software on general-purpose computers, but in those that do, we wish to avoid the special danger that patents applied to a free program could make it effectively proprietary. To prevent this, the GPL assures that patents cannot be used to render the program non-free.

The precise terms and conditions for copying, distribution and modification follow.

TERMS AND CONDITIONS

0. Definitions.

   "This License" refers to version 3 of the GNU General Public License.

   "Copyright" also means copyright-like laws that apply to other kinds of works, such as semiconductor masks.

   "The Program" refers to any copyrightable work licensed under this License. Each licensee is addressed as "you". "Licensees" and "recipients" may be individuals or organizations.

To "modify" a work means to copy from or adapt all or part of the work in a fashion requiring copyright permission, other than the making of an exact copy. The resulting work is called a "modified version" of the earlier work or a work "based on" the earlier work.

A "covered work" means either the unmodified Program or a work based on the Program.

To "propagate" a work means to do anything with it that, without permission, would make you directly or secondarily liable for infringement under applicable copyright law, except executing it on a computer or modifying a private copy. Propagation includes copying, distribution (with or without modification), making available to the public, and in some countries other activities as well.

To "convey" a work means any kind of propagation that enables other parties to make or receive copies. Mere interaction with a user through a computer network, with no transfer of a copy, is not conveying.

An interactive user interface displays "Appropriate Legal Notices" to the extent that it includes a convenient and prominently visible feature that (1) displays an appropriate copyright notice, and (2) tells the user that there is no warranty for the work (except to the extent that warranties are provided), that licensees may convey the work under this License, and how to view a copy of this License. If the interface presents a list of user commands or options, such as a menu, a prominent item in the list meets this criterion.

1. Source Code.

   The "source code" for a work means the preferred form of the work for making modifications to it. "Object code" means any non-source form of a work.

   A "Standard Interface" means an interface that either is an official standard defined by a recognized standards body, or, in the case of interfaces specified for a particular programming language, one that is widely used among developers working in that language.

   The "System Libraries" of an executable work include anything, other than the work as a whole, that (a) is included in the normal form of packaging a Major Component, but which is not part of that Major Component, and (b) serves only to enable use of the work with that Major Component, or to implement a Standard Interface for which an implementation is available to the public in source code form. A "Major Component", in this context, means a major essential component (kernel, window system, and so on) of the specific operating system (if any) on which the executable work runs, or a compiler used to produce the work, or an object code interpreter used to run it.

   The "Corresponding Source" for a work in object code form means all the source code needed to generate, install, and (for an executable work) run the object code and to modify the work, including scripts to control those activities. However, it does not include the work's System Libraries, or general-purpose tools or generally available free programs which are used unmodified in performing those activities but which are not part of the work. For example, Corresponding Source includes interface definition files associated with source files for the work, and the source code for shared libraries and dynamically linked subprograms that the work is specifically designed to require, such as by intimate data communication or control flow between those subprograms and other parts of the work.

The Corresponding Source need not include anything that users can regenerate automatically from other parts of the Corresponding Source.

The Corresponding Source for a work in source code form is that same work.

2. Basic Permissions.

   All rights granted under this License are granted for the term of copyright on the Program, and are irrevocable provided the stated conditions are met. This License explicitly affirms your unlimited permission to run the unmodified Program. The output from running a covered work is covered by this License only if the output, given its content, constitutes a covered work. This License acknowledges your rights of fair use or other equivalent, as provided by copyright law.

   You may make, run and propagate covered works that you do not convey, without conditions so long as your license otherwise remains in force. You may convey covered works to others for the sole purpose of having them make modifications exclusively for you, or provide you with facilities for running those works, provided that you comply with the terms of this License in conveying all material for which you do not control copyright. Those thus making or running the covered works for you must do so exclusively on your behalf, under your direction and control, on terms that prohibit them from making any copies of your copyrighted material outside their relationship with you.

   Conveying under any other circumstances is permitted solely under the conditions stated below. Sublicensing is not allowed; section 10 makes it unnecessary.

3. Protecting Users' Legal Rights From Anti-Circumvention Law.

   No covered work shall be deemed part of an effective technological measure under any applicable law fulfilling obligations under article 11 of the WIPO copyright treaty adopted on 20 December 1996, or similar laws prohibiting or restricting circumvention of such measures.

   When you convey a covered work, you waive any legal power to forbid circumvention of technological measures to the extent such circumvention is effected by exercising rights under this License with respect to the covered work, and you disclaim any intention to limit operation or modification of the work as a means of enforcing, against the work's users, your or third parties' legal rights to forbid circumvention of technological measures.

4. Conveying Verbatim Copies.

   You may convey verbatim copies of the Program's source code as you receive it, in any medium, provided that you conspicuously and appropriately publish on each copy an appropriate copyright notice; keep intact all notices stating that this License and any non-permissive terms added in accord with section 7 apply to the code; keep intact all notices of the absence of any warranty; and give all recipients a copy of this License along with the Program.

You may charge any price or no price for each copy that you convey, and you may offer support or warranty protection for a fee.

5. Conveying Modified Source Versions.

   You may convey a work based on the Program, or the modifications to produce it from the Program, in the form of source code under the terms of section 4, provided that you also meet all of these conditions:

   a. The work must carry prominent notices stating that you modified it, and giving a relevant date.

   b. The work must carry prominent notices stating that it is released under this License and any conditions added under section 7. This requirement modifies the requirement in section 4 to "keep intact all notices".

   c. You must license the entire work, as a whole, under this License to anyone who comes into possession of a copy. This License will therefore apply, along with any applicable section 7 additional terms, to the whole of the work, and all its parts, regardless of how they are packaged. This License gives no permission to license the work in any other way, but it does not invalidate such permission if you have separately received it.

   d. If the work has interactive user interfaces, each must display Appropriate Legal Notices; however, if the Program has interactive interfaces that do not display Appropriate Legal Notices, your work need not make them do so.

      A compilation of a covered work with other separate and independent works, which are not by their nature extensions of the covered work, and which are not combined with it such as to form a larger program, in or on a volume of a storage or distribution medium, is called an "aggregate" if the compilation and its resulting copyright are not used to limit the access or legal rights of the compilation's users beyond what the individual works permit. Inclusion of a covered work in an aggregate does not cause this License to apply to the other parts of the aggregate.

6. Conveying Non-Source Forms.

   You may convey a covered work in object code form under the terms of sections 4 and 5, provided that you also convey the machine-readable Corresponding Source under the terms of this License, in one of these ways:

   a. Convey the object code in, or embodied in, a physical product (including a physical distribution medium), accompanied by the Corresponding Source fixed on a durable physical medium customarily used for software interchange.

   b. Convey the object code in, or embodied in, a physical product (including a physical distribution medium), accompanied by a written offer, valid for at least three years and valid for as long as you offer spare parts or customer support for that product model, to give anyone who possesses the object code either (1) a copy of the Corresponding Source for all the software in the product that is covered by this License, on a durable physical medium customarily used for software interchange, for a price no more than your reasonable cost of physically performing this conveying of source, or (2) access to copy the Corresponding Source from a network server at no charge.

c. Convey individual copies of the object code with a copy of the written offer to provide the Corresponding Source. This alternative is allowed only occasionally and noncommercially, and only if you received the object code with such an offer, in accord with subsection 6b.

d. Convey the object code by offering access from a designated place (gratis or for a charge), and offer equivalent access to the Corresponding Source in the same way through the same place at no further charge. You need not require recipients to copy the Corresponding Source along with the object code. If the place to copy the object code is a network server, the Corresponding Source may be on a different server (operated by you or a third party) that supports equivalent copying facilities, provided you maintain clear directions next to the object code saying where to find the Corresponding Source. Regardless of what server hosts the Corresponding Source, you remain obligated to ensure that it is available for as long as needed to satisfy these requirements.

e. Convey the object code using peer-to-peer transmission, provided you inform other peers where the object code and Corresponding Source of the work are being offered to the general public at no charge under subsection 6d.

A separable portion of the object code, whose source code is excluded from the Corresponding Source as a System Library, need not be included in conveying the object code work.

A "User Product" is either (1) a "consumer product", which means any tangible personal property which is normally used for personal, family, or household purposes, or (2) anything designed or sold for incorporation into a dwelling. In determining whether a product is a consumer product, doubtful cases shall be resolved in favor of coverage. For a particular product received by a particular user, "normally used" refers to a typical or common use of that class of product, regardless of the status of the particular user or of the way in which the particular user actually uses, or expects or is expected to use, the product. A product is a consumer product regardless of whether the product has substantial commercial, industrial or non-consumer uses, unless such uses represent the only significant mode of use of the product.

"Installation Information" for a User Product means any methods, procedures, authorization keys, or other information required to install and execute modified versions of a covered work in that User Product from a modified version of its Corresponding

Source. The information must suffice to ensure that the continued functioning of the modified object code is in no case prevented or interfered with solely because modification has been made.

If you convey an object code work under this section in, or with, or specifically for use in, a User Product, and the conveying occurs as part of a transaction in which the right of possession and use of the User Product is transferred to the recipient in perpetuity or for a fixed term (regardless of how the transaction is characterized), the Corresponding Source conveyed under this section must be accompanied by the Installation Information. But this requirement does not apply if neither you nor any third party retains the ability to install modified object code on the User Product (for example, the work has been installed in ROM).

The requirement to provide Installation Information does not include a requirement to continue to provide support service, warranty, or updates for a work that has been modified or installed by the recipient, or for the User Product in which it has been modified or installed. Access to a network may be denied when the modification itself materially and adversely affects the operation of the network or violates the rules and protocols for communication across the network.

Corresponding Source conveyed, and Installation Information provided, in accord with this section must be in a format that is publicly documented (and with an implementation available to the public in source code form), and must require no special password or key for unpacking, reading or copying.

7. Additional Terms.

   "Additional permissions" are terms that supplement the terms of this License by making exceptions from one or more of its conditions. Additional permissions that are applicable to the entire Program shall be treated as though they were included in this License, to the extent that they are valid under applicable law. If additional permissions apply only to part of the Program, that part may be used separately under those permissions, but the entire Program remains governed by this License without regard to the additional permissions.

   When you convey a copy of a covered work, you may at your option remove any additional permissions from that copy, or from any part of it. (Additional permissions may be written to require their own removal in certain cases when you modify the work.) You may place additional permissions on material, added by you to a covered work, for which you have or can give appropriate copyright permission.

   Notwithstanding any other provision of this License, for material you add to a covered work, you may (if authorized by the copyright holders of that material) supplement the terms of this License with terms:

   a. Disclaiming warranty or limiting liability differently from the terms of sections 15 and 16 of this License; or

b. Requiring preservation of specified reasonable legal notices or author attributions in that material or in the Appropriate Legal Notices displayed by works containing it; or

c. Prohibiting misrepresentation of the origin of that material, or requiring that modified versions of such material be marked in reasonable ways as different from the original version; or

d. Limiting the use for publicity purposes of names of licensors or authors of the material; or

e. e) Declining to grant rights under trademark law for use of some trade names, trademarks, or service marks; or

f. Requiring indemnification of licensors and authors of that material by anyone who conveys the material (or modified versions of it) with contractual assumptions of liability to the recipient, for any liability that these contractual assumptions directly impose on those licensors and authors.

All other non-permissive additional terms are considered "further restrictions" within the meaning of section 10. If the Program as you received it, or any part of it, contains a notice stating that it is governed by this License along with a term that is a further restriction, you may remove that term. If a license document contains a further restriction but permits relicensing or conveying under this License, you may add to a covered work material governed by the terms of that license document, provided that the further restriction does not survive such relicensing or conveying.

If you add terms to a covered work in accord with this section, you must place, in the relevant source files, a statement of the additional terms that apply to those files, or a notice indicating where to find the applicable terms.

Additional terms, permissive or non-permissive, may be stated in the form of a separately written license, or stated as exceptions; the above requirements apply either way.

8. Termination.

You may not propagate or modify a covered work except as expressly provided under this License. Any attempt otherwise to propagate or modify it is void, and will automatically terminate your rights under this License (including any patent licenses granted under the third paragraph of section 11).

However, if you cease all violation of this License, then your license from a particular copyright holder is reinstated (a) provisionally, unless and until the copyright holder explicitly and finally terminates your license, and (b) permanently, if the copyright holder fails to notify you of the violation by some reasonable means prior to 60 days after the cessation.

Moreover, your license from a particular copyright holder is reinstated permanently if the copyright holder notifies you of the violation by some reasonable means, this is the first time you have received notice of violation of this License (for any work) from that copyright holder, and you cure the violation prior to 30 days after your receipt of the notice.

Termination of your rights under this section does not terminate the licenses of parties who have received copies or rights from you under this License. If your rights have been terminated and not permanently reinstated, you do not qualify to receive new licenses for the same material under section 10.

9. Acceptance Not Required for Having Copies.

   You are not required to accept this License in order to receive or run a copy of the Program. Ancillary propagation of a covered work occurring solely as a consequence of using peer-to-peer transmission to receive a copy likewise does not require acceptance. However, nothing other than this License grants you permission to propagate or modify any covered work. These actions infringe copyright if you do not accept this License. Therefore, by modifying or propagating a covered work, you indicate your acceptance of this License to do so.

10. Automatic Licensing of Downstream Recipients.

    Each time you convey a covered work, the recipient automatically receives a license from the original licensors, to run, modify and propagate that work, subject to this License. You are not responsible for enforcing compliance by third parties with this License.

    An "entity transaction" is a transaction transferring control of an organization, or substantially all assets of one, or subdividing an organization, or merging organizations. If propagation of a covered work results from an entity transaction, each party to that transaction who receives a copy of the work also receives whatever licenses to the work the party's predecessor in interest had or could give under the previous paragraph, plus a right to possession of the Corresponding Source of the work from the predecessor in interest, if the predecessor has it or can get it with reasonable efforts.

    You may not impose any further restrictions on the exercise of the rights granted or affirmed under this License. For example, you may not impose a license fee, royalty, or other charge for exercise of rights granted under this License, and you may not initiate litigation (including a cross-claim or counterclaim in a lawsuit) alleging that any patent claim is infringed by making, using, selling, offering for sale, or importing the Program or any portion of it.

11. Patents.

    A "contributor" is a copyright holder who authorizes use under this License of the Program or a work on which the Program is based. The work thus licensed is called the contributor's "contributor version".

    A contributor's "essential patent claims" are all patent claims owned or controlled by the contributor, whether already acquired or hereafter acquired, that would be infringed by some manner, permitted by this License, of making, using, or selling its contributor version, but do not include claims that would be infringed only as a consequence of further modification of the contributor version. For purposes of this definition, "control" includes the right to grant patent sublicenses in a manner consistent with the requirements of this License.

Each contributor grants you a non-exclusive, worldwide, royalty-free patent license under the contributor's essential patent claims, to make, use, sell, offer for sale, import and otherwise run, modify and propagate the contents of its contributor version.

In the following three paragraphs, a "patent license" is any express agreement or commitment, however denominated, not to enforce a patent (such as an express permission to practice a patent or covenant not to sue for patent infringement). To "grant" such a patent license to a party means to make such an agreement or commitment not to enforce a patent against the party.

If you convey a covered work, knowingly relying on a patent license, and the Corresponding Source of the work is not available for anyone to copy, free of charge and under the terms of this License, through a publicly available network server or other readily accessible means, then you must either (1) cause the Corresponding Source to be so available, or (2) arrange to deprive yourself of the benefit of the patent license for this particular work, or (3) arrange, in a manner consistent with the requirements of this License, to extend the patent license to downstream recipients. "Knowingly relying" means you have actual knowledge that, but for the patent license, your conveying the covered work in a country, or your recipient's use of the covered work in a country, would infringe one or more identifiable patents in that country that you have reason to believe are valid.

If, pursuant to or in connection with a single transaction or arrangement, you convey, or propagate by procuring conveyance of, a covered work, and grant a patent license to some of the parties receiving the covered work authorizing them to use, propagate, modify or convey a specific copy of the covered work, then the patent license you grant is automatically extended to all recipients of the covered work and works based on it.

A patent license is "discriminatory" if it does not include within the scope of its coverage, prohibits the exercise of, or is conditioned on the non-exercise of one or more of the rights that are specifically granted under this License. You may not convey a covered work if you are a party to an arrangement with a third party that is in the business of distributing software, under which you make payment to the third party based on the extent of your activity of conveying the work, and under which the third party grants, to any of the parties who would receive the covered work from you, a discriminatory patent license (a) in connection with copies of the covered work conveyed by you (or copies made from those copies), or (b) primarily for and in connection with specific products or compilations that contain the covered work, unless you entered into that arrangement, or that patent license was granted, prior to 28 March 2007.

Nothing in this License shall be construed as excluding or limiting any implied license or other defenses to infringement that may otherwise be available to you under applicable patent law.

12. No Surrender of Others' Freedom.

    If conditions are imposed on you (whether by court order, agreement or otherwise) that contradict the conditions of this License, they do not excuse you from the conditions of this License. If you cannot convey a covered work so as to satisfy simultaneously your obligations under this License and any other pertinent obligations, then as a consequence you may not convey it at all. For example, if you agree to terms that obligate you to collect a royalty for further conveying from those to whom you convey the Program, the only way you could satisfy both those terms and this License would be to refrain entirely from conveying the Program.

13. Use with the GNU Affero General Public License.

    Notwithstanding any other provision of this License, you have permission to link or combine any covered work with a work licensed under version 3 of the GNU Affero General Public License into a single combined work, and to convey the resulting work. The terms of this License will continue to apply to the part which is the covered work, but the special requirements of the GNU Affero General Public License, section 13, concerning interaction through a network will apply to the combination as such.

14. Revised Versions of this License.

    The Free Software Foundation may publish revised and/or new versions of the GNU General Public License from time to time. Such new versions will be similar in spirit to the present version, but may differ in detail to address new problems or concerns.

    Each version is given a distinguishing version number. If the Program specifies that a certain numbered version of the GNU General Public License "or any later version" applies to it, you have the option of following the terms and conditions either of that numbered version or of any later version published by the Free Software Foundation. If the Program does not specify a version number of the GNU General Public License, you may choose any version ever published by the Free Software Foundation.

    If the Program specifies that a proxy can decide which future versions of the GNU General Public License can be used, that proxy's public statement of acceptance of a version permanently authorizes you to choose that version for the Program.

    Later license versions may give you additional or different permissions. However, no additional obligations are imposed on any author or copyright holder as a result of your choosing to follow a later version.

15. Disclaimer of Warranty.

    THERE IS NO WARRANTY FOR THE PROGRAM, TO THE EXTENT PERMITTED BY APPLICABLE LAW. EXCEPT WHEN OTHERWISE STATED IN WRITING THE COPYRIGHT HOLDERS AND/OR OTHER PARTIES PROVIDE THE PROGRAM "AS IS" WITHOUT

WARRANTY OF ANY KIND, EITHER EXPRESSED OR IMPLIED, INCLUDING, BUT NOT LIMITED TO, THE IMPLIED WARRANTIES OF MERCHANTABILITY AND FITNESS FOR A PARTICULAR PURPOSE. THE ENTIRE RISK AS TO THE QUALITY AND PERFORMANCE OF THE PROGRAM IS WITH YOU. SHOULD THE PROGRAM PROVE DEFECTIVE, YOU ASSUME THE COST OF ALL NECESSARY SERVICING, REPAIR OR CORRECTION.

16. Limitation of Liability.

    IN NO EVENT UNLESS REQUIRED BY APPLICABLE LAW OR AGREED TO IN WRITING WILL ANY COPYRIGHT HOLDER, OR ANY OTHER PARTY WHO MODIFIES AND/OR CONVEYS THE PROGRAM AS PERMITTED ABOVE, BE LIABLE TO YOU FOR DAMAGES, INCLUDING ANY GENERAL, SPECIAL, INCIDENTAL OR CONSEQUENTIAL DAMAGES ARISING OUT OF THE USE OR INABILITY TO USE THE PROGRAM (INCLUDING BUT NOT LIMITED TO LOSS OF DATA OR DATA BEING RENDERED INACCURATE OR LOSSES SUSTAINED BY YOU OR THIRD PARTIES OR A FAILURE OF THE PROGRAM TO OPERATE WITH ANY OTHER PROGRAMS), EVEN IF SUCH HOLDER OR OTHER PARTY HAS BEEN ADVISED OF THE POSSIBILITY OF SUCH DAMAGES.

17. Interpretation of Sections 15 and 16.

    If the disclaimer of warranty and limitation of liability provided above cannot be given local legal effect according to their terms, reviewing courts shall apply local law that most closely approximates an absolute waiver of all civil liability in connection with the Program, unless a warranty or assumption of liability accompanies a copy of the Program in return for a fee.

END OF TERMS AND CONDITIONS

How to Apply These Terms to Your New Programs

If you develop a new program, and you want it to be of the greatest possible use to the public, the best way to achieve this is to make it free software which everyone can redistribute and change under these terms.

To do so, attach the following notices to the program. It is safest to attach them to the start of each source file to most effectively state the exclusion of warranty; and each file should have at least the "copyright" line and a pointer to where the full notice is found.

> *<one line to give the program's name and a brief idea of what it does.>*
>
> Copyright (C) <year> <name of author>
>
> This program is free software: you can redistribute it and/or modify it under the terms of the GNU General Public License as published by the Free Software Foundation, either version 3 of the License, or (at your option) any later version.

This program is distributed in the hope that it will be useful, but WITHOUT ANY WARRANTY; without even the implied warranty of MERCHANTABILITY or FITNESS FOR A PARTICULAR PURPOSE. See the GNU General Public License for more details.

You should have received a copy of the GNU General Public License along with this program. If not, see *<http://www.gnu.org/licenses/>*.

Also add information on how to contact you by electronic and paper mail.

If the program does terminal interaction, make it output a short notice like this when it starts in an interactive mode:

<program> Copyright (C) <year> <name of author>

This program comes with ABSOLUTELY NO WARRANTY; for details type 'show w'. This is free software, and you are welcome to redistribute it under certain conditions; type 'show c' for details.

The hypothetical commands 'show w' and 'show c' should show the appropriate parts of the General Public License. Of course, your program's commands might be different; for a GUI interface, you would use an "about box".

You should also get your employer (if you work as a programmer) or school, if any, to sign a "copyright disclaimer" for the program, if necessary. For more information on this, and how to apply and follow the GNU GPL, see *<http://www.gnu.org/licenses/>*.

The GNU General Public License does not permit incorporating your program into proprietary programs. If your program is a subroutine library, you may consider it more useful to permit linking proprietary applications with the library. If this is what you want to do, use the GNU Lesser General Public License instead of this License. But first, please read *<http://www.gnu.org/philosophy/why-not-lgpl.html>*.

APPENDIX M

The Open Software License, Version 3.0

The Open Software License (OSL), Version 3.0

This Open Software License (the "License") applies to any original work of authorship (the "Original Work") whose owner (the "Licensor") has placed the following licensing notice adjacent to the copyright notice for the Original Work:

1. **Grant of Copyright License**. Licensor grants You a worldwide, royalty-free, non-exclusive, sublicensable license, for the duration of the copyright, to do the following:
    a. to reproduce the Original Work in copies, either alone or as part of a collective work;
    b. to translate, adapt, alter, transform, modify, or arrange the Original Work, thereby creating derivative works ("Derivative Works") based upon the Original Work;
    c. to distribute or communicate copies of the Original Work and Derivative Works to the public, with the proviso that copies of Original Work or Derivative Works that You distribute or communicate shall be licensed under this Open Software License;
    d. to perform the Original Work publicly; and
    e. to display the Original Work publicly.
2. **Grant of Patent License**. Licensor grants You a worldwide, royalty-free, non-exclusive, sublicensable license, under patent claims owned or controlled by the Licensor that are embodied in the Original Work as furnished by the Licensor, for the duration of the patents, to make, use, sell, offer for sale, have made, and import the Original Work and Derivative Works.

3. **Grant of Source Code License.** The term "Source Code" means the preferred form of the Original Work for making modifications to it and all available documentation describing how to modify the Original Work. Licensor agrees to provide a machine-readable copy of the Source Code of the Original Work along with each copy of the Original Work that Licensor distributes. Licensor reserves the right to satisfy this obligation by placing a machine-readable copy of the Source Code in an information repository reasonably calculated to permit inexpensive and convenient access by You for as long as Licensor continues to distribute the Original Work.
4. **Exclusions From License Grant.** Neither the names of Licensor, nor the names of any contributors to the Original Work, nor any of their trademarks or service marks, may be used to endorse or promote products derived from this Original Work without express prior permission of the Licensor. Except as expressly stated herein, nothing in this License grants any license to Licensor's trademarks, copyrights, patents, trade secrets or any other intellectual property. No patent license is granted to make, use, sell, offer for sale, have made, or import embodiments of any patent claims other than the licensed claims defined in Section 2. No license is granted to the trademarks of Licensor even if such marks are included in the Original Work. Nothing in this License shall be interpreted to prohibit Licensor from licensing under terms different from this License any Original Work that Licensor otherwise would have a right to license.
5. **External Deployment.** The term "External Deployment" means the use, distribution, or communication of the Original Work or Derivative Works in any way such that the Original Work or Derivative Works may be used by anyone other than You, whether those works are distributed or communicated to those persons or made available as an application intended for use over a network. As an express condition for the grants of license hereunder, You must treat any External Deployment by You of the Original Work or a Derivative Work as a distribution under section 1(c).
6. **Attribution Rights.** You must retain, in the Source Code of any Derivative Works that You create, all copyright, patent, or trademark notices from the Source Code of the Original Work, as well as any notices of licensing and any descriptive text identified therein as an "Attribution Notice." You must cause the Source Code for any Derivative Works that You create to carry a prominent Attribution Notice reasonably calculated to inform recipients that You have modified the Original Work.
7. **Warranty of Provenance and Disclaimer of Warranty.** Licensor warrants that the copyright in and to the Original Work and the patent rights granted herein by Licensor are owned by the Licensor or are sublicensed to You under the terms of this License with the permission of the contributor(s) of those copyrights and patent rights. Except as expressly stated in the immediately preceding sentence, the Original Work is provided under this License on an "AS IS" BASIS and WITHOUT WARRANTY, either express or implied, including, without limitation, the warranties of non-infringement, merchantability or fitness for a particular purpose. THE ENTIRE RISK AS TO THE QUALITY OF THE

ORIGINAL WORK IS WITH YOU. This DISCLAIMER OF WARRANTY constitutes an essential part of this License. No license to the Original Work is granted by this License except under this disclaimer.

8. **Limitation of Liability**. Under no circumstances and under no legal theory, whether in tort (including negligence), contract, or otherwise, shall the Licensor be liable to anyone for any indirect, special, incidental, or consequential damages of any character arising as a result of this License or the use of the Original Work including, without limitation, damages for loss of goodwill, work stoppage, computer failure or malfunction, or any and all other commercial damages or losses. This limitation of liability shall not apply to the extent applicable law prohibits such limitation.

9. **Acceptance and Termination**. If, at any time, You expressly assented to this License, that assent indicates your clear and irrevocable acceptance of this License and all of its terms and conditions. If You distribute or communicate copies of the Original Work or a Derivative Work, You must make a reasonable effort under the circumstances to obtain the express assent of recipients to the terms of this License. This License conditions your rights to undertake the activities listed in Section 1, including your right to create Derivative Works based upon the Original Work, and doing so without honoring these terms and conditions is prohibited by copyright law and international treaty. Nothing in this License is intended to affect copyright exceptions and limitations (including 'fair use' or 'fair dealing'). This License shall terminate immediately and You may no longer exercise any of the rights granted to You by this License upon your failure to honor the conditions in Section 1(c).

10. **Termination for Patent Action**. This License shall terminate automatically and You may no longer exercise any of the rights granted to You by this License as of the date You commence an action, including a cross-claim or counterclaim, against Licensor or any licensee alleging that the Original Work infringes a patent. This termination provision shall not apply for an action alleging patent infringement by combinations of the Original Work with other software or hardware.

11. **Jurisdiction, Venue and Governing Law**. Any action or suit relating to this License may be brought only in the courts of a jurisdiction wherein the Licensor resides or in which Licensor conducts its primary business, and under the laws of that jurisdiction excluding its conflict-of-law provisions. The application of the United Nations Convention on Contracts for the International Sale of Goods is expressly excluded. Any use of the Original Work outside the scope of this License or after its termination shall be subject to the requirements and penalties of copyright or patent law in the appropriate jurisdiction. This section shall survive the termination of this License.

12. **Attorneys' Fees**. In any action to enforce the terms of this License or seeking damages relating thereto, the prevailing party shall be entitled to recover its costs and expenses, including, without limitation, reasonable attorneys' fees and costs incurred in connection

with such action, including any appeal of such action. This section shall survive the termination of this License.

13. **Miscellaneous**. If any provision of this License is held to be unenforceable, such provision shall be reformed only to the extent necessary to make it enforceable.
14. **Definition of "You" in This License**. "You" throughout this License, whether in upper or lower case, means an individual or a legal entity exercising rights under, and complying with all of the terms of, this License. For legal entities, "You" includes any entity that controls, is controlled by, or is under common control with you. For purposes of this definition, "control" means (i) the power, direct or indirect, to cause the direction or management of such entity, whether by contract or otherwise, or (ii) ownership of fifty percent (50%) or more of the outstanding shares, or (iii) beneficial ownership of such entity.
15. **Right to Use**. You may use the Original Work in all ways not otherwise restricted or conditioned by this License or by law, and Licensor promises not to interfere with or be responsible for such uses by You.
16. **Modification of This License**. This License is Copyright © 2005 Lawrence Rosen. Permission is granted to copy, distribute, or communicate this License without modification. Nothing in this License permits You to modify this License as applied to the Original Work or to Derivative Works. However, You may modify the text of this License and copy, distribute or communicate your modified version (the "Modified License") and apply it to other original works of authorship subject to the following conditions: (i) You may not indicate in any way that your Modified License is the "Open Software License" or "OSL" and you may not use those names in the name of your Modified License; (ii) You must replace the notice specified in the first paragraph above with the notice "Licensed under <insert your license name here>" or with a notice of your own that is not confusingly similar to the notice in this License; and (iii) You may not claim that your original works are open source software unless your Modified License has been approved by Open Source Initiative (OSI) and You comply with its license review and certification process.

INDEX

We'd like to hear your suggestions for improving our indexes. Send email to *index@oreilly.com*.

C

D

E

F

G

H

I

J

K

L

M

N

O

P

Q

R

S

T

U

V

W

Z

About the Author

Van Lindberg is a software engineer and practicing attorney. What he does most, though, is translate from "lawyer" to "engineer" and back. He likes working with computer and legal code to get things done. Van's current work touches traditional intellectual property and the emerging field of open source law, where he advises businesses and open source groups on intellectual property issues.

Colophon

The cover image is composed of two stock photos overlaid with artwork by Monica Kamsvaag. The cover font is in various weights of Helvetica Neue. The text font is Adobe's Meridien; the heading font is ITC Bailey; and the code font is LucasFont's TheSansMonoCondensed.

Related Titles from O'Reilly

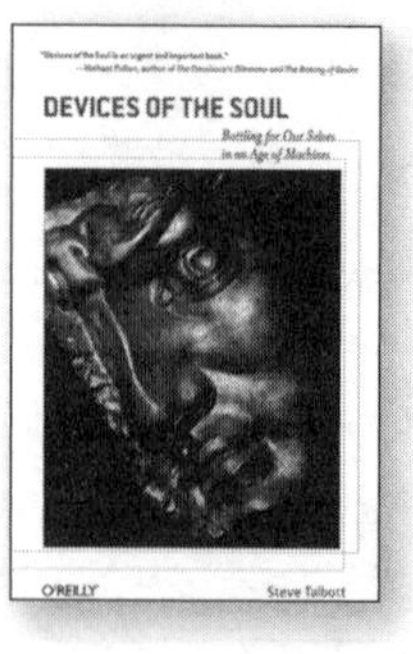

Technology and Society

Devices of the Soul

Just a Geek

Open Sources

Open Sources 2.0

Revolution in the Valley

Spam Kings

The Cathedral & the Bazaar

The Myths of Innovation

We the Media